The Mass

Other Titles of Interest from St. Augustine's Press

St. Augustine, *On Order [De Ordine]*

St. Augustine, *The St. Augustine LifeGuide™*

Thomas Aquinas, *Commentary on the Epistle to the Hebrews*

Thomas Aquinas, *Commentaries on St. Paul's Epistles to Timothy, Titus, and Philemon*

Thomas Aquinas, *Commentary on Aristotle's Nicomachean Ethics*

Thomas Aquinas, *Commentary on Aristotle's De Anima*

Thomas Aquinas, *Commentary on Aristotle's Metaphysics*

Thomas Aquinas, *Commentary on Aristotle's Posterior Analytics*

Thomas Aquinas, *Commentary on Aristotle's Physics*

Thomas Aquinas, *Disputed Questions on Virtue*. Translated by Ralph McInerny

John of St. Thomas, *Introduction to the Summa Theologiae of Thomas Aquinas*. Translated by Ralph McInerny

John Poinsot, *Tractatus de Signis*

Aristotle, *Aristotle – On Poetics*. Translated by Seth Benardete and Michael Davis.

Plato, *The Symposium of Plato: The Shelley Translation*. Translated by Percy Bysshe Shelley.

Francisco Suarez, *On Creation, Conservation, & Concurrence: Metaphysical Disputations 20–22*. Translated by A.J. Freddoso

Francisco Suarez, *Metaphysical Demonstration of the Existence of God*. Translated by John P. Doyle

John Paul II, *The John Paul II LifeGuide™*

Josef Pieper and Heinz Raskop, *What Catholics Believe*

Josef Pieper, *Scholasticism: Personalities and Problems*

Josef Pieper, *The Silence of St. Thomas*

Josef Pieper, *The Concept of Sin*

Josef Pieper, *Death and Immortality*

C.S. Lewis, *The Latin Letters of C.S. Lewis*

Jacques Maritain, *Natural Law*

Gabriel Marcel, *The Mystery of Being* (in two volumes)

Dietrich von Hildebrand, *The Heart: An Analysis of Human and Divine Affectivity*

Dietrich von Hildebrand, *The Dietrich von Hildebrand LifeGuide™*

Florent Gaboriau, *The Conversion of Edith Stein*. Translated by Ralph McInerny.

Ralph McInerny, *The Defamation of Pius XII*

Henry of Ghent, *Henry of Ghent's Summa of Ordinary Questions: Article One: On the Possibility of Human Knowledge*. Translated by Roland Teske, S.J.

James V. Schall, S.J., *The Sum Total of Human Happiness*

James V. Schall, S.J., *The Regensburg Lecture*

Peter Kreeft, *The Philosophy of Jesus*

Peter Kreeft, *Jesus-Shock*

Servais Pinckaers, O.P., *Morality: The Catholic View*. Translated by Michael Sherwin, O.P.

The Mass
The Presence of the Sacrifice of the Cross

Charles Journet

Translated by Fr. Victor Szczurek,
O. Praem.

St. Augustine's Press
South Bend, Indiana

Manufactured in the United States of America.

1 2 3 4 5 6   25 24 23 22 21 20 19

Library of Congress Cataloging in Publication Data
Journet, Charles.
[Messe. English]
The mass: the presence of the sacrifice of the cross / Charles Journet; translated by Victor Szczurek.
p. cm.
Includes bibliographical references and index.
ISBN-13: 978-1-58731-494-0 (clothbound: alk. paper)
ISBN-13: 978-1-58731-499-5 (paperbound: alk. paper)
1. Mass. 2. Lord's Supper. 3. Jesus Christ – Crucifixion. I. Title.
BX2230.3.J6813 2008
234'.163 – dc22 2007040719

∞ The paper used in this publication meets the minimum requirements of the American National Standard for Information Sciences - Permanence of Paper for Printed Materials, ANSI Z39.48-1984.

St. Augustine's Press
www.staugustine.net

Epigraphs

As often as the memorial of this Victim is celebrated, the work of our redemption is wrought. Roman Missal

The celebration of this sacrament is called the immolation of Christ by reason of the effect of Christ's Passion; for, by this sacrament we become partakers of the fruit of the Passion of the Lord. St. Thomas Aquinas

One unique Host, offered only once on the Cross, which remains by manner of immolation, through the daily repetition of the rite instituted by Christ in the Holy Eucharist . . .

The Mass is celebrated not to add anything to the offering on the Cross, but as the vehicle of the remission of sins obtained by Christ on the Cross. Cajetan

Although the external bloody offering and immolation have passed, nevertheless it endures in God's act of receiving and preserves its power; such that it is no less efficacious today before the Father than on the day when the Blood of Christ flowed from the wound in His side. Therefore we offer with Christ the same Host of the Cross, just as did those who were present at the foot of the Cross. Melchior Cano

One sacrifice . . . which applies to us the saving power of the bloody sacrifice of the Cross for the remission of sins which we commit each day. Council of Trent

There is not here a supplement to the sacrifice of the Cross; there is not a reiteration, as if it were imperfect. There is, on the contrary, while regarding it as most perfect, a perpetual application . . . a continued celebration. Bossuet

The divine arrangement of the Redeemer has willed that the sacrifice consummated one time on the Cross be made perpetual and uninterrupted. Leo XIII

Men have perpetually needed the Blood of the Redeemer to destroy the sins which offend divine justice.

The sacrifice of the altar is a supreme instrument by which the merits of the Cross are communicated to the faithful. Encyclical *Mediator Dei*

Contents

CHAPTER II

**The Unbloody or Sacramental Presence of the one
Redemptive Sacrifice at the Last Supper and the Mass:
Revealed Doctrine and Protestant Innovation**   **29**

CHAPTER III

CHAPTER IV

CHAPTER V

The Offering of the Mass   **93**

FIRST SECTION   93

Who Offers the Mass?   **93**

CHAPTER VIII

Communion   185

Chapter IX

Appendix ii

Preface

In the last of his fourteen encyclicals, *Ecclesia de Eucharistia*, our beloved late Holy Father, Pope John Paul II, spoke of his desire to rekindle a sense of profound amazement and gratitude toward the mystery which is the Eucharist (cf. n. 6). One can almost detect a certain sense of urgency in his words as he makes reference to "shadows" which have crept into certain sectors of the Church with regard to attitudes and practices related to the Eucharist. Among these, he mentions an "extremely reductive understanding of the Eucharistic mystery," that is, one which strips the Eucharist of its sacrificial meaning and celebrates it "as if it were simply a fraternal banquet" (n. 10).

At the same time, the Holy Father speaks of "lights" bearing witness to a renewed appreciation of and devotion to the Eucharist, such as a more conscious, active and fruitful participation of the faithful in the celebration of Mass resulting from the liturgical reforms inaugurated by the Second Vatican Council, the growing popularity of the practice of adoration of the Blessed Sacrament, and the revival of the Eucharistic procession on the Solemnity of the Body and Blood of Christ, which "is a grace from the Lord which yearly brings joy to those who take part in it" (n. 10). Finally, in his Apostolic Letter *Mane nobiscum Domine*, Pope John Paul II declared October 2004 to October 2005 to be the "Year of the Eucharist," concluding with the eleventh Ordinary General Assembly of the Synod of Bishops on the theme, "The Eucharist: Source and Summit of the Life and Mission of the Church." The Pope's proclamation has been received with much attention and enthusiasm throughout the Catholic world, leading to a greater impetus for a renewal of Eucharistic devotion, even as the Church and the world mourned his passing away and rejoiced at the election of his successor, Pope Benedict XVI, during the very Year of the Eucharist which he proclaimed.

It is within the context of this singular historical moment of the Church's life that Fr. Szczurek's translation of Cardinal Journet's treatise on the Sacrifice of the Mass makes its appearance. Charles Journet (1891–1975) was a man steeped in the Church's Tradition; this present work demonstrates in particular just how thoroughly conversant he was in Sacred Scripture, the Fathers and Scholasticism. Yet at the same time he was sensitive to conveying the eternal truths of the faith in ways more immediately understandable to people of his time. In short, he had a true Catholic sense of continuity and development of the faith.

The availability of this scholarly work to the English-speaking world, therefore, could not be timelier. Cardinal Journet presents the great classic themes of the Catholic theology of the Eucharist in a cohesive way, explaining complicated points of doctrine in a clear and intelligible manner. He sheds light on our understanding of the Mass as a sacrifice which perpetuates in time the one historical sacrifice of Christ. His treatment of the "presences" of Christ's sacrifice provides an exceptional help to the modern mind for grasping this fundamental truth of the Catholic faith, which acknowledges the ineffable mystery of God and time: with God, all time is present.

For all of its elucidation on this great mystery, though, *The Mass: The Presence of the Sacrifice of the Cross* does not exempt us from considering the contemporary age in which we live and the various challenges present therein. Such would be the case, for example, with the need for the Church to teach clearly and authoritatively the Catholic understanding of this sacrament, while at the same time continuing ecumenical dialogue and working for Christian unity; and also the need for the Church to preserve the authentic historical spirit and form of Catholic liturgy, while allowing for some degree of appropriate adaptation in certain cultures. Such a balance strengthens the Church for fulfilling her mission of heralding the Good News of salvation to the world, and it necessitates knowing the Church's Tradition and being firmly rooted in it. Indeed, without this, one of two extremes would be inevitable: either closure to any notion of development whatsoever, such that the Church's liturgy would no longer communicate the immutable truths of the faith as effectively as it could and should; or, rejection of any sense of the need to respect and preserve Tradition, thus reducing what is to be worship of the one, true God to mere novelty, entertainment and self-expression. Neither would be in keeping with the mind and spirit of Cardinal Journet.

The election of Pope Benedict XVI has brought a renewed impetus to the direction set by his predecessor, and augurs well for the Church's faithful response to the Lord's call to her to sanctify all in the truth. Fr. Szczurek has done the English-speaking Catholic world a great service in making this work accessible at this time. A thoughtful reading of this text will contribute to the authentic Eucharistic renewal so desired by Popes John Paul II and Benedict XVI. Happily, it will also help promote a wider knowledge of the writings and person of Charles Cardinal Journet, a great theologian from whom we have much to learn in our own time.

Most Rev. Salvatore Cordileone
Auxiliary Bishop of San Diego

Introduction

The first fact of faith—without prejudice to truths or even probabilities which can conceal an evolving vision of the world—is that it is divinely certain that we live not in a universe of nature, but in a universe of redemption. The entire religious history of humanity, beginning with the morrow after the original catastrophe, is reassumed, recapitulated in the sacrifice which Christ, with tears and a great cry, would offer for it to God on the Cross. This unique sacrifice would not be able to recapitulate human destiny if it did not draw it into participation, first by anticipation during the period prior to the Cross, then more intimately, more mysteriously by derivation during the period after the Cross *(Chapter I)*.

The redemptive sacrifice is unique: the Epistle to the Hebrews insists on this. But we find that the Savior Himself prescribed the reiteration of what He did at the Last Supper, in memory of Himself and until He returns. And what did He do? He changed bread into His Body, which was handed over for us, wine into His Blood, which was poured out for the multitude for the sake of the remission of sins. He invited the Apostles to unite themselves through Communion to His Body, which was handed over, and to His Blood, which was poured out, in the way, St. Paul tells us, that Israel united itself to the victims offered to the true God, and the Gentiles to the victims offered to idols. There was, then, a sacrifice at the Last Supper and a union with the sacrifice through Communion. Thus the Cross offers a unique sacrifice; the Last Supper also offers a true and proper sacrifice. Are these two affirmations of the Faith reconcilable? Here is the problem. One can suppress it by saying that at the Last Supper there was neither a sacrifice nor a communion with that sacrifice, but only the promise of the remission of sins; then all becomes very simple. But how does one reconcile them if one wishes to preserve the two given Scripture passages with all the depth of their mystery? *(Chapter II)*.

The one redemptive sacrifice began the very night the Savior was handed over and the Last Supper was instituted. The words of transubstantiation at the Last Supper established not another sacrifice, but another presence of the same sacrifice. It was present naturally, under its proper appearances; in addition, it became present sacramentally, under the borrowed appearances of bread and wine. The Last Supper is a true and proper sacrifice because it renders present under unbloody appearances Christ, together with the same reality of His bloody sacrifice *(Chapter III)*.

At the Last Supper, the same Priest, the same Victim, the same sacrificial act are present in two ways: first under their proper appearances, then under their borrowed or assumed appearances. The Council of Trent reminds us that there are equally, under the species of the unbloody sacrifice, the same Priest and Victim at the Mass as on the Cross; and is there not also the same sacrificial act as on the Cross? The explanation of the doctrine of the Eucharist has clarified that each consecrated host is Christ because transubstantiation multiplies in space the real substantial presence of the one Christ. Can it not also clarify that each Mass is a real and true sacrificial act because it multiplies in time the real efficient, operative presences of the one redemptive sacrifice? Here is how it looks from this point of view. One could say that at the Mass we have the glorious Christ Who comes to us; but He comes to meet us through His Cross. The sacramental appearances bring to us the real substantial presence of the glorious Christ and the real operative presence of His bloody sacrifice. The glorious Christ ratifies eternally in heaven the unique redemptive sacrifice by which He willed to save all men, first by anticipation in the ancient economy of salvation, then and more intimately by derivation in the new economy. When He comes to us at that very moment in which transubstantiation repeats the unbloody sacrifice of the Last Supper, it is in order to touch us through the Cross, to valorize and actualize for us His one redemptive sacrifice, always present and actual with respect to God, in which are pre-contained all the graces of the new economy of salvation. But is the redemptive sacrificial act accomplished? If it is always present in the divine eternity, can it always be present to us who are carried along in the flow of time? The response is that this act is related to us under different aspects, at once accomplished and present, in time and beyond time. In time: it is an irreversible moment of Christ's temporal life. Beyond time: touched by divinity it is capable of reaching by its spiritual power, its contact, its presence, all succeeding generations as they come into existence. Each consecration, renewing the unbloody sacrifice of the Last Supper, renders substantially present the now glorious Christ; but the sacramental species of bread and wine, which remind us of the Body of Christ handed over for us and His Blood poured out for us, show and testify that the grace hidden in each Mass is the very grace of redemption, a ray of redemption as it were. Like the Last Supper, the Mass is a real and true sacrifice: not another sacrifice than the one redemptive sacrifice, but another presence to us, a sacramental presence of that unique sacrifice. The unbloody sacrifice neither stands in juxtaposition to nor substitutes itself for the bloody sacrifice; it subordinates itself to the latter in order to transport its power to us. To multiply Masses is to multiply the points of application among us, the real operative presences among us of the one redemptive sacrifice: *As often as the memorial of this Victim is celebrated, the work of our Redemption is wrought (Chapter IV).*

If, by repetition of the unbloody sacrifice instituted at the Last Supper, the Mass is the full existential entrance of the Church at every moment of her life into the bloody redemptive sacrifice of the Cross, where her place is marked out beforehand, then to the first question— "Who offers Mass?"— one must respond by distinguishing first of all the primordial, enveloping, infinite offering of Christ, and the secondary, enveloped, finite offering of the Church. One should insist on the distinction between the order of worship and the order of charity, both being necessary here below. On the ordering of worship to charity: *When I deliver my body over to the flames, if I have not charity, it avails me nothing.* In the order of worship, or the order of the validity of the offering, one finds first the ministerial hierarchical power of the priests, which alone is the "transubstantiator," then the ministerial non-hierarchical power of the baptized and confirmed. In the order of charity, or the order of the holiness of the offering, which is the superior order, all the faithful are urged to make an offering, and the last can be the first. The Church in heaven with her angels and saints is united, in a certain way, to the Church here below. To the second question—"What is offered at Mass?"—one must respond that the supreme offering is Christ Himself, into Whom the bread and wine will become transubstantiated, and Who draws unto Himself His Church and the whole world by the Cross on which He has been lifted up (*Chapter V*).

At each Mass, whatever be the holiness of the minister, Christ in glory comes to us in order to touch us by His Cross—the universal, superabundant, infinite cause of the world's salvation. At each Mass the Church herself enters into the drama of the redemptive Passion in a finite manner and in proportion to her faith and love. Furthermore, at each Mass the Church, thus united to the Passion of Christ, begs for the salvation of the world: that which she obtains, which she draws in, and which redounds in blessing upon men is what theologians call the fruits of the Mass. We can distinguish here the intention or general application of the Church praying at each Mass for all the living and dead among the faithful and for the salvation of the entire world (general fruit); the intention or application of the celebrant, considered not simply as a particular or immediate minister of Christ who pronounces the transubstantiating words, but as the immediate minister of the hierarchical powers who accomplishes the liturgy (special fruit); the intention or personal application of the celebrant and of the faithful (particular fruits) (*Chapter VI*).

The corporal presence of Christ, once capable of suffering, assembled men around the redemptive sacrifice; the corporal presence of Christ, now glorious, continues to assemble them around that same sacrifice valuable for all time. This is why before leaving us in order to *pass to the Father,* Jesus, *on the night before He was handed over, took the bread, gave thanks, broke the bread saying: "This is My Body for you; do this in memory of Me."* Before the consecration it was bread; after the consecration what is seen is still the species or appearances of bread, what is believed is the Body of Christ. From the very beginning the Church has accepted this mystery of the Real Presence, immediately revealed in Scripture. How is it possible? Only by transubstantiation. It is still not comprehended; it must be discovered gradually. In the notion of the Real Presence is necessarily included the hidden notion of transubstantiation, a little like the way in which all the properties of a triangle, which are discovered only later, are necessarily included in the definition of a triangle. In recognizing this inclusion we see that the notion of transubstantiation was revealed from the beginning, implicitly not explicitly, mediately not immediately; and that consequently it could be defined as such by the Church. The notion of contact, of presence, taken in its proper and true sense, is, we insist, analogical, proportional: God is present to all things; an angel can be present in the place in which it acts; a body is present in a place. Even corporal presence can be analogical: one presence is the presence of bread before consecration; the other presence is the presence of the Body of Christ in the same place after consecration. Before consecration the substance of bread, sustaining the appearances of bread, exists in a place by space and dimension, each part of its proper extension being coextensive with the corresponding part of the surrounding body. After consecration the substance of the Body of Christ, with the Word Who is personally united to it, is contained under those same appearances of bread: no longer directly by sustaining the appearances, but indirectly by borrowing, as it were, the veil of those appearances; no longer by space and the coextensivity of its dimensions with that of the surrounding body, but in a totally different manner—the entire Body of Christ being present under each particle of the species or appearances and each particle of the species or appearances having reference to the entire Body of Christ. This is what is called the presence in a place by mode of substance and not of space. As the notion of transubstantiation is necessarily included, as we have said, in the notion of the Real Presence, the counter-proof is made by saying that the negation of the first notion carries with it the negation of the second. Those who deny transubstantiation ought, in effect, to hold that under the appearances of bread the substance of bread is either annihilated or remains. In both cases one must posit an adduction of Christ's Body. Two ways present themselves. According to the first, one must attribute to Christ as many bodies as there are consecrated hosts; then enclose each of these bodies in the dimensions of a small host. According to the second way, one would affirm that the Body of Christ is one but spread out all over, although it would not be distinguishable by us except in the consecrated bread; or, that the bread joins Christ in a new body. Both ways lead to absurdity. The only way out then would be to shun the mystery of Holy Thursday: the Gospel would have spoken only figuratively. Others have also said the same of the very mystery of Christmas (*Chapter VII*).

One's incorporation into the Passion of Christ begins at Baptism and is consummated in the Eucharistic Communion. Baptism is the sacrament of Christian initiation. The grace which it communicates is a participation in the grace which Jesus sent forth at His Passion, Death and Resurrection. It pre-contains in itself, as a seed does the plant, the final stages of the spiritual life. The Eucharistic Communion, the sacrament of the consummation of the spiritual life, is a more immediate invitation to enter into the drama of the Passion, Death and Resurrection. The triple symbolism of the Eucharist discloses to us its effects. The appearances of bread and wine signify that Christ, now glorious, meets us by means of His bloody sacrifice, to which one must unite oneself not only by faith and charity but also by consuming the Victim; these same appearances signify the spiritual repast and spiritual intoxication which comes to the soul through the gift of love; they signify the unity of all those who communicate in the one Bread: *There emerges from the natural Body of our Savior a stamp of unity which gathers together the Mystical Body and condenses it into one.* In the measure that the Church goes forth in time she becomes always more explicitly aware of the dispensation, according to which He Who founded the Church by His corporal presence wills to accompany her by that same corporal presence, now glorious, but accessible under the mere signs of the Passion. In the relation between the Cross of Christ and the glory of Christ the Church learns to penetrate the secret of her destiny (*Chapter VIII*).

The work of historians and of liturgists allows us to conclude with a look at the order of the Mass in the first centuries, to introduce the question regarding the diversity of rites and liturgical languages, and to explain the order of prayers which form the present Roman rite of the Mass. The mystery of the Mass is transcendent in relation to its liturgical expressions. Legitimate and necessary as they may be, these liturgical expressions remain inadequate. They represent but partial truths. A tension rises between them. It reappears at the very interior of each of the great rites. To the eyes of the contemplative, the mystery of redemption continued in each Mass is one, perfect and immutable; and men, surpassed by it, move about its environs. But the order of discipline and of social comportment venture forth in time and space, stressing in turn the various aspects of the unique mystery (*Chapter IX*).

Luther, followed by all of Protestantism, broke with the traditional doctrine of the Eucharist on two essential points: he denied the sacrificial character of the Last Supper and of the Mass; and, he denied the transubstantiation of bread and wine into the Body and Blood of Christ. He intended nevertheless to profess the evangelical and Pauline doctrine of the Real Presence; but the rejection of transubstantiation dragged immediately along with it, in Zwinglism and Calvinism, the rejection of the Real Presence.

The doctrines of transubstantiation and the Real Presence had already reached their state of clarification when they were rejected by Protestantism. The doctrine of the sacrificial character of the Last Supper and of the Mass, on the contrary, although firmly taught and believed, was still at an implicit stage. The Council of Trent—constantly cited in the pages which follow—in defining the first two points holds up as essential a doctrine which had already been clarified. On the other hand, in defining the sacrificial character of the Last Supper and of the Mass, it can be said that by making use of previous theological explanations—notably those of Cardinal Cajetan—the Council needed to proceed in a certain measure toward a first clarification. On this point the Protestant negation worked as a stimulus; it brought about the doctrinal development.

The clarification that the Council of Trent began seems in no way complete. It calls for the work of theologians; and their task is a difficult one. If St. Thomas Aquinas, while on his death bed, asked pardon of Him Whom he lovingly called the "price of his soul's redemption," the "Viaticum of his pilgrimage," for what he might have said against Him out of ignorance, and left all to the correction of the Roman Church, then how could theologians dare speak without fear of ignorance of a revelation at once so near and so hidden?

Fribourg, Evening of Easter

CHAPTER 1

The One Redemptive Sacrifice

1. A Universe of Redemption

We do not live existentially in a universe of nature; we live existentially in a universe of redemption.

a) The Hypothesis of a Universe of Nature

Cannot the human species be regarded as the point of natural issue and the supreme ascensional impulse, which brings about in the universe forms of life always more lofty and spiritual?

By ordering on a chart its data, its findings, intuitions, conjectures and projections, science today can outline the great traits of a genesis of the earth, of life, of humanity. It shows us that our planet has become capable, after millions of years, of receiving life; then, the progression from vegetative forms and animals; the successive appearances of fish, amphibians, reptiles, birds, mammals, the cerebral development which hastens into the order of primates, above all the anthropoids. It is in the midst of, but distinct from these, that emerged the human species—though one cannot say exactly how. This latter group demonstrates from the outset an original and ever-springing source of life, which overflows successively into waves and pools emerging and disappearing: first of all, at the lower quaternary (100,000 years before our era), the wave of the pithecathropus and the sinanthropus (this is already the *homo faber* with his fire and tools); then, at the medium quaternary (50,000 years), the Neanderthal wave (graves); finally, the high quaternary (30,000 years), the wave of *homo sapiens* (art), the wave of modern man with three races: white, black and yellow. The Mesolithic Age (15,000 years) and the Neolithic Age (or the polished rock) give the appearance of the birth of civilization (agriculture, raising of animals, etc.), which would open indefinite avenues for human progress.

One could bring forward reasons of the scientific order, which are not without their value, in order to explain that humans emerged from anthropoids beginning with one point of humanization, such that all of humanity can truly be considered as the offspring from the same phylum (monophylitism). One could add that paleontology knows the species only by the age of the *groups*, and this always rather far off from the moment of birth, so that the question of an original *couple* (monogenism) escapes it, but that some consideration of a higher order could allow the question to be resolved positively.[1]

Let us suppose that, in retracing the stages of the birth of the universe, we outline furthermore, as a correct philosophy demands, the irreducible differences which separate minerals, vegetables, animals and man; that we insist especially on the immediate creation of each human soul by God; that we characterize man as a being who is, from the awakening of his psychical life, a religious animal. Will we be authorized to say that this table, *which presents to us the concrete and existential state of humanity as a normal and natural fruit of the development of life on our planet*, "a humanization of the will of the living universe," *and therefore as a normal and natural state*—will we be able to say that this is an exact and truthful table?

To this question we must respond in the negative.

b) The Revelation of the Universe of Redemption

The vision of the birth and progress of humanity, which we have just related, undoubtedly contains some extremely precious data—be it truly scientific, highly probable or simply conjectural and provisory—the value of which one would be foolish to ignore; and this information ought to be gathered together. It would never cease to err, however, nor would it ever obtain its proper significance or become truly instructive, until it is transposed into a far more mysterious vision of the origins of humanity, one which would cast a decisive and indelible clarity on the concrete and existential condition of humanity.

In place of the idea of a *universe of nature*, which would have been possible, one must substitute the idea of a *universe of redemption*, it alone being real and existential. Man, of whom we are all descendents, does not appear naturally in the series of living beings. God no doubt would have been able to bring forth man with his one essence of a rational animal as a *horizon between two worlds,* as St. Thomas says—the world of nature and the world of the spirit. It would have existed in what theologians call the state of pure nature, that is in a dramatic state, experiencing from the very beginning the conflicts between the soul and the body, the reason and the passions, the human person and the world. But God did not act thus.

Well before the time of the paleontologists' first subdivisions of the *homo faber*, the "point of life's humanization," man—the first human couple—appeared in a privileged state of harmony, clothed with sanctity and justice: the life of grace, faith and charity introduced him into the

---

1   See Fr. Teilhard de Chardin, *Le groupe zoologique humain, Structures et directions évolutives* (Paris: Abin Michel, 1956); *Le phénomène humain* (Paris: Seuil, 1956), chap. 2, "L'expansion de la vie," pp. 108–152.

divine friendship and made him a child of God. Above all it strengthened in him the triple domination—in itself frail—of soul over body, reason over the passions, the human person over exterior nature, such that he suffered no sickness or death, no troubled passions, no hostility of the surrounding world.

This privileged state of original justice was short-lived. It was destroyed by the first sin. It shot by like lightning. It is vain to search for traces of it with paleontology. The consequences of this fall, however, are inscribed forever in the heart and flesh of humanity.[2] Every vision of the world which presents the concrete and existential condition of humanity as natural and normal is radically aberrant. It is, on the contrary, the concrete and existential condition of a being who has shattered in himself a wonderful gift, who has fallen irreparably from his first state of sanctity and harmony, who finds in his relapse a state more dramatic than if there had been a state of pure nature where the conflicts would have risen at all stages between the soul and the body, the reason and the passions, the human person and the universe; but the first anticipations of the unknown and extraordinary redemptive grace of Christ would come to visit man in this fallen condition immediately, in order to help him recommence his entire history.

c) Catastrophe and Redemption: Their Constant Existential Overlapping

According to St. Paul the concrete and existential state of humanity in no way represents a natural and normal state, but rather the catastrophe of a privileged state, where man had been in grace and outside the reaches of death. It is therefore a state not of a simple "absence" of grace, but of a "privation" of grace, a state of *sin*, where death appears as a *chastisement*: "The wages of sin is death" (Rom 6:23); nevertheless it is not a desperate state, but, on the contrary, *a state where all hope of humanity hangs on the redemption of Christ*: "The wages of sin is death; but the free gift of God is life eternal in Christ Jesus our Lord" (Rom 6:23).

The sin of Adam—to which was attached death: "With respect to the tree of knowledge of good and evil … the day on which you shall eat of it, you shall die the death" (Gen 2:17)—has passed to his descendents. It is by reason of this transmission that they die, and not by reason of their own personal sins, since they died even before Moses, when no divine

---

2   Pascal thought that the grandeurs and miseries which are in man are capable of *demonstrating* if not the very mystery of original sin—which can only be an object of faith—then at least the existence of an initial catastrophe in humanity. According to St. Thomas, philosophical reflection can furnish here only a *probability*. Cf. our work *Vérité de Pascal* (Œuvre Saint-Augustin: Saint-Maurice, 1951), pp. 119 and 139–146.

law punished personal sins with death: "As sin came into the world through one man and death through sin, and so death spread to all men because all men sinned—sin (personal) indeed was in the world before the law was given, but sin is not imputed (by death) where there is no law (which punishes it by death); death, nevertheless, reigned from Adam to Moses, even over those whose sins were not like the transgression of Adam (and therefore they in no way sinned by transgressing a divine law which is sanctioned by punishment by death), who was a type of the One who was to come" (Rom 5:12–14). And it is still by reason of this transmission of Adam's sin that small infants die who have not sinned personally.

In consideration of his first state, there is a state of catastrophe, a condition of sin and death, which humanity inherits from Adam. But the first Adam is a "figure" or "type" of the Second: the catastrophe of the first Adam calls forth the redemption of the Second Adam. The latter is not a return to the first state, but an entrance into a much more mysterious state, one which will be totally better: "But the free gift is not like the trespass. For if many died through *one man's trespass*, much more *have the grace of God and the free gift in the grace of that one man Jesus Christ* abounded for many. And the free gift is not like the effect of that one man's sin. For *the judgment following one trespass* brought condemnation, *but the* free gift following many trespasses *brings justification*. If, because of one man's trespasses, *death reigned through that one man*, much more will *those who receive the abundance of grace and the free gift of righteousness reign in life through the one man Jesus Christ*" (Rom 5:15–17).

Far from living in a normal existential state, humanity lives in one which is mysterious, where a mystery of trespass and condemnation coexists with a mystery of pardon and justification: "Then, as one man's trespass led to *condemnation* for all men, so one man's act of righteousness leads to *justification* and life for all men. For as by one man's disobedience many *were made sinners*, so by one man's obedience many *will be made righteous*" (Rom 5:18–19).

d) The Unexpected Arrival of Sin Enables the Advent of a Totally Better World

According to St. Paul the trespass of Adam and the redemption of Christ cannot answer each other equally, the latter simply restoring that which the former had plundered. God, in fact, does not permit evil except that He might use the occasion to bring forth an unexpected and greater good. The promise to Abraham was followed by the law of Moses "which entered in order to increase (by reason, alas, of human perversity) the trespass. But, *where sin increased, grace abounded all the more*, so that as *sin reigned* in death, so *grace reigned* through righteousness to eternal life through Jesus Christ our Lord" (Rom 5:20–21).

To the question, "Why did God permit it, why did He allow the first catastrophe?," there is but one response: He knew that it would be able to be compensated in superabundance by the drama of the Cross. The head of the humanity of innocence was only the first Adam; the Head of the humanity of redemption is the Second Adam, the Word made Flesh. In short, "the state of redemption is worth a hundred times more than that of innocence."[3]

e) The Grace of Christ Before Christ

It is unthinkable that God could have abandoned fallen humanity to its own fate for even one moment. The catastrophe was not permitted except insofar as redemption was foreseen along with it. The grace which came to man secretly after the Fall, and which accompanied him under the regimes that theologians would call the law of nature and then the Mosaic law, is already Christic. It is granted by God in consideration of the future Passion of Christ. It is an initial anticipation of the supreme redemption, which would take place in the Blood of the Cross (Col 1:20) at the threshold of the regime of the New Law.

Here we have the universe of redemption. This is our existential universe. The Christian, whether he be a philosopher or not, knows no other. It is in the perspective of this universe that all the valuable findings of philosophy and the disciplines which study the evolution of the world and of life, must order and integrate themselves, whether they are about proved data scientifically founded, or highly probable views, or even simple conjectures.[4]

The universe of redemption depends from its birth, and throughout and even until the end of its history, on the Cross of Christ. It is dominated by the bloody Passion of a God made man and Who died for man.

---

3   St. Francis De Sales, *Traité de l'amour de Dieu*, Book II, chap. 5.

4   "In short, we do not see the legal incompatibility between the two groups of the following data attributed to the first man: on one hand, a physical type different from the current type, more primitive but in no way degenerate, and a potential for technical evolution not yet deployed; on the other hand, with the goodness of divine assistance in his first stages in the world, the possession by Adam of an interior life, the knowledge of God and of the moral order, the sense of familial unity and of the responsibility of the first father of all men— lights which do not depend solely on the natural gift of intelligence, but on the gratuitous intervention of a revealing God. The coming of man was marked by the loftiest gifts in the order of his supernatural destiny; nevertheless, God left to his natural faculties the care of organizing the world; their culture would be refined through the exercise and transmission of knowledge. God immediately and magnificently raised man above himself by granting him that which he could not attain; but his toil needed to realize slowly what he was capable of by the forces of his nature." M. Grison, *Problèmes d'origines, l'univers, les vivants, l'homme* (Paris: Letouzey et Ané, 1954) p. 282.

2. Why Salvation by Redemption?

a) Man Is Not Only "Saved" but "Redeemed"

After the original Fall, which definitively destroyed the first state of humanity, what could God do but grant pardon?[5] And this could have been done, no doubt, in different ways. He could have, for example, pretended to forget the offense of the sin and granted us again the life of grace and no more; but then this first offense would have remained without compensation, and it would have been forever true that the insult rendered to God by His creation was on the whole greater than the love He received from it.[6]

It is here that the plan of redemption appears. Flesh having offended God, the Son of God would become Flesh. He would take on a body in the womb of the Virgin. By it He would then be able to raise from the earth toward heaven an adoration and a love (a created adoration and love no doubt) of extraordinary intensity, which, by reason of the divinity of the Person, would be divine-human, theandric, vested with an infinite power and capable of compensating superabundantly for the outrage of all men's sins. From there the world gives to God—through Christ Who takes on a human nature—an honor incomparably greater than the offense it caused. "He properly atones for an offense who offers something which the offended one loves equally, or even more than he detested the offense. But by suffering out of love and obedience, Christ gave more to God than was required to compensate for the offense of the whole human race."[7]

b) Why Such Sufferings of Christ?

The price of the drama, however, was unspeakable. In the wonderful painting at the Prado, where El Greco depicts the Redemption, the Father seems to be overwhelmed with distress. One might say that He is discovering unexpectedly the excessive pain of His Son and that He is repenting of having sent Him to such a martyrdom. Why did the redemptive sufferings of Christ have to be so terrible?

5   "It was necessary that, in establishing a secret dispensation, the immutable God, Whose will never acts without benignity, accomplish by a more hidden economy the primitive disposition of His goodness." St. Leo the Great, *Deuxième sermon pour Noël*, no. 1. Sources chrétiennes, no. 22, p. 77.
6   Man, said St. Thomas, would have been *delivered*; he would not have been *redeemed*, "for redemption carries with it a sufficient satisfaction." *III Sent.*, dist. 20, qu. 1, a. 4, quaest. 1, ad 1.
7   St. Thomas, *Summa Theologiae* III, qu. 46, a. 3. In Christ "the dignity of man was honored; for as man was overcome and deceived by the devil, so also it should be a man that should overthrow the devil; and as man deserved death, so a man by dying should vanquish death. Hence it is written (1 Cor 15: 57): *Thanks be to God Who hath given us the victory through our Lord Jesus Christ.*"

To this question there is no other response than His love. He willed, in order to espouse humanity completely, to descend to the very depths of its tragedy. He did not come at this first parousia to eliminate our distress, but to assume it and illuminate it. He bore it entirely on Himself: "He was tempted in every respect, and like us in every way except sin" (Heb 4:15). God, writes St. Paul, "shows His love for us in that while we were yet sinners Christ died for us" (Rom 5:8). Christ, writes St. John, "loved us and washed us of our sins in His own Blood" (Apoc 1:5). He Himself said: "Greater love than this no man hath, than to lay down his life for his friends" (Jn 15:13).

How could we have conjectured such a solicitude in God, such a need of our salvation? It is before the abyss of Jesus' agony that we begin to fathom God's love for us.

To the objection that the greatest sign of love which the Son of God could have given would have been to become incarnate in each of the individuals of human nature, St. Thomas does not content himself with responding that the natural order would have then been destroyed. He adds: "The love of God to men is shown not merely in the assumption of human nature, but especially, *praecipue*, in what He suffered in human nature for other men, according to Rom 5:8: *God shows His love for us in that while we were yet sinners Christ died for us*, which would not have taken place had He assumed human nature in all men."[8]

c) The Contemplative and Redemption

No one could go further into the thick of it, to penetrate, in a sense, experientially into the understanding of the redemptive plan, except in the measure in which he burned with the desire to save the world for God. Beatrice reminds Dante of this:

> *Brother, no eye of man not perfected,*
> *Nor fully ripen'd in the flame of love*
> *May fathom this decree.*[9]

Such would be the teaching of St. John of the Cross. He explains that it is to the soul which has entered into the spiritual marriage that are revealed, in a manner yet unknown, the secrets of the Bridegroom, that is the mysteries of the Incarnation and Redemption.[10] They are by nature unfathomable: "So that whatever mysteries and wonders which the holy

8   *Summa Theologiae* III, qu. 4, a. 5, ad 2.
9   *Questo decreto, frate, sta sepulto*
    Agli occhi di ciascuno, il cui ingegno
    Nella fiamma d'amor non è adulto. Paradiso, VII, 58–60.
10 *Cantique Spirituel*, XXVIII, édit. Silverio, T. III, p. 136; XXIX, trad. (Lucien de S. Joseph: Desclée de Brouwer) p. 863.

doctors may have discovered and holy souls may have heard in this life, their principle still remains to be spoken and understood."[11]

If the true name of Christian contemplation, in contrast to the contemplation of philosophers, has "entered into the states of God, of the God Incarnate,"[12] how then could it tend, under the pretext of loving God better, to push aside from its view the mysteries of Christ, of the Blessed Virgin, of the Church? St. Teresa rose up against one such fatal illusion.[13] We can say here that, unlike the way of beginners, who ascend from the bottom up to God through Christ (and this is for some time the way of all souls), the privileged way of the contemplative is to pass at times from God to Christ. It is granted them, therefore, to know the mysteries of the redemptive Incarnation, the Blessed Virgin, the Church, a little in the way that God sees them: from on high, by descending from great divine simplicity toward the multiplicity of the universe which needs to be rescued. Scripture shows us the angels themselves "desiring to look into" the things of the Gospel (1 Pet 1:12) and the heavenly powers discovering the infinitely manifold wisdom of God through the Church (Eph 3:10).

And how would the love of God, when it is intense, not rediscover the divine intention of saving all men? Fr. Elijah of the Martyrs hands on to us the thought of St. John of the Cross: "It is an evident truth that compassion for our neighbor increases the more that the soul unites itself to God by love; for, the more it loves, the more it desires that this same God be loved and honored by all. And the more it desires Him, the more it labors for Him, both in prayer and by all the other necessary means possible. And in those who are so possessed by God the fervor and force of their charity is such that they are unable to be content with and limit themselves to their own profit alone. Rather, as it seems to them a small thing to go to heaven alone, they search with agony, with a love which is completely heavenly, and with extraordinary diligence to lead to heaven with them a great number of souls. And this is born from the great love which they have for their God. It is the proper fruit and effect of perfect prayer and contemplation."[14]

The supreme act by which Jesus establishes the universe of redemption by dying on the Cross is what He Himself calls "His hour."

3. The Hour of Jesus

a) Jesus Announces It

All of our Savior's life is dominated by the thought of that which He calls "His hour," the hour of His Passion and His passage to the Father.

11 *Ibid.*, XXXVI, édit. Silverio, T. III, p. 162; XXXVII, trad., p. 897.
12 Jacques Maritain, "Action et Contemplation," in *Questions de Conscience* (Paris: Desclée de Brouwer, 1938) p. 107.
13 *Vie,* chap. 22, Silverio, T. I, p. 165. *Demeures,* chap. 7, Silverio, T. IV, p. 147.
14 *Œuvres de saint Jean de la Croix*, Silverio, t. IV, p. 351, trad. Lucien de S. Joseph, p. 1370.

At Cana, "His hour had not yet come" (Jn 2:4). If for the sake of the Blessed Virgin He desires to hasten His public manifestation, He knows that it advances at the same time the hour of His death.

This hour is not in the power of men; it depends on the Father: "So they sought to arrest Him; but no one laid hands on Him, because His hour had not yet come" (Jn 7:30; cf. 8:20).

This hour marked Jesus' entrance by death into a glory to which He would draw all of His own: "The hour has come for the Son of man to be glorified. Truly, truly, I say to you, unless a grain of wheat falls into the earth and dies, it remains alone. . . . Now my soul is troubled. And what am I to say? 'Father, save me from this hour?' No, for this purpose I have come to this hour" (Jn 12:23, 27). "Father, the hour has come; glorify Thy Son that the Son may glorify Thee, since Thou hast given Him power over all flesh, to give eternal life to all whom Thou hast given Him" (Jn 17:1–2). It is the hour of His passage to the Father. "Before the feast of Passover, Jesus knowing that His hour had come to pass from this world to the Father ..." (Jn 13:1).

b) It Preoccupies Him

Jesus knew this hour in advance. He foretold it to His disciples: "You know that after two days the Passover is coming, and the Son of Man will be delivered up to be crucified" (Mt 26:1–2).

He knew all its circumstances. When the disciples asked Him where He would celebrate the Passover, He responded: "Go into the city, and a man carrying a jar of water will meet you. Follow him, and wherever he enters, say to the master of the house: 'The Teacher says, Where is my guest room, where I am to eat the Passover with My disciples?' And he will show you a large upper room furnished and ready" (Mk 14:13–15).

This hour preoccupied Him. It colored His earlier actions with its mystery—the steps of His public life, as well as the silence of His hidden life. It weighed upon the first Christmas. This is the sense of Hebrews 10:4–9: "It is impossible that the blood of bulls and goats should take away sins. Consequently, when Christ came into the world, He said, 'Sacrifices and offerings Thou hast not desired, but a body hast Thou prepared for Me. . . . Lo, I have come to do Thy will, O God.'"

Ever since the entrance of Christ into the world, His Passion, His hour seemed to fascinate Him.

c) It Sums Up His Temporal Life

The entire life of Christ, therefore, glows by anticipation with the fires of His Passion.

In return, His Passion is enriched with His whole earlier life. It condenses, it recapitulates in itself the power of all His past actions. "With respect to merit and satisfaction one must consider the entire life of Christ, although it be composed of many partial actions, as one complete act which finds its fulfillment in His Passion. In fact, since Christ came to redeem the sin of Adam, the consequence of which was death (Rom 5:12), it was fitting that He should bring about the full satisfaction of sin in His death...

"It would be insufficient to say that the Passion of Christ had simply more meritorious and satisfactory value than the preceding acts of Christ; for certainly it is by the Passion alone that our redemption is accomplished. Also, Sacred Scripture always attributes our redemption to the Passion: God established Christ as an instrument of propitiation by faith in His Blood (Rom 3:15); we have been reconciled to God by the death of His Son (Rom 5:10), etc.

"If, then, by reason of the person of Christ each of His acts have by their nature an infinite value, nevertheless, each act was in fact offered as a part of the whole which the Passion needed to perfect."[15]

d) It Sums Up the History of the World

The Passion of Christ draws unto itself and recapitulates in itself not only the life of Christ, but all the earlier periods, indeed the entire history of the world recommenced after the original Fall.

St. Irenaeus writes: "The Lord Himself said to those who should afterwards shed His Blood, 'All righteous blood shall be required which is shed upon the earth, from the blood of righteous Abel to the blood of Zachariah the son of Barachiah, whom you slew between the temple and the altar. Truly I say to you, all these things shall come upon this generation' (Lk 11:50; Mt 23:35). *He thus points out the* recapitulation *that should take place in His own person of the effusion of blood from the beginning, of all the righteous men and of the prophets,* and that by means of Himself there should be a *requisition* of their blood. Now this blood could not be *required* unless it also had the capability of being *saved*; nor would the Lord have *summed up* these things in Himself, unless He had Himself been made flesh and blood from the beginning, *saving in His own person at the end that which had in the beginning perished in Adam.*"[16]

The same teaching is found in St. Jerome: "The entire economy which preceded the world and which afterwards was restored in the world for both visible and invisible creatures proclaimed the coming of the Son of God. . . . *It is therefore in the Cross of the Lord and His Passion that all things have been* recapitulated, *all things have been enveloped in this* recapitulation."[17]

e) It Opens Up Onto the Resurrection and the Ascension

1. Nevertheless, the Passion of Christ was the end only of His pilgrimage; it was not the end of His life. It was a death pre-containing the

---

15   Dominic Soto, *IV Sent.*, dist. I, qu. 3, a. 5 (Venice, 1584) p. 74.
16   St. Irenaeus, *Adversus haereses*, V, chap. 14, n° 1; PG VII, 1161.
17   St. Jerome, *Comm. ad Ephes.*, I, 10; PL XXVI, 454.

Resurrection, a suffering pre-containing happiness, an apparent loss pre-containing a manifest victory. And it is as such—that is as uniting in itself all these opposing elements—that the Passion is the cause of our salvation. Indeed, the Passion, Death, Resurrection and Ascension were, speaking here in the strict sense, moments of one unique act, begun in sorrow and completed in glory, by which the Lord descended into the very depths of humanity held captive in order to raise it up on high.[18]

The Passion sums up in itself alone our entire salvation—insofar as it comprises the earlier life of Christ, and above all insofar as it opens up to the Resurrection and Ascension, which touch us by means of the Passion, and which conjointly with the Passion cause our deliverance.

2. For the Apostle, the Passion and the Resurrection are as two sides of the same mystery: "He was handed over for our iniquities, and He was raised up for our justification" (Rom 4:25); "We have been buried with Him through baptism into His death, so that, just as Christ was raised from the dead by the glory of the Father, we too might live a new life" (Rom 6:4).

The same goes for the Passion and the Ascension: "He ascended on high, He took a host of captives. . . . What does this mean but that He had first descended into the lower regions of the earth?" (Eph 4:8–10).

The grace of the Passion is a grace of death but in view of the Resurrection, a grace of the Crucifixion but in view of the Transfiguration. It is destined to break forth into glory, and the Apostle knows this. Brothers, he says, "I professed to know nothing among you but Jesus Christ and Him crucified" (1 Cor 2:2); but in the same epistle St. Paul proclaims the glory of Christ, Who in the end will hand over the Kingdom to our God and Father."[19]

3. The command of the Father is that Jesus lay down His life in order that He may take it up again (Jn 10:18). What our Lord Himself calls His hour, then, is the Passion which opens up into glorification and as such is identified with it. "When Judas went out, Jesus said: 'Now the Son of Man has been glorified, and God has been glorified in Him'" (Jn 13:31).

f) It Is in Time but Dominates Time, Be It by Anticipation or by Derivation

Christ's hour, when He would glorify the Father through that power over His flesh which had been conferred on Him (Jn 13:12), is the world's solemn hour. It is in time but it dominates all times. The Cross of Christ

---

18 The Roman Canon of the Mass does not separate these mysteries: "We celebrate, O Lord, we Thy people and Thy ministers, the Passion, Resurrection and glorious Ascension into heaven of this same Christ, Thy Son our Lord…" The *Suscipe sancta Trinitas* expresses the very same thought.

19 For this paragraph, see *L'Église du Verbe Incarné* (Paris: Desclée De Brouwer, 1951), t. II, p. 175.

extends its arms over the past and the future. Its luminous shade precedes it and stretches back even to the first days after the Fall. Its hidden light follows it and descends again even unto the world's final days.

The Cross saves the previous ages by *anticipation*: all the graces granted under the law of nature and under the Old Law were in view of the Cross. At His death Christ's soul brought the Beatific Vision to the souls of the just held in Limbo.

The Cross saves the ages which follow in a more intimate manner, *by application or derivation*: all the graces of the New Law flow down from the Cross. "Without the shedding of blood there is no forgiveness" (Heb 9:22). This Law continues to have power: not by the blood of bulls or rams, but by the Blood of the Lamb. If, therefore, after the flowing of Blood from the Cross, which happened once for all, sin begins again and continues in each generation, it would be necessary that that flowing forth from the Cross—once with respect to Christ but inexhaustibly with respect to men—begin again and continue to touch each generation.

When time ceases, sin will cease, the flowing forth of Christ's Blood will cease, and the reconciliation of the world will cease. Then it is Christ's glory alone which will fall upon the reconciled world. The priesthood of Christ, completed with respect to its redemptive action, will last eternally through its fruits.[20]

4. The Ascending Mediation and the Descending Mediation of Christ the Priest

Christ is a Priest in the most sovereign sense.

The office proper to the priest is to give people to God and God to the people.[21]

Christ gives men to God by raising up in their hearts an offering, a supplication which He draws forth and elevates to Himself, incorporating it into His own offering, to His own theandric supplication, in order to present it to God. This is the ascending mediation of Christ. It acts as a moral cause, that is, by way of supplication. It procures our salvation by way of merit, sacrifice, satisfaction and redemption.

Christ also gives God to men. For, "having been heard because of His reverence" (Heb 5:7), He drew unto Himself, in order then to pour them out on the world, the greatest treasures of grace which God held in reserve for us since the beginning of the world. In sign of which, and in proof that He delivered all to us, there flowed from His pierced side blood and water (Jn 19:34). This is the descending mediation of Christ. It acts by way of efficient causality.[22]

20 St. Thomas, *Summa Theologiae*, III, qu. 22, a. 5, ad 1.
21 St. Thomas, *Summa Theologiae* III, qu. 22, a. 1.
22 *Ibid.*, III, qu. 48, a. 6, ad 3.

The Cross is the place of passage to God for all the prayer of the world and for all of God's responses to the world. These are the two inseparable and complementary aspects of one unique mediation.

5. The Mediation of Christ On the Cross is Simultaneously a Sacrifice and an Act of Love

a) Sacrifice and an Act of Love

The Passion of Christ which saved the world—lost as it was since the first sin—that same Passion which also established a universe of redemption, is indissolubly a *sacrifice* and an *act of love*.

It is a sacrifice, an exterior cultic act, a liturgy, but insofar as it envelops the purest and most intense love which would ever come forth from a human heart. It is an act of love, but insofar as it is enveloped in a voluntary sacrifice, an exterior cultic act, a liturgy. The Church sings of the "Love Priest" immolating His own body, *Almique membra corporis Amor sacerdos immolat*.[23]

It is a *sacrificial act*: "The Father loves Me because I lay down my life to take it up again. *No one takes it from me, I lay it down freely*. I have the power to lay it down and the power to take it up again. This command I received from my Father" (Jn 10:17–18).[24] It is by reason of the absolutely privileged power of His human will over His nature and over every nature, that Christ was able to make of His life a sacrifice in the proper sense, to be at the same time the Priest and the Victim of this sacrifice, *to change the horrible death on the Cross into an adorable sacrifice*.[25] Jesus is "the Victim of propitiation for our sins, and not for our sins only, but for those of the whole world" (1 Jn 2:2). The abrogation of the ancient sacrifices by

---

23 Hymn from the Pascal Season, *Ad regias Agni dapes*. ["The Love Priest immolates the members of His bountiful Body."]

24 On this passage St. Thomas writes: *"In no pure man does nature obey the will, since nature, like the will, is from God; and therefore it is necessary that the death of any pure man be natural. In Christ, however, His nature and every other nature are obedient to His will, like a work of art to the will of the craftsman*. And therefore according as He sees fit, He could lay down His life and take it up again when He wished; something which no pure man can do, even though the latter can voluntarily inflict the cause of death upon himself." *Commentary on John*, X, 17–18. In his third *Jentaculum*, which he wrote in 1524 to Poznan, Cajetan, faithful to this doctrine, mentions how, unlike a simple martyr who is a sacrifice only in the metaphorical or spiritual sense, the Savior's death is a sacrifice in the true sense. Cf. *L'Église du Verbe Incarné*, t. I, second edition, 1955, pp. 74–75.

25 With respect to the will of those who were instigators or executors, the death of Christ is certainly not a sacrifice; but with respect to the will of Christ, Who freely accepted death, it is a sacrifice. Cf. St. Thomas, *Summa Theologiae* III, qu. 22, a. 2, ad 2; qu. 48, a. 3, ad 3.

the one sacrificial act of the Cross is the central theme of the Epistle to the Hebrews: Unlike the Levitical priests, Christ does not need to offer sacrifices each day, "He did this once for all *when He Offered Himself*" (Heb 7:27); "*Having offered one sacrifice for sins*, He now sits at the right hand of God" (Heb 10:12).

And the Passion is *one act of love*: "Before the feast of Passover, Jesus realized that the hour had come for Him to pass from this world to the Father. He had loved His own in this world, and would show His love for them to the end," even to the end of love (Jn 13:1). "As the Father has loved Me, so I also have loved you" (Jn 15:9; cf. 17:23). "There is no greater love than this: to lay down one's life for one's friends" (Jn 15:13). "The way we came to know love was that He laid down His life for us" (1 Jn 3:16).

These two acts, that of sacrifice and of love, are really but one: "Follow the way of love, even as *Christ loved you*; and He gave Himself up for you *as an offering to God*, a gift of pleasing fragrance" (Eph 5:2). Water is never presented alone, nor the vase alone, said St. Catherine of Siena, but the water in the vase: the vase is the sacrifice, the water the love. The two are inseparable here below. The content, however, is more precious than the vase, love more than sacrifice: "When I hand my body over to the flames, if I have not charity, it profits me nothing" (1 Cor 13:3). One day the vase will break: the sacrifice will not overstep the threshold of the Fatherland, there will be no temple in the Holy City, "the Lord, God the Almighty, is its temple—He and the Lamb" (Rev 21:22). The content however shall endure: "Charity never fails" (1 Cor 13:8).

b) Christ Is Consecrated Priest in the Line of Worship and Saint in the Line of Love

Assumed by the Person of the Word, the humanity of the Savior is enriched with a double consecration in view of His twofold mission.

His humanity was consecrated *in the line of cultic validity*, having the mission to establish the new sacrifice commanded by God: "Christ did not glorify Himself with the office of High Priest; He received it from the One Who said to Him (Ps 2:7): 'You are my Son; this day I have begotten You'; just as He says in another place (Ps 110:4): 'You are a priest forever, according to the line of Melchizedek'" (Heb 5:5–6).

And His humanity was consecrated *in the line of the sanctity of love*, having the mission to pour out on the world a great and extraordinary effusion of grace: "I have come to cast fire upon the earth, and how I wish it were already aflame!" (Lk 12:49). "I have given them the glory that You gave Me... that the world may know that You sent Me, and that You loved them as You loved Me. . . . I have revealed to them Your name, and I will continue to reveal it, so that Your love for Me may live in them and I in them" (Jn 17:22–23, 26).

The consecration and mission of worship is at the service of the consecration and mission of love.

6. The Four Ends of Christ's Sacrifice

Christ on the Cross was one with the Father *to Whom* the sacrifice was offered; He made Himself one with them *for whom* the sacrifice was offered; He was Himself *the one Who* offered and *He Who was offered.*[26] The sacrifice of Christ could only be announced and prefigured by that which was pure in the sacrifices of the law of nature and in those of the Mosaic law. Being theandric, it is the only one to realize in a perfect manner the four ends of sacrifice: latrial, propitiatory, eucharistic, impetratory.

1. The sacrifice of Jesus on the Cross is first of all adoration; it is *latrial*. The obeisance which, in submission to the eternal divine decree, led Jesus even to the gift of His life, is the consequence, the manifestation, the expression of the most humble, the most humiliating, the most loving act of *adoration* which would ever go forth from earth to heaven.

"'The Father loves Me because *I lay down my life*. . . . No one takes it from me, *I lay it down freely.* I have the power to lay it down and the power to take it up again: *such is the command I received from my Father'*" (Jn 10:17–18). "He *emptied* Himself and took the form of a slave, being born in the likeness of men . . . He *humbled* Himself, *obediently accepting death*, death on a Cross" (Phil 2:8).

The holocaust is the hallmark of adoration.

2. The sacrifice of Jesus on the Cross is *propitiatory*. It appeases God Who was angered because of sin; it solicits His pardon; it calls forth His mercy: "We have an advocate before the Father, Jesus Christ the just one. He is Himself a *victim of propitiation* for our sins, and not for our sins alone, but for those of the whole world" (1 Jn 2:2). The Passion of Christ, counterbalancing sin, redeems us and reconciles us: "You were *redeemed* ... not by any diminishable sum of silver or gold, but by Christ's Blood beyond all price, the Blood of a spotless, unblemished Lamb" (1 Pet 1:18–19). "We have been *reconciled* with God through the death of His Son" (Rom 5:10). "God *reconciling* the world to Himself in Christ, not counting men's transgressions against them ..." (2 Cor 5:19). "It pleased God *to reconcile* through Him everything in His person, *making peace* through the Blood of His Cross" (Col 1:20).

3. The sacrifice of Jesus on the Cross is *eucharistic*. It is the greatest *act of thanksgiving*, thanking God especially for His plan of mercy on the world. At the moment that Jesus Himself instituted the memorial of His sacrifice, He rendered thanks to God by making a Eucharist of bread and wine (Lk 22:19; Mt 26:27).

---

26 St. Thomas, *Summa Theologiae* III, qu. 48, a. 3, citing here St. Augustine.

4. The sacrifice of Jesus on the Cross is *impetratory*. It is the greatest supplication, a supreme appeal to the largess of the divine goodness. Christ, "in the days of His flesh, offered prayers and supplications with loud cries and tears to God, Who was able to save Him from death, and He was heard because of His reverence" (Heb 5:7).

If the ends of sacrifice, which is a cultic act, are to adore God, to implore His pardon, to render Him thanks, to solicit His gifts, then they will be obtained in proportion to the charity vivifying the sacrifice; and there is no charity comparable to that of Jesus on the Cross.

7. The Redemptive Sacrifice Is Offered Once For All, but in Order to Be Actualized Unceasingly

1. The redemptive sacrifice is offered once in order to save, to recapitulate all ages. It occupies but a moment of time; but being the sacrifice of God, it is clothed with divine eternity, which, touching the sacrifice by its power, renders it capable of illuminating all time: the past by anticipation; the future by derivation. "'When I am lifted up from the earth *I will draw all men to Myself*.' He said this to indicate the sort of death He would suffer" (Jn 12:33). "Christ . . . entered *once for all* into the sanctuary, not with the blood of bulls or goats, but with His own Blood, *and achieved eternal redemption*" (Heb 8:12). "Now He has appeared at the end of the ages to take away sins *once for all* by His sacrifice" (Heb 9:26). "After being offered up *once* to take away the sins of many, He will appear a second time not to take away sin but to bring salvation to those who eagerly await Him" (Heb 9:27). "Wherefore, on coming into the world, Christ said, 'Sacrifice and offering You did not desire, but a body You have prepared for Me. . . . I have come to do Your will, O God ...' By this will we have been sanctified through the offering of the Body of Jesus Christ *once for all*" (Heb 10:5–10). "Having offered *one sacrifice* for sins, He sits forever at the right hand of God" (Heb 10:12). "By *one oblation* He has *forever* perfected those who are being sanctified" (Heb 10:14).

2. The conclusion is that "where sins have been remitted, there is no further offering for sin" (Heb 10:18).[27] And nevertheless, if with the passing of generations sins must continue, they will not be able to be remitted except by the presence, the application, the actualization continued in each generation of this one oblation of Christ. Concerning the words of St. Paul, "Every time, then, you eat this bread and drink this cup, you proclaim the death of the Lord until He comes" (1 Cor 11:26), St. Ambrose would write the following: "If we proclaim the death of the Lord, we proclaim as well the remission of sins. If every time His Blood is poured out

---

27 The Mass multiplies not the *one sacrifice*, but the *presences* of the one sacrifice. This is misunderstood by Protestant commentators, who since Luther and Calvin, avail themselves of this verse in order to condemn the Mass.

it is poured out for the remission of sins, then I must always receive it in order that it may always remit my sins. I, who sin always, always need a remedy."[28] There is not *another* oblation for sin; but a *presence*, an *application*, *an actualization of that one oblation*. In such a way is proclaimed the death of the Lord, until He comes again.

8. Christ, a Priest According to the Order of Melchizedek, His Priesthood and His Sacrifice Obliterate the Priesthood and Sacrifices of the Old Law

1. Jesus, explains the Epistle to the Hebrews, "has become, according to the order of Melchizedek, a High Priest forever" (Heb 6:20). The imperfect priesthood of the Old Law is blotted out before the perfect priesthood of Christ.

Christ is called a Priest "according to the order of Melchizedek," not according to the order of the Old Law. There are many reasons for this: 1) The mystery which surrounds Melchizedek, whose genealogy is not told to us (Gen 14:18), prefigures the mystery of the Son of God, Who is without genealogy, and Who therefore is designated a priest not by way of carnal succession, but by divine decree (Heb 7:3). 2) Then, we see Abraham, from whom issues forth the Levitical priesthood, offering a tithe—as an inferior to a superior—to Melchizedek, the King of Salem and priest of the Most High (Gen 14:20). 3) Finally, Melchizedek going before Abraham brings forth bread and wine (Gen 14:18), thus prefiguring the sacrifice of the Last Supper and the Mass. Psalm 110 (verse 4), cited by the Epistle to the Hebrews, already hailed the Messiah as a Priest forever, according to the example of Melchizedek.

It is by comparing the priesthood of the Old Law according to Aaron to the new priesthood of Christ according to the order of Melchizedek, that the Council of Trent begins its teaching on the sacrifice of the Mass: "The Old Testament cannot, as the Apostle Paul bears witness (Heb 7:2, 19), by reason of the *imperfection of the Levitical priesthood*, result in consummation; it was necessary, according to the mind of God the Father of Mercies, that there come forth *another Priest, according to the order of Melchizedek*, our Savior Jesus Christ, Who would be able to bring to their consummation and perfection all those who needed to be sanctified (Heb 10:14)."[29] This is why we see at the Last Supper Christ, "declaring Himself a Priest for all eternity, offering to God His Father, His own Body and Blood under the species of bread and wine."[30]

2. Just as the priesthood of Christ blots out the ancient priesthood, Christ's sacrifice blots out the ancient sacrifices: "It is impossible for the

---

28 *De sacramentis*, IV, chap. 6, no. 28, *Source chrétiennes*, no. 25.
29 Session XXII, chap. 1, Denz., 938.
30 *Ibid.*

blood of bulls and goats to take away sins. Wherefore, on coming into the world, Christ said, 'Sacrifice and offering You did not desire, but a body You have prepared for Me. . . . I have come to do Your will, O God.' He abrogates the first Covenant in order to establish the second" (Heb 10:5–10).

A question arises here. Has the worship of the previous ages been totally abrogated? Has it been preserved in any way?

9. The One Redemptive Sacrifice Recapitulates In Itself Any Good Offerings Men Have Ever Made

a) Retrospective Recapitulation

1. The cultic economy of the Old Law secretly and obscurely expressed faith in a Savior Who would come, *qui cultus erat in fide venturi*; and under this aspect it became obsolete with the coming of the Savior, *jam veniente eo qui venturus erat*. Under another aspect, nevertheless, it was perfected and accomplished in the New Law—the figure giving way to the truth.[31]

When, therefore, one says that the priesthood and the sacrifice of Christ abrogate the priesthood and the sacrifices of the Mosaic law—and those of the law of nature, such as the sacrifices of Abel (Gen 4:4), of Noah (Gen 8:20) and of Abraham (Gen 12:8; 22:1–14), etc.—it is *with respect to the* still figurative and imperfect *cultic form* of this priesthood and its sacrifices. The priesthood and sacrifice of Christ, however, do not abrogate the ancient priesthood and sacrifices *insofar as the latter announce and contain the truth;*[32] they do not abrogate them, but rather fulfill and recapitulate them. The sacraments of the Old Law, said St. Augustine, announced Christ; at His coming they were abrogated because they were fulfilled, *ideo ablata quia impleta.*[33]

2. In the immediate wake of the Fall the Cross was already raised up on the horizon of history, and it is in consideration of the future Passion of His Son that God sent to men a secret inspiration, *interior instinctus,*[34] making known to them the worship which they would have to render to Him. To the extent that they become docile to this divine impulsion (indeed, they can pervert it, derail it even quite horribly, and the devil is there to assist them in this!), and offering themselves as sacrifices, their sacrifices will be Christic—no doubt obscurely, but truly, drawing from Christ by *anticipation* their power of supplication and their salutary strength. Such

---

31 St. Thomas, *Summa Theologiae* I-II qu. 103, a. 3, ad 1 and 3.
32 The liturgical precepts of the Old Law had a twofold end: 1st, to render to God the legitimate worship *needed for that time;* 2nd, *to prefigure* the messianic salvation. St. Thomas, *Summa Theologiae* I-II, qu. 102, a. 2. Under the second aspect they are abolished; under the first they are fulfilled.
33 St. Augustine, *Contra Faustum*, XIX, 13. Cf. St. Thomas, *Summa Theologiae* III, qu. 61, a. 4, sed contra.
34 St. Thomas, *Summa Theologiae* III, qu. 60, a. 5, ad 3.

that, when Christ will be lifted up from the earth (Jn 12:32), it will be in order to raise up the desire, and to bear the burden of the previous thousands of years of history. According to St. Irenaeus, we have seen "the recapitulation" of all the blood of the just and the prophets, poured out in Abel and since the beginning of the world, "fulfilled" when the blood of Jesus was poured out.[35] Likewise, St. Thomas sees in the pouring out of the blood of all the just who have ever lived and whom Christ would visit in Limbo, "a prefiguration of the pouring out of Christ's Blood."[36]

b) Prospective Recapitulation

The one redemptive offering raises up in advance, assumes, recapitulates most mysteriously, intimately and completely, future offerings, this time by way *of application, of derivation*: the sign of which was the flow "of blood and water" (Jn 19:34) from the pierced side of Jesus; "for the Spirit had not yet been given, since Jesus had not yet been glorified" (Jn 7:39).[37] And it is in order to assure the integrity of this application and this derivation, unknown to previous ages, that the sacrificial rite of the Last Supper would be instituted.

10. The Sacrifice of the Cross Does Not Take Place Without the Participation of Humanity

If, according to the mind of St. Irenaeus, Christ recapitulates and requires (*exquirit*) the blood of the just of previous ages, where only the shadow of the Cross had extended over the world, in order to save it; if, furthermore, by the founding of a new economy, He recapitulates in advance the supplication of subsequent ages, where the memorial of His death will be perpetuated until He comes again; if, in short, the Cross is the tree where there changes into blood all that has ever had value in human offerings, then it must be said that that redemptive sacrifice, the offering of Christ for the world's salvation, was not an offering of Christ alone, isolated from men, but rather the offering of Christ incorporating as well the offering of men. The sacrifice of Christ does not take place without the participation of humanity. Humanity is called to immerse itself in the sacrifice, to be redeemed, to offer Christ the Redeemer, to follow Him in the offering which He makes of Himself, to strive to be coredemptrix in

---

35 St. Iranaeus, *Adversus haereses*, V, chap. 14, n 1; PG VII, 1161.
36 St. Thomas, *Comm. Ad Hebr.*, XII, 24.
37 "The blood attests to the reality of the Lamb's sacrifice offered for the salvation of the world; and the water, a symbol of the Spirit, attests to its spiritual fecundity. *By the blood we have the water of the Spirit* (St. Hippolytus). Numerous Fathers of the Church have seen in the water the symbol of Baptism, in the blood that of the Eucharist, and in these two sacraments the sign of the Church, the New Eve being born from the side of the New Adam." D. Mollat, S.J., *Saint Jean* (Paris: Édit. Du Cerf, 1953), p. 189.

Him and through Him. Insofar as that happens humanity constitutes at each of its stages the Church, which is the Body of Christ.

11. The Participation of the Blessed Virgin and St. John at the Sacrifice of the Cross[38]

1. Christ is the Head, the Church His Body. He does not *evacuate* the Church; He *pulls it along* in His wake. What He does in a sovereign manner as Head, she must do in dependence on Him, vivified by Him, carried by Him as His Body.

a) The Blessed Virgin and St. John prefigure the Church at the foot of the Cross. To His infinite theandric offering Christ unites their created finite offering. He envelops it, sustains it, raises it up; similar to the way in which the Infinite Being envelops, sustains and raises up finite beings. "Christ being the Head of the Church, grace was given to Him not only as an individual person, but also in view of overflowing onto His members, such that the works of Christ have value for Him and for His members, as the works of a man, who possesses grace, have value for himself."[39]

Certainly this does not mean that the offering of the Blessed Virgin and St. John could add anything intensively to Christ's offering; but it could be expanded, deepened, vivified, sanctified by this contact. This offering, united to the supplication of Jesus, represents the unspeakable distress of very loving creatures, torn by the spectacle of evil which seems to drown the world. It can, from then on, become a coredemptrix for the world—no doubt to various degrees. For the Blessed Virgin, her offering is coredemptive of all that is Christ's the Redeemer; her intercession is universal. The offering of St. John is more restricted.

b) At the same time that He pulls them along in the offering of His ascending mediation, Christ pours out on the Blessed Virgin and St. John—that is, on the heart of the Church of that time—the treasures of a definitive and fully Christ-conforming grace. "The human nature of Christ," says St. Thomas, "is the instrument of the divinity; consequently, all the actions and passions of Christ act instrumentally, under the motion of the divinity, in order to procure men's salvation. The Passion of Christ is thus the efficient cause of our salvation."[40]

2. At the moment when the drama of the world's redemption is completed on the Cross, Christ desires that the Church, the Church of that time, be engaged in it in the measure that she is capable. The participation in the oblation of the Cross, which is at once liturgical, bloody and loving, happens then *by immediate contact*, that is without recourse to sacramental signs and an unbloody rite.

---

38   See below, p. 94.
39   St. Thomas, *Summa Theologiae* III, qu. 48, a. 1.
40   St. Thomas, *Summa Theologiae* III, qu. 48, a. 6.

At the Last Supper and at the Mass it is, on the contrary, *under sacra-mental signs and an unbloody rite* that the entrance into the sacrificial drama is proposed, first to the Apostles, then to Christians of future ages.

One must remember, therefore, two manners by which the Church participates fully in the redemptive drama: one of them, passing, by immediate contact with the bloody sacrifice—that of the Church at the very foot of the Cross, that of the Blessed Virgin and of St. John; the other, permanent, bringing to us the bloody sacrifice in the envelopment of the unbloody sacrifice, instituted at the Last Supper by the Savior in order to be reproduced by His disciples—that of the Church in waiting for the return of Christ.

CHAPTER 2

The Unbloody or Sacramental Presence of the One Redemptive Sacrifice at the Last Supper and the Mass: Revealed Doctrine and Protestant Innovation

Regarding the relationship between the one sacrifice of the Cross and the unbloody sacrifice of the Last Supper and the Mass, we can recall the mysterious revelation of Scripture, note its reaffirmation and clarification by the Council of Trent, and outline the meaning of the Lutheran innovation.

1. The Teaching of Sacred Scripture: The Event of the Bloody Sacrifice and the Institution of the Unbloody Sacrifice

The sacrifice of the Cross is a unique event; the sacrifice of the Last Supper is a permanent institution. Is it necessary to choose between the Cross and the Last Supper, between the *event* and the *institution*?

a) The Unicity and Non-Reiterability of the Redemptive Sacrifice

Scripture reveals to us the unicity and non-reiterability of the redemptive sacrifice. This is the great theme of the Epistle to the Hebrews: "By one offering Christ has perfected forever those who are sanctified" (Heb 10:14).

The Epistle to the Hebrews' insistence upon the redemptive sacrifice's unity to the multiplicity of the Old Law's bloody sacrifices is sufficiently accounted for by the nature of things and by the importance of the revolution which established a new age of worship.

It is even exegetically more clear if one grants that this Epistle is addressed—perhaps by Apollo—to a group of ancient priests who had just converted to the Faith of Christ (Acts 6:7), having been chased out of Jerusalem by the persecution which followed the death of Stephen, having taken refuge in a small town near the sea, such as Caesarea or Antioch, and now bearing with difficulty the lack of spectacular and numerous actions of the old cult and its sacrifices: "Accustomed to the splendors of the Levitical cult, and reduced to laity status, these priests were tempted to return to Judaism and the Mosaic liturgy. The Epistle to the Hebrews responds to this psychology by justifying the totally spiritual and interior character of the new religion which, however, hardly supplies sensible support. Before their conversion, for example, these priests had the right to eat a part of the immolated victims; in the future they would be excluded from the altars from which their old confreres would still nourish themselves. In reality they have one altar, Christ in person, but in which one participates only by faith (Heb 13:10). The wording of the phrase contrasts two categories of priests: those who remain faithful to the customary Levitical law; and those who are excluded from it. The truism of Hebrews 10:18, which concludes the doctrinal argumentation of the Epistle: *Now where there is forgiveness of these, there is no longer an offering for sin*, is understood perfectly in its absolute formulation,[1] if it is addressed to Judeo-Christian priests preserving the nostalgia of their ancient ministry. There is no longer an offering to be fulfilled, no longer sacrifices to be presented. The priesthood of Jesus Christ has provided for all the remission of sins once and for all."[2]

b) The Necessity to Repeat the Unbloody Sacrifice of the Last Supper

1. Sacred Scripture also reveals to us, with no less force, the *obligation of reproducing the unbloody sacrifice of the Last Supper*. Here are three passages.

1) First of all *the very account of the Last Supper*. It is a sacrifice: it contains under a sacramental and unbloody envelopment *Christ insofar as He is actually offered and immolated*. And it is as such that *it is necessary to reproduce it*: "And having taken bread, He gave thanks and broke, and gave it to them saying, 'This is My Body, which is being given for you; *do this in remembrance of Me*'" (Lk 22:19; 1 Cor 11:24). "'This cup is the New Covenant in My Blood; *do this as often as you drink it, in remembrance of Me*'" (1 Cor 11:25).

In memory of Jesus, then, something must not only be *said*, but *done*. What? That which He Himself had just come to do. He had just come (this much the Lutherans understand) to render His Body present in the Eucharist. More precisely still (here the Lutherans cease to understand), that which He just came to render present in the Eucharist is, say St. Luke, *My Body given for you*, and St. Paul, *My Body for you*; it is, say St. Mark (Mk 14:24) and St. Matthew (Mt 26:28), His Blood, the Blood of the Covenant, *poured out for many*; and, in fact, the Passion has already

---

1   On the profound and permanent theological sense of this phrase, see above, chap. 1, no. 7, paragraph 2.

2   C. Spicq, "L'Épître aux Hébreux," Introduction, *Bible de Jérusalem* (Paris, 1950), p. 11,.

3   "This Covenant is properly called the Testament of Jesus, Who would die and shed His Blood. This Blood is poured out in the present, but represents the future with respect to the reality of the deed . . . But from that moment, this effusion is considered a sacrifice, and it is in the quality of Blood poured out that the Blood of Jesus appears in the cup." M.-J. Lagrange, *Évangile selon Marc* (Paris: Gabalda, 1911), p. 355.

begun, it is in the process of being completed.[3] Therefore, in memory of Christ and in commemoration of Him, the disciples would have to render present in the Eucharist His Body *insofar as it was given for us*, His Blood *insofar as it was poured out for many*. St. Matthew adds here that this Blood is poured out *for the remission of sins*, which accentuates all the more the sacrificial and propitiatory character of the Last Supper. In short, they would have to render present in the Eucharist Christ *insofar as He offers Himself and immolates Himself for the remission of sins*.

There would be multiplied, then, according to the will of Christ, sacramental and unbloody offerings and immolations, unbloody sacrifices, containing the one bloody sacrifice. Like the ancient Passover, the new Passover would be a sacrificial memorial—not the simple keepsake of a sacrifice, but a true sacrifice. This would happen certainly not by the impossible reiteration of the unique sacrifice, but by the reiteration of the presence of the unique sacrifice under the unbloody rite.

2) The second passage does not concern the institution of the Last Supper. It brings us to the year AD 55. *What is taking place in the Church of God in Corinth?* St. Paul speaks of a table which is an altar; of a bread which is the Body of the Lord, of a cup which is the Blood of the Lord; of a union of faithful united in this Body and Blood through its consumption, the way in which the Jews participated in the sacrifices of the Mosaic law and the Gentiles in the sacrifices to idols. Neither the sacrifices of the Gentiles nor those of Israel, however, are permitted any longer, under pain of provoking the Lord to jealousy. Today Christians have their own sacrifice, where they participate by drinking of the Lord's chalice and sharing in His table. Here is the text: "The cup of blessing that we bless, is it not the sharing of the Blood of Christ? And the bread that we break, is it not the partaking of the Body of the Lord? Because the bread is one, we though many, are one body, all of us who partake of the one bread. Behold Israel, according to the flesh, are not they who eat of the sacrifices partakers of the altar? What then do I say? That what is sacrificed to idols is anything, or that an idol is anything? No; but I say that, what the Gentiles sacrifice, 'they sacrifice to devils and not to God'; and I would not have you become associates of devils. You cannot drink the cup of the Lord and the cup of devils; you cannot be partakers of the table of the Lord and the table of devils. Or are we provoking the Lord to jealousy? Are we stronger than He?" (1 Cor 10:16–22).

Note the parallelism of opposition between:

- The *victims* offered in Israel and the meat sacrificed to idols
- The *altar* of Israel and the table of demons
- *Those who eat* either the victims of Israel's altar or the idolaters'

- The *bread* which we break, the cup which we bless
- The *table* of the Lord
- *Those who eat* of the table of the Lord and drink of His cup

If the "bread" and the "cup" of Christ were not offered to God in sacrifice, says Cajetan, St. Paul's entire argument would crumble.

3) That passage from chapter 11 must be included where, after having narrated the mysterious institution of the Last Supper, St. Paul declares that he who approaches this banquet unworthily will be *"guilty of the Body and Blood of the Lord,"* namely—it is clear—of Christ insofar as He is immolated (1 Cor 11:27).

He had just said immediately beforehand: "For as often as you shall eat this bread and drink this cup, *you proclaim the death of the Lord, until He comes"* (1 Cor 11:26). Because it contains the Body and Blood of Christ, that is to say Christ Who comes to us under the signs of His immolation, the Eucharist *proclaims* and makes present throughout time *the death of the Lord,* which took place once in time in order to save all times, *until He comes* to judge all times. It must be renewed with the passing of generations, which need to be immersed in the Blood of Christ as they go forth in time and for as long as they exist. Its redemptive role will not cease except at the end of history, when Christ will come in glory to transfigure the universe.

2. What can we conclude? If Scripture is the rule of our faith, it is necessary to believe by its authority on one hand the absolute perfection of the one bloody sacrifice, the sacrifice-event of the Cross, and on the other hand the necessity of reproducing until the end of time the unbloody sacrifice, the sacrifice-institution of the Last Supper.

2. Is the Necessity of Reproducing the Sacrifice of the Last Supper Compatible or Incompatible With the Perfection of the One Sacrifice of the Cross?

a) Two Opposing Conceptions of the Relation Between the Cross and the Mass

1. When Scripture teaches us first, that the redemptive sacrifice is unique, offered once for all, perfect, and then, that it is necessary to reproduce the unbloody sacrifice of the Last Supper, we know well that it is not throwing us into contradiction, but that it is opening to us a mystery—the *mysterium fidei* as the liturgy calls it. We do not choose between the sacrifice of the Cross and that of the Last Supper, between the *sacrifice-event* and the *sacrifice-institution*; we preserve all of Scripture. The sacrifice-institution, in our eyes, does not multiply the sacrifice-event; *it multiplies the real presences of the sacrifice-event.*

2. Others (the Protestants), however, pose as a rule that, if the offering, if the sacrifice of the *Cross* is perfect, then there can be no question under any pretext of a sacrifice, of an offering, be it at the *Last Supper* or *a fortiori* at the *Mass.* Christ saved the faithful by one *unique sacrifice,* how could they place their confidence in *another sacrifice?*

It is, first of all, the interpretation of the texts of Scripture concerning the *Last Supper* which would begin to change. They would not be able in any way to signify a sacrifice or an offering of Christ.

Then comes violence done to the *Mass*. It is a "scandal," wrote Luther, to think "that the Mass is, as is everywhere believed, a sacrifice offered to God."[4] For Calvin, Satan alone was able to blind "almost all the world with this pestilent error, which says that the Mass is a sacrifice and oblation for asking for the remission of sins. . . . There would never rise up a more powerful machine for combating and demoralizing the reign of Jesus Christ."[5]

b) The Mass Juxtaposed With the Cross

1. What is the immediate reason for such a brutal rupture?

It is furnished for us by the Reformers themselves. They deliberately *juxtapose* in their mind the notion of the unbloody sacrifice of the Last Supper and the Mass with the one sacrifice of the Cross. The former, therefore, could not appear but as the notion of *another* sacrifice, a *rival* to the latter, *bringing about injury* to the latter. One would have to choose between the bloody sacrifice and the unbloody sacrifices; and then the choice was made.

In such a way Calvin endeavored to prove that the Mass, in whatever way it might be "dressed and adorned," greatly dishonors Jesus Christ, oppresses and enslaves the Cross, makes one forget Christ's death and steals away the fruit with which that death provides us.[6] At the Mass, according to Calvin, a mortal priest *is substituted* for the eternal Priest, *another* sacrifice *is added* to that of the Cross, now considered as *imperfect*, a *new redemption* and *another remission* than that of the Cross is proposed to us.[7]

2. From that point of view one ceases to understand that that which Christ Himself rendered present at the Last Supper was His Body *handed over* for us, His Blood *poured out* for the many, *for the sake of the remission of sins.*

One forgets that the Christians of Corinth distinguished between the sacrifices of the Jews and Gentiles and a sacrifice in which they would participate by drinking of the Lord's cup and sharing in His table; and that it was necessary *to proclaim the death of the Lord* by communicating in *His Body and His Blood.*

One ends up fabricating an exegesis destined to destroy the Scriptural notion—already distorted—of the unbloody sacrifice. It is denied that by

4   Martin Luther, *De captivitate babylonica Ecclesiae praeludium*, 1520; chap. "De Coena Domini." Édition d'Iéna, 1566, pp. 261 and ff.
5   John Calvin, *Institution chrétienne*, IV, chap. 18, nos. 1 and 18; edit. De Genève 1888, revised and corrected in the French edition of 1560.
6   *Ibid.*
7   *Ibid.*, nos. 2 and 6.

the words, *Do this in memory of Me*, Christ was able to make the Apostles priests and ordain them and other priests "to offer His Body and His Blood"; and it is denied that the Mass is "the offering of a real and true sacrifice to God." If one happens to speak of the Mass as an offering of Christ, "it is simply that His Body is given as nourishment"; it is nothing other "than a pure commemoration, *nuda commemoratio*," a non-sacrificial commemoration of the sacrifice completed on the Cross, etc.[8]

These are the reasons by which the Lutherans and Calvinists upset the profound evangelical and Pauline mystery of the Last Supper and the Mass.

3. It is clear that the Reformers conceived but one way to compare the unbloody sacrifice, whether that of the Last Supper or of the Mass, to the bloody sacrifice of the Cross: *juxtaposition*, addition, concurrence, substitution. They never thought to, or never wanted to give any attention to the idea of *subordination*. Because of such a prejudice, they see it as praiseworthy to find in the Epistle to the Hebrews the condemnation of the sacrifice of the Last Supper and the Mass. It is precisely this prejudice, however, which shuts down their understanding of the unbloody sacrifice and makes their exegesis stray from the right path, for which we reproach them first and foremost.[9]

c) The Mass Subordinated to the Cross

It is folly, in our eyes, to see in the sacrifice of the Last Supper or the Mass a sacrifice which can compete with the sacrifice of the Cross, a sacrifice *juxtaposed*, joined, substituted for the sacrifice of the Cross. The entire substance of the Church's teaching on this point, the fundamental intuition which she proclaims against Protestantism, is, on the contrary, that the Mass is in its essence a sacrifice which depends on the sacrifice of the Cross—totally *subordinated* and in complete reference to the sacrifice of the Cross, uniquely destined to perpetuate, to prolong even unto us the perfect sacrifice which was offered on the Cross once and for all. The repetition of the unbloody sacrifice multiplies among us the real presences of the bloody sacrifice; the repetition of the sacrifice-institution multiplies among us the real presences of the sacrifice-event.

---

8   These are the theses to which are directly opposed the first, second and third canons of the Council of Trent regarding the sacrifice of the Mass, session 22, Denz. 948, 949, 950. The preparatory discussion was about the thirteen theses; cf. Ehses, *Acta Concilii Tridentini*, Friburgi Brisgoviae, t. VIII, p. 719. The following are the main principles from the dogmatic point of view: 1) Is the Mass a simple commemoration of the sacrifice completed at the Last Supper, and not a true sacrifice? 2) Does the sacrifice of the Mass depart from the sacrifice at the Last Supper? 3) By the words, "Do this in memory of Me," did Christ ordain the Apostles to offer His Body and Blood at Mass? Is saying that Christ is immolated mystically for us simply to say that He is given to us to eat?

9   On the general signification of the Lutheran innovation, see below, p. 56.

We see no contradiction whatsoever in believing that the redemptive sacrifice—fulfilled in one thrust with respect to the Savior, Who is the Head, the Leader, but incomplete with respect to the men who are His members, as long as they need to be saved, to be incorporated into the sufferings and death of their Head—we see no contradiction in believing that the redemptive sacrifice continues to take place through the Mass, continues to be accomplished certainly not intensively but extensively, until Christ's Body the Church be fully built up.

Such is the substance of the teaching of the Council of Trent.

3. The Doctrine of the Council of Trent on the Essential Identity and Modal Difference Between the Sacrifice of the Cross and the Mass

a) An Overall View

The Council of Trent[10] begins by recalling the doctrine of the Epistle to the Hebrews, according to which Christ, by offering Himself once for all on the Cross, obtained for us an eternal redemption. According to that same Epistle, however, the priesthood of Christ could not be annulled.[11] The one bloody sacrifice of the Cross, therefore, would need to be actualized for each generation. This will be the role of the unbloody sacrifice, first instituted at the Last Supper, in order to be later reproduced at each Mass.

With regards to the unbloody sacrifice the Council affirms two things. First, it is at the *Last Supper* that Christ offers to God His Father His Body and His Blood under the species of bread and wine:[12] which signifies that the Last Supper was—the Reformers did not see this—an offering, a sacrifice. Second, today at the *Mass* a real and true sacrifice is offered to God.[13]

If there is but one sole redemptive sacrifice in the New Covenant, that of the Cross, how could the *Last Supper* be a true sacrifice? There can be only one response: The Last Supper was not *another* sacrifice than that of the Cross; it was the very same sacrifice of the Cross, *already begun at that hour* and made present, as it would need to be henceforth, under the appearances of bread and wine.

And if there is but one redemptive sacrifice in the New Covenant, that of the Cross, how can the *Mass* be a true sacrifice? Again, there can be only one response: The Mass is not *another* sacrifice than that of the

---

10 September 17, 1562, Session XXII, chap. 1, Denz. 938.
11 "But He (Christ), because He lives forever, has an everlasting priesthood. Therefore He is able at all times to save those who come to God through Him, since *He lives always to make intercession for them.*" Heb 7:24–25.
12 Council of Trent, Chap. 1, Denz. 938.
13 Council of Trent, Chap. 1, Denz. 948.

Cross. The sacrifice, in both cases, is substantially identical; the Victim is identical. It differs only accidentally, modally, that is with respect to the mode of presentation. For on one hand, Christ, present under His natural and proper appearances, offered Himself in a bloody manner and without the use of any ministry; and, on the other hand, Christ, present under the sacramental or borrowed appearances, offers Himself in an unbloody manner by using the ministry of priests.[14] It is impossible for the sacrifice of the Mass to be in rivalry with that of the Cross; for the entire work of the Mass represents to us, makes present to us the bloody sacrifice, and applies to us its saving power for the remission of sins which we commit each day.[15] It is by means of the unbloody oblation that the fruits of the bloody oblation are abundantly received.[16]

b) The Texts

Below are the texts of the Council which concern the relations between the sacrifice of the Cross and the sacrifice of the Mass.

"Although He was once and for all to offer Himself through death on the altar of the Cross," Christ during the Last Supper "offered to God His Father His own Body and Blood under the species of bread and wine," in view of leaving to His Bride the Church "a visible sacrifice, by which the bloody sacrifice which He was once for all to accomplish on the Cross would be *represented*, and its memory *perpetuated* until the end of the world and its salutary power *applied* for the forgiveness of the sins which we daily commit."[17]

"In this divine sacrifice which is celebrated in the Mass, *the same Christ Who offered Himself once in a bloody manner on the altar of the Cross is contained and immolated* in an unbloody manner. Therefore, the holy Council teaches that this sacrifice is truly propitiatory, so that, if we draw near to God with an upright heart and true faith, with fear and reverence, with sorrow and repentance, through it 'we may receive mercy and find grace to help in time of need' (Heb 4:16). For the Lord, appeased by this oblation, grants grace and the gift of repentance, and He pardons wrong-doings and sins, even grave ones."[18]

At the Cross and at the Mass, *a)* "the Victim is one and the same, *b)* the same Jesus Who then offered Himself on the Cross, now offers Himself through the ministry of priests, *c)* only the manner of offering is different, *sola offerendi ratione diversa.*"[19]

---

14   Chap. 2, Denz. 940.
15   Chap. 1, Denz. 938.
16   Chap. 2, Denz. 940.
17   Chap. 1, Denz. 938.
18   Chap. 2, Denz. 940.
19   *Ibid.*

"The fruits of this oblation are received in abundance through this unbloody oblation, *per hanc incruentam*; by no means, then, does the latter detract from the former."[20]

c) Conclusion

Such is the doctrine which the Council of Trent, in opposition to the fatal innovation of the Reform and proposes to the Catholic Faith, soaring beyond the tumult of the theological opinions of the time and laying bare the initial evangelical revelation. It is enough to feed the gaze of loving contemplation, which will never penetrate to its base. It in fact opens up onto the very mystery of the redemptive sacrifice: on one hand, from the part of its *unicity* and its *infinite intrinsic perfection*; on the other hand, from the part of its presence and its *actualization* for each of the succeeding generations. For the Mass is not *another* sacrifice than that of the Cross and one which *juxtaposes itself* to it. It is a sacrifice only by *identifying itself* with it with respect to its content, namely Christ, Priest and Victim; and by *subordinating itself* to it with respect to its sacramental and unbloody container, destined throughout time to represent it, to perpetuate its memory and to apply its salutary power.

The Reform was in the process of no longer understanding that the unbloody sacrifice of the Mass is the means by which the bloody sacrifice of the Cross enters into full and direct contact with later generations, and touches the flow of time in order to purify it.

4. The General Signification of the Lutheran Innovation

a) Is the Mass Only a Promise Like Those of the Old Testament, but More Perfect?

1. Luther affirmed, as we do, that God, Who could have saved the world from the heights of heaven, saved it nevertheless through the contact of His bloody Passion. Luther's innovation took place when he assured that it is enough that the redemptive sacrifice entered into contact with the world in the past; that it is useless that it touch by means of an unbloody rite men from all countries and of all times; that it suffices that it be recalled to them through preaching. The doctrine of the real and perpetuated presence of the very sacrifice of the Cross by way of contact is what he needed to deny. The Mass becomes for him but a sermon; it recalls the promise which God made to pardon sin (in the Lutheran sense of pardoning, that is by simply not imputing it and without actually removing it).

"The Mass," writes Luther in his *Prelude to the Church's Babylonian Captivity*, "is the act of kindness of the divine promise proposed to all men through the hands of the priests. There is in the Mass but two things: the

20 *Ibid.*

divine promise and human faith, the latter receiving what the former promises.

"The Mass is nothing other than the divine promise or testament of Christ, enriched by the sacrament of the Body and Blood. The Mass, in its substance, is really nothing other than the words of Christ—*Take and eat*, etc. As if He said: 'Here, O sinful and damned man, on account of the pure and gratuitous charity with which I love you, and by the will of the Father of mercies, I promise you by these words, before any merit and desire on your part, the remission of all your sins and eternal life. And in order to make you most certain of My irrevocable promise, I will give My Body and pour out My Blood, confirming My promise by death, and leaving you both of these as a sign and memorial of this promise.'

"*Few people know this: the Mass is but a promise, like the promises made to Adam, to Noah in the rainbow, to Abraham, to Moses, but more perfect than these; for it promises not temporal goods but the remission of sins. It is not a sacrifice. Nothing is offered to God there. If one does not agree with this,*" adds Luther, "*the entire Gospel is lost.*"

2. Is it true? Let us reread the Gospel texts: "This cup is the New Covenant in My Blood" (Lk 22:20; 1 Cor 11:25).[21] The cup is the Covenant, the Testament, because it contains the Blood of Christ, because in it is present the price of the world's redemption. Two other evangelists employ the direct style: "Taking the cup . . . He said to them: 'This is My Blood of the Covenant, shed for the multitude" (Mk 14:23–24) "for the remission of sins'" (Mt 26:20). What is present at the Last Supper is the Blood of Christ *having the power to bring about the redemption of the world*, the Blood of Christ *with its effect, which is the remission of the sins of the many*. The Body and Blood are therefore truly *offered*; they are truly *given* to God for us, if it is true that at that moment the redemptive sacrifice is already begun. The Body and Blood which are present under the sacramental appearances *are the Body and Blood already engaged in the bloody sacrifice*, which would find its end on the Cross. The Gospel expressly says: "This is My Body . . . *given*, διδόμενον for you" (Lk 22:19); "This is My Blood . . . *poured out*, ἐκχυννόμενον, for many," that is to say for the multitude (Mk 14:24 and Mt 26:28). And if the Last Supper must be repeated, this is what it will bring forth each time for every generation. If one does not agree with this, it is Scripture itself which is destroyed.

21 In accordance with the grammar it should read: "This cup is the New Covenant *because it* contains My Blood," rather than: "This cup *which* contains My Blood is the New Covenant." E.-B. Allo, O. P., *Première Épître aux Corinthiens* (Paris: Gabalda, 1935), p. 280.

b) Is the Redemptive Sacrifice Met as Something Present by Way of Contact, or as Something Absent by Way of Remembrance?

1. We now consider the importance of Luther's innovation. The Church proclaims the redemptive sacrifice unique, but its salvific power echoes from age to age in order to reach out and draw to itself all men. Luther wished to close up that redemptive sacrifice in the past, cut it off from contact with future ages, preach it as a thing entirely past, which faith must know as absent: at this price only, he thinks, is the redemptive sacrifice unique.

Luther did not go much further. However, what he would say against the permanence of the sacrifice of the Cross in our midst, others would begin to say against the permanence of Christ Himself in our midst. When Zwingli would hold that the bodily presence of Christ must be pushed back totally into the past, that it is not continued under sacramental veils, that it furthermore serves us nothing, that it must be preached as a pure fact of history and not as a contemporary fact distinct from the faith which we have in it—when he would hold all this he would drag along after him the majority of Protestantism. It is in vain that, in order to defend the Eucharistic presence, Luther would refer to Scriptural texts which he held to be unshakable.

2. Following the traditional conception, the drama of the redemptive Incarnation is brought about at the very beginning of the New Covenant, in order to perpetuate itself throughout history until Christ comes in glory. And God, Who so loved the world that He gave it the corporal presence of His bloody Passion, loved the world enough to leave it this presence and not take it away. This is the sense of the mystery of the first Supper and the Mass, where to us is revealed the fullness of God's love for the men of our time.

Following the new [i.e. Protestant] conception, on the contrary, the drama of the redemptive Incarnation is produced at the very beginning of Christianity in order to be immediately taken back into the heavens, and to leave in history no more than the greatest of memories, the most solemn of promises. The Last Supper and the Mass—when we keep them—are quickly reduced to nothing but purely commemorative symbols. From then on, everything which pretends to perpetuate the corporal presence of Christ or His redemptive sacrifice appears as an imposture, an invention of Satan. According to this conception, the purity of the Cross must be defended against the impurity of the Mass.

c) Ignorance of Change in the Economy of Salvation Brought About by the New Law

1. The faith of the ancient just, who are proposed to us as examples in the eleventh chapter of the Epistle to the Hebrews—the faith of Abel, Noah,

Abraham, Isaac, Jacob, Joseph, Moses—that faith is, without a doubt, of the same nature, of the same *species* as the faith of the New Testament. It is distinguished from it, nevertheless, by its *state*, by something which dwells exterior to it, and which is due to the different historic conditions of believers.[22]

The ancient just awaited the coming among men of a *still absent* Reality, one which had been proposed to them only under pure signs, pure figures—at the most, capable of promising it but incapable of receiving it. In the New Testament, the disciples believe in a Reality *present* among them, certainly not revealed as it is in heaven, but hidden under the veil of signs and figures. The ancients, through faith, touched Christ in spirit, *corporally distant and absent*; in the New Testament the disciples, through faith, touch Christ in spirit, *corporally present in their midst*, first under His natural appearances, then under sacramental appearances. This corporal presence of Christ, which makes the innate difference between the Old and New Testaments, is an inexpressible favor: "Truly, I say to you, many of the prophets and the just desired to see what you have seen, and did not see it, and to hear what you have heard, and did not hear it" (Mt 13:16).

2. It is from the Cross where He was lifted up, that Christ draws all men to Himself (Jn 12:32). But He does this in different ways: by *anticipation* for the previous ages, where grace was granted in expectation of Christ's future Passion; by *derivation* for later ages, where grace is given as an outpouring from the opened side of Christ on the Cross. The sacraments of the Old Law were but simple practical *signs* of grace, indicating the subjects to whom God would give it directly and by reason of the future Passion. The sacraments of the New Law are, in addition, the *instruments* which Christ uses in order to lead in a superabundant manner the grace of His past Passion into each soul.[23]

3. From this point of view, Protestantism, which tries to appeal to "contact by faith" in the redemptive Promise in order to declare useless the "corporal contact" of the redemptive Passion, appears as an ignorance of the very nature of the New Testament, as an unconscious nostalgia for the Old Law, as a return to the past, as a recoiling before the exigencies of the law of the Incarnation. And Liberal Protestantism, which ends by being horrified at the very mystery of the Word made Flesh, must pass not for an improved form of Protestantism, but for its extreme form and its eternal temptation.

4. From a higher point of view, the Christian must finally grant that the great errors and schisms are permitted for some mysterious progress

---

22   Faith, says St. Thomas, is the same in the Old and New Testaments; it differs in *state* (*Summa Theologiae* I-II, qu. 107, a. 1, ad 1) by reason of the condition of believers (*Summa Theologiae* II-II, qu. 4, a. 6, ad 2).

23   Cf. Council of Florence, *Decretum pro Armenis*, 22 November 1439, Denz. 695.

of truth and unity in the world; whence the troubling words of the Master: "It is necessary that scandals come, but woe to the man by whom they come" (Mt 18:7); to which the Apostle makes an echo: "It is necessary that there be divisions among you, in order to reveal those among you who overcome the trial" (1 Cor 11:19).

The Protestant deviation has given place to a more explicit awareness of the revealed teaching on the unbloody sacrifice, be it of the Last Supper or of the Mass. By placing ourselves at the crux of the doctrine of the Council of Trent, we shall try to clarify some points concerning first the Last Supper, then the Mass.

5. Since Her Beginning the Church Confesses the Mystery of the Unity of the Sacrifice at the Cross, the Last Supper and the Mass

First, however, it will be useful to present in chronological order some texts where there appeared the interior conviction of the primitive Church, previous to any theological elaboration.

When the Council of Trent defined that the Mass is a true and proper sacrifice, it intended to confess what Scripture had revealed and what the Church had always believed. The opposing contemporary doctrines affirmed, on the contrary, that, by seeing in the Mass a sacrifice, one departs from the sacrifice of the Cross and substitutes a human invention for the Gospel, that we cannot offer the Body and Blood of Christ, that we simply commemorate His death, and that the Fathers called it a sacrifice only in a metaphorical sense.

Let us take a look then at the testimony of the Fathers.

a) Justin and Irenaeus

1. St. Justin († c. 165) tried to explain to Trypho, a Jew, that the grain offering for the purification of lepers in the Old Testament was "the figure (*the type*) of the bread of thanksgiving (*of the Eucharist*) which Jesus Christ our Lord enjoined us to make in commemorating His Passion," which He underwent in order to purify the leper from sin. "We thank God at the same time for having created the world for us with all that it contains, for having freed us from the evil in which we are, for having definitively destroyed the principalities and powers of evil through Him Who suffered according to His will." Regarding the sacrifices formerly offered in the Temple, continues Justin, God said through the mouth of Malachi (Mal 1:10–11), that He would no longer accept them; "On the contrary, *regarding the sacrifices which we, the Gentiles, everywhere offer Him, namely the bread of thanksgiving and likewise the cup of thanksgiving*, He proclaimed beforehand, saying that we shall glorify His Name which you profane."[24]

---

24 St. Justin Martyr, *Dialogue With Trypho*, chap. 41, 1–3.

Thus the sacrifice of the Passion is commemorated by the sacrifice of bread and wine, the sacrifice of thanksgiving, which perfects and abolishes the ancient sacrifices. In this text the thanksgiving, or eucharist, and the sacrifice are one and the same; and, no doubt, every thanksgiving is not a sacrifice in the proper sense, but every true sacrifice is ordained toward thanksgiving.

2. St. Irenaeus recalls that God, Who was not pleased with the sacrifices of the Old Testament, "gave His disciples the counsel to offer to Him the first fruits of His creation; not that He has any need of them, but in order that they themselves might not be fruitless or ungrateful. Also, having taken the bread which comes from His creation, and having given thanks, He says: 'This is My Body.' And likewise, having taken the cup, which comes from the creation of which we are, He declares it His Blood, *instituting the oblation of the New Testament. The Church received it from the Apostles, and throughout the whole world it offers it to God*, from Whom we receive all nourishment. Such are the first fruits of His gifts in the New Law. The Prophet Malachi (Mal 1:10–11) had announced this offering, *and noted that at the time when the former people would cease from their sacrifices, a pure sacrifice would be offered in all places to God*, the name of Whom is glorified among the Gentiles."[25] Thus, according to Irenaeus, the sacrifices of the Old Testament are abolished, but the sacrifice has not ceased: the Body and Blood of the Lord is offered by the Church throughout the entire world.

b) Hippolytus of Rome and Cyprian of Carthage

1. The *Apostolic Tradition* (c. 215–220) of Hippolytus of Rome speaks thus about the institution of the Eucharist: "Whereas He (Jesus Christ) delivered Himself up voluntarily to suffering in order to destroy death and break the chains of the devil, to bring hell to its knees, to enlighten the just, to establish the Covenant and manifest His Resurrection, He took some bread and having rendered Thee thanks, He said: 'Take, eat, this is My Body which is broken for you.' He took also the cup and said: 'This is My Blood which is poured out for you. When you do this, you do it in memory of Me.' *We commemorate then His Death and Resurrection, we offer to Thee, O God, the bread and wine*, by rendering Thee thanks for having judged us worthy to come before Thee and to serve Thee."[26] The offering begun by Christ at His Passion can be continued at each of our Masses through the rite of the Last Supper.

2. At Carthage, St. Cyprian (✝ 258), in his *Letter to Cecil*, affirms first the sacrificial character of the Last Supper: "Who, in fact, was a greater

---

25   St. Irenaeus, *Adversus haereses*, IV, chap. 17, no. 5; PG VII, 1023–1024.
26   Edited by Dom B. Botte, O.S.B., *Source chrétiennes*, no. 11 (Paris, 1946), p. 32.

High Priest than our Lord Jesus Christ, *Who offered a sacrifice to God His Father*, the same which Melchizedek had offered, *namely bread and wine, that is to say His Body and His Blood?*"[27]

The Church must continue to offer the Blood of Christ and to celebrate the sacrifice of the Lord, which is a reply, so to speak, to the Passion. "On the eve of His Passion, the Lord, taking the cup, blessed it and gave it to His disciples saying: 'Drink of it. This is the Blood of the Testament, *which will be offered for the many for the remission of sins.* . . .' We see here that the cup which the Lord offered was mixed,[28] and that that which He calls Blood had been wine. It follows that *the Blood of Christ is not offered* if there is no wine in the cup, and that *the sacrifice of the Lord is not legitimately celebrated if our oblation and our sacrifice does not relate to the Passion.*"[29] In the very same passage St. Cyprian calls the Lord's sacrifice "the sacrifice of God the Father and of Christ."

The sacrifice by which Christ ransomed us is the same one which is continued among us: "*As Christ bore us all, bore our sins*, we see that the water symbolizes the people, the wine the Blood of Christ. When, therefore, water is mixed with the wine in the cup, *it is the people who are mingled with Christ*, and the crowd of believers who join themselves and unite themselves to Him in Whom they believe. This mingling, this union of wine and water in the Lord's cup is indissoluble. Thus the Church, that is the people who are in the Church and who faithfully and firmly persevere in the faith, cannot ever be separated from Christ; she will always adhere to Him, and the love which makes them one will always endure."[30]

The unity of the sacrifice of Christ and of the priests is strongly affirmed: "If Christ Jesus our Lord and God is Himself the High Priest of His divine Father, and if He first offered Himself to this Father in sacrifice, *if He instructed that the same be done in memory of Him*, then certainly that priest fills the role of Christ who imitates what Christ did, *and he offers to God the Father, in the Church, the truth and fullness of the sacrifice only insofar as he offers it as Christ offered it.*"[31]

By what clearer texts could be confessed the truth of the sacrifice of Christ at the Passion, the Last Supper and the Mass?

c) Cyril of Jerusalem

The *Catecheses* of St. Cyril of Jerusalem date from the years 348–350. The twenty-third catechesis, in a celebrated passage which we have translated in its entirety, speaks of the conversion of bread and wine, of the

---

27 "Lettre LXIII," chap. 4, no. 1; édit. *Les Belles Lettres* (Paris, 1925).
28 Certain persons wanted to suppress the wine and keep only the water.
29 *Ibid.*, chap. 9, nos. 2 and 3.
30 *Ibid.*, chap. 13, nos. 1 and 2.
31 *Ibid.*, no. 4.

unbloody sacrifice, of the offering for the living and the dead: "After we are sanctified by the spiritual hymns (the preface of the Mass), we beseech the loving God of men to send the Holy Spirit on the gifts placed on the altar, in order that the bread might become the Body of Christ and the wine the Blood of Christ. For absolutely all that the Holy Spirit touches is sanctified and transmutated (μεταβάλλεσθαι).

"*The spiritual sacrifice, the unbloody cult* (αναιμαντος) *having been accomplished, we beseech God, over this host of propitiation,* to obtain a common peace for all the Churches; for the good order of the world, the emperors, soldiers and their allies; for the sick, the weak, the afflicted; and we pray in a general way and *offer this host* for all those in need of help.

"We then commemorate all those who have died: first of all the patriarchs, the prophets, the apostles and martyrs, so that through their intercession and prayers God might deign to hear ours; then, for the ancestors who passed on in a holy manner, the bishops and all those who have gone before us in death. We believe that a very great help is granted to the souls for whom we make this prayer, *in the very presence of the holy and redoubtable Victim.*"[32]

d) Gregory of Nazianzen and John Chrysostom

1. Around 383, St. Gregory of Nazianzen wrote to Amphilochius, Bishop of Iconium: "O pious adorer of God, do not omit to be in prayer and embassy for us, when, through one word, you bring down the Word, *and when, using the word as a sword, you divide by an unbloody division the Body and Blood of the Lord.*"[33]

2. St. John Chrysostom (344–407) speaks on many occasions of the Eucharistic sacrifice. In De sacerdotio (lines 381–385) we read: "*When you see the Lord immolated and stretched out, and the priest bowed over the sacrifice in prayer, and all the people reddened by that most precious Blood,* do you think you are still on earth among men? Are you not rather transported into the heavens, having left behind every carnal thought in order to contemplate what is taking place, with the soul naked and the spirit purified? O miracle, O divine philanthropy! He Who is seated next to the Father is at that very moment in the hands of all; He gives Himself to those who wish to clasp and embrace Him; and all do so with the eyes of faith."[34]

In the eighth homily on the *Letter to the Romans,* where he advises mutual charity for Christians, the saintly doctor writes: "Reverence then, reverence this table at which we all participate, *and Christ, placed on it in sacrifice, immolated for us.*"[35]

---

32 *Catechesis XXIII,* 5° *mystagogique,* chap. 7, 8, 9; PG XXXIII, 1113–1116.
33 *Epistola CLXXI;* PG XXXVII, 280–281.
34 *De sacerdotio,* III, no. 4; PG XLVIII, 642.
35 *In Epist. ad Rom.,* hom. VIII, no. 8; PG LX, 465.

And here is a text which would become the common good of the theologians of the Middle Ages and the echo of what we find in St. Thomas: "Christ is offered once for always. . . . But do we not offer Him each day? *Yes, we offer, but in order to commemorate Christ's death.* It is one, not many. It, in fact, has been offered one time only. The High Priest entered once a year into the Holy of Holies. Therein is a type with which this corresponds. *It is the same Victim which we offer always,* not today one sheep and tomorrow another; but the same Victim always. This is why the sacrifice is one. If Christ is offered in several places, is this to say that there are many Christs? No. The one Christ is everywhere. He is totally here and there, having one Body. *And as He Who is offered in many places is one sole Body and not many bodies, so the sacrifice is one.* Our Pontiff offered the sacrifice which purifies us. *And we now offer still that same sacrifice once offered before, and which cannot be destroyed.* We do it in memory of what has been done. *We do not offer another sacrifice,* as did the High Priest, *but always the same one*; or better yet, it is a commemoration of the sacrifice which we make."[36]

e) Ambrose

St. Ambrose (✝ 397) relates in *De sacramentis* a text of the anamnesis almost identical to that of our own Roman Canon: "Recalling, therefore, His most glorious Passion, His Resurrection from the dead and His Ascension into heaven, *we offer Thee this unblemished host, this spiritual host, this unbloody host,* this sacred bread and cup of eternal life, and we ask Thee and pray Thee to *accept this offering* from the hands of Thy angels around Thy altar in heaven, as Thou deigned to accept the gifts of Thy just servant Abel, the sacrifice of Abraham our father, and that which was offered by Thy High Priest Melchizedek."

To the words of the Apostle (1 Cor 11:26), *"Every time you eat this bread . . . you proclaim the death of the Lord,"* Ambrose adds these lines wherein is contained the mystery of the Mass: "If we proclaim the death of the Lord, we proclaim the remission of sins. *If each time that His Blood is poured out, it is poured out for the remission of sins, I must always receive it, so that He might always take away my sins.* I, who always sin, must always have a remedy."[37]

In these texts, separated by time and place, is expressed the same certitude, the same faith prior to all theology, and one which never disappears: it is the sacrifice accomplished one time only on the Cross, which the Savior has enclosed in the unbloody rite of the Last Supper, in order that it might be carried to each succeeding generation.

---

36 *In Epist. ad Hebr.,* hom. XVII, no.3; PG LXII, 131.
37 *De sacramentis,* IV, chap. 5, nos. 27–28.

CHAPTER 3

The Unbloody Sacrifice of the
Last Supper

1. Two Economies of the World, According to Which the Redemptive Sacrifice Is Either Awaited or Possessed

The greatest hour of the world, that of the redemptive sacrifice, divides time into two economies: the one, *that of anticipation*, which proceeds toward the Cross; the other, *that of derivation*, which ensues from the Cross and prepares the world for the greatest encounter of the Parousia.

In the ancient economy, the redemptive sacrifice is indicated by signs and awaited through an obscure premonition.[1] In the new economy, which it inaugurates, the redemptive sacrifice remains present under the veils of the unbloody sacrifice. The unbloody sacrifice is instituted at the Last Supper by Christ in order to be reproduced at the Mass by His disciples.

2. The Bloody Sacrifice of the Cross Is Begun When the Last Supper Is Instituted

The bloody sacrifice, which would be consummated on the Cross at the ninth hour, is already begun when Jesus institutes the Last Supper.

1. The hour of Jesus is come: "Before the feast of Passover, *Jesus knowing that His hour had come to pass from this world to the Father*. He had loved His own in this world, and would show His love for them until the end," even unto the end of love (Jn 13:1).

The account of the washing of the feet follows (v. 2 and following), then the announcement concerning the betrayal of Judas (v. 21 and following). At the moment when it has been decided, Jesus is handed over, His Passion is begun, and so is His glorification into which His Passion opens up: "Immediately after Judas had eaten the morsel he went out. It was

---

1   Regarding the law of nature, one can appeal to the Bible itself, and see, for example, with the Fathers in the killing of Abel, or in the sacrifice of Isaac, types of the sacrifice of Christ.

   More recent studies, however, such as those of Mircea Eliade, regarding the metahistorical and spiritual signification of myth and symbol among men of "archaic and traditional cultures," offer to a theology certain of its principles a new field of investigation. See for example our article "Sur Mircea Eliade et l'histoire des religions," in *Nova et Vetera* (Fribourg-Genève: 1955), p. 305.

night. Once Judas left, Jesus said: *'Now is the Son of Man glorified and God is glorified in Him.* If God has been glorified in Him, God will, in turn, glorify Him in Himself, and will glorify Him soon'" (Jn 13:30–32).

2. St. Paul similarly brings together the moment of the institution of the Last Supper and that of the Passion: "I received from the Lord what I handed on to you, namely, that the Lord Jesus, *on the night in which He was betrayed*, took bread, and after He had given thanks, broke it and said, 'This is My Body, which is for you . . .'" (1 Cor 11:23–24).

3. Likewise, following the Gospel account, the Body of Christ is given already at the Last Supper, His Blood is already poured out, which is to say that the act by which He offers them is put in place: "Then, taking bread and giving thanks, He broke it and gave it to them, saying, 'This is My Body *given for you*; do this as a remembrance of Me.' Then, taking the cup in like manner after eating, He gave it to them, saying, 'This cup is the New Covenant in My Blood *poured out for you*'" (Lk 22:19–20). "This is My Blood, the Blood of the Covenant, *poured out for the many* for the remission of sins" (Mt 26–28).

Thus according to Scripture, the unique redemptive sacrifice is one act, beginning when Jesus instituted the Last Supper.

3. The Last Supper Does Not Multiply the Bloody Sacrifice, but Its Mode of Presence

1. At the moment when the bread and wine are changed into the Body and Blood of Christ through transubstantiation, that is to say through a change affecting not Christ but only the substance of bread and wine, the species of which remain, it is not Christ Who is made two but rather the presence of Christ. There are not two distinct *Christs* at that moment but two distinct *presences* of the same and unique Christ: on the one hand there is the natural presence under its proper and normal appearances; on the other hand there is the sacramental presence under its foreign and borrowed or assumed appearances.

The sacramental appearance completely corresponds, primarily and immediately, to the natural presence. If Christ is naturally in His glory, He will be sacramentally in His glory. If He is naturally in a state of sacrifice and immolation, He will be sacramentally in a state of sacrifice and immolation. If the one redemptive sacrifice is actually taking place when Jesus institutes the Last Supper, it is the one redemptive sacrifice which will be present under the sacramental appearances.

2. There are not two *sacrifices* juxtaposed at the Last Supper, but two distinct *presences* of one unique sacrifice: on one hand a presence under its *natural* bloody appearances; on the other hand a presence under its *sacramental* unbloody appearances. Under these two presences, one manifest, the other secret, *the redemptive sacrifice is numerically one, identical*. The Blood of the Cross, which obtains eternal redemption for us

(Heb 8:12), is that very one which fills the cup of the New Covenant (Lk 22:20).

4. The Last Supper Is a Sacrifice in the Real and Proper Sense

1. Was the Last Supper an offering, a sacrifice?

The Reformers, we said, denied it on one hand from fear of departing from the unity of the Cross; on the other hand, from fear of having to grant that the Mass, where the Last Supper is repeated, is itself an offering, a sacrifice.

But how is it a question for those who understood that *the great bloody offering*—where Christ offers it, offers Himself to the Father and incorporates us into His own offering—*begins with this sacrificial Passover which He had had a great desire to eat with His disciples the night He was betrayed*; and that through transubstantiation, through changing the bread and wine into His Body and Blood, *that which became present under the sacramental and unbloody species of bread and wine was precisely Christ, at the moment when He entered into the one redemptive bloody oblation* completed on the Cross? Thus it is explained that, in instituting the Last Supper, Christ spoke of His Body *given* for us, His Blood *poured out* for the many *for the remission of sins*. Therefore, there are not, we repeat, two offerings, two oblations, two distinct and juxtaposed sacrifices; there are two distinct presences— the one natural, bloody and manifest, the other sacramental, unbloody, hidden and mysterious—of the one bloody sacrifice.

2. The Last Supper is a sacrifice of Christ in the true and proper sense.

We can speak of a sacrifice of Christ in the proper sense and in the improper sense. In the *proper* sense, the sacrifice of Christ is the one redemptive sacrifice. In the *improper*, metaphoric sense, we would call the sacrifices of Christ all the interior acts of adoration, praise and offering of His temporal life. We must carefully distinguish between these two senses if we wish to avoid equivocation.

If the unbloody sacrifice of the Last Supper sacramentally contains the reality of Christ and His bloody sacrifice already begun, it must be said for that same reason that it is a true and proper sacrifice—not *another* sacrifice than the unique sacrifice but another *presence* of this unique sacrifice. To speak formally, the notion of *presence* is analogous: first a natural presence, then a sacramental presence of the one sacrifice; the notion of Christ's *sacrifice* is not analogous but rather univocal. We ought to speak of the Mass as we do of the Last Supper: it is a true and proper sacrifice if it is a real presence of Christ and His one sacrifice.

Similarly, if each consecrated host is Christ, because what it contains is really, truly, substantially Christ, then it is the notion of Christ's presence, natural in heaven, sacramental in the tabernacle, which is analogous; this is not to be confused with the always univocal notion of Christ Himself.

5. The Testimony of St. Cyprian: The Sacrifice of the Last Supper and the Passion Is Offered in the Church

That there was a sacrifice at the Last Supper, the same one as at the Passion, St. Cyprian, as we have seen, bears witness in his *Letter LXIII* to Cecil. One is struck by the insistence with which he identifies the unbloody sacrifice of the Church with the Passion.

His intention is entirely practical: to recall that we must observe "in the consecration of the Lord's chalice" what Jesus, "the author and teacher of the sacrifice," observed (1,1).

On "the eve of His Passion" He blessed the chalice. We must, there-fore, offer wine in the chalice; for "what the Lord called Blood had been wine." "The Blood of Christ is not offered . . . the sacrifice of the Lord is not legitimately celebrated, if our oblation and our sacrifice do not corre-spond to His Passion, *nisi oblatio et sacrificium nostrum responderit Passioni*," that is, like the Last Supper, totally bound up with the Passion, inseparable from the Passion, which brings the Passion to us. How do we drink the fruit of the vine in heaven "if in the sacrifice of God the Father and Christ we do not offer up wine?" (X, 2 and 3). This is the sacrifice of God and Christ, and it is we who offer it.

If Christ Jesus "is Himself the High Priest of His divine Father, and first offered Himself to this Father in sacrifice, if He instructed that the same be done in memory of Him, certainly the priest fills the role of Christ who imitates what Christ did, *ille sacerdos vice Christi vere fungitur qui id quod Christus fecit imitatur*; and he offers to God the Father, in the Church, the true and complete sacrifice, *sacrificium verum et plenum tunc offert in Ecclesia Deo Patri*, only insofar as he offers it as Christ offered it" (XIV, 4).

"And because we make mention of His Passion in all our sacrifices—the Lord's Passion is in fact the sacrifice we offer, *Passio est enim Domini sacrificium quod offerimus*—we need to do nothing other than what He did" (XVII, 1).

It is not a theological clarification which we must expect from these texts of St. Cyprian, but something more fundamental, more precious. They bear witness to a certitude of faith and of magisterial teaching. The bishop of Carthage knew and proclaimed that there continues to be offered in the Church a sacrifice which is the very same one as that of the Last Supper, as well as that of the Passion.

6. At the Last Supper the Unbloody Sacrifice Is the Exclusive Effect of Christ; At the Mass it is the Principal Effect of Christ and the Ministerial Effect of the Priests

We can compare the role of Christ to that of the disciples; the former at the Last Supper, the latter at the Mass.

1. At the Last Supper, Christ acted alone, to the exclusion of the disciples, in order to transubstantiate the bread and wine into His Body and Blood and to render His redemptive sacrifice present under sacramental signs. What did the disciples do? They communicated with the Body and Blood of Christ. They entered, therefore, by this means into the very drama of His bloody sacrifice. *And this is the manner in which all the baptized can act today at Mass.* They became one with Christ in order to offer and be offered through Him, with Him and in Him: "Consider Israel according to the flesh, are not they, who eat the sacrifices, partakers of the altar?" (1 Cor 10:18).

2. At the Mass there are some differences regarding this matter. Christ gives *to those of His disciples who are to be priests*, along with His omnipotent help, the power to celebrate *ministerially* the unbloody rite of consecrating the bread and wine—something which He did alone at the Last Supper. Christ grants this power that they might celebrate it for the good of the entire community "in memory of Him" (Lk 22:19), "until He comes again" (1 Cor 11:26). The power of the priests at Mass is a power purely ministerial, instrumental, dependent. It is Christ Who, in each transubstantiation, continues to act, no longer alone as at the Last Supper but as principal agent, without Whose motion the power of the ministers would be totally inefficacious.

7. Transubstantiation Is an Unbloody Offering Made at the Last Supper by Christ Alone; At Mass by Christ and His Priests

1. The redemptive offering, already present and actual under its natural and proper appearances, is, in addition, made present at the Last Supper through transubstantiation under the sacramental and borrowed appearances of bread and wine.

Transubstantiation has for its effect a new unbloody presence of the bloody offering; this is why it is called an unbloody offering.

Christ offered Himself in a bloody manner. He offers Himself furthermore in an unbloody manner, not by *another offering* but by *another modality*, by *another presence* of the same offering.

2. The Council of Trent teaches that, at the Last Supper, Christ "offered His Body and His Blood under the species of bread and wine to God His Father."[2]

The same Council also teaches that at the Mass, "He will Himself be immolated by the Church, by means of the priests, under visible signs";[3] that He offers Himself therefore "through the ministry of priests" in an "unbloody offering."[4]

---

2 Session XXII, chap. 1, Denz., 938.
3 *Ibid.*
4 *Ibid.*, chap. 2, Denz., 940.

8. The Last Supper Is Ordered Toward the Mass

Thus the unbloody rite of the Last Supper is instituted in order to contain and subsequently to perpetuate the unique redemptive sacrifice of the Cross, multiplying each time that it is repeated, not that unique sacrifice but its presence in our midst: "As often as the memorial of this Victim is celebrated," says the Liturgy, "the work of our Redemption is wrought."[5] Such that the Savior would not leave His Church, His beloved Bride, without leaving her a sacrifice: not an invisible sacrifice, a sacrifice in only a spiritual and metaphorical sense, but a sacrifice in the proper sense, a sacrifice which would be visible, as human nature requires.

9. The Doctrine of the Council of Trent on the Last Supper

Let us hear the doctrine of the Council of Trent on the Last Supper: "He, then, our Lord and God, was once and for all to offer Himself to God the Father by death *on the altar of the Cross*, in order to obtain an everlasting redemption for those who needed to be sanctified. But, because His priest-hood was not to end with His death (Heb 7:24, 28), *at the Last Supper,* 'on the night He was betrayed,' in order to leave His beloved Spouse the Church a visible sacrifice (as the nature of man requires) ... declaring Himself constituted 'a priest forever after the order of Melchizedek' (Ps 109:4):

"He *offered* to God the Father His Body and Blood under the species of bread and wine;

"He *distributed* them under the same signs in order to be consumed by the Apostles (whom He then established as priests of the New Covenant);

"And *ordered* them and their successors in the priesthood *to offer His Body and Blood*, saying: '*Do this as a memorial of Me*' (Lk 22:19; 1 Cor 11:24), as the Catholic Church has always understood and taught."[6]

10. The Jewish Passover, the Christian Passover, the Heavenly Passover

The will of Jesus was that His Last Supper and Passion completely coincide with the Passover: "On the first day of Azymes, when it was customary to sacrifice the Paschal lamb, His disciples said to Him, 'Where do You wish us to go to prepare the Passover supper for You?'" (Mk 14:12). And when evening came, He said to them, "I have greatly desired to eat this Passover with you before I suffer" (Lk 22:15). Clearly, Jesus wished to superimpose on the Jewish Passover another Passover, of which the former was but a figure, and which would be more mysterious and solemn.

1. The *Jewish Passover* began the night when the Israelites immolated the lamb, the blood of which would preserve them from death (Ex 13), and abandoned the country of servitude in order to head for the Promised

---

5　Secret from the ninth Sunday after Pentecost.
6　Session XXII, chap. 1, Denz., 938.

Land. The lamb would be immolated again, the unleavened bread eaten again, the cup blessed again. This was not a pure and simple commemoration; this was the commemoration of a former symbolic sacrifice through a similar sacrifice.

2. It prefigured *another Passover*. But what kind of love could have imagined such a thing?

a) The Lamb would be the immolated Savior: "Christ, our Pasch, has been immolated" (1 Cor 5:7), the bones of Whom, like those of the pascal lamb, would not be broken (Jn 19:36), and Who would give Himself to be eaten under the appearances of the bread and the cup (Lk 22:19–20).

b) The mission of the Lamb would be to preserve us from a death other than corporal death. The Baptist, who first announced Him as a terrible Judge (Mt 3:11–12), would cry out upon seeing Him, "Behold the Lamb of God, Who takes away the sins of the world" (Jn 1:29).[7] A "new canticle" would have to be sung in His honor: "You were slain, and with Your Blood You purchased for God men of every race and tongue, of every people and nation" (Rev 5:9).

c) The "journey" of this new Passover would first be that of Jesus to the Father (Jn 13:1); then, that of those whom He draws to Himself by His grace. For, the memorable journey of the Israelites from slavery to the Promised Land, as prodigious as it was in itself, and so charged with a spiritual sense as it appeared to the better among them—who knew that "the intention of God was not to have an entire people born of Abraham so that He could simply lead them into an abundant land"—that memorable journey was still more, as St. Paul tells us, *the messianic proclamation, the figure, the "type"* of the most solemn passage of all of humanity from the state of condemnation to the state of redemption (1 Cor 10:1–11).

3. The Council of Trent also draws a comparison between the Jewish Passover and the Christian Passover: "For, after He celebrated the *old Pasch*, which the multitude of the children of Israel immolated to celebrate the memory of the departure from Egypt (Ex 12:1), Christ instituted a *new Pasch*, namely Himself to be offered by the Church through her priests under visible signs in order to celebrate the memory of His passage from this world to the Father, when by the shedding of His Blood He redeemed us, 'delivered us from the dominion of darkness and transferred us to His Kingdom'" (Col 1:13).[8]

4. The Christian Passover, celebrated under sacramental signs in the exile of faith, announces in its turn the *heavenly Passover of the world beyond*, the banquet of the *eschatological kingdom*, where the sacramental signs will disappear in order to give way to the beatific satiation of vision

---

7   On this interior illumination of the Baptist, read F.-M. Braun, O. P., "Le baptême d'après le quatrième Évangile," in *Revue Thomiste*, 1948, pp. 347–351.

8   Session XXII, chap. 1, Denz. 938.

and intoxication of love: "I will not eat again this Passover until it is fulfilled in the Kingdom of God. . . . I will not drink of the fruit of the vine until the coming of the Kingdom of God" (Lk 22:16, 18).

11. The Christian Passover, a Messianic and Eschatological Mystery

1. In thus comparing the Jewish Passover, the Christian Passover and the Passover of heaven, we join St. Thomas in speaking of the economy of the Old Law, the New Law and of the Fatherland: "The *state of the New Law* is midway between the *state of the Old Law*, the figures of which would be fulfilled in the New Law, and the *state of glory* where the whole truth will be made clearly and fully manifest. And at that time there will be no sacraments. Now, however, as long as 'we know through a mirror and images,' as it is said in 1 Corinthians 13, it is necessary for us to come to spiritual things through sensible signs; which is the reason for the sacraments."[9]

Placed between the messianic promise and the eschatological fullness, the economy of the New Testament is, to speak with the words of the Poet: "*This hour which is between the spring and summer—Between this evening and tomorrow, the only hour left—Sleep without any sleep until the Sun returns . . .*"[10]

2. Insofar as it is announced in the Mosaic Law[11] and hinted at even in the law of nature,[12] the Christian Passover, the Last Supper, the Mass, is a *messianic mystery*. And insofar as it announces in its turn that which is

---

9 *Summa Theologiae* III, qu. 61, a. 4, ad 1. In a parallel passage St. Thomas speaks of the worship of the blessed which is without signs or temple, *nihil erit figurale ad divinum cultum pertinens, Summa Theologiae* I-II, qu. 103, a. 3. See Thomas a Kempis, *The Imitation of Christ*, IV, chap. 11, no. 2.

10 Paul Claudel, *La Cantate à trois voix*.

11 One could cite here, after the Council of Trent, session XXII, chap. 1, Denz., 939, the prophecy of Malachi (1:10–11), comparing to the legal sacrifices of the Temple a sacrifice offered in spirit and in truth throughout the whole earth. "I find no pleasure in you, says the Lord of hosts, neither will I accept any sacrifice from your hands. For from the rising of the sun to its setting My name is great among the Gentiles. And everywhere they bring sacrifice to My name, and a pure offering. For great is My name among the Gentiles, says the Lord of hosts." The Christian Passover, the Council of Trent explains, is itself, in fact, "a pure offering, which cannot be sullied either by the unworthiness or the evil of those who offer it."

12 There is an offering of the Law of nature, which, according to the Council of Trent, "at the time of Nature and of the Law, was prefigured by various types of sacrifices. For it includes all the good that was signified by those former sacrifices; it is their fulfillment and perfection. *Loc. cit.* We are reminded—with respect to that which is of the Law of nature—of the offering of Abel (Gen 4:4) of Noah (Gen 8:20) and of Abraham (Gen 12:8; 22:2), etc.

to come and demonstrates under symbols the fullness and intoxication of the Fatherland, it is an *eschatological mystery*. It is instituted at the threshold of the world's final age, in order to color with the Blood of Christ the flow of time before it flowers into eternity.

That immense hope, which had stirred the Old Testament, the all too brief coming of the Messiah only inflamed the more, and carried it to a point of intensity which consummates it in the heart of the saints. They summon the second Parousia more fervently than the prophets awaited the first: "The *Revertere* of the Bride is the Church's true canticle, as these other words, '*Come, approach, show Thyself, pierce the clouds,*' are the canticle of the Synagogue. The latter has not yet seen Him; but the Church has seen Him, has heard Him, has touched Him, and He quickly left. She left all for Him. '*Behold,*' says St. Peter the Apostle, '*we have left all to follow Thee.*' Jesus then espoused her, taking her poverty and nakedness as a dowry. Immediately after He espoused her, He died. And if He rises, it is in order to return from where He came. He leaves His chaste Spouse on earth a young desolate widow, who remains without support. Can she do anything else but cry out, '*Revertere, revertere.*' 'Return, return, O Divine Bridegroom; hasten that return which Thou hast promised!' It is because of this that the very depths of the Bride's being do not cease to sigh after the second coming of Jesus Christ."[13]

---

13 Bossuet, *L'amour de Madeleine*, édité par J. Bonnet, (Paris: Librairie des Saints-Pères, 1909). On the desire which the Church has for the Parousia, see our work *Destinées d'Israël* (Paris: Luf, 1945), pp. 392 and ff.; "Les destinées du Royaume de Dieu," in *Nova et Vetera*, 1935, pp. 105 ff.

CHAPTER 4

The Unbloody Sacrifice of the Mass

1. The Viewpoint of Faith and the Theological Question

a) The Viewpoint of Faith

The teaching of the Council of Trent concerning the Mass opens up, one recalls, onto the very mystery of the redemptive sacrifice: on one hand by its *unicity*, for, being perfect, it has been offered once for all; on the other hand by the necessity of its *actualization* to the extent that man begins to sin again: proclaiming the death of the Savior, that is for St. Ambrose, pouring out His Blood: "If each time that His Blood is poured out, it is poured out for the remission of sins, I must always receive it so that He might always take away my sins."[1]

The Mass is precisely this actualization, continually recommenced, of the one redemptive sacrifice. It is a sacrifice only by identifying itself with the latter through the *content*. We recall the words of St. Cyprian: "The Passion of the Lord is, in fact, the sacrifice which we offer."[2] The Mass does not differ from this sacrifice except in the *mode* of the offering: the bloody sacrifice of the Cross is not repeated; the unbloody mode of offering is repeated, not in order to substitute for the bloody sacrifice but to subordinate itself to it, and to bring it to us whole and entire under the envelopment where Christ is hidden as at the Last Supper.

This view is sufficient, we believe, to open up to contemplation an ocean of mystery in which it may lose itself.

b) The Theological Question

1. At the *Last Supper* the unbloody sacrifice contains the bloody sacrifice. That which is contained under the sacramental species is Christ, Priest and Victim, Who offers Himself, Who gives His Body and pours out His Blood for the redemption of the world—Christ in the very act of accomplishing His redemptive sacrifice. The same Priest, the same Victim and *the same sacrificial act are* twice present: first under their proper appearances, then under their borrowed appearances.

---

1   *De sacramentis,* IV, chap. 6, no. 28, *Source chrétiennes,* no. 25.
2   St. Cyprian, *Epistola LXIII,* chap. 17, no. 1.

2. At the *Mass*, recalls the Council of Trent, there is likewise, under the species of the unbloody sacrifice, the same Victim as on the Cross. Is it not also *the same sacrificial act* as on the Cross?

In other words, does the unity of the Mass and the Cross result from the one identity in both places of Priest and Victim? Or is there between the Mass and the Cross a numerical unity of the sacrifice, of the sacrificial redemptive act?

The difficulty comes from the fact that Christ, the Redeemer on the Cross, has now entered into His glory. Is He present at the Mass *with* or *without* His redemptive act? In the first case the words of the Council of Trent hold true, which speak of an *application*, at the Mass, of the salutary power of the Cross's bloody sacrifice for the remission of sins which we commit each day.[3] An *application* of the power of the sacrifice of the Cross is in fact, according to St. Thomas,[4] a daily *contact* with us of the bloody sacrifice of the Cross, a real daily *presence* to us of the bloody sacrifice of the Cross.[5]

At each Mass, Christ, coming to us in glory with all the power of His Cross, causes that same power to be *applied* to us, to be *made present* to us in proportion to the intensity of our desire.

3. It ought to be clearly understood that it is in no way for the purpose of laying a reckless and sacrilegious hand on the mystery that the theologian poses these questions; it is rather out of fear of failing to see—because of lack of attention—the point of clarification (which certainly exists) from where the mystery of the Mass will appear at once detailed and simplified, and from where one will be able to see, moreover, all the specious obscurities dissipated. The explanation of the teaching on the Eucharist states precisely that each consecrated host is Christ, because transubstantiation multiplies in space the real substantial presences of the one Christ. Could we likewise say that each Mass is a true and sacrificial act, because it multiplies in time the real efficient operative presences of the one redemptive sacrifice?

2. The Substantial Presence of Christ the Priest and Victim, and the Operative Presence of His Sacrificial Act

a) The Substantial Presence and Operative Presence

Right from the very beginning of this fourth chapter we must appeal to a fundamental truth, one which will throw further light on the question of transubstantiation and the Real Presence. The ignorance of this truth, or even the simple placing it in parenthesis, would be disastrous. The truth

---

3   Session XXII, chap. 1, Denz., 938.
4   *Summa Theologiae* III, qu. 83, a 1.
5   In the second case, one would have either to call the state of the glorious Christ a *sacrificial state;* or at least see a *sacrificial act* in the simple changing of bread and wine into Christ *formerly* sacrificed but *now* glorious. As a result, it would therefore be difficult not to equivocate the word "sacrifice."

about which we speak is: the notion of contact or presence is not univocal, but analogous—by an analogy of proportion.[6]

Let us fix our attention for a moment on two forms of presence which are important for describing with clarity the *substantial presence* and the *efficient or operative presence*. The word "presence" is taken in the two cases not in a metaphorical sense, but in a true and proper sense; and nevertheless, in both cases the signification of the word "presence" is in no way univocal. It is essentially different and proportionately similar, that is to say analogous. There is a relation between the two presences, a proportion: the substantial presence is for being in the ontological order, the operative presence is for acting in the dynamic order.

b) The Substantial Presence and Operative Presence of God

1. With regards to God we can speak of a substantial presence and a virtual or operative presence.

Insofar as He immediately sustains in existence the substantial being of things by a conserving action, which is a continuation of His creative action,[7] God is present to these things by His essence, by *His substance*.

Insofar as He grants to things not only their being but also their action as secondary causes and all that is real in their action, God is present to them by *His power, by His strength*. These two presences are proportional: as in the ontological order the being of God is present to the substantial being of things, so in the dynamic order the act of God is present to their activity.

2. The presence of God to things of time is a mystery.[8]

Compared to each other, the things of time are really past, present, future; and God sees them as really past, present and future in relation to each other.

But considered in relation to God, all are equally present; all coexist in His eternity. If one were able to imagine successive moments in divine eternity, yesterday would coexist with the first of these moments, today with the second, and tomorrow with the third. But divine eternity excludes precisely all such succession. Yesterday, today and tomorrow coexist with the simultaneity of its unique and unchanging instant. Yesterday, which is a memory for us, is not so for God, but rather a vision; tomorrow, which is for us a prevision, is not so for God, but

---

6   See below, p. 162.

7   "To preserve things in being is for God nothing other than to grant them being continuously; such that if He were to withdraw His influence, they would sink completely into nothingness. St. Thomas, *Summa Theologiae* I, qu. 9, a. 2. "The preservation of things by God is not a new action, but the continuation of that action by which He gives them their being." *Summa Theologiae* I, qu. 104, a. 1, ad 4.

8   See below, pp. 66, 78, 90.

rather a vision. All things which for us have been, are or will be, God knows in their presentiality, in the actuality of the instant wherein they are existing.[9] And it is from all eternity that He grants them being by His substantial presence and action by His operative presence; but He does this only for the moment and time wherein they act and exist.

3. Therefore, the redemptive sacrificial act of Christ on the Cross, where the world is given to God and God to the world, is known by God from all eternity in its presentiality.

It is in itself transitory and immersed in time. It appeared at the end of the ancient economy of salvation, at the threshold of the new economy.

One question can be asked: Can the omnipotent divine power, by touching this transitory act of Christ and by using it as an instrument— can it extend the application, the spiritual power, the contact and the presence not only to immediate contemporaries, but also to the succeeding generations of the new economy of salvation?

c) The Substantial Presence and Operative Presence of Christ Insofar as He Is Man

1. Christ insofar as He is man was present *substantially* in the house of Simon the Pharisee, where the sinful woman threw herself at His feet (Lk 7:36–50). But He was present *efficiently* only in the house of the centurion whose servant He cured—present by His action and His power, and without entering into the house itself (Lk 7:1–10). Between these two real and true presences of Jesus, the one substantial and the other efficient and operative, there is an analogous, and not a univocal, relation.

2. At Calvary, Jesus as man was present *substantially* on the Cross, where He was nailed. And He is present *efficiently*, spiritually, by His action and His power, in the hearts of the Virgin and St. John, in order to draw them along in the wake of His offering and to pour out on them redemptive grace. He is at a distance from the Virgin and St. John by His substantial presence; He is in the Virgin and St. John by His virtual presence.

At the Last Supper Christ is present *substantially* twice: first, naturally and under His proper appearances, and, in such a way, He is in the midst of His disciples; second, sacramentally and under the borrowed appearances

---

9   St. Thomas, *Summa Theologiae* I, qu. 14, a. 13. Cf. Commentary of Cajetan, XII: "The first instant of this hour is within the eternal instant; the last instant of this hour, while certainly not in the first, is also, however, in the same eternal instant."

     In addition, the very touching passage of *Jeanne d'Arc*, where Charles Péguy, envies the saints who will have seen Jesus twice—during His mortal life and in glory—this passage supposes the univocal relation of these two knowledges of Jesus and forgets the supereminence of the Beatific Vision, where the elect will see all succession of the things of this world from the viewpoint of God, in their native freshness, in their *presentiality*.

of bread and wine, under which He gives His Body to be eaten and His Blood to be drunk. These two real and true substantial presences of the Body of Christ, the one natural and the other sacramental, are not univocal—we shall again insist on it in Chapter VII—but analogous. And Christ at the Last Supper is still present *efficiently*, spiritually by His action and His power in the souls of the Apostles, pulling them mysteriously into the drama of His Passion which has begun. The disciples at Emmaus leave it for us to guess what took place in them: "Were not our hearts burning within us while He opened to us the Scriptures?" (Lk 24:32). Here then at the Last Supper are the two orders of presence of Christ in the world: the one substantial, be it natural or sacramental; the other operative, spiritual, by action when He rejoins His disciples to unite them to His sacrifice.

At the Mass there is, under the appearances of bread and wine, the *substantial* presence of Christ now glorious. And there is under the same appearances the *efficient, operative* presence of His one redemptive sacrifice. Not without reason does Christ, now glorious, come to us under the appearances of His Body given for us, of His Blood poured out for the remission of sins; it is in order to signify that He comes to us with the application, the contact, the power and the presence of His one redemptive sacrifice.

d) The Operative Presence of the One Sacrificial Redemptive Act on the Cross, at the Last Supper and the Mass

On the Cross, at the Last Supper and at the Mass, the very same Christ, Priest and Victim, is present to the world *substantially*.

It is clear that on the Cross and at the Last Supper Christ is present to the world *insofar as He is Priest and Victim*, in the very act of His offering Himself to God and saving the world; it is clear, in other words, that there is for the contemporary faithful, in addition to the substantial presence of Christ, *the operative presence of the one redemptive sacrifice*: this is precisely the time when that sacrificial act which redeems the world is accomplished in its transitory reality.

But at the Mass? Christ is glorious. Can He be present to us *insofar as He is Priest and Victim?* The one sacrificial redemptive act is for us *past*. How could it be *present* to us efficiently? How was it able to be such for the Apostles at the Last Supper? For the Blessed Virgin and St. John at the Cross? This is the problem.

If it is to be resolved,[10] the Mass will be, like the Last Supper, a true and real sacrifice, but *another presence*, an operative presence—when it is

---

10 If the problem were unsolvable, in order to explain that the Mass is a true and real sacrifice, it would be necessary—the sacrificial redemptive act being unique—to appeal to another sacrificial non-redemptive act, be it of Christ Himself or of the Church united to Christ.

a question not of a substance but of an act, the operative presence is the only thing which can be the cause—an operative presence of the unique redemptive sacrifice; a sacramental and unbloody presence of the unique bloody sacrifice. One could say that, just as each consecrated host is substantially Christ because it multiplies the real substantial presences of the one Christ, so proportionately each Mass is a true and real sacrifice because it multiplies the real operative presences of the unique redemptive sacrifice.

3. Christ Is Present at the Mass in His Glorious State

The change which takes place in transubstantiation in no way affects Christ. It begins with bread and wine and ends with Christ, Who preexists and remains unchanged.

By this, Christ is made present under the sacramental species according to the state in which He is at that time.[11] And as He has now entered into His glory, the transubstantiation which takes place at each Mass renders Him sacramentally present primarily and immediately in His glorious state.

Hence we cannot understand Christ's role at Mass if we do not understand His role in heaven.

4. The Eternal Priesthood of the Heavenly Christ

a) The Scriptural References

The heavenly Christ continues to intercede for us: "Who shall bring any charge against God's elect? It is God Who justifies; who is to condemn? It is Christ Who died, yes, Who was raised from the dead, Who *is at the right hand of God, Who intercedes for us!*" (Rom 8:34). "If anyone sins, *we have an advocate before the Father, Jesus the just one.* He is the victim of propitiation for our sins, and not for ours only but also for those of the whole world" (1 Jn 2:1–2).

Jesus is "the great High Priest forever" (Heb 6:20), "a priest forever according to the order of Melchizedek" (Heb 7:17). The priests of the Old Law "were many in number, because they were prevented by death from continuing in office; *but He holds His priesthood permanently, because He continues for ever.* Consequently, He is able for all time to save those who draw near to God through Him, since *He always lives to make intercession for them*" (Heb 7:23–25). "But when Christ appeared as a *High Priest of the good things to come.* . . . He entered once for all into the sanctuary . . . thus acquiring for us an eternal redemption" (Heb 9:11–12).

---

11   Let us suppose that Christ is living, or dead, or glorious, or beaten, bruised, or even crucified, He would be such under the sacramental species; but breaking, crucifying or destroying the sacramental species will not break, crucify or destroy Christ. The violence done to Christ would be present under the sacramental species; but the violence done to the species would not be able to touch Him physically. Cf. St. Thomas, *Summa Theologiae* III, qu. 81, a. 4.

The Apocalypse shows us that near Him Who is seated on the throne there is "a *Lamb, standing, as though it had been slain,* with seven horns and with seven eyes, which are the seven spirits of God sent out into all the earth" (Rev 5:6). And in the new canticle in praise of the Lamb it is said: "Worthy art Thou to take the scroll and to open its seals, for Thou wast slain and by Thy Blood didst ransom men for God from every tribe and tongue and people and nation, and hast made them a kingdom and priests for our God, and they shall reign on the earth" (Rev 5:9–10).

b) Three Ways in Which the Priesthood of Christ Is Eternal

The priesthood of Christ is eternal under three aspects.

1) First, in the sense that the supreme goods which He can obtain for us are not present goods, but future goods (Heb 9:11) which are eternal. The priesthood of Christ, therefore, is eternal *in its outcome, in its fruits, its consummation.*[12]

2) Furthermore, it is eternal in the sense that, insofar as history continues to unfold, Christ, Who is always living, continues to intercede for us (Heb 7:25), to be our Advocate before the Father (1 Jn 2:1–2).

How does He intercede? Is it by *repeating His Passion and Death*? No. The redemptive oblation, being perfect, can only be unique (Heb 10:14). "Christ, having been raised from the dead, will never die; death no longer has dominion over Him" (Rom 6:8).

Is it by living perpetually in a *sacrificial state*? No. The Apocalypse (5:6) does not say that the Lamb is slain, but "as slain;" and this signifies, as the text explains, that *"He was slain,"* and that He *"has redeemed* by His own Blood" (5:9) men of every race. The figure of the Lamb "as slain, having seven heads and seven eyes, which are the seven spirits of God, sent throughout all the earth," is related to the Johannine tract on the blood and water coming forth from the side of Jesus (Jn 19:34), that is to say the Redemption, the sole source of the outpouring of the Spirit.[13] In the thought of John, the Spirit is symbolized by water and given by blood: "There are three that bear witness: the Spirit, the water and the blood, and these three agree" (1 Jn 5:7–8).

The love of the heavenly Christ is no longer a *meritorious, satisfactory, redemptive* love, as was the love of Christ the pilgrim; merit ceases with the state of pilgrimage. The intercession of the heavenly Christ consists in *presenting to the Father*[14] *the unique sacrificial act* by which is accomplished one

---

12 St. Thomas, *Summa Theologiae* III, qu. 22, a. 5.
13 See above, p. 25, note 37.
14 This is a *supereminent presentation* (Theologians would say "interpretative"); for the sacrificial act of the Cross, we said, is not a *memory* in God, but a *vision*. God does not cease to see it in the actuality of the instant where it existed; and, insofar as He is man, Christ, by the beatific vision, knows it also as present.

time the redemption and salvation of the entire world, and in *dispensing* to the world the riches of this one redemption.[15]

The priesthood of Christ, therefore, is eternal in a second sense, by continuation as long as the world remains, by its mediating function of *intercession and dispensation.*

3) The priesthood of the heavenly Christ cannot consist in presenting *to God* another sacrifice than that of the Cross. There is no other. God eternally sees this sacrifice in its presentiality and cannot forget it.

Hence the meritorious, satisfactory, redemptive power (the power of efficiency as well) of the sacrifice of the Cross is without limit *with respect to us*: it is able to suffice, and far more than suffice for all generations.[16] The heavenly Christ does not need, therefore, to substitute another sacrificial offering for the sacrificial offering of the Cross. He confirms this unique offering by an eternal act. His intercession and His mediation consist in willing eternally that which He willed on the Cross, namely to save all men *by this one Cross.*

In this third sense the priesthood of Christ is eternal: *it ratifies, it valorizes progressively throughout history the one sacrifice of the Cross, the power of which is inexhaustible, and therefore eternal.*

We shall focus our attention on the second, and most especially the third aspects of the heavenly Christ's priesthood.

5. The Glorious Christ Is Present at the Mass With His Redemptive Act

We said that at Mass Christ is made present under the sacramental species by transubstantiation, primarily and immediately as He is in Himself, that is, in His glorious state.

But if in heaven He continues to desire to save us, as He so desired once and for all by the very act of His Passion and His Death, it is in exactly this same way that He will be present to us at Mass. He will come in His glorious state; however, certainly not in order to touch us by His glory, but in order to "proclaim His death," to actualize according to our intention the unique act of redemption. He will come *with* His redemptive act. Between His glory and our sin he will interpose His bloody Cross.

And since His heavenly intercession and His will to save us by the unique redemptive sacrifice cannot divert from this same sacrifice, but rather it has for its sole end the unceasing amplification of that sacrifice, so this same heavenly intercession, rendered sacramentally present at Mass through transubstantiation, will not divert the redemptive intercession of

15   On the position of St. Robert Bellarmine, see below, pp. 76 and 82, note 54.
16   "Neither the Passion nor the Death of Christ can happen again; but the *power* of this offering, *offered one time only,* lasts eternally." St. Thomas, *Summa Theologiae* III, qu. 22, a. 5, ad 2.

the Cross, and will have as its end the amplification and actualization of that redemptive intercession among us. "In the manner," says Cajetan, "in which, according to the Epistle to the Hebrews, Christ entered into the heavens by His own Blood and continues to be a priest forever, interceding for us, in such a manner He continues to be with us through the Eucharist under a mode of immolation, interceding for us. And as the supreme sufficiency and efficacy of the sacrifice offered on the altar of the Cross does not exclude in heaven the continuity of the function of Christ's intercession for us, so it does not exclude the presence of Christ among us, interceding, under a mode of immolation."[17]

The efficacy of the sacrifice of the Cross, being supreme, does not need to be completed, but rather applied, actualized in the course of time by the heavenly Christ.

6. The Interposition of the Cross

It is the heavenly and glorious Christ Who, by the changing of the bread and wine into His Body and His Blood, is rendered substantially present at Mass under the sacramental species. He comes, however, to proclaim and apply His death to us.

What a mystery! Our irrepressible desire, from the moment that we learn that He has preceded us into heaven in order to prepare a place for us (Jn 14:3), is to enter into His glory without having to pass through the Cross or death. We would like—it is the cry of St. Paul—not to strip ourselves of the earthly body, "not to unclothe ourselves, but to be further clothed, so that what is mortal may be swallowed up by life" (2 Cor 5:4). Since Christ has died for us, why must we ourselves still have to die? Why does He not immediately give us this glory for which He begged with such love on our behalf before the Father Who refuses Him nothing?

When at Mass, Jesus is present before us with His glory in the small host, and we know that there is but a blanket of sacramental appearances which separates us from Paradise, we desire to throw ourselves at His feet in order to embrace them, as did the Magdalene on Easter Morning in the little garden of the Resurrection; and we desire to beg Him to bring us near to Himself, to put a sudden end to our temptations, to our trials, to our duplicity, to abolish as well our contact with death and its pains. Alas, for us it is not yet the time of vision in the fatherland, but the time of faith and pilgrimage, the time for us—as for the Magdalene—of *Noli me tangere*. The mysterious word of Jesus casts a shadow in our hearts. We recall the words of Pascal: "It seems to me that Jesus Christ allowed only His wounds to be touched after His Resurrection."[18]

---

17 *De Missae sacrificio et ritu, adversus Lutheranos, ad Clementem VII Pont. Max.,* Rome, May 3, 1531, chap. 6.

18 Pascal, *Pensées,* ed. Brunschvicg, no. 554. See below, p. 210.

Jesus, now glorious, comes to us only through His Cross; and there is no other way to come to Him except through the Cross. He interposes His Cross between Himself and us; and the more He presses us close to His heart, the more deeply the Cross penetrates into our flesh to crucify us: "I am crucified with Christ" (Gal 2:19).

This Cross is the actualization for us of the redemptive act.

7. Eternal Acts and Transitory Acts of Christ

1. Jesus as God possesses uncreated knowledge and charity, by which God knows Himself and loves Himself always, by one rigorously eternal act in Himself, without beginning, without succession, without end, identical with His own substance.

Jesus as man possesses in addition a created knowledge and charity. From the first instant of His Incarnation, His intelligence and His will, elevated by divine grace, enter into immediate contact with the divine essence by an act of beatific vision and love. These two initial acts are never extinguished in the soul of Christ. They are above all the vicissitudes of His temporal life. They are not touched, therefore, by the agony and death on the Cross. They continue to subsist uninterrupted in the glorious Christ. They are in that sense two acts, which are in themselves eternal.

Beneath these two acts of the immediately theological order there is in the holy soul of Christ an act of adoration, of dependence, of offering; it also is in itself uninterrupted and eternal. This act, however, cannot be regarded as a sacrificial act in the proper sense.

2. The sacrificial act, the sacrificial offering takes place at the moment called by Christ, "His hour," when He actually gives His life by His redemptive passion and death on the Cross. This sacrificial act is animated and vivified by the eternal acts about which we have just spoken, and the flame of which burns unceasingly in the heart of Christ. It is not in itself, however, an eternal act of Christ, an act made to endure and last forever in the very life of Christ. It lasted but a moment. In this sense the redemptive sacrificial act is a transitory act. Other transitory acts have preceded it (the work in Nazareth, preaching, miracles), and others have followed it (apparitions to Mary Magdalene and the Apostles).

8. How the Redeeming Sacrificial Act of the Cross Is at Once Both in Time and Out of Time

a) It Is in Time and Out of Time

1. The mystery of the redemptive act of the Cross is summed up with one simple and profound glance.

We said that with respect to God the redemptive act of the Cross is in no way something of the past but rather always present. It subsists perpetually in the divine acceptance, not in the condition of a memory but in the condition of an actual object of vision. God knew it in its presentiality from all eternity.[19]

With respect to us and the things of the world, the redemptive act is simultaneous and under two different aspects: both in time and outside of time. *In* time, if we consider its sensible reality; it is a transitory moment of the life of Christ. *Outside of* time, if we consider its spiritual redemptive power; whence its power to redeem and to reconcile by contact not only the world, which is contemporary with it, but also all times to come.

2. Christ came, according to the words of St. Gregory the Great, by successive leaps: from heaven into the womb of a Virgin, then into a manger, then onto the Cross, then into the tomb, in order to return to heaven. His mission was consummated by His Passion on the Cross. It is this last and short space of time which He calls His hour. It is a moment, the supreme moment of His pilgrimage among us. Under this aspect it is *in time*; it has passed and is irreversible.

3. But how will Christ's hour be moved along by the flow of time? It is touched and inhabited by divine eternity. And by this fact it is *outside of time*; it seeks to extend its power, to be actualized for all time to come. It takes place in time, but in order to agitate it, and, as a rock thrown into a lake, to bring forth infinite waves. Christ's hour recapitulates in advance and contains beforehand all the grace that will subsequently pass to the world. It has the power, as generations pass, to communicate to His Body the Church the drama which was accomplished once in Christ the Head.

4. Here we can see what differentiates the ancient economy of salvation from the new.

In the ancient economy of salvation, the Passion of Christ was already present, but *by anticipation*: all the graces were then offered and granted by God *immediately*, but in view of the merits of the future Passion. The Passion was not able to act in time before existing in time: "Unlike the

---

19 Both past and future things are known by God *as past or future with respect to other things,* but *as present* to *Him;* for He knows them in His eternity, which exists at every instant of time. It is on this profound Thomistic doctrine which Marguerite De Veni D'Arbouze nourished her contemplation: "We know that the events of the birth, life and death of the sons of God were one time present and are no longer with respect to us. But in God, Who is an eternity without succession of time, the same things are in act and all of them together have been from all eternity and will be so forever. For us, Jesus was born and will not be born again; He died and will die no more. . . . According to this, the soul can place itself at the foot of the Cross by meditating on the Passion of its Savior and by seeing how He suffered. *But by seeing this mystery in God, the soul sees it in act before Him Who gives us His Son through love, raising Him up to death on the Cross for the expiation of our sins." Traité de l'oraison mentale,* edited by Dom Bonaventure Sodar,(Paris: Desclée De Brouwer, 1934), p. 12. See below, pp. 78, 90; and above, p. 61.

final cause," clarifies St. Thomas apropos of this question, "the efficient cause cannot move before it comes into existence."[20]

In the new economy of salvation, the Passion is present *by derivation*: all the graces merited by the Passion are granted to us *through and by means of* the Passion.

The solemn words of the Savior, "When I am lifted up from the earth, I will draw all men to Myself" (Jn 12:32), cover both economies of salvation. Between the two there is not a univocal relation, but one which is analogical. Before Christ, the shadow of the Cross is over the world; after Christ, the light of the Cross.

b) The Redemptive Act Recapitulates the New Economy in Advance

1. Christ, while dying on the Cross in order to redeem retrospectively the previous ages and to inaugurate a new age of salvation, knew all things which concerned Him, *omnia quae ad ipsum spectant*,[21] that is to say, the entire existentiality of the world, *omnia existentia secundum quodcumque tempus*. He also knew all the secret thoughts of men.[22] And He did this by seeing them in the Word with the knowledge of the blessed. The following words of Pascal are true: "I thought of you in My agony, I spilt drops of Blood for you."[23] Christ's knowledge bore the weight not only of past ages, but also of the whole new economy of the world.

2. And Christ, while dying on the Cross, was able, on the brink of this new economy, to reach all future times and places in order to communicate to them His grace. Just as the principal cause elevates the instrument in order that it might be joined and proportioned to ends which would otherwise surpass it, so the divinity was able to use the human nature of the Savior, His intelligence, His liberty, His senses, as a conjoined instrument, *instrumentum conjunctum*, in order to transmit grace to the world.[24] It follows that, by divine power, which is beyond space and time, the sacred humanity of Christ was able to touch instrumentally by contact all places at the very hour of His Passion, even though sacred humanity was

---

20 *Summa Theologiae* III, qu. 62, a. 6. Is this an impossibility *in view of the plan of actual providence?* Is this a *metaphysical* impossibility? We will not prejudge the response. Some have thought that God, by a mode of eternity, *could* make the sacrificial act of Calvary present in times prior to when it actually took place.

21 St. Thomas, *Summa Theologiae* III, qu. 10, a. 2.

22 *Ibid*. To see *in the Word* is to see with the eyes of God Who, in a singular instant of His eternity, does not see *successive things as simultaneous*, but *sees successive things simultaneously*. To this vision, writes Cajetan, "omnia secundum suas existentias simul, simultate instantanea aeternitatis, sunt praesentia." *Summa Theologiae* I, qu. 14, a. 13, XII.

23 Pascal, *Pensées*, edit. Br., no. 553.

24 St. Thomas, *Summa Theologiae* III, qu. 8, a. 1; qu. 13, a. 3; qu. 43, a. 2; qu. 62, a. 5.

in a place. It also follows that, even though it was in time, this same sacred humanity was able to touch instrumentally by contact all times, present and future. "The principal Cause of man's salvation is God. But, from the fact that Christ's humanity is the instrument of the divinity, it follows that all the actions and passions of Christ operate instrumentally in virtue of the divinity, for the salvation of humanity. In this sense the Passion of Christ is the efficient Cause of the salvation of humanity."[25]

c) The Mass Is the Existential Entrance of a Generation into the Drama of the Passion, Where Its Place Was Marked Out in Advance

Thus all the graces of the new economy are pre-contained in the Passion of Christ.

These graces would touch each and every generation according to modes, degrees and measures planned and indicated by Christ. Immediately, the immediate contemporary generation: the Apostles at the Last Supper, the Blessed Virgin and St. John at the foot of the Cross, and each of the succeeding generations in turn.

These graces would have as a result the rousing and incorporation of all generations into the drama of Calvary: on one hand, by integrating them into Christ's unique act of offering, where their place had been marked out in advance (by the ascending mediation of Christ); and on the other hand, by opening them up to the unique effusion of charity obtained when the side of Christ was opened, but in order to be dispensed progressively (by the descending mediation of Christ).

The Mass—where each time the death of the now glorious Christ is announced, He is made present to us under the sacramental species—is the power of the Cross ready to pour out its heart, so to speak, upon a generation in order to make it enter existentially, with all its faith and love, into the drama of the Passion, where its place had been marked out in advance.

d) Two Presences at the Sacrifice of the Mass: One Temporal, the Other by Spiritual Contact

At the Mass we enter into the redemptive drama; we become present to it.

But can one speak of a rigorous and real *presence* of us at a sacrifice offered only once, and twenty centuries ago? We preserve its *memory*: is this not the only way for us to encounter it?

1. It is here that we distinguish, in contrast to a pure memory, two types of presences: one temporal, the other spiritual.

The first is that of all the contemporaries gathered around the Cross: the Blessed Virgin and St. John certainly; but also the actors and

---

25   *Ibid.*, qu. 48, a. 6.

spectators of the drama. It is a presence of coexistence in time, a *presence of contemporaneity.*

The second presence is the privilege of the Blessed Virgin and St. John. *They have been touched by the spiritual power which descends from the Cross.* They adhere to the mystery accomplished before their eyes. They enter by the knowledge of their faith and the impulse of their charity into the interior of the redemptive sacrifice: on one hand, in order to unite themselves presently to the theandric offering of Christ; on the other hand, to open themselves up presently to the graces which He desires to pour out upon the world. Here we have the *presence of spiritual contact.*

2. It is clear that the presence of contemporaneity is excluded from us. It is contradictory for us to coexist with that which for us happened two thousand years ago. But this presence—as regards both the friends and the enemies of Christ—does not matter here. The only presence which counts is that which constituted the privilege of the Blessed Virgin and St. John, the presence of spiritual contact. And there is no contradiction in saying that this extends even to us. The ray of the bloody Cross, which touched the Blessed Virgin and St. John, moves with each succeeding generation in order to touch us at each Mass. It leads us into the interior of that redemptive sacrifice, where our place is marked out in advance, in order that we might be able to implore with Christ and to be blessed and satisfied in Christ.

e) The Spiritual Presence Is Enveloped in the Unbloody Rite

1. The great condescension which governs the economy of salvation since the Fall wills that God bring to man spiritual things in the envelopment of corporal things, which are connatural to him and which all too often seduce him.[26] He began to teach us His mysteries through the images of the human language. He Himself would personally come to us by being incarnate in a human nature. Finally, He would signify and communicate His graces to us in the sacraments.

2. If, therefore, the glorious Christ eternally ratifies in heaven the unique redemptive act by which He willed to save us; if He decides to actualize it, to amplify it for us continuously, it would be necessary then, in conformity with His law of condescension, that the spiritual ray of His bloody Cross come to us in a sensible envelopment, capable at once of signifying and transmitting it.

Therefore, regarding the unbloody rite of sacrifice instituted at the Last Supper: the sacramental species of bread and wine, which recall the Body of Christ given for us and His Blood poured out for the remission of sins, manifest and bear witness that the grace hidden in each Mass is the very grace of Redemption, that each Mass is an operative presence, a real

---

26   Cf., St. Thomas, *Summa Theologiae* III, qu. 61, a. 1.

and true presence of the Redemption: "As often as the memorial of this Victim is celebrated, the work of our Redemption is wrought."[27]

9. The Unbloody Sacrifice Does Not Substitute but Rather Subordinates Itself to the Bloody Sacrifice; It Multiplies Not the Sacrifice but Rather Its Presences

The unbloody sacrifice does not substitute the bloody sacrifices; it subordinates itself to it.

The unbloody rite of the Mass is, as the unbloody rite of the Last Supper, a real and true sacrifice, because Christ and His same sacrifice of the Cross are not only there in figure but also really and truly rendered present.

In virtue of the words of transubstantiation, Christ Himself, now glorious, is present to us *substantially*. But He signifies to us, by the sacramental appearances of His Body given and His Blood poured out, that He comes only by means of His Cross to touch us and to apply to us the very *power* of His bloody sacrifice, as He did to the Apostles at the Last Supper. Such that at each Mass He brings to us, really and truly, under the unbloody species, the *substantial presence of the glorious Christ* and the *efficient presence of His bloody sacrifice*.

As each consecrated host is really and truly *Christ*, because transubstantiation multiplies not the one Christ but rather the real *substantial* presences of the one Christ, so each Mass is really and truly the *sacrificial act of Christ*, because transubstantiation multiplies not the one sacrificial act of Christ but rather the real operative presences of His one sacrificial act.

It is in order to multiply not the supreme sacrifice, but rather the presences of that sacrifice among men that Jesus, on the night He was betrayed, having taken bread and broken it, said, "This is My Body given for you." He added, "Do this in memory of Me," and that having taken the cup, saying, "This cup is the New Covenant in My Blood," He added, "Do this, as often as you drink it, in remembrance of Me." The Church, therefore, has received the power to renew the unbloody rite of Holy Thursday, capable not only of representing but also of rendering present to us—in the only manner in which it can be rendered present to us, namely operatively—the unique bloody immolation. "*There is one Host, and not many*," writes St. Thomas, "which Christ offered and which we offer in our turn, *because Christ was offered but once*."[28]

The redemptive sacrifice—completed with one stroke with respect to the Savior Who is the Head, but incomplete with respect to men who are the members, insofar as they still need to be saved, to be incorporated into the sufferings and death of their Head—the redemptive sacrifice

---

27 Secret from the ninth Sunday after Pentecost. It is cited in the encyclical *Mediator Dei*, AAS, 1947, 551.
28 *Summa Theologiae* III, qu. 83, a. 1, ad 1.

continues "to be perfected" by the Mass; it continues to incorporate the succeeding generations until the Body of Christ, which is the Church, be completely built.

10. The Mass and the Sacraments

Earlier[29] we distinguished in the priestly mediation of Christ two distinct but inseparable movements: an ascending movement by which He gave the world to God; and a descending movement by which He gave God to the world.

This double movement is found again, but in a different and unequal manner, in the Mass and in the sacraments.

a) Ascending Mediation and Supplication

1. In the order of ascending mediation, *the Mass* alone really acts in the manner of a sacrifice of adoration, expiation, impetration and thanksgiving. It grants us under the veil of an unbloody sacrifice the now glorious Christ, but coming to us now in order to associate us with the very act of His redemptive sacrifice.

By this fact the Mass constitutes an incomparable presence, *a supplication of infinite power.* The entire role of the Church will be—insofar as it possible—to appropriate to herself this supplication, to make it her own, to attach herself to it, to engulf herself in it.

Even in the case where the minister is unworthy, this suppliant and redemptive presence of Christ will not be annulled. And from this point of view one could say that the sacrifice of the Mass is efficacious *ex opere operato*, that is, independently of the good or bad dispositions of its minister.[30]

The Mass, according to the Council of Trent, is "the pure offering which is unable to be sullied by either the unworthiness or the malice of them who offer it, and about which the Lord foretold through Malachi

---

29   P. 18, see below, p. 102.
30   In his *De Missa*, bk. 2 ch. 4, St. Robert Bellarmine defines the notions of efficacy *ex opere operantis* and efficacy *ex opere operato* in order to apply them to the very *sacrifice* of the Mass.

"Something," he says, "*occurs ex opere operantis* when it takes its power from the goodness or devotion of him who does it . . . It occurs *ex opere operato* when, accomplished according to the prescriptions, it is efficacious in itself, independently of the good or bad dispositions of the minister who applies it." (Not, we add, independently of the dispositions of the subject who receives it.)

This admitted, the doctor would say "that the sacrifice of the Mass, insofar as it is offered *by Christ*, occurs *ex opere operantis* but infallibly; for it pleases God by reason of the goodness, forever equal and constant, of Christ Who offers it. But that, insofar as it is offered *by the minister*, it occurs *ex opere operato;* for it is pleasing to God even if the minister who offers it is displeasing to Him." See below, p. 119.

1:11, that it will be a pure offering, in every place, to His Name, which is great among the Gentiles."[31]

2. In this same order of ascending mediation what do the *sacraments* of the New Law represent? They have been instituted by Christ. They bear the marks of the Passion, which were sacrificial, meritorious, satisfactory and propitiatory.[32]

By approaching, receiving and accomplishing the acts of worship necessary to receive them, they are, in a way, adorned with the marks of the Passion, presented to the Father in the very name of the Son; and they move Him to grant pardon.

There is, then, in the sacraments of the New Law, a prayer, a supplication. Nevertheless, as powerful as it may be, this manner of imploring proper to the sacraments, and what modern theologians have called the moral causality of the sacraments, represents only an indirect and diminished participation in the immediate sacrificial supplication of the Mass. One could, therefore, on this same plane of supplication, introduce a radical distinction between the Eucharist considered as *sacrifice* and the Eucharist considered as *sacrament*.

b) Descending Mediation and Benediction

1. The Mass brings us Christ's Passion. Yet the Passion of Christ accomplishes our salvation not only by way of supplication but also by way of efficiency: "The principal Cause of our salvation is God. But, from the fact that the humanity of Christ is the instrument of the divinity, all the actions and passions of Christ operate instrumentally, in virtue of the divinity, in order to accomplish the salvation of the human race. In this sense the Passion of Christ is the efficient cause of our salvation."[33] This efficiency of the Passion is infallible. And it too is brought to us by means of the Mass, certainly not independently of the dispositions of those whom it saves, but independently of the dispositions of the minister's sanctity.

It is necessary to understand this efficiency of the Passion. It is the efficiency of a Source which wishes to be poured out. One has to draw near to it by faith and the sacraments. St. Thomas compares the Passion to a remedy made by a doctor, but which needs to be applied to each particular case.[34] The Passion of Christ, he says, must precede, "being the universal cause of the remission of sins, *ut causa quaedam universalis remissionis peccatorum*; it is necessary also that it be brought in particular to each person for the abolition of his own sins, *necesse est quod singulis adhibeatur ad deletionem propriorum peccatorum*; which happens at

31 Session XXII, chap. 1; Denz., 939.
32 The sacrament of the New Law is "a sign which recalls that which has preceded, namely the Passion of Christ." St. Thomas, *Summa Theologiae* III, qu. 60, a. 3.
33 St. Thomas, *Summa Theologiae* III, qu. 48, a. 6.
34 *Ibid.*, qu. 49, a. 1, ad 3.

Baptism, Penance, and the other sacraments, which draw their power from the Passion of Christ."[35]

2. How should we understand the efficiency of the *sacraments* of the New Law vis-à-vis the efficiency of the Mass? "We make use," says St. Thomas, "of two types of instruments: one is separated from us, like a stick; the other is joined to us, like a hand. The first is moved by the second, as the stick is moved by the hand. The principal efficient Cause of grace is God; the humanity of Christ is the conjoined instrument (joined to the divinity); the sacraments are the separated instruments. Thus the sanctifying power travels to us from the divinity of Christ, through His humanity, into the sacraments."[36] But Christ saved us by His Passion. "It is clear then that the sacraments of the Church take their power especially from the Passion of Christ. The power of the Passion is conferred on us in some way by the reception of the sacraments: the sign of which is, that from the side of Jesus suspended on the Cross flowed forth water and blood, signs of Baptism and the Eucharist, that is, the two principal sacraments."[37] St. Paul teaches that we have been baptized "into the death of Christ" (Rom 6:3).

Hence we see that the general, total and undivided application of the Passion to each celebration of the unbloody rite (which takes place at the Mass) differs essentially from the personal, determined and particularized application procured by each of the sacraments of the New Law. We find again, but this time on the level of the descending mediation, the distinction between the Eucharist considered as a *sacrifice* and the Eucharist considered as a *sacrament* of the New Law.

11. The Necessity of a Permanent Presence of the Sacrifice of the Cross

1. When He appears as "the Great High Priest of the good things to come," Christ makes "once and for all an offering of His own Body" and "obtains for us an eternal redemption" (Heb 9:11, 12; 10:10). It was in the predestined offering of a moment that the eternal God and the still incomplete unfolding of the ages were reconciled. *The bloody Cross remains forever planted at the center of the true religion.*

The Cross revives perishing souls. It dispenses life. It dissolves the hardness of hearts. As Yahweh said through His prophet: "I will pour out on the House of David and upon the inhabitants of Jerusalem a spirit of grace and mercy, and they will turn toward Me; and they will look upon him whom they have pierced, and they shall mourn for him as for an only child." It purifies from sin: "At that time there will be a fountain opened

---

35   *Ibid.*, ad 4. See below, pp. 78, 117.
36   *Ibid.* St. Thomas, *Summa Theologiae* III, qu. 62, a. 5.
37   *Ibid.*

for the House of David and for the inhabitants of Jerusalem to cleanse them from sin and uncleanness" (Zech 12:10; 13:1). The Cross is the fountain of Eden, the fountain of the sweetness and sorrows which flourish in the garden of the Church. Its presence is necessary.

2. "Lord, if You had been present, my brother would not have died." And Jesus did not deny this. He even said to His disciples something similar: "Lazarus is dead, and for your sake I rejoice that I was not there, so that you may believe." But when they came to Him—the two sisters, one after the other—when Mary was at His feet and He "saw her weeping, her and the Jews who accompanied her," then "He was deeply moved in spirit and troubled, and said: 'Where have you laid him?'" (Jn 11). There are supplications which are resisted from afar but which are not resisted from close up. Martha and Mary knew this. God knows this as well. It is for this very reason that the Word was made Flesh and dwelt among us. And it is for this that, being nailed to the Cross with the plan of drawing all men to Himself, *He would desire that that very Cross would not stand at a distance, but be present, and that it would be carried on the waves of time*. Having considered that the supreme sacrifice had begun, He established a mysterious institution which would see to the conveyance of that sacrifice and the perpetuation of its power.

The Liturgy of Holy Thursday, which the disciples would have to reproduce "in memory of Him," would, in effect, truly carry to succeeding generations His Body "given for us," and His Blood "of the New Covenant" "poured out for us" (Lk 22:19–20) "for the remission of sins" (Mt 26:28). Those who "eat this bread and drink of this cup proclaim the death of the Lord" (1 Cor 11:26) until He comes to substitute for that meal—where the realities dwell veiled under sacramental signs—the meal where they will be made manifest and where the faithful will drink of the vine of love and the unmixed cup "in the kingdom of His Father" (Mt 26:29).

In summary, the bloody sacrifice is conveyed to us by the renewal of the unbloody rite instituted at the Last Supper, around which the Church is built.

12. The Thought of St. Thomas Aquinas

a) Two Ways: For or Against the Continual Efficiency of the Redemptive Act

1. Must it be said that the glorious Christ, substantially present, whether it be in heaven under His own appearances or at Mass under sacramental appearances—must it be said that He continues to desire to touch men who live in time by means of the act of redemption, an act transitory in itself but permanent in its effects? And must it be said that the redemptive act can be made present for us by its power and in order to touch us?

The Mass, therefore, explains itself completely. It is the real presence of the one redemptive sacrifice now consummated under the sacramental veils, as the Last Supper was the real presence of the one redemptive sacrifice on the way to being accomplished under the same sacramental veils. Such is the thought of St. Thomas. It reveals to us by the same stroke the mysteries of redemption, of the Mass and of the new economy of salvation in their ultimate depths.

To the objection that the Passion, being past, can no longer operate in the present, the response is made that the motion of God, Who is eternal, can act above all subsequent succession of time by a transitory instrument, like the Passion of Christ.

2. Must we, on the contrary, recoil before this doctrine of the presence to the world of the bloody sacrifice under the veil of the unbloody sacrifice? Is it necessary to posit a contradiction where St. Thomas sees a mystery, to declare his thought inadmissible, to search for facile solutions?

One would say then, with numerous theologians of the Baroque and Modern periods, that the Passion of Christ, existing no longer in itself, would be unable to continue to act on generations, and that we would be saved not by the very Passion, Death and Resurrection of Christ, as St. Thomas said, but by the glorious Christ Who formerly suffered, died and rose.

All from that point on appears simple. There would no longer be a question of seeing in the Mass the very presence of the redemptive act. The Mass would not be a sacrifice from the fact that it brings to us the sacrifice of the Cross; it would be admitted without a doubt that it applies sacrifice to us, that it communicates to us the power; but this application, this power would cease to appear as it really is, namely as the true presence of the sacrificial redemptive act of the Cross. From then on, the Mass would not be able to become a sacrifice except in virtue of another act, of a sacrificial act of the glorious Christ and of the Church uniting herself to Him. But it is here precisely that the difficulties begin.[38]

---

38 According to St. Robert Bellarmine, *De Missa*, bk. II, chap. 4, this sacrificial act of the glorious Christ, different than the unique sacrificial and fully sufficing act of the Cross, would no longer be in itself meritorious or satisfactory, but only impetrative. See below, p. 82, note 54. Also Suarez, Commentary on the *Summa Theologiae* III, qu. 83, a. 2; disp. 76, sect. 1, no. 5; edit. Vivès, t. XXI, p. 682, sees in the Mass a sacrifice "specifically and essentially" different from that of the Cross; and he criticizes Dominic Soto, according to whom, as said in as said in *IV Sent.*, dist. 13, qu. 2, a. 1, edit. Venice, 1584, p. 634, "our daily sacrifice of the Mass is not dis-tinct from that of the Cross, but exactly the same, *idem prorsus.*"

 Can an act of the glorious Christ be sacrificial in the proper sense? The unbloody rite of the Last Supper was a real and true sacrifice because it rendered Christ sacramentally present to the disciples *with* the act of His unique redemptive sacrifice. Would the unbloody rite of the Mass be a real and true sacrifice if it rendered to us Christ sacramentally present *without* the act of His unique redemptive sacrifice? It would be in itself not a *sacrifice*, but an *offering*. Cf. St. Thomas, *Summa Theologiae* II-II, qu. 85, a. 3, ad 3.

b) The Passion of Christ Touches Us by a Spiritual Contact Despite the Distance of Time

1. We know the great texts from Scripture: "By one single oblation Christ has perfected forever those whom He sanctifies" (Heb 10:14). "This is My Blood, the Blood of the Covenant, poured out for the multitude, for the remission of sins" (Mt 26:28). Jesus Christ "loved us and washed away (deleted) our sins in His own Blood" (Rev 1:5). God, through Christ, reconciled all things "by making peace through the Blood of His Cross" (Col 1:20). "Christ, while we were still sinners, died for us" (Rom 5:8). God raised "from the dead Jesus Christ our Savior, Who was put to death for our sins and raised for our justification" (Rom 4:24–25); etc.

If one wishes to give to these revelations all their profundity, says St. Thomas, he must say that since God, according to the plan of the Incarnation, willed to use the sacred humanity of Christ in order to communicate grace, then it is by a power coming forth from the one redemptive drama, from the very Passion of the Savior, from His Death heralding His Resurrection; then it is by this power that we continue to be saved and will one day rise. It is truly by a ray coming forth from His bloody Passion that Christ willed on the Cross, and continues to will now in heaven, to touch all men since the restoration of the economy of the New Alliance.

2. We reproduce here three texts of St. Thomas concerning the Passion, Death, and Resurrection of the Savior.

1) "Whether Christ's Passion Brought About Our Salvation Efficiently?"[39]—Here is the response: "The principal efficient cause of man's salvation is God. But since Christ's humanity is the instrument of the divinity, therefore all Christ's actions and sufferings operate instrumentally in virtue of His divinity for the salvation of men. Consequently, then, the Passion of Christ is the efficient cause of men's salvation, *et secundum hoc Passio Christi efficienter causat salutem humanam.*"

To the objection that a corporeal agent does not act efficiently except by contact and therefore Christ's Passion was not able to touch men nor bring about their salvation efficiently, *sed Passio Christi non potuit contingere omnes homines, ergo non potuit efficienter operari salutem omnium hominum,* St. Thomas responds that "Christ's Passion, although corporeal, has yet a spiritual effect from the united divinity; and therefore it secures its efficacy by spiritual contact, *et ideo per spiritualem contactum efficaciam sortitur*—namely, by faith and the sacraments of faith, as the Apostle says (Rom 3:25): 'Whom God hath proposed to be a propitiation, through faith in His Blood.'"[40] These last words of St. Thomas are explained elsewhere: "The power of Christ's

---

39 St. Thomas, *Summa Theologiae* III, qu. 48, a. 6. English translation by Fathers of the English Dominican Province (New York: Benziger Brothers, Inc., 1947).
40 *Ibid.,* ad 2. See above, p. 73, and below, p. 117.

Passion is united to us by faith and the sacraments, but in different ways; because the link that comes from faith is produced by an act of the soul; whereas the link that comes from the sacraments is produced by making use of exterior things. It is therefore clear that the sacraments of the New Law do reasonably derive the power of justification from Christ's Passion, which is the cause of man's righteousness; whereas the sacraments of the Old Law did not, *manifestum est quod a Passione Christi, quae est causa humanae justificationis, convenienter derivatur virtus justificativa ad sacramenta novae Legis, non autem ad sacramenta veteris Legis.*"[41]

2) "Whether Christ's Death Conduced in Any Way to Our Salvation?"[42]—The response makes a distinction between the act of tending toward death, *mors in fieri*, and the state of death, *mors in facto esse.*

The transitory act of dying, it must be said, is, like the Passion, the *meritorious* and *efficient* cause of our salvation.

When death occurs the body "cannot be the cause of our salvation by way of *merit*, but only by way of *efficiency* . . . and therefore, whatever befell Christ's Flesh, *quidquid contigit circa carnem Christi*, even when the soul was departed, was conducive to salvation in virtue of the united divinity." Cajetan wrote here: "From the fact that the Deity used the Body of Christ as an instrument, it follows that It made use of His Body deprived of life as an organ for causing in us the destruction of the double death of the soul and the body, according to what was said: 'He destroyed our death by His own,' *Qui mortem nostram moriendo destruxit.*"

3) "Whether Christ's Resurrection Is the Cause of the Resurrection of Our Bodies?"[43]—The response: "The Word of God first bestows immortal life upon that body which is naturally united with Himself, and through it works the resurrection in all other bodies."

Will there immediately follow here the question of Christ *arisen* from His own Resurrection, but not of Christ *resurrecting*? Let's look at the following texts. The third objection maintains that Christ's Resurrection cannot be the efficient cause of ours, "for an efficient cause acts only through contact, whether spiritual or corporeal. Now it is evident that Christ's Resurrection has no corporeal contact with the dead who shall rise again, owing to distance of time and place, *propter distantiam temporis et loci*; and similarly it has no spiritual contact, which is through faith and charity, because even unbelievers and sinners shall rise again." To which St. Thomas responds: "Just as all other things which Christ did and endured in His humanity are profitable to our salvation through the power of the Godhead, so also is

41 *Summa Theologiae, Summa Theologiae* III, qu. 62, a. 6. St. Thomas explains here, as we saw above, p. 94, that *unlike the final cause, the efficient cause cannot move before existing. Before Christ*, the Passion was able to act in the manner of a *final* cause; it is only *since Christ* that it can act moreover as an *efficient* cause.
42 St. Thomas, *Summa Theologiae* III, qu. 50, a. 6.
43 St. Thomas, *Summa Theologiae* III, qu. 56, a. 1.

Christ's Resurrection the efficient cause of ours, through the Divine power whose office it is to quicken the dead; and this power by its presence is in touch with all places and times;[44] and such virtual contact suffices for its efficiency, *quae quidem virtus praesentialiter attingit omnia loca et tempora, et talis contactus virtutis sufficit ad rationem hujus efficientiae.*"

The first objection of this same article holds that, if Christ's Resurrection were the cause of man's, all the dead would be returned to life at the same time as Christ. St. Thomas responds that the Resurrection of Christ works its effects throughout time, according to the decree of the divine will: "Christ's Resurrection is the cause of ours through the power of the united Word, Who operates according to His will. And consequently, it is not necessary for the effect to follow at once, but according as the Word of God disposes, namely, that first of all we be conformed to the suffering and dying Christ in this suffering and mortal life; and afterwards may come to share in the likeness of His Resurrection."[45]

c) The Mass Allows Us to Enter Into the Drama of Christ's Passion and Bloody Sacrifice

At the end of the tract on the Eucharist St. Thomas asks: "Whether Christ is Sacrificed in This Sacrament?"[46] He poses, as we see, a burning question. It is strange that his response, as succinct as it is, brushes by the subject and fails to plumb the depths of his knowledge.

1. Three objections are raised: 1) according to Hebrews 10:14, the oblation, that is, the sacrifice of Christ, is unique; 2) the sacrifice of the Cross was a crucifixion, but Christ cannot be crucified again; 3) at the Cross, Christ is Priest and Victim; at Mass, another priest appears.

---

44 Cf. St. Thomas, *Summa Theologiae* I, qu. 14, a. 13: "All things that are in time are present to God from eternity, not only because He has the types of things present within Him, as some say; but because His glance is carried from eternity over all things as they are in their presentiality," in their existentiality.

45 Suarez mentions the opinion, according to which Christ's humanity made use of His past actions as physical instruments in order to bring about our justification and resurrection. He speaks of Thomists who see there a *mysterium reconditae theologiae.* (It's a question of nothing less than the mystery of redemption continued among us, that is to say the mystery of the Mass, less sublime than that of the Trinity, but as hidden in the bosom of God as the mystery of the Incarnation or the Eucharist.) For him, this thesis conceals an impossibility. There is not even a mystery; all is simple and is reduced to saying that Christ's humanity, formerly subjugated to the Passion and Resurrection, is today the instrument of our salvation. *De Incarnatione,* disp. 31, sect. 8, no. 5 and ff; edit. Vivès, t. XIX, p. 613. It is the thought of Suarez which would prevail, even among those who are called Thomists, and the view of St. Thomas would be forgotten. Suarez, as we said, would be led to see in the Mass a sacrifice specifically and essentially distinct from that of the Cross.

46 St. Thomas, *Summa Theologiae* III, qu. 83, a. 1.

2. In a contrary sense, we offer some words—those which we italicize—of St. Augustine, where he explains that the sign often takes the name of the thing signified; do we not say, for example, that tomorrow is the day of the Passion, that is, the day when we celebrate the anniversary of the Passion? *"Was not Christ sacrificed one time only in Himself,* in seipso, *and nevertheless He is sacrificed* for the people *in the sacrament,* in sacramento, not only each Feast of Easter, but *everyday;* and they do not lie who, when asked, respond, 'He is sacrificed.'"[47]

2. The response of St. Thomas is twofold.

1st: The celebration of the sacrament, of the Eucharistic mystery, is called an immolation of Christ in this sense: that "it is as *an image representing the Passion of Christ,* which is His true sacrifice." This response is meant to give an initial justification of certain patristic texts, such as one attributed to St. Ambrose and which St. Thomas cites here,[48] or the one of St. Augustine which we have related. It is not, for St. Thomas, a sufficient response: the image of a true sacrifice is still not a true sacrifice. In stopping there one would be able to say, all the same, that the figures of the Old Testament, for example the sacrifice of the Pascal lamb, were already sacrifices of Christ.

2) Here now is the proper response: "It is called a sacrifice in respect of the effect of His Passion; because, by this sacrament, we are made partakers of the fruit of our Lord's Passion. Also, it is said in one of the Sunday secrets: As often as the memorial of this Victim is celebrated, the work of our redemption is wrought.[49]

Thus, Christ is sacrificed at the Mass because the Mass brings us the effect of His Passion; it actualizes for us His Passion; it makes us partakers of the fruits of His Passion; it accomplishes each time the work of our redemption.[50] Let us take note here. We see here the same thought and

47 St. Augustine, *Epist. XCVIII,* no. 9. St. Augustine, who speaks here of the Eucharist only by way of comparison, wishes to explain that, since we call the *Body and Blood* of Christ the *sacrament* of Christ's Body and Blood, we would also have the right to call *faith Baptism,* which is the sacrament of faith; such that the godparent would be able to say of the infant who receives Baptism, that he has the faith. The difficulty proposed by St. Augustine bears solely on this point of the liturgy.

48 "In Christ, the host always capable of saving us has been offered one time only. Yet what do we do? Do we not offer it everyday? Yes, but by making a memorial of His death." This passage, attributed to St. Ambrose by Peter Lombard, *IV Sent.* dist. 12, no. 7, is in fact a fragment of a commentary of St. John Chrysostom, *Ad Hebr.,* homil. 17, no. 3; PG LXIII, 131. See this text above, p. 45.

49 Secret from the ninth Sunday after Pentecost.

50 "The august sacrifice of the altar is the perfect instrument, *velut eximium instrumentum,* by which the merits coming forth from the Cross of the Divine Redeemer are distributed to the faithful: *As often as the memorial of this Victim is celebrated, the work of our redemption is wrought."* Encyclical *Mediator Dei,* 20 November 1947, AAS 1947, 551.

words of St. Thomas, which he used in his work when he taught that the Passion of Christ, insofar as it is an instrument of His divinity, worked our salvation in a manner of efficiency; and, that it exercises its efficiency by a spiritual contact despite the distance of time and space, that it can touch all times in their presentiality, in their existentiality. Where Christ's Passion is really present, Christ's sacrifice is really present. Here we have the direct response of St. Thomas to the direct question that he posed.

In other words, the Mass brings us not only the *substantial presence* of Christ in His glorious *state*, but also the *operative presence* of His redemptive sacrificial *act*. Christ desires now, as He desired on the Cross (and until the end of the world), that the ray from His bloody Cross touch and redeem every moment of time by this contact.

d) The Mass Communicates to Us the One Sacrifice of Christ

The doctrine indicated by St. Thomas was not entirely explicit; the responses which he gives to the objections preserve a rather general character. We must try to clarify them.

To the objection taken from Hebrews 10:14 on the unicity of the oblation and sacrifice of Christ, St. Thomas responds with a text attributed to St. Ambrose:[51] "There is but one Victim, namely that which Christ offered, and which we offer, and not many victims, because Christ was offered but once: and this latter sacrifice is the pattern (*exemplum*) of the former. For just as what is offered everywhere is one Body, and not many bodies, so also is it but one sacrifice." We clarify: just as the Eucharist multiplies not the Body of Christ but the substantial presences of Christ's Body, so the Mass multiplies not the sacrifice of Christ but the operative presences of Christ's sacrifice.

To the second objection, namely that Christ can be neither sacrificed nor crucified again, the response is made that, at the Mass the bloody sacrifice is not repeated, but *re-presented*: the altar, where the death of Christ is signified by the sacramental appearances, represents the Cross where Christ was sacrificed under His own appearances. We should add (and this will be the key response) that the bloody sacrifice is then *applied* to us, made present, and that the Mass multiplies not this unique sacrifice but the real presences of this unique sacrifice.

To the third objection, namely that on the Cross Christ was Priest and Victim, we respond that, at the Mass also Christ is not only the Victim Who is offered, but the Priest Who offers as well: "It is in His name, in fact, and by His power that priests who represent Him pronounce the words of consecration." We add that the unbloody sacrifice, accomplished through the ministry of the priests, is intended to apply and make present to us the bloody sacrifice where Christ is offered and offers Himself to us.

---

51   It is given as such in the third part of the *Décret*, dist. 2, c. 53, *In Christo semel*, then in Peter Lombard, etc. See above, p. 80, note 48.

Thus, as St. Thomas says elsewhere, "it is a true sacrifice of Christ which is communicated to the faithful under the species of bread and wine."[52]

e) The Way Opened by St. Thomas and the Divergent Way

The two aspects of the Mass noted by St. Thomas, namely that it *represents* the Passion and *applies* its fruits to us, are taken up by the Council of Trent.[53] With that, approval is granted.

Either, however, one sees in this application a real presence of the Passion and redemptive sacrifice of the Cross—and thus St. Thomas responded to the problem proposed (the entire teaching of the saintly doctor on the infinite power of the sacrifice of the Mass would confirm this view); or, one sees in the doctrine of the presence of the Passion at all times and places an impossibility—in which case *a)* St. Thomas failed in teaching this doctrine in his tract on redemption; *b)* He left the question which he so well proposed without a response, apropos of the Mass; *c)* One would have to find for the Mass another sacrificial act than the one about which the Letter to the Hebrews speaks, and which nevertheless would be according to the exigencies of the Council of Trent: 1) a *true* sacrifice of Christ, and not only the ritualistic and sacramental representation of a true sacrifice of Christ; 2) a sacrificial offering of Christ in the *proper* sense, and not only in the improper sense; 3) a truly satisfactory and *propitiatory* sacrifice;[54] *d)* Finally, one would have to regard the application of the fruits of the Passion which are produced at the Mass as a consequence of this new sacrificial act of Christ.

---

52   "Unde etiam in nova Lege, verum Christi sacrificium communicatur fidelibus sub specie panis et vini." St. Thomas, *Summa Theologiae III*, qu. 22, a. 6, ad 2.
53   Session XXII, chap. 1, DS 938.
54   "Sacrificium istud vere propitiatorium esse." Session XXII, chap. 2 and c. 3, Denz., 940, 950.
     For St. Robert Bellarmine, the sacrifice of the Mass is, properly speaking, only impetrative: "*The sacrifice of the Cross* has been truly and in itself meritorious, satisfactory and impetrative; for Christ in His own mortal life was able to merit and to make satisfaction. The *sacrifice of the Mass*, properly speaking, is only impetrative; for Christ, now immortal, can neither merit nor make satisfaction." *De Missa*, bk 2, chap. 4.
     It is correct, as we said above, pp. 89 and 106, that the *intercession of the heavenly Christ* is no longer meritorious nor satisfactory nor redemptive. The conclusion which must be made, with St. Thomas, *Summa Theologiae* III, qu. 22, a. 5, *is that it* [i.e. Christ's intercession in heaven] *is not a sacrifice*, it *distributes* the fruits of the sacrifice, it is a *dispenser* of the fruits of the sacrifice.
     St. Bellarmine seeks in the Mass another sacrifice than that of the Cross by qualifying the *sacrificial dispensing* mediation of the heavenly Christ. But he demonstrates his own perplexity. We have here then a true sacrifice of Christ, which nevertheless is neither meritorious, nor satisfactory, and which consequently is lacking the two ends recognized in the sacrifice of Christ.
     To adopt the way which we call divergent is not without its difficulties.

13. An Analysis of Cajetan's Teaching

The Lutherans, if they reject transubstantiation, remain faithful neverthe-less to confessing the Real Presence of Christ in the Eucharist. However, they use the Letter to the Hebrews to deny that the Last Supper, and *a fortiori* the Mass, was a true sacrifice, a true offering to God. It was in order to dissipate their objections that Cajetan would recall the Catholic teach-ing on the nature of the Mass in the sixth chapter of his small work *De Missae sacrificio*,[55] thirty-one years before the twenty-second Session of the Council of Trent, which treated *The Most Holy Sacrifice of the Mass*, 17 September 1562.[56] In addition to supplying clarifications integrated into the teaching of the Council of Trent, Cajetan's work brings with it invalu-able contributions to the subject.

a) The Same Victim or Offering Is Offered Under Different Modes, the One Bloody the Other Unbloody, On the Cross and at Mass

"The basis," writes Cajetan, "which explains and allows one to under-stand the diverse passages of Sacred Scripture regarding the sacrifice and priesthood of the New Testament is the unity of the Victim: on one hand sacrificed absolutely, *simpliciter et absolute*, one time only on the Cross by Christ insofar as He is in Himself; and on the other hand sacrificed in a certain manner, *secundum quid*, each day in His Church by Christ, by means of the ministers; such that there is in the New Testament a *bloody Victim* and an *unbloody Victim*.

"The bloody Victim is Jesus Christ offered one time only on the altar of the Cross for the sins of the entire world; the unbloody Victim instituted by Christ is His Body and Blood under the species of bread and wine.

---

55   *De Missae sacrificio et ritu, adversus Lutheranos, ad Clementem VII, Pontificem Maximum*, Rome, 3 May 1531. At the request of Clement VII, Cajetan, as the the-ological consultant of Nonce, wrote against those (*the Zwinglians*) who held that the Body and Blood of Christ are not present in the Eucharist except by symbol. Having read a *Lutheran* work, which recognized that Christ's true Body and true Blood are present in the Eucharist but denied that the Mass is a sacrifice, he real-ized his duty to respond spontaneously. We note here that the first writing of Cajetan had for a title *De erroribus contingentibus in Eucharistiae sacramento*. It was dated from 1525 and treated very precisely the twelve theses of Zwingli. In chapter 9, Cajetan declares that at the Mass *Christ* is signified and contained, while the *death of Christ* is signified but not contained. He wants to establish here the fact that one cannot cite the Letter to the Hebrews against the Mass. The Mass reiterates not the *one bloody sacrifice*, but the *unbloody sacrifice*, which trans-ports the former to us. There are not as many *deaths* of Christ as there are Masses, but as many *presences* of His one death. Christ's death, then, is not contained in the Mass as *repeatable*; but it is contained therein *as present*. And this is the teach-ing which is found in *De Missae sacrificio*.

56   Cajetan died on 10 August 1534, the same year in which the Council of Trent would open.

"The bloody and unbloody Victim, nevertheless, *are not two victims*, but one only; for, that which is the Victim, *res quae est hostia*, is one and the same. The Body of Christ on our altar is none other than the Body of Christ offered on the Cross; and the Blood of Christ on our altar is none other than the Blood of Christ poured out on the Cross. However, the manner of immolating, *modus immolandi*, this one and the same Victim is different.

"In fact, the one, substantial, original mode of sacrifice, *ille unicus substantialis ac primaevus immolandi modus*, was bloody. It is under its proper appearances that the Blood was poured out on the Cross by the breaking of the Body. Whereas the daily, external, adjunctive mode of the sacrifice, *iste vero quotidianus externus accessoriusque modus*, is unbloody. It represents, under the species of bread and wine and by way of immolation, *immolatitio modo*, Christ offered on the Cross."

b) The Unbloody Mode Is Not Juxtaposed but Subordinate to the Bloody Mode; Whence the Unicity of the Sacrifice on the Cross and of the Mass

"Thus the bloody Victim and unbloody Victim of the New Testament is one with respect to the thing offered, *ex parte rei oblatae*; and there is diversity with respect to the mode of offering, *ex parte modi offerendi*.

"This unbloody mode, however, is instituted not for itself, *secundum ipsum*, as a disparate mode of sacrifice,[57] but uniquely, as referring to the bloody Victim of the Cross, *ut refertur ad cruentem in Cruce hostiam*.

"Then, for all who can understand and see that a thing which does not exist except for another is but one thing with that other, *ubi unum nonnisi propter alterum, ibi unum dumtaxat est*—for such as these it is evident that one cannot affirm the existence in the New Testament of two sacrifices, two victims, two oblations, two immolations (whatever term one employs), just by the fact that the bloody Victim is Christ on the Cross and the unbloody Victim is Christ on the altar.[58] There is rather only one Victim, offered once only on the Cross, which endures by way of immolation, by the daily repetition of the rite instituted by Christ in the Eucharist, *sed esse unicam hostiam, semel oblatam in Cruce, perseverantem modo immolatitio, quotidiana repetitione ex institutione Christi in Eucharistia*.

"The permanence of the Victim offered on the Cross is *figured* on the altar; it is *possessed* of the identity of the thing offered on the Cross and on the altar. If Christ's Body, one and the same, is offered on the Cross and on the altar, it is clear that the Victim is not one thing on the Cross and another on the altar; and that the same Victim offered once on the Cross remains, but in another manner on the altar. With Christ having

---

57   The Old Testament, which *repeated* sacrifices, presupposed *disparate* victims; the New presupposes the *continuation of one Victim only*.

58   Another reading: ". . . by the fact that there is in the bloody Victim Christ on the Cross, and in the unbloody Victim Christ on the altar."

said, 'Do this in memory of Me,' that which was then broken and poured out now endures under the appearance of bread and wine in memory of Christ."

c) The Sacrifice Is Not Repeated, but Endures by the Repetition of the Unbloody Rite

Having recalled these principles, Cajetan then considers some difficulties.

1) The Letter to the Hebrews contrasts the one oblation of the Cross with the numerical multiplicity of the ancient sacrifices. If each of our Masses presupposed a sacrifice distinct from that of the Cross, the multiplicity (at least numerical) of the sacrifices would appear in the New Testament. Here is Cajetan's response: "There is not in the New Testament a repetition of the sacrifice or oblation, *non repetitur sacrificium seu oblatio*, but the one sacrifice offered once for all, continued by manner of immolation, *sed perseverat immolatitio modo unicum sacrificium semel oblatum*. The repetition occurs in the manner, *modus*, under which it endures, and not in the thing, *res*, which is offered; and this manner concurs with the sacrifice not for itself, *propter se*, but in order to commemorate in an unbloody manner the oblation of the Cross."

When the Letter to the Hebrews declares that Christ entered into heaven "not to offer Himself repeatedly, as the high priest enters the sanctuary each year with blood not his own," it is clear, adds Cajetan, that it is the repetition of the bloody sacrifice which it wished to exclude, and that this appears also in what follows: "In this case, then, He would have had to suffer many times since the foundation of the world" (Heb 9:25–26).

2) Was not the offering of Christ, then, more than sufficient?—The fact that "Christ *poured out His Blood once on the Cross* with a superabundance and super-sufficiency," is not in any way incompatible with the fact that "this unique and super-sufficient bloody effusion on the Cross *endures in the Eucharist by way of immolation*."

3) It is because the sacrifices for sin were insufficient that they needed to be repeated in the Old Testament. But this is no longer suitable— "We grant that, to speak properly, it is not suitable in the New Testament to speak of a victim-for-sins which must be repeated, *quam oportet repetere*; for, at the Mass the Victim is not repeated, *non repetitur in Missa hostia*, but the same Victim is offered on the Cross, and remains by way of immolation and is commemorated."

4) Christ's sacrifice made satisfaction for the sins of the entire world. One insults Him by juxtaposing to Him another victim for sin—"May the faithful guard themselves from thinking that the Mass is celebrated in order to supply what is lacking to the efficiency of the Victim offered on the Cross! It is, in fact, celebrated as the vehicle of the remission of sins brought about by Christ on the Cross, *tamquam vehiculum remissionis peccatorum per Christum in Cruce facta*. And as it is not another victim, so it does not bring another remission of sins, *quemadmodum non est alia hostia, ita non aliam affert remissionem peccatorum*."

5) "Where sin has been remitted, there is no longer an offering for sin" (Heb 10:18). It is made clear by the Letter to the Hebrews, that the supreme sufficiency and efficacy of the sacrifice of the Cross does not exclude Christ's heavenly intercession; nor, as a consequence, does it exclude His Eucharistic intercession by way of immolation.

This last response, common among Catholics, certainly sheds some light on the subject, but it does not resolve the problem. Is, in fact, the heavenly *intercession* of Christ a true and real *sacrifice*? On the contrary, the Eucharistic intercession of Christ at Mass most certainly is.[59]

d) Conclusions

The great teaching of the Council of Trent is laid out in this small work. Some theological clarifications accompany it.

1) The numerical unity of the sacrifice of the Cross and of the Mass is strongly confirmed.

2) In fact, the unbloody mode of offering does not multiply the sacrifice; for *a)* it is subordinated as "adjunctive" to the bloody mode which is "substantial"; *b)* it has no value in itself, but has reference to the bloody Victim of the Cross.

3) There is no recurrence at the Mass, no repetition *of the sacrifice, Victim, oblation, and immolation* of the Cross. There is the unbloody *rite* instituted by Christ, which alone is repeated; and by this repetition the sacrifice of the Cross *endures*.

4) The Mass is the *vehicle* of the remission of sins brought about by Christ on the Cross; it brings us this remission and no other.

One can see here the direction of Cajetan's thought. There seems to be very little to do in order to bring it to completion. We pose just two questions: *a)* Does the repetition of the unbloody rite, which allows *the sacrifice to endure among us,* bring us not only the *substantial presence* of Christ now glorious, but also the *contact*, the *operative presence* of the redemptive sacrificial act of the Cross? *b)* Does the Mass, *which transports to us the remission of sins obtained by Christ*—does it put us in direct contact with Christ? *Is it an operative and real presence of the same sacrifice of the Cross?*

The principles set down by St. Thomas allow us to respond to these two questions in the affirmative.

14. The Central Vision of Melchior Cano

We can point out here, without going into detail, the central point of the Eucharistic doctrine of Melchior Cano (1509–1560), found in his *De locis theologicis*, book XII, chapter 12.[60]

59 See above, p. 83.
60 Cano was sent by the Emperor to the Council of Trent, and remained there from 1551 to 1553. The thirteenth session, *De Eucharistia*, took place on October 11, 1551. We cite Cano here according to the Padua edition, 1734.

"If one considers the effect which results from it, the Blood of Christ is poured out at the sacrifice of the altar, just as if it were now on the Cross; and His Body is broken, just as if it were now on the Cross for us."[61]

"If Christ's Body is living in the Eucharist and united to His Blood, it nevertheless is not offered by us as living and united to His Blood: the Body is offered as immolated, the Blood as poured out on the Cross. . . . Although the offering and the external bloody immolation have passed, it nevertheless endures in the acceptance of God and perpetually preserves its power; such that it is not less efficacious today before the Father than on the day when Christ's Blood flowed from the wound in His side. We therefore offer with Christ the same Victim of the Cross, *just as those who were present at the foot of the Cross*. The difference is that, having before their eyes the living reality, they had no need of a symbol; whereas for us, the same Victim is made present under the sacrament. The sign and the sacrament, however, in no way prevent us from offering now the same Blood which Christ poured out on the Cross, as if it were now visibly poured out."[62]

"The Fathers call this sacrifice unbloody, this sacrifice which is equal to no other and without precedent, and by which, if one considers the effect which results from it, Christ is sacrificed for us, just as He was formerly for those who were at the foot of the Cross. If the Fathers called it unbloody, it is because it happens not by a visible effusion of Blood but by an application of the Blood poured out for all."[63]

"This commemoration is neither something futile nor a shadow, but works what it signifies. We do not put to death the risen Christ Who dies no more; but we do apply Christ's death as if it were contemporaneous to us. This application is brought about not only by faith and words, but by sacramental symbols."[64]

"The power of Christ and His Gospel is such that He was able to attach to sacramental signs and symbols the same power as the signified realities would have, if they were to take place at that very moment."[65]

15. A Text of Bossuet

Preoccupied more with his episcopal duty of preaching the great common doctrine of the Church than conceptually clarifying the riches still hidden therein, Bossuet, in order to respond to the Protestant attacks against the sacrifice of the Mass, uses, according to need, diverse explanations proposed by writers after the Council of Trent; such that his theological teaching on the very essence of the sacrifice remains eclectic. There is, however, a passage

61 P. 410.
62 P. 419.
63 *Ibid.*
64 P. 424.
65 *Ibid.*

where he spontaneously recalls the simple and profound view, which we believe to be that of St. Thomas.

He writes in his *Explication de quelques difficultés sur les prières de la Messe*,[66] dedicated to *un nouveau catholique*: "There is not here, as your ministers made you to believe, a *supplement* to the sacrifice of the Cross; there is not a *reenactment*, as if it had been imperfect. There is, on the contrary, while supposing it to be most perfect, a *perpetual application*, similar to that which Jesus Christ does continuously in heaven before the eyes of His Father; or rather, there is a *continued celebration*: such that there is no need to be astonished if we call it, in a certain sense, a sacrifice of redemption, in accordance with that prayer which we make: 'Grant to us, we beseech Thee, O Lord, that we may worthily celebrate these mysteries; for, as often as the memorial of this Victim is celebrated, the work of our Redemption is wrought';[67] that is to say, *by applying it we continue and consummate it.*"[68]

16. The Mass Is a "Renewal" of the Unbloody Sacrifice of the Last Supper and a "Perpetuation" of the Bloody Sacrifice of the Cross

1. If we consider the rite or *unbloody sacrifice*, it is necessary to say that it was instituted by Christ at the Last Supper in order to be repeated, reenacted, renewed with each generation until the Parousia.

There is a repetition, a reenactment, a renewal, and hence a numerical multiplicity: 1st, of the unbloody sacrifices; 2nd, of generations to whom the unbloody sacrifices apply the one bloody sacrifice. In this sense "the plurality of Masses multiplies the oblation of the sacrifice."[69]

It is, then, rigorously exact to say that the Mass multiplies (numerically, not specifically), repeats, reenacts and renews the unbloody sacrifice of the Last Supper.

2. But it does not multiply the *bloody sacrifice* of the Cross.

At the Last Supper, the unbloody rite made present to the disciples, in a sacramental and unbloody manner, the *commenced* bloody sacrifice. At the Mass, the unbloody rite makes present to later generations, in a sacramental and unbloody manner, the *completed* bloody sacrifice.

The Last Supper was not, numerically speaking, another *sacrifice* than that of the Cross, but rather a *presence* (not natural but sacramental) numerically and specifically distinct from the bloody sacrifice. Likewise, the Mass is not numerically another *sacrifice* than that of the Cross, but a *presence* (not natural but sacramental) numerically and specifically distinct from the bloody sacrifice.

66 *Explanation of Some Difficulties with The Prayers of the Mass.*
67 Secret from the ninth Sunday after Pentecost.
68 Chap. 14.
69 In pluribus Missis multiplicatur sacrificii oblatio et ideo multiplicatur effectus sacrificii et sacramenti." St. Thomas, *Summa Theologiae* III, qu. 79, a. 7, ad 3.

The bloody sacrifice of the Cross, *numerically one and the same*, is hidden under the envelopment of the sacramental species, be it at the Last Supper or the Mass.

Properly speaking, the bloody sacrifice of the Cross is in no way multiplied, reenacted or renewed at the Mass.

3. The Mass, however, by reenacting and renewing the unbloody sacrifice of the Last Supper, reenacts and renews the *presences* of the bloody sacrifice of the Cross.

This permits one to say, if one so wishes, (*in a derived, material, improper sense, and using a figure of speech*) that the Mass multiples, reenacts and renews the bloody sacrifice of the Cross.[70]

This is to say simply: *a)* that the unbloody rite which makes the sacrifice of the Cross present is continuously repeated, renewed; *b)* that the generations to whom it becomes present are continuously repeated, renewed.

Whatever the case may be, we have here a material and improper way of speaking.

4. The encyclical *Mediator Dei* of Pius XII, 20 November 1947, speaks in a more proper manner both of the Last Supper and the unbloody rite, and of the sacrifice of the Cross.

a) The Last Supper is *renewed*—"The culminating point and center of the Christian religion is the Mystery of the Most Holy Eucharist, which Christ, the Great High Priest, in former times instituted, and which He desired to see perpetually *renewed* in the Church through His ministers, *quamque per suos administros perpetuo in Ecclesia renovari jubet.*"[71] "Every time, in fact, that the people renew what the Divine Redeemer accomplished at the Last Supper, the sacrifice is truly consummated."[72]

b) The unbloody rite is *reenacted*—Transubstantiation makes present the Body and Blood of Christ, and the Eucharistic species under which they are found symbolize the bloody separation of the Body and Blood. "Thus the commemorative representation of His death, *memorialis demonstratio ejus mortis*, which was real on Calvary, is reenacted, *iteratur*, in every sacrifice on the altar; since the distinction of the species signifies and indicates Christ Jesus in the state of a victim."[73]

c) The sacrifice of the Cross is *manifested*—The sacrifice of the altar, "quite far from diminishing the dignity of the bloody sacrifice . . . on the

---

70 "All of the power of expiation depends on Christ's *one* bloody sacrifice, which, without interruption of time, *renews* itself in an unbloody manner on our altars, *ab uno Christi cruento sacrificio* pendere, quod sine temporis intermissione, in nostris altaribus incruento modo, *renovatur* . . ." Pius XI, encyclical *Miserentissimus Redemptor*, 8 May 1928, AAS 1228, 171. The words which we italicized demonstrate sufficiently what we are trying to express here.

71 AAS 1947, 547.

72 *Ibid.*, p. 557.

73 *Ibid.*, pp. 548–549.

contrary, uncovers and renders more manifest its grandeur and necessity, as the Council of Trent guarantees. By the fact that it is immolated each day, *dum quotidie immolatur*, it reminds us that there is no other salvation than in the Cross of our Savior Jesus Christ; and if God willed that the continuation of this sacrifice (of the altar) be guaranteed from sunrise to sunset, it is in order that the hymn of praise and thanksgiving which men owe the Creator would never cease. They have, in fact, a continuous need of His help in order to blot out the sins which provoke His justice; they are in need of the Blood of the Divine Redeemer."[74]

5. Leo XIII spoke in proper terms of the perpetuity and perennial character of the sacrifice of the Cross in the Eucharistic sacrifice: "The expiation offered on the Cross for mortals was perfect and absolute. *There is in the Eucharistic sacrifice not another expiation, but the very same one.* As it was necessary that a sacrificial rite accompany religion throughout history, the divine disposition of the Redeemer willed that *the sacrifice consummated once on the Cross be perpetual and uninterrupted.* The reason of this perpetuity is found in the Most Holy Eucharist, which brings us not only a simple figure or a mere souvenir of the Cross, *but its very truth,* although under dissimilar appearances; and this is why the efficacy of this sacrifice, be it for supplication or for expiation, follows completely from Christ's death."[75]

17. On the Text of Marguerite de Veni d'Arbouze

1. We recalled above the teaching of St. Thomas,[76] according to which God knows the things of time as really past, present, future, *each in relation to each other*: it would be contradictory if He knew as present to us that which is past or future to us. *In relation to Him,* however, He knows past things not as past (there is not past in Him), and future things not as future (there is not future in Him). He knows each of them as coexisting, in their fleeting existential reality; and He knows them in one moment of His eternity, or, if you will, as coexisting with one of the supposed moments which the imagination can number, in the one and indivisible existential moment of eternity, which contains (by exceeding them) all the moments of time, being for them a measure—not an "adequate" but an "excessive" measure.[77]

We said as well that, in this regard, Marguerite de Veni d'Arbouze loved to consider Christ's Passion not only in its relation to us, to whom it appears irrevocably as an event of the past, *but also in its relation to God,*

---

74   *Ibid.,* pp. 551–552.

75   Leo XIII, encyclical *Caritatis studium,* July 25, 1898.

76   St. Thomas, Summa *Theologiae* I, qu. 14, a. 13. See above, pp. 59, 66, 78.

77   *Mensura non adaequata, sed excessiva*: These are the words of Cajetan, Commentary on the *Summa Theologiae* I, qu. 14, a. 13, XII, which explain with that very passage that the first and last instants of the hour where we are, are both contained, but as distinct and separate from each other, in the one indivisible instant of eternity.

to Whom it continuously appears as existing and in its presentiality; and it is as such that it appears perpetually to Christ Himself, to Whom it is granted by the Beatific Vision to see it in the sight of God. The soul, she says, gazes on this mystery of the Passion in God; "it sees the mystery in act before Him, Who grants us His Son through love, delivering Him up to death on the Cross for the expiation of our sins."[78]

2. St. Thomas, however, in addition to this profound insight, provides a second. Christ's Passion, that supreme moment of the world's history, that time which Jesus called His hour, is too lofty to be totally immersed in a moment of duration equal to the others, juxtaposed to others, pulled along like the others by the irreversible flow of time; but touched by the divine power which transcends space and time and uses it as an organ, *it can touch as present, by its efficacious spiritual contact, all the generations of the world's new economy*, partially by the sacraments of the New Law, and fully in the Mass: *"Passio Christi per spiritualem contactum efficaciam sortitur. . . . Quae quidem virtus attingit omnia loca et tempora."*

Therefore, for the one who tries to contemplate by faith what God sees from the bosom of His eternity, and what He reveals to Christ and the elect through the Beatific Vision—for such a one the Passion of the Savior appears not only as always present and in its existentiality, in its concrete and transitory reality at the unique instant of the divine eternity, subsisting perpetually in the divine acceptance, not in the state of a memory but in the state of the actual object of vision; but also, for such a one it appears *as present, by its efficiency and its spiritual contact, to each succeeding moment of time.* The ray which goes forth from the bloody Cross touched by divinity will strike in turn each of the generations of the new economy of salvation as they come into existence. We can reread then the words of Marguerite de Veni d'Abouze on the Passion—this time by superimposing a new sense (one followed by St. Thomas as well), but this time in relation *to the perpetuity, in regard to us, of the presence of the sacrifice of the Cross*: "Regarding this mystery in God, the soul sees it in act before Him Who grants us His Son through love, delivering Him up to death on the Cross for the expiation of our sins." The soul sees God continuing, by love, to give His Son, to deliver Him up to death on the Cross, seeing that henceforth each generation, as it comes into existence, can enter mysteriously into the drama of the bloody Redemption.

At each Mass, Christ in glory comes to us with the same act of His redemptive sacrifice, ready to apply it to us, to render it present to us according to the intensity of our desire.

78 See above, p. 67, note 19—It is thus that in heaven we will see in their *presentiality* the Passion of Christ and all the events of the past. They will not be reduced to the state of *memories*, as Péguy thought. They will be seen in the perpetual freshness of the sight of God, in Whom there is, properly speaking, neither *memory* nor *pre-vision*, but only *vision*.

CHAPTER 5

The Offering of the Mass

We shall divide this chapter into two sections: I. Who offers the Mass? II. What is offered at Mass.

FIRST SECTION
WHO OFFERS THE MASS?

1. The Mass: Christ's Sacrifice or the Church's Sacrifice?

Is the Mass Christ's sacrifice or the Church's? This is the first question which we meet when we inquire about who offers the Mass. The response is to reject immediately this dilemma which can lead one astray.[1]

The choice between Christ's sacrifice and that of the Church is imposed on neither the Cross, nor the Last Supper, nor the Mass. In these three cases there is a sacrifice of Christ and a sacrifice of the Church: a sacrifice of Christ which takes in the Church; a sacrifice of the Church which is taken up by Christ.

It is true that the part of the Church is larger, though not more intense, at the Mass than at the Last Supper and at the Cross. The Mass, however, remains first of all the sacrifice of Christ, and secondarily, dependently, the sacrifice of the Church. If Christ is both Priest and Victim at the Mass, according to the Council of Trent, then He holds the first place, and the Church the second. No consideration is capable of prevailing against this order of values.[2]

---

1   This dilemma is at the heart of the work (quite profound nevertheless) of Maurice de la Taille, who compares the sacrifice *of the Lord* instituted at the Last Supper, consummated on the Cross and continued in heaven, with the *ecclesiastical* sacrifice of the Mass. *Mysterium fidei, De augustissimo corporis et sanguinis Christi sacrificio atque sacramento* (Paris: 1921).

2   It is from a purely external and non-theological point of view which Joseph-André Jungmann writes in his *Missarum sollemnia, Explication génétique de la Messe romaine* (Paris: 1951): "In the theological controversies at the time of the Reform and in later theology . . . it was necessary to establish that the Mass is before all else the sacrifice of Christ. However, as soon as the apologetic interest receded and *the question once again arose as to the meaning and purpose of the Mass in the midst of the Church's life*, it was necessary to give back to the sacrifice of the Church its value, *and even grant it pride of place*. It is sufficient to glance quickly at the text of the Roman Mass and of the other liturgies, and nothing appears more clearly than this idea: that the Church, the people of God, the community assembled together, offers the sacrifice to God . . . In the ordo of the Roman Mass

We shall try to view the part of the Church in the sacrifice of Christ, at the Cross, at the Last Supper, and at the Mass.

2. The Church's Participation in the Bloody Sacrifice of the Cross[3]

When His hour came, Christ, we said, saved the world by one sacrifice, one worship, one liturgy enveloping the act of His supreme love—or by the act of His supreme love enveloped in one sacrifice, one worship, one liturgy. The contained is greater than the container, love more than sacrifice.

The redemptive sacrificial mediation of the Cross can be considered from then on under the precise aspect of the cultic validity, and under the aspect of the redemptive love.

1. In the *line of worship* Christ alone is capable of offering and restoring on the Cross the redemptive sacrifice, which at one and the same time perfects and abrogates the worship and sacrifices of the Old Law. In fact, He alone is consecrated High Priest according to the new order of Melchizedek (Heb 7:1); He alone has the power over His own life in order to give it and take it up again (Jn 10:18), thus offering to God a theandric sacrifice, the power of which is infinite. *Torcular calcavi solus, et de gentibus non est vir mecum.*[4]

2. This sacrifice, however, is the envelopment of *the redemptive love*, which seeks to descend again upon men in order to make of them the members and the very Body of Christ. In this line, Christ on the Cross pours out around Himself the first outpourings of salvific graces coming from His Passion. He draws unto Himself especially the offering of the Blessed Virgin and St. John, having first imbued it with His charity. This offering thus becomes through Him, with Him, in Him—fully in the Virgin, partially in St. John—the coredemptrix of the world of which He is the one Redeemer.

That which the Virgin and St. John—supported by the theandric offering of Christ-offer through Him, with Him and in Him is not only their own lives, for such an offering never constitutes (except in the case of Christ) a sacrifice in the proper sense;[5] *it is before all else what*

---

it is only assumed that the Mass is the sacrifice of Christ, but this is not stated expressly." We respond by saying that this is blatantly contrary to the words of consecration. (The italics are ours.)

The competence of liturgists as such in doctrinal matters is secondary. Pius XII reminds us that the axiom *Lex orandi, lex credendi*, is derived; the original axiom was *Lex credendi, lex orandi*. Encyclical *Mediator Dei*, AAS 1947, 541. See below, chap. 9, no. 5, *b*.

3　See above, p. 26.

4　Cf. Isaiah 63:3, cited in a sense accommodated to First Vespers of the Feast of the Precious Blood.

5　See above, p. 20.

Christ offers, the bloody sacrifice of the Cross. They *participate by their coredemptive love in every "yes" which redemptive Love pronounces to God from the Cross*. By an immediate contact, a pure spiritual contact of love, they enter, as profoundly as possible for the members of Christ, into the interior of the liturgical, sacrificial, bloody and loving oblation of the Cross.

There is here the Church's great entrance into Christ's redemptive Passion. It will remain until the end of the world the type, the model—forever unequal—of all the entrances into Christ's Passion by which our Masses are supremely defined.

3. The Church's Participation in the Unbloody Sacrifice of the Last Supper

What happened at the Last Supper? The hour of Jesus came. The redemptive sacrifice was inaugurated.

1. In the *line of worship* Jesus alone enters His life into this bloody drama which men seem to conduct, but which He has the power to change into a sacrifice perfected on the Cross.

In the line of worship Jesus always acts alone, to the exclusion of His disciples, in order to transubstantiate the bread and wine into His Body and Blood. In this way the redemptive sacrifice, already begun under its own proper and bloody appearances, becomes, in addition, present under the sacramental and unbloody appearances. Transubstantiation is, at the Last Supper, a true and real sacrifice, an unbloody sacrifice, not by multiplying the redemptive sacrifice, but by multiplying the real presence of the redemptive sacrifice: the true Body of Christ is given there, the true Blood of Christ is there poured out under sacramental and unbloody appearances.

Thus Jesus alone is active in the upper room in the line of worship, as regards both the bloody offering and the unbloody offering.

2. In the *line of charity* there is at that solemn hour of the Last Supper a profound participation by the disciples in the redemptive sacrifice. On one hand the institution of the unbloody rite, which permits them sacramental communion through physical consumption, manifests the Savior's express intention of drawing them into the drama of His bloody Passion. On the other hand their desire to follow Jesus is evident. Recall the washing of their feet: "'You shall never wash my feet,' Peter said to Him. Jesus answered him, 'If I do not wash you, you have no part in Me.' Simon Peter said to Him, 'Lord, wash not my feet only but also my hands and my head!'" (Jn 13:8–9).

3. The Last Supper is thus the living entrance of the apostles by *love* into the very heart of the redemptive sacrifice, without which they would have to intervene in the *cultic* celebration of either the bloody or unbloody sacrifice.

4. What the Mass Is

1. The Mass is, *by the repetition of the unbloody sacrifice* instituted at the Last Supper, *the full existential entrance of the Church at every one of her moments into the redemptive bloody sacrifice, where her place is marked out in advance.*

It gives us *Christ*, now in His glorious state, *Who does not cease to draw His Church unto Himself* by means of the redemptive act of His bloody Passion—no doubt localized and transitory in itself, but universalized and perpetuated by the divine power which penetrates it and transports it to us in the envelopment of the unbloody rite.

And the Mass presents to us *the Church insofar as she is drawn into this offering of Christ*; detached from this supreme offering which rouses and sustains her, the offering of the Church would instantly lose its power and intelligibility.

2. Christ's offering is charged with too many riches not to be complex.

It has value, we said,[6] in the order of cultic validity and in the order of redemptive love.

Moreover, the redemptive bloody offering has been enveloped by Christ in an unbloody rite, which is destined to bring that same offering to us through repetition.

It should be shown, at every step, which is Christ's part and which the part of the Church.

3. It will be important never to forget that the entire order of the cultic validity, so divine and rigorously necessary as it may be, exists for the order of redemptive charity, which is still more divine and necessary; one must not forget *that the cultic sacrifice is for the manifestation of redemptive love, and the Church's worship for the Church's charity*: "If I give my body to the flames, but have not charity, I gain nothing" (1 Cor 13:3).

5. Who Offers the Mass in the Line of Worship?

a) The Bloody Sacrifice and the Unbloody Sacrifice

Let us dwell first of all on the strictly ritualistic, liturgical and cultic perspective, where the Christian cult is not seen under the immediate aspect of its sanctity but rather its validity. And let us consider successively the bloody sacrifice and the unbloody sacrifice, which envelops the former and renders it present.

1. If we consider the *redemptive bloody sacrifice of the Cross*, made present at each Mass, Christ was the only one able to offer it, He being the only one able to give His life and take it up again.

2. Such is not the case if we consider the *unbloody sacrifice of the Mass*, which is a true and proper sacrifice, not through multiplying the one redemptive sacrifice, but through multiplying its real presence. This unbloody sacrifice, where the bread and wine are transubstantiated

6   See above, p. 19.

into the Body and Blood of Christ, is offered in the line of worship simultaneously, but on essentially different levels: by Christ, by the priests and by the faithful.

b) The Role of Christ in the Cultic Unbloody Offering

1. Insofar as He is God Christ is the First Cause; insofar as He is man He is the "conjoined instrumental cause." Without these two, no transubstantiation would take place, no unbloody sacrifice would be offered. He is by this fact the sovereign priest with the privilege of an "intransmissible priesthood" (Heb 7:24), both with regards to the bloody sacrifice as well as the unbloody sacrifice. Christ, the priest at the Cross, is also at the Mass, says St. Thomas, "for it is in His name and by His power, *in cujus persona et virtute*," that the words of consecration are pronounced.[7]

To the objection that, since Christ is the unique Priest, then the succession of priests proper to the Old Testament ought not to begin again in the New Testament (Heb 7:23–24), Cajetan replies in the same manner that, "Christ, the one Priest of the New Testament, is present at the altar; for it is not in their own name, *in personis propriis*, but in the name of Christ, *in persona Christi*, that the ministers consecrate Christ's Body and Blood, as the words of consecration attest. Such that they make the offering as Christ's representatives, *vices Christi agentes offerunt*. In fact, the priest does not say, 'This is the Body of Christ,' but rather, 'This is My Body,' making Christ's Body present in the name of Christ, *in persona Christi*, under the species of bread, according to His commandment."[8]

This was already the teaching of St. Ambrose in the well-known text *De sacramentis*: "By what words then does the consecration take place and to whom do they belong? The Lord Jesus. In fact, all that precedes is said by the priest: praises are offered to God, prayers for the people, for kings, for others. As soon as the venerable sacrament is about to be confected, the priest ceases to use his own words and instead applies the words of Christ. *It is, then, the words of Christ which bring about this sacrament.* Which word of Christ? Ah well, that by which all has been made. . . . You see how efficacious is the word of Christ. If then there is in the word of the Lord Jesus so great a power that that which was not has come to be, how much more efficacious is it to make that which already was exist and change into another thing. . . . Before the consecration there was not the Body of Christ, but after the consecration, I tell you that there is henceforth the Body of Christ."[9]

This great view of *the priority of Christ's initiative over that of the Church in the very offering of the unbloody sacrifice* is taught by the Council of Trent. Apropos of the sacrifice of the Mass, which it compares to the sacrifice of

---

7   St. Thomas, *Summa Theologiae* III, qu. 83, a. 1, ad 3.
8   *De Missae sacrificio . . .* , chap. 6.
9   *De sacramentis*, bk. IV, chap. 4, 14–16. See below, p. 144.

the Cross, the Council relates Christ to the priests as the principal to the instrumental causes: "It is the same [Christ] Who *offers* now by the *ministry* of the priests, Who then offered Himself on the Cross, *idem nunc offerens, sacerdotum ministerio, qui seipsum tunc in Cruce obtulit.*"[10]

2. Seeing such things with the eyes of flesh, it could seem that the first initiative of transubstantiation would come from the priest, who sets out by his own will the words of Christ; but seeing them with the eyes of faith, it is clear that the first initiative comes from Christ, Who, by His beatific knowledge, knows from the beginning all times, and on Whom depends the life and death of all priests along with the radiance of their works.

"The priest, in truth, is the minister of God, making use of the word of God, through God's order and institution; but here God is the principal Author and invisible Agent to Whom submits all that He wills, Who is obeyed by all whom He commands."[11]

c) The Role of the Church and that of the Priests in the Cultic Unbloody Offering

The Church intervenes through her priests in the cultic unbloody offering on two essentially distinct levels: as she is the bearer of the voice of the Bridegroom, or as she makes heard her own voice as Bride.

1. *Through transubstantiation* the Church acts through her priests, *in persona Christi*, in the very name of Christ.[12] It is the voice of the Bridegroom which she makes heard, and not that of her own. The words of consecration, St. Ambrose recalls, contrary to those which precede and follow them, are pronounced in the very name of Christ. The priest does not say: "This is the Body of Christ, this is the Blood of Christ"; he makes the offering by taking the role of Christ, *vices Christi agens offert*. His own role is hidden before that of Christ: "This is My Body, this is My Blood." The sacramental character of Orders, explains St. Thomas, is an instrumental spiritual power, *potentia spiritualis instrumentalis*.[13] The priest is, at the moment of consecration, purely an instrument in the hands of Christ, capable of transmitting the elevating power which comes from the principal agent, but incapable of acting by himself.[14]

It is clear that "to celebrate," in the sense of to transubstantiate, is a privilege of the priest alone; but we must always remember that this privilege is

---

10   Session XXII, chap. 2, Denz, 940.

11   *De imitatione Christi*, IV, 5.

12   At the Mass the priest is Christ Jesus, "cujus sacram personam ejus administer gerit." Encyclical *Mediator Dei*, AAS 1947, 548.

13   St. Thomas, *Summa Theologiae* III, qu. 63, a. 2.

14   The act, always present to the divine eternity, by which Jesus at the Last Supper ordains the Apostles and their successors to transubstantiate the bread and wine, commands all future transubstantiations, where the priests act as "separated instruments."

a service. It is also clear that "to concelebrate," in the sense of validly pronouncing with the priest the transubstantiating words, as newly ordained priests do at their Ordination, is likewise a privilege exclusive to priests.

2. *Before and after transubstantiation* the Church acts through her priests in her own name, *in propria persona*. It is her own voice, that of the Bride, which she makes heard when, through the authority of her canonical power prudentially assisted—and sustained, in that which touches upon revealed teachings, by the superior infallible authority and absolute declarative power—it is her voice which is heard when she arranges the priests and the ceremonies of the Mass. Here she acts as a secondary cause, no doubt divinely assisted, but with her own responsibility. The priests here are no longer ministers as before, that is to say, in the sense of purely the instruments of Christ the Bridegroom; they are ministers in the sense of the servants of the Church the Bride, who is grateful for them.[15] This new privilege, though less, is still great. It also is, as all privileges in the Church, ordained to the common ends of charity.

d) The Role of the Church and the Faithful in the Cultic Unbloody Offering

1. The sacramental characters of Baptism and Confirmation are also participations in Christ's priestly power.[16] They allow the faithful to accomplish validly certain acts of the Christian cultus. The character of Confirmation consecrates them in view of continuing this witness to the Truth, which is one of the aspects of Christ's priesthood.[17] The baptismal character renders them suitable on one hand to receive validly the other sacraments, and on the other hand to contract a sacramental marriage; or still more, to unite themselves to the priest in order to offer with him the unbloody sacrifice of the Mass. In the early Church the catechumens were sent out after the first part of the Mass, and the baptized alone remained to participate in the sacrifice.

2. How do we characterize this cultic participation of the baptized in the offering of the Mass? We say that Baptism, unlike Holy Orders, in no way confers the power to intervene under the divine motion *in* the very act of transubstantiation; but that, if it grants the power to intervene *after* transubstantiation to receive validly the Body and Blood of Christ, it must grant equally the power to intervene *before* transubstantiation in order to participate ritually in the prayers of offering which prepare for

---

15 See below, pp. 105 and 128.
16 "Participationes sacerdotii Christi ab ipso Christo derivatae." St. Thomas, *Summa Theologiae* III, qu. 63, a. 3.
17 "Confirmatus accipit *potestatem* publice fidem Christi verbis profitendi, *quasi ex officio*." St. Thomas, *Summa Theologiae* III, qu. 72, a. 5, ad 2.

transubstantiation. Hence the words of the Roman Canon: *Hanc igitur oblationem servitutis nostrae, sed et cunctae familiae tuae* . . . ,[18] where *servitus* and *familia* signify "the celebrant and the assistants, or better still the Church,"[19] the clergy and the gathering of Christians.[20]

3. The liturgical and cultic participation of the faithful in the unbloody offering is described in the encyclical *Mediator Dei*. Pius XII points out several passages of the Ordo of the Mass, where the priest unites himself to the people for praying and offering: "Pray, my brothers, that my sacrifice *and your sacrifice* be acceptable to God the Almighty Father"; "Be mindful, Lord, of Thy servants . . . for we who offer Thee, *or those who offer Thee* this sacrifice of praise . . ." "This offering, then, which we present to Thee, we Thy servants *and with us Thy entire family*, we beseech Thee, Lord, to accept with kindness. . . ." "This is why, we Thy servants, *and with Your holy people*, we present to Thy glorious Majesty, an offering chosen from among the goods which Thou hast granted, a pure host, a holy host, an immaculate host . . ." And furthermore, the preface begins with a solemn dialogue between the people and the celebrant.

The Sovereign Pontiff adds: "It is not astonishing that Christians be elevated to such dignity. By the laver of Baptism, in fact, Christians in virtue of a prerogative which is common to them, become in the Mystical Body members of Christ the Priest, *membra Christi sacerdotis*; the character which is as a mark on their soul ordains them for the divine cultus; *such that they participate, according to their condition, in the very priesthood of Christ.*"[21]

e) Can One Speak of a "Concelebration of the Faithful"?

Would we be able, then, to speak of a "concelebration of the faithful"?

1. Yes, if one means that the faithful, in virtue of their baptismal character, can contribute in *preparing* the cultic and liturgical offering of the unbloody sacrifice, which the priest, in virtue of the sacramental character of Orders, can alone *finish*. From this point of view P. Clérissac can write: "A member of the Mystical Body of Christ, having been baptized, becomes a concelebrant of the one sacrifice with the Church and

---

18   *"This offering, therefore, which we present to Thee, we Thy servants, and with us Thy entire family . . . "*

19   Mgr. Pierre Batiffol, *Leçons sur la Messe* (Paris: Gabalda, 1920), p. 250, who notes that St. Augustine, *De civitate Dei*, I, 35, grants to the Church the qualificator of "redempta *familia* Domini Christi."

20   Dom Bernard Botte, O.S.B., *L'ordinaire de la Messe, Texte critique, traduction et études* (Paris: edit. du Cerf, 1953), p. 79.

21   AAS 1947, 554–555. The encyclical then speaks of a very mysterious participation of the faithful in the sacrifice of Christ. We believe that it then quits the order of strict cultic validity in order to enter into the order of charity. See below, p 147.

Christ: *Unde et memores nos servi tui sed et plebs tua sancta* (*Therefore, we remember, we Thy servants, and with us Thy holy people* . . .). This participation in the Church's priesthood . . . constitutes henceforth its true royalty: *Gens sancta, regale sacerdotium* (a holy race, a royal priesthood, 1 Peter 2:9)."[22]

2. No, if to concelebrate means to participate in the very consecration of the bread and wine into the Body and Blood of Christ, to pronounce validly with the priest the words of transubstantiation. In the encyclical *Mediator Dei*, Pius XII vehemently condemns the error of those who think that "the members of the Church accomplish the visible liturgical rite in the same manner as the priest himself";[23] those who pretend "that the people enjoy a true priestly power, *vera perfrui sacerdotali potestate*,[24] and that the priest acts only in virtue of a function which is delegated to him by the community, *solummodo agere ex delegato a communitate munere*"; those who conclude "that the Eucharistic sacrifice is, in the proper sense, a concelebration, *veri nominis concelebrationem*, and that it

---

22 Humbert Clerissac, *Le mystère de l'Église*, chap. 4, "La vie hiératique de l'Église" (Paris: Crès, 1918), p. 80.

Elsewhere, addressing some nuns, the same author said the following: "Even from your part, you who do not have the power of Orders, the Mass is a concelebration: all Christians are concelebrants, and this greatly elevates human dignity: 1) The true Priest, the one Priest is our Lord; the priest who celebrates is but His representative, His minister. Now we are Christ's members, we are all in Him. He offers us, then, with Himself to His Father, and it is in this way that we all concelebrate with Him. 2) Christians, however, the faithful, are no longer separated from the minister in his act: there is a very real participation in the assisting at the divine oblation. The proof of this is that the priest speaks in the plural: *Offerimus* . . . *rogamus* . . . *gratias agimus* . . . *deprecamur* . . . At Baptism we truly receive a priestly anointing: all Christians are "priests." How this consideration ought to incite us to bring to the Mass the most perfect dispositions! Let us go, if not to celebrate, at least to concelebrate, let us go to offer *our* sacrifice, *our* host." *La lumière de l'Agneau*, Lyon, edit, de l'Abeille, 1943, pp. 31–32.

We will find the first consideration again when speaking of the *order of charity*. The second concerns the *cultic order;* and so it is not exact to say with P. Clérissac, in the same place, that the priest is "the representative and the delegate of the great family of God." Properly speaking, the priest, in the order of worship, is the representative and delegate of Christ with respect to divine law, and of the hierarchical powers with respect to ecclesiastical law.

23 AAS 1947, 556.

24 The three sacramental characters are, according to St. Thomas, *participations in the priesthood* of Christ, derivations of Christ's priesthood, St. Thomas, *Summa Theologiae* III, qu. 63, a. 3, but unequally. The character of Baptism and that of Confirmation are *common* to the faithful. Only the character of Orders is *hierarchical*. Usually—and such is the case here—the priestly power means *the hierarchical priestly power,* conferred by the sacrament of Orders.

would be preferable if the priests, instead of offering the sacrifice in private and in the absence of the people, would come among the people in order to concelebrate in union with them, *ut sacerdotes, una cum populo adstantes concelebrant.*"[25]

On the practical level it would be better, therefore, to avoid the expression "concelebration of the faithful," or not use it except with a precision which would dismiss any possibility of equivocation.

6. Who Offers the Mass in the Line of Redemptive Love?

a) The Cultic Union Is Ordered to the Sanctifying Union

The transubstantiating unbloody rite is a sacrifice only because it brings to us Christ, Who is now glorious but continues to desire to save us by means of the unique act of His bloody Passion, which inaugurated a new form of worship and manifested His supreme love.

The valid form of worship and the fire of His love, the container and the contained, are inseparable in the sacrifice of the Mass; but the rite is for love, and not the other way around. More important than cultic validity is redemptive charity; and hence, according to the evangelical reversal of values, the last will be first, and the most humble in worship will be the most elevated in love.

Under this one aspect, which is most important, the Mass is, through the repetition of the unbloody sacrifice, the existential entering of each generation of the Church into the drama of redemptive charity, charity which is present in its Source and whose place has been marked out in advance.

b) The Order of Supplication and the Order of Blessing

1. That which in the order of supplication took place at the Last Supper for the Apostles and at the Cross for the Blessed Virgin and St. John, when Christ—having accomplished by Himself and without anyone else that which in the line of validity extended to a sacrificial rite, both bloody and unbloody—when Christ drew the love of the newborn Church into the fire of His redemptive love for the world, that which was produced then, is reproduced in all its perfection at the Mass at each moment of the Church's life. For each Mass truly opens up to that act by which the now glorious Christ desired at one time "to draw to Himself" the one love of all generations for the moment when they would come into existence.

Christ has truly incorporated into the offering which He then made of His life this offering predicted by Him, by which we solemnly unite

---

25 *Ibid.*, p. 553. On concelebration in the proper and improper senses, see below, p. 244.

ourselves to Him with all the strength of our faith, participating in our turn in His bloody sacrifice by a mysterious but true dispensation.[26]

2. The ray of blessing which came forth from the bloody Cross in order to fall upon the Blessed Virgin and St. John was pre-contained in the very Source, and was of the same nature as the ray of blessing which falls upon us today with each repetition of the unbloody rite.

It follows that, according to the teaching of St. Thomas, the Passion officially works the salvation of all men by its spiritual contact; that the divine power which passes through it can touch in their present moment all times and places; that this spiritual contact by which we are rendered partakers in the fruits of the Lord's Passion is such that one must say that the very bloody immolation of Christ is made present to us, or better, that it is we who become present at it.

If the Blessed Virgin and St. John had closed their eyes at the foot of the Cross, and if we close ours at the moment of consecration, it is for both the same real presence of the bloody Passion. While they, however, were able to raise their eyes to the real and bloody appearance of the redemptive sacrifice accomplished by the suffering Christ, we raise ours to the unbloody sacramental appearance of the very same redemptive sacrifice, which Christ in glory does not cease to grant to us again and again.

By this dialectic of supplication and blessing, the Mass—from the ascending of our love toward God and the descending of His love toward us—draws the Church into the inner depths of the mystery of Christ's Passion.

c) The Last in Worship Are Able to Be the First in Love

1. Moses alone had the privilege of striking the rock, but it was in order to bring forth a source from which the people and himself could drink. Likewise, in the ministerial celebration of the *unbloody sacramental rite*, the *priests* have a privileged part. This celebration, however, is a service. In making sacramentally present the naturally bloody sacrifice, the rite opens the door by which the *baptized faithful*, and with them the priests, can freely enter into the *sacrificial and loving drama of the bloody Passion*, according to the intensity of their supplication.

---

26 If He was able to bear our sins, He was able to take up our offering: "If, for the sake of our future but foreseen sins, the soul of Christ became sorrowful unto death, there is no doubt that it had from that moment received some consolation by our acts of reparation, these also being foreseen . . . Such that we can and ought, even now, by a mysterious but true dispensation, *mira quidem sed vera ratione*, console the Sacred Heart, constantly wounded by the sins and ingratitude of men." Pius XI, Encyclical *Miserentissimus Redemptor*, AAS 1928, 174.

2. In this line of charity's ardor and of the coredemption of the world it happens that the offering of the faithful, especially those "friends of God" either dispersed about the world or hidden in the cloisters, can, by being united to the personal offering of the priest, support it, elevate it, even go beyond it. They can, perhaps—and more than they realize— follow Jesus into the mystery, now made present, of His agony on the Cross. They can plummet into the knowledge of the tragedy of their own age and take upon themselves the boundless distress of humanity in order to hand it over to the very Host which they hold in their hands. They will seem in a way to rob humanity of its distress in order to present, as less unworthy, that same humanity to the heavenly Father and lift it up to heaven.

3. It is a teaching of Tauler that the more ardent the charity the more it elevates beyond their own value the works which are done by others with a lesser love, granting them a new life and energy; such that these works are more to those who do them with love than to those who simply do them, and that God receives them more from the hands of the former than from those of the latter. "From the moment," writes Tauler, "that I love the good of my brother more than he himself does, that good is more truly mine than his."[27]

Thanks to these friends of God, thanks to these transformed souls, by whom and in whom the entire Church is the Bride in a most eminent manner,[28] *each Mass in Christendom will never be deprived of love.* "Ah," continues Tauler, "how many psalters, how many nocturnes recited, how many Masses— low and sung—how many great sacrifices performed, the benefits of which will not count at all for those who perform the acts, but are attributed completely to him who has the charity of which we speak. All this good he piles up in his vessel. Nothing in the world escapes him. . . . Love absorbs also all the good which is found in heaven in the saints and angels, the sufferings of the martyrs. It draws into itself all the good in all the creatures of heaven and earth, so great a part of which is lost or at least seems to be lost. Charity allows nothing to be lost. . . . It is in this way that the measure of overflowing hearts is poured out upon the entire Church, on the good as well as the bad. They bring back into the Divine Font all the good that has ever been done. They allow nothing to be lost, whether

---

27 *Sermons de Tauler*, edit. de la Vie Spirituelle (Paris, 1930), t. II, p. 207.

28 "See in the Bridegroom Christ, in the Bride without stain or wrinkle the Church, about whom it has been written: *In order to appear before Him, this Church, without stain or wrinkle or anything of the sort, but holy and immaculate.* With respect to those who, although faithful, are not yet such that we can say the same about them, but nevertheless seem to have made some progress on the way to salvation, these are identified as the young daughters of the Bride's cortege." Origen, *Homélies sur le Cantique des Cantiques*, SC, nos. 37 and 61.

great or small, not the littlest prayer or pious thought, not the smallest act of faith. They bring back all to God with an active love, and offer all to the Father of heaven. . . . My children, if we did not have these persons, we would be in a terrible situation."[29]

Tauler again: "There are only some men who are able to consecrate or bless the sacred Body of Jesus, and no one else. In a spiritual manner, however . . . a woman can offer this sacrifice just as a man, and whenever she wants, night or day. She needs to penetrate into the Holy of Holies and leave behind anything of the world. She must enter alone, that is to say enter into herself with a recollected spirit, and there, having left outside all things sensible, she must offer to the Father of Heaven for all that she desires and for all her intentions the all-lovable sacrifice, His own beloved Son, with all His works and words, with all His sufferings and holy life. She must, with a great devotion, include in this prayer all men, poor sinners, the just, those imprisoned in purgatory."[30]

4. From the perspective of charity, the concerns of each of the faithful can be extended to all the Church. It is true, as Tauler explains, that the entire Church can be more or less intensely enclosed in each heart, born in each heart.

It is also true, however, that the Church, who is the Bride, carried along toward the parousia by the wind of Pentecost, contains all her children and even the whole world; and she is holier than her greatest saints (and they themselves know this).

d) The Personal Role and Ministerial Role of the Priest in the Sanctifying Offering

1. His personal role. At each Mass Christ now glorious infallibly comes to us, ready to draw us—as He did the Blessed Virgin and St. John—into the movement of His redemptive offering, in order that we might become by Him and in Him co-redeemers of our contemporary world. And He anticipates us, moving us interiorly to consent to His invitation by the gift of our heart.

In this order of love, which is supreme here below and where the dialogue with God is immediate, the priest is but one of the faithful, the first of those invited into the multitude who come to the banquet.

2. His ministerial role. The officiating priest, however, is in addition mandated by the Church, that is to say by the hierarchical powers, to pronounce the liturgical prayers composed and arranged by these same powers–prayers which have been deemed suitable for expressing the entire Church's (the Bride's) sentiments of offering, adoration, supplication and thanksgiving at the moment when Christ comes to visit her.

29 *Sermons de Tauler*, t. II, pp. 189, 190, 193.
30 *Ibid.*, p. 239.

He himself acts, then, in the line of worship, but in order to guide the interior devotion of the faithful, to direct their faith, their contemplation, their love. It is, therefore, clear that the priest is a *minister*: not the immediate minister of *Christ*, as at the moment when he pronounces the transubstantiating words of consecration; but the immediate minister of the Church, the Bride, endowed with all her hierarchical powers. He is the servant of the Church, which prescribes and arranges the liturgical prayers for the good of the Christian people.[31]

e) A Text from the Encyclical "Mediator Dei"

The faithful's common offering of love, directed by the liturgical prayer which the priest pronounces, can be recognized, we believe, in a passage of *Mediator Dei*, where it outlines the part which the faithful take in the sacrifice by offering it not *through the hands of the priest as at the moment of transubstantiation,*[32] but *at the same time as the priest*: "The people offer with the priest himself, *una cum ipso sacerdote* . . . , when gathering together their desires of praise, impetration, expiation and thanksgiving, they unite them to the prayers and intentions of the minister, and even to those of the High Priest. His plan then is to present them to God the Father, contained as they are in the oblation of the Victim and the external sacrificial rite. The external rite of the sacrifice must, in effect, manifest by its very nature the internal worship. More precisely, however, the sacrifice of the New Law signifies that supreme homage where honor and veneration due to God are rendered unto Him through the principal Offerer, Who is Christ, and with Him and in Him, all His mystical members."[33]

31　He is not superior to the *Church*, if one includes in the Church the jurisdictional powers to which he submits. Is he superior to the *simple faithful*? Yes, insofar as he transmits to them the jurisdictional decisions. The entire jurisdictional order, however, is itself at the service of charity, which holds primacy. For St. Robert Bellarmine on this see note 33 below.

32　Concerning this offering St. Thomas writes: "The priest represents Christ, in Whose name and by Whose power he pronounces the words of consecration." St. Thomas, *Summa Theologiae* III, qu. 83, a 1, ad 3. The priest then, the Encyclical would say, represents Christ insofar as the Head offers in the name of His members. In other words, all the members offer it through the priest representing Christ.

33　AAS 1947, 556.

On the role of the priest in the offering of the sacrifice, the encyclical *Mediator Dei* (AAS, 1947, 553) makes reference to St. Robert Bellarmine (*De Missa*, II, chap. 4), without, however, constraining itself to follow him.

The holy doctor, considering the offering of transubstantiation, distinguishes three agents: Christ, the priest, the Church. *Christ* is the principal priest; the *priest* is His minister in the proper sense. And the *Church*? He considers her only in the *line of worship* and by abstracting from her her *hierarchical powers* of order and jurisdiction. She is simply the *faithful people*. Restricted to this point

7. ". . . In Memory of Me"

a) *The Memory of the Cult and the Memory of Love*

1. The solemn words of the Savior at the Last Supper, "Do this in memory of Me," gave the Apostles the command, and hence the power, to do what He had just done, namely to change the bread and wine into His Body and Blood, in memory of Him, until He comes again at the Parousia. This applies first and foremost *to the order of cultic validity.*

2. It applies again, in a no less mysterious and essential manner, *to the order of coredemptive charity.* The transubstantiating words had been pronounced by Christ at the Last Supper in a supreme act of love, which would move Him to hand over His life for the glory of His Father and the salvation of the world: "Now before the feast of the Passover, when Jesus knew that His hour had come to depart out of this world to the Father, having loved His own who were in the world, He loved them to the end" (Jn 13:1); "I have desired with a great desire to eat this Pasch with you before I suffer" (Lk 22:15); "Greater lover has no man than this, that he lay down his life for his friends" (Jn 15:13); "I sacrifice Myself that they also may be consecrated in truth" (Jn 17:19).

That which Jesus did with so great a love He asks be done "in memory of Himself," that is to say with a desire equal to His own—insofar as it is possible—for the glory of His Father and the salvation of men. He expects that the words of consecration be pronounced by the priests and listened to by the faithful with hearts in agreement with His own. What a pressing, demanding and formidable invitation! It is understood by the most loving—priests or faithful—but it is addressed to all. All Christians are invited at the Mass to "have these same sentiments within themselves which were in Christ Jesus, Who, being in the form of God, did not deem equality with God something to be grasped at, but He emptied Himself

---

of view, the priest is superior to the Church, that is to say, to the people: the Church, the people, offer through the priest as the inferior through the superior.

The encyclical distinguishes two offerings of the people: the one which is made *through the hands* of the priest; the other which is made *at the same time as* the priest: 1) Concerning the first, it is said that the priest does not represent the people (*vices gerit*), except by the fact that he acts in the person of Christ (*personam gerit*), Who, being the Head of all the members, offers Himself for them (p. 553); and that the faithful offer the sacrifice through the hands of the priest, for the latter acts in the person of Christ the Head, Who offers in the name of all His members, "such that the entire Church is said with good reason to present the offering of the Victim through Christ" (p. 556). 2) In addition to this offering, which the people make *per sacerdotis manus*, the Encyclical acknowledges that the people have another manner of offering, *una cum ipso sacerdote.* It is this one about which we are speaking here.

and took the form of a slave, being born in the likeness of man; and being found in human form He humbled Himself and became obedient unto death, even death on the Cross" (Phil 2:5–8).

If the Mass brings to us the very reality of the bloody Passion under the veil of unbloody appearances, how do we approach it without the fear of hearing the reproach of Jesus: "And so, could you not watch with Me one hour?" (Mt 26:40).

b) The Encyclical "Mediator Dei"

That the Mass would not proceed without a union of love between the faithful and the sacrifice of the Cross is the very teaching of the encyclical *Mediator Dei*: "Christ truly is a Priest, but for us, not for Himself; for, it is in the name of the whole human race that He presents to the Eternal Father the desires and acts of religion. He is also the Victim, but for us, since He puts Himself in place of guilty man. The exhortation of the Apostle, *Have in yourselves the same sentiments which were in Christ Jesus* (Phil 2:5), demands then that all Christians reproduce in themselves, insofar as is humanly possible, the sentiments which the Divine Redeemer animated when He offered Himself up in sacrifice, namely His sentiments of humility and submission of spirit, adoration, veneration, praise and thanksgiving to the Sovereign Majesty of God. It demands furthermore to take up in some sense the condition of victim, to renounce their very selves, conforming to the precepts of the Gospel, to give themselves spontaneously and lovingly to penitence, to detest and expiate their own faults. Finally it demands all to die mystically on the Cross, in union with Christ, such that we might be able to make our own the maxim of the Apostle (Gal 2:19): 'I am crucified with Christ.'"[34]

c) A Contemporary Text

"Those persons who return from Mass talking and laughing believe that they have not seen anything extraordinary. They don't suspect anything because they have not taken the pains to see. One would say that they just assisted at some simple and natural thing; and this thing, if it had happened but once, would suffice to throw into ecstasy a passionate world.

"They come back from Golgotha and they speak about the weather.

"This indifference keeps them from becoming fools.

"If one would tell them that St. John and Mary descended from Calvary speaking of frivolous things, they would say that that's impossible. They, nevertheless, act no differently.

"They just assisted at a capital execution; after a moment they no longer consider it. This lack of imagination keeps them from dizziness and from dying.

34   AAS 1947, 552–553.

"They would say that what the eyes do not see has no importance; in reality there is only that which has importance, and there is only that which exists.

"They have been in the Church for twenty-five minutes without understanding what is taking place. . . . Some remain seated.

"There are those who stand during the elevation. I do not know what is of greater wonder, the elevation itself or the attitude of those who see it.

"As if that elevation were but a symbol of truth! But it is Truth itself presented under an aspect which is proportionate to human weakness. The Jews were not able to bear the brilliance of Moses' countenance, and Moses was but a man. Manuel feared dying for having seen the face of His Creator (Judg 12:22), but he had seen only an Angel. What is hidden under the species of bread and wine? Certainly more than an Angel and more than Moses. One of the most astonishing characteristics of the Mass is that it does not *kill* those who assist at it.

"They hear the Mass calmly, without tears, without commotion; that's admirable. What would it take to move them? Something common.

"In order to see to what degree they are poor of heart it would be necessary to examine what is done on their account, what is done every day all over the world in order to save their inattentive souls. Their poverty of heart is neither great nor small; it is infinite. Powers, Thrones and Dominations are less powerful than this imbecility of soul.

"If they could be astonished they would be saved; but they make their religion from their own customs, that is to say something vile and natural. It is custom which damns the world."[35]

8. The Church of Heaven

Christ invites not only the earthly Church, but also the entire heavenly Church of the saints and angels to participate—according to their own proper mode—in the offering to God, which He Himself makes at every Mass for the salvation of men.

a) The Angels

1. He is Lord of the angels. He sits at the right hand of God in the heavens, "above every Principality, Power, Virtue, Domination, and above every name that is named, not only in this present world, but also in the world to come" (Eph 1:20–21). He orders their legions (Mt 26:53); He lets them share His concerns for the temporal destiny of His Kingdom, entrusting to them the protection of His little ones (Mt 18:10); they are present at His agony (Lk 22:43) and His Resurrection (Mt 28:2); they will

---

35 Théophile Delaporte, *Pamphlet contre les catholiques de France*, October 15, 1924, nos. 38–50; reprinted in *Cahiers du Rhône*, 15(54) (Neuchatel, La Baconnière, 1944). The author who borrows this transparent name is Julian Green.

come into His glory with Him (Mt 16:27) in order to separate the good from the bad (Mt 13:41, 49). How could they not unite themselves to the most solemn of prayers, they who gather around the Cross in order to mount up from earth to heaven?

Not that they are able *in the proper sense* to co-sacrifice with us, to co-offer with us the very sacrifice of the Mass. Their prayer, in fact, is no longer meritorious; and it has never made satisfaction or expiation. They are able, however, *to intercede* for us who walk in the night of time, in order to ask and obtain that our offering be more intensely meritorious, satisfactory, expiatory and coredemptive, and that we might participate with a more magnanimous heart in the Passion of the Savior.

2. At the *Preface*, the earthly Church unites her thanksgiving to the praise that the whole heavenly host renders through Christ to the all powerful and eternal God.

A little further on, at the *Per intercessionem*, she asks that through the intercession of St. Michael the Archangel and the elect, subordinate to the greater intercession of Christ, God might deign to bless and accept the incense, a symbol of the prayers which she will send up to heaven.

A bit later, at the *Supplices te rogamus*, thinking of the prayers of the saints, which, according to the Apocalypse (8:3–4), ascend from the hands of the Angel to the throne of God, she asks again through the greater intercession of Christ that the offerings, that is to say that Christ Himself veiled under the appearances of bread and wine already transubstantiated, might be carried through the hand of the angel to the altar of heaven, that is, in order that they might be received by God. These saints are not separated from us, as the pure is separated from the impure, but joined to us—we who have known too much evil to pray and to make offerings.[36]

In order to understand the heart of this prayer, writes Bossuet, "it is necessary always to remember that these things of which we speak are truly *the Body and Blood of Jesus Christ*; but they are this Body and this Blood *with us all, and with our vows and our prayers*; and that the entire gathering composes the same oblation which we wish to make pleasing to God in every way: both from Jesus Christ's part, Who is the One offered, and from the part of those who offer it and who offer themselves with Him. In this plan, what greater thing can be done than to ask again the society of

---

36   It is the intercession of all the angels which is represented by the angel of the Apocalypse, as the ancient text given by St. Ambrose bears witness, *De sacramentis*, IV, chap. 6, no. 27: "We recall then His most glorious Passion, His Resurrection from the dead, and His Ascension into heaven. We offer Thee this pure host, this spiritual host, this unbloody host, this sacred bread and the cup of eternal life. And we beseech Thee and pray that Thou wouldst accept this oblation through the hands *of Thy angels* on Thy altar on high, as Thou didst deign to accept the gifts of Thy servant Abel, the sacrifice of our father Abraham, and that offered by the great priest Melchizedek."

the angel who presides at the prayer, and in him all the holy companions of his beatitude, in order that our present offering, when it is presented in this blessed company, might quickly and most pleasingly ascend to the altar in heaven?"[37]

b) The Saints

1. It is, again, through Christ that the earthly Church asks both before consecration at the *Suscipe sancta Trinitas* and the *Communicantes*, and after at the *Libera nos quaesumus*, that God might deign to take into account the past merits and present prayers of the Blessed Virgin, the apostles and martyrs, in order to purify her offering.

We must understand, says Bossuet, "that there truly are in heaven intercessors who pray and offer with us; but that they are not listened to except through the supreme Intercessor and Mediator Jesus Christ, through Whom alone all have access, both angels as well as men, as well as the saints who reign and those who fight."[38]

2. Thus Christ, Who at the moment of the Mass engages heaven and earth in order to reconcile them in the Blood of His Cross, arouses in His heavenly Church the desire to intervene through an offering (according to the improper use of that term), by interceding for the earthly Church; and He arouses in this latter which offers (in the proper sense of the term) the need to implore the help of the saints and angels.

SECOND SECTION
WHAT IS OFFERED AT MASS?

1. The Multiplicity and Unity of the Offering

There is only one thing offered at Mass. Christ allows us, as He had done for the Blessed Virgin and St. John, to offer with Him His own life, which He alone could give.

All things, in a certain sense, are offered here. The sole and unique offering which Christ makes of Himself on the Cross, and which is rendered present to us at Mass, draws all things to itself: firstly and immediately, *that which is required for the preparation, celebration and accomplishment of the unbloody rite*; secondly and elsewhere, *all which* at each moment of time *will be saved for heaven*. "When I am lifted up from the earth I will draw all men to Myself" (Jn 12:32). "God was pleased that the fullness should dwell in Him, and through Him to reconcile all things for Him, whether in heaven or on earth, making peace through the Blood of His Cross" (Col 1:19–20).

The multiplicity of things offered, however, does not multiply the sacrifice. The Church offers the *bread* and the *wine*; she offers *Christ*; she offers *her*

---

37 *Explication de quelques difficultés sur les priers de la Messe*, chap. 38.
38 *Ibid.* chap. 39. See below, p. 130.

very self. There are not three independent offerings, three distinct sacrifices, one of bread and wine, one of Christ, and one of the Church. The bread and wine are offered only in order to be changed into the Body and Blood of Christ, Who, offering Himself, gathers around Himself His Church, which is His Body.[39]

There is but one supreme offering, that of Christ, in which the Church is engulfed along with all who depend on her.

2. All Ascends Toward or Descends From Christ's Offering

a) The Offering of Bread and Wine

1. The first sense of the word "offerings," *oblata*, in the liturgical prayers refers to the bread and wine. Such is it used, at least frequently enough, in the secret prayers of the offertory and in the *Te igitur*, with which the canon of the Mass begins: "Most merciful Father, we humbly beseech and ask Thee through Jesus Christ Thy Son, our Lord, to accept and bless these gifts here present, these holy and stainless offerings."

2. Initially the preparation of the bread and wine were not yet a ritual act. The early Church seemed concerned with clashing with the too materialistic sacrificial rites of the Gentiles and Jews. Her glance passes over the bread and wine in order to focus immediately on the supreme offering. Beginning with the second century, however, with St. Irenaeus, we sense a need to insist on the value of earthly creation, against the false spiritualism of the Gnostics. Creation is the heavenly gift's point of departure. "The movement toward God, by which are offered the Body and Blood of the Lord, begins also to communicate itself to the material offerings; these offerings take place in the liturgical action. Tertullian teaches us that the faithful brought gifts, and he employs for this action the word *offerre* to offer to God. Likewise in St. Hippolytus of Rome . . . the bread and wine which the deacons bring to the bishop before the Eucharist are called *oblatio*, from the name given to the offerings already consecrated, *oblatio sanctae Ecclesiae* . . ."[40]

3. The *Quam oblationem* of the canon of the Mass will clarify this, however. The bread and wine are not offered except by passing immediately beyond to Christ, Who will take their place: "May Thee, our God, deign to bless, accept and fully approve this offering; render it perfect and worthy to please Thee; and may it become for us the Body and Blood of Thy Beloved Son, our Lord Jesus Christ."

---

39 "The Church, who offers *the bread and wine* so that it may become the Body and Blood, and who then offers again *this Body and Blood* after they are consecrated, does so only in order to accomplish the third oblation, by which she offers *her very self.*" Bossuet, *Explication de quelques difficultés . . .*, chap. 36.

40 Joseph-André Jungmann, *Missarum sollemnia, Explication génétique de la Messe romaine* (Paris: Aubier, 1951–1954), t. II, p. 272.

b) The Offering of Christ

1. Then come the words of consecration. They reiterate the rite where Christ, at the Last Supper, made His own bloody sacrifice present sacramentally under the unbloody appearances of bread and wine:

"On the night before His Passion, He took bread in His sacred and venerable hands, and raising His eyes to heaven,[41] to Thee, O God, His almighty Father, giving Thee thanks, He blessed it, broke it, and gave it to His disciples saying: TAKE AND EAT, FOR THIS IS MY BODY. *In like manner, after they had eaten, He took the cup in His sacred and venerable hands, gave Thee thanks again, blessed it and gave it to His disciples saying:* TAKE AND DRINK OF IT, FOR THIS IS THE CUP OF MY BLOOD, THE BLOOD OF THE NEW AND ETERNAL COVENANT—THE MYSTERY OF FAITH[42]—WHICH WILL BE POURED OUT FOR YOU AND FOR THE MULTITUDE OF MEN, FOR THE REMISSION OF SINS."

"As often as you do this, you do it in memory of Me."

Henceforth, from the *Unde et memores*, the bread and wine have given place to the Body and Blood of Christ: "Wherefore, in memory, Lord, of Christ Thy Son and our Lord's blessed Passion and Resurrection from the dead, and His glorious Ascension into heaven, we Thy servants (the clergy) and with us Thy holy people, present to Thy glorious Majesty—an offering chosen from among the goods which Thou hast given us—the perfect, holy and spotless Victim, the sacred bread of eternal life and the cup of eternal salvation."

2. The prayers of the *Supra quae* and the *Supplices te*, where we continue to ask that these offerings be pleasing, as were the sacrifices of Abel, Abraham and Melchizedek, and the blessings which we continue to make over these offerings, concern the offerings not *insofar as they are now Christ,* but *insofar as they are presented by hearts as poor as ours.*

It is clear, writes Bossuet, that what we wish to compare here is "not *gift with gift,*[43] since the Eucharist is continually—in a certain sense—above the ancient sacrifices; but rather *persons with persons,* and this is why we name

41 During the first multiplication of bread the Synoptics note that Jesus "having taken five loaves and two fish, *and having raised His eyes to heaven,* blessed them ..." (Mk 6:41). This first multiplication of loaves is what, according to St. John (chap. 6), prepares the proclamation of the Eucharist.

42 "This expression, borrowed from St. Paul, is to be understood in its Pauline sense: the Eucharist is *the* mystery of faith, that is to say that it contains and reveals the entire economy of salvation." Dom Bernard Botte, *L'ordinaire de la Messe* ... , p. 81. The same interpretation is found in Jungmann, *Missarum sollemnia* ... , t. III, p. 118.

43 That is to say, not on one hand the gift offered by Abel, Abraham and Melchizedek, and on the other hand the gift offered at Mass, namely Christ; but rather, on one hand the piety of Abel, Abraham and Melchizedek, and on the other hand our need.

the holiest of men: Abel, the first of the just; Abraham, the common father of all believers; and the last place is reserved for Melchizedek, who was above Abraham, since to him Abraham offered a tenth of his goods, and who received at the same time with them bread and wine, the first fruits of the sacrifice of the Eucharist."[44]

The blessings and signs of the Cross, which continue to be made after consecration over the Body and Blood of Christ, are explained in the same manner: "When the gifts (the bread and wine) are blessed *before* the consecration, this blessing has two effects: with regard to the sacrament itself which is to be consecrated, and with regard to the man who is to be sanctified by the sacrament. *After* the consecration, however, the blessing has already been consummated with regard to the sacrament, and hence exists only with regard to the man, who must be sanctified by participation in the mystery. This is why the signs of the Cross which are made after the consecration over the consecrated "bread" and "wine" are accompanied by this prayer: *In order that we might receive from this altar the Body and Blood of Thy Son, and be filled in Jesus Christ with every grace and spiritual blessing.* It is clear that there is in no way here a blessing over things already consecrated, but rather a prayer where we ask that such things, being holy in themselves, might bring blessings and grace on those who participate in them."[45] Let us say that the blessings with the sign of the Cross have a double meaning: before the consecration it descends from heaven to the host; after the consecration it rises up again from the host to us.

If we distinguish, as we did before, four principle moments in the canon of the Mass: the *thanksgiving*, the recitation of the *institution*, the *anamnesis* or commemoration of this institution, and the *epiklesis* (in the wide sense of an invocation for the community),[46] it is to this last moment which refer the prayers and benedictions in question.

c) The Offering of the Church

The invocation of the divine benevolence upon the community, which is united in Christ to offer Christ, is at the same time an invocation made to this same community to offer itself with Christ, in Christ and through Christ.

How could Christ, drawing the Church into His own offering, not call her at the same time to give her very self? "There proceeds from the natural Body of our Savior a force of unity to gather and reduce all into one Mystical Body. The mystery of Christ's Body is fulfilled when all the members are united to offer themselves in Him and with Him. Thus the

---

44   Bossuet, *Explication de quelques difficultés . . .* , chap. 37. "The perfection of this sacrifice is not only that we offer and receive *holy things*; but still more, that *we*, who offer them and participate in them, *become holy.*" *Ibid.*

45   *Ibid.*, chap. 41.

46   Dom Bernard Botte, O.S.B., *L'ordinaire de la Messe . . .* , p. 16.

Church has a share in His sacrifice, such that this sacrifice will never reach its perfection except when it is offered by the saints."[47]

The secret prayer from the Mass of the Blessed Trinity beseeches God that, being pleased to change the bread and wine into Christ's Body and Blood, He in addition transform His Church in the offering: "O Lord our God, sanctify, we beseech Thee, through the invocation of Thy holy Name, the Host which we offer Thee; and, through It, make us all an eternal gift for Thyself, *et per eam nosmetipsos tibi perfice munus aeternum.*"

At the Cross, said St. Augustine, Christ Jesus is the Priest: "He is Himself the one Who offers; He is Himself the offering. And He wished that the sacrifice of the Church be the daily sacrifice of this reality. The Church, the Body of which Christ is the Head, learns to offer herself through Him, *seipsam per ipsum discit offerre.*"[48]

Thus the bread and wine are offered only in view of Christ's sacrifice, around which the Church and all who will be saved in the world are assembled: "When I am lifted up from the earth, I will draw all men to Myself" (Jn 12:32).

b) A Text from Leibniz

We read in the *Systéme théologique* of Leibniz: "As God is infinite, and all which comes from us is in no way proportionate to His perfection, a victim capable of appeasing Him cannot be found except Him Who possesses an infinite perfection. Whence it happens, by a wonderful means, that Christ, always giving Himself to us anew in this sacrament every time a consecration takes place, is also always able to be offered anew to God, and thus *He represents and confirms the perpetual efficacy of His first sacrifice on the Cross*. For there is not in this sacrifice of propitiation, unceasingly repeated for the remission of sins, a new efficacy added to that of the Passion; but *all its power consists in the representation, the application of that first bloody sacrifice which is totally consummated, once and for all*,[49] and the fruit of which is the divine grace accorded to all who, assisting at this formidable sacrifice, *unite themselves to the priest in order to worthily offer this holy oblation.*

"Furthermore, in addition to the remission of eternal punishment and the application of Christ's merits for eternal life, we can ask God for still additional salutary things for ourselves and for others, both living and dead; above all we can solicit the sweetening of that paternal chastisement due to every sin, even after the penitent re-enters into grace; it is clear and

---

47 Bossuet, *Explication* . . . , chap. 36.
48 *De civitate Dei*, X, chap. 20.
49 Repeated with respect to the *unbloody rite* which transports it to us and to all *generations* who participate in it; but unique and unable to be repeated *in itself*. See above, p. 88.

certain that there is nothing in our worship more precious and more efficacious for obtaining such favors than the sacrifice of this divine sacrament, where the very Body of the Lord is rendered present to us. *No offering on our part has a greater price in the eyes of God and rises before His throne as a most pleasing fragrance than a pure heart, humbled at the foot of the altar where He Himself comes down.*"[50]

---

50 *Système theologique*, chap. 15, *Le sacrifice de la Messe*, § 1, *En quoi consiste le sacrifice de la Messe*, translated by Prince Albert de Broglie, Tours, 1870, pp. 334–335. According to Jean Baruzi, the *Système* was meant not to present the personal thought of Leibniz, but to prepare the union of the churches by clarifying principal points of controversy. *Leibniz et l'organisation religieuse de la terre*, Paris, 1907, pp. 242–243.

CHAPTER 6

The Infinite Power of the Mass

1. The Source Is Infinite; The Participation Is Finite

The contents of this chapter are summed up in two lines. The power of the Mass, which is nothing other than that of the Cross, is infinite *in itself*. Nevertheless, each Mass bears *in reality* only a limited help—limited, that is, on one hand by the devotion of those who contribute to the offering in one degree or another, and on the other hand by the devotion of those for whom it is offered.

2. The Teaching of St. Thomas

a) The Passion, the Universal Cause of Salvation, Must Nevertheless Be Applied Through Faith and the Sacraments

In the order of ascending mediation, Christ's Passion, being that of a God, raises up to heaven a supplication the power of which is infinite. In the order of descending mediation, it marks that moment when Christ, the universal principle of all graces[1] and whose grace is in this sense infinite,[2] pours out uponmen the superior reserves of His heart. Christ's Passion, therefore, has fully freed us from sin.[3] Why then is it necessary to have recourse to faith and to the sacraments of the New Law?

To this question St. Thomas responds, that the Passion of Christ brings the remission of sins in the manner of a universal cause, *ut causa quaedam universalis remissionis peccatorum*. This universal cause of salvation, however, must be applied to each individual person for the destruction of his own sins.[4] This application happens in two ways, the second of which perfects the first. First of all, through living *faith*, vivified by charity,[5] according to the words of St. Paul: "God has destined Christ Jesus to be, through His Blood, a propitiation by means of faith" (Rom 3:25); then, through the *sacraments* of the New Law:[6] "Are you not aware that, having been baptized in Christ Jesus, all you have been baptized in His death?" (Rom 6:3).

1 "Conferebatur ei gratia tanquam cuidam universali principio in genere habentium gratiam." St. Thomas, *Summa Theologiae* III, qu. 7, a. 9.
2 St. Thomas, *Summa Theologiae* III, qu. 7, a. 11.
3 St. Thomas, *Summa Theologiae* III, qu. 49, a. 1.
4 *Ibid.*, ad 4.
5 *Ibid.*, ad. 5.
6 *Ibid.*, ad 4.

"The Passion of Christ was a sufficient and superabundant satisfaction for the sins of the whole human race, *sufficiens et superabundans satisfactio pro peccatis totius humani generis*. . . . The Passion of Christ obtains its effect in those to whom it is applied through faith and charity and through the sacraments of faith, *sortitur effectum suum in illis quibus applicatur per fidem et charitatem, et per fidei sacramenta*."[7]

A little further on St. Thomas will write similarly: "The power of Christ's Passion is brought to us (*copulatur nobis*) through faith and the sacraments, but in different ways. For, the application (*continuatio*) which depends on faith happens by an (interior) act of the soul. While the application which depends on the sacraments happens through recourse to an exterior rite, *continuatio autem quae est per sacramenta fit per usum exteriorum rerum*."[8] The sacraments of the New Law confer grace *dependently* of the subject's disposition, but *going beyond* these dispositions, and *proportionately* to these dispositions; such that he who approaches them with two or three, receives four or six. Thus *the Passion of Christ is infinite, but the Church participates in it in a finite manner*, according to the intensity of her faith and love.

b) We Must Speak of the Mass in the Same Way as the Passion: It Is Infinite but Participated in a Finite Manner

1. If we have thus far interpreted exactly the thought of St. Thomas on the essence of the sacrifice of the Mass, if the unbloody rite of the Mass is sacrificial because it brings us Christ now glorious, by means of the act of His bloody sacrifice, if each new Mass is a new presence among us of the unique sacrifice of the Cross, it would be necessary to speak of the Mass as one speaks of the Cross, and to say that, in the lines of ascending and descending mediation, *the power of the Mass is infinite, but that it is participated in by the Church only in a finite manner*, according to the intensity of her love at a given moment in time, and that it is *applied to each generation through the mediation of faith and the sacraments*—in the present case through the sacrament of the Eucharist, instituted by Christ for this end. Such, in fact, is the teaching of St. Thomas.

2. Speaking in the *Summa* of the effects of the Eucharist, St. Thomas distinguishes the sacrifice from the sacrament. The sacrifice refers to those who offer it and for whom it is offered; the sacrament, to those who receive it.

What are the effects of the sacrifice? "The Eucharist, insofar as it is a sacrifice, has satisfactory power. In the satisfaction, however, the affection of him who makes the offering matters more than the grandeur of the offering—the Lord says of the widow who gave two pieces, that she gave more than all the others (Lk 21:3). Thus, although this offering with regard to its power, *ex sui quantitate*, suffices to make satisfaction for all

---

7   St. Thomas, *Summa Theologiae* III., qu. 49, a. 3, and ad 1. See above, pp. 73, 78.

8   St. Thomas, *Summa Theologiae* III, qu. 62, a. 6.

punishment, it is not effectively satisfactory for those who offer it or for whom it is offered except according to the intensity of their devotion, *secundum quantitatem suae devotionis.*"[9]

The power of the Mass, as that of the Cross, is infinite, but it is received by the Church only according to the intensity of her devotion: "Just as Christ's Passion is sufficient for the remission of sins and the attainment of grace and glory for all men, *prodest omnibus quantum ad sufficientiam*, but produces its effect only in those who join themselves to it through faith and charity; so this sacrifice, the memorial of the Lord's Passion, produces its effect only in those who join themselves to this sacrament through faith and charity. . . . And it profits them more or less according to the intensity of their devotion, *illis tamen prodest plus vel minus secundum modum devotionis eorum.*"[10]

Let us say: At each Mass Christ comes with all His Cross, ready to apply it to us, to make it present to us, according to the measure of our desire.

3. The Efficacy of the Mass with Respect to Validity

a) Christ is Made Present at Each Mass Despite the Unworthiness of the Minister; Considered, Therefore, With Respect to the Minister the Mass Is Efficacious "Ex Opere Operato"

During transubstantiation Christ—now glorious and the one Who eternally ratifies what He willed already on the Cross—is made present on the altar in order to actualize and apply to us the unique act of His bloody Passion by which He truly saved all men once and for all.

---

9   St. Thomas, *Summa Theologiae* III, qu. 79, a. 5.—On this passage Cajetan writes: "Two points are to be noted: 1st The offering of the Eucharist, by reason of its own power, *ex sui quantitate,* suffices to make satisfaction for all punishment; 2nd This offering is satisfactory for those who offer it and for whom it is offered according to the intensity of their devotion. It follows from the first point that the Mass is in itself, *ex parte sui,* satisfactory for the punishment of all sinners, both living and dead. As such its power is infinite, *ut sic est valoris infiniti;* for Christ is offered here. It follows from the second point that one sole Mass loses nothing of its satisfactory power by being offered by *one, two or three persons;* for the quantity of one person's devotion does not harm that of another."

This is exactly right concerning the offering which they (i.e. both priest and faithful) make in a private manner. Where we disagree with Cajetan is when he speaks about the offering which the priest makes insofar as he is a minister of the Church; for there the offering will lose its wholeness if it is divided among several intentions.

Cajetan, who wrote his commentary on the Summa in 1522, is here referring back to a work he wrote in 1510, The Celebration of the Mass.

10   St. Thomas, *Summa Theologiae* III, qu. 79. a. 7, ad 2.

In his Commentary on John, VI, 52, St. Thomas seems to indicate by the word "sacrament" the entire Eucharistic "mystery," namely both the sacrifice and sacrament at the same time:

This mysterious coming of the glorious Christ into our midst in order to unite us to His Passion is accomplished each time a priest, whatever be his personal sanctity, validly repeats the unbloody rite of the Last Supper. If, therefore, we call efficacious *ex opere operato* the rite, the validity of which remains independent of the minister's sanctity, we would say that the offering of the Mass acts ex opere operato.[11] It is in thinking of the dispositions of the priest as *minister* in the celebration of the unbloody rite that one must read this text of St. Bellarmine: "The sacrifice of the Mass, insofar as it is offered by Christ, is efficacious *ex opere operantis*, but infallibly; for it is pleasing to God in reason of the sanctity of Christ, Who offers it; it is supreme and cannot be diminished or increased. But insofar as it is offered by a man, it is efficacious *ex opere operato*; for it is pleasing to God even when he who offers it is not."[12]

b) The Mass Is an Offering Which Is Pure and Without Stain, Whatever Be the Minister in Himself (1st Sense). A Text from the Council of Trent on the Prophecy of Malachi

Regarding the subject of the Mass, the Council of Trent would declare, "that it is a pure offering, which cannot be stained either by the unworthiness or the malice of those who offer it; and concerning it the Lord had foretold

---

"The utility of the Eucharist is great and universal.

"It is great: the Eucharist, being the sacrament of Christ's Passion, contains in Itself the Christ Who suffered; such that every effect of the Lord's Passion is also the effect of the sacrament, which is nothing other than the application which is made to us of the Lord's Passion, *nihil aliud est hoc sacramentum quam applicatio dominicae Passionis ad nos . . . .*

"It is universal: for the life which it confers is not only that of one man, but regarding this life in itself (*quantum in se est*) it is the life of the whole world, for which Christ's death can suffice, according to 1 John 2:2: *He Himself is the propitiation for our sins, not only for our own but for those of the whole world.*

"There is, in fact, a difference between this sacrament and the others. The others have particular effects. Thus at Baptism the baptized alone receives grace; but in the immolation of this sacrament the effect is universal, *in immolatione hujus sacramenti est universalis effectus.* It does not stop with the priest alone. It passes over to those for whom he prays and to all the Church, the living and the dead."

11   "The act which draws its power from the goodness or devotion of him who performs it has value *ex opere operantis.* . . . The act which has value in itself, by the very fact that it is validly performed, whatever be the goodness or malice of the minister in itself, has value *ex opere operato*; here the effect remains the same and does not become better through the minister's goodness nor worse through his malice." St. Robert Bellarmine, *De Missa*, bk. II, chap. 4. See above, p. 72.

The value *ex opere operato* is defined in this text according to the *minister* of the sacrament. It would still need to be defined according to the *subject* of the sacrament. This would be done later by John of Saint Thomas. See below, p. 124.

12   *Ibid.*

through Malachi that it would be offered pure in every place in His Name, which would be great among the gentiles."[13]

4. The Efficacy of the Mass With Respect to Sanctity: 1) Ascending Mediation

At Mass Christ comes to actualize for us the act of His bloody Passion, both in the line of ascending mediation and descending mediation.

a) At Mass Christ Actualizes the Offering Which He Made of Us On the Cross

In the line of ascending mediation, where it is an adoring, eucharistic, impetrative and propitiatory sacrifice, the Passion of Christ acts in the manner of a universal, sufficient and superabundant cause, in view of the world's salvation. Christ, therefore, unites to His redemptive offering (an offering which is theandric, divine and human, and infinite) the offering which will rise up from all future generations as they come into existence, in order to purify it, elevate it and render it co-redemptive.

When He comes to us at Mass it is precisely in order to lift up from us the offering which will actually allow us to enter—as once did the Blessed Virgin and St. John—into His bloody offering of the Cross, where a place has been marked out in advance; in order, according to the words of the Apostle, to complete in our flesh "that which is lacking to the sufferings of Christ, for His Body the Church" (Col 1:24).

Our participation in the offering of Christ on the Cross can happen either through faith and charity only, or additionally by the sacraments, that is to say—in the present case—by Eucharistic Communion.

---

13 Session XXII, chap. 1, Denz., 939. Here is the celebrated passage of Malachi on the rejection of the Jews' sacrifices and the pure offering of the Gentiles: "I have no pleasure in you, saith the Lord of hosts; and I will not receive a gift of your hand. For from the rising of the sun even to the going down, My name is great among the Gentiles, and in every place there is sacrifice, and there is offered to My name a clean oblation; for My name is great among the Gentiles, saith the Lord of hosts" (Mal 1:10–11).

Without a doubt, writes Père Lagrange, the veil of the future was not completely lifted for the prophet, "and we do not pretend that he saw with his own eyes the offering of the Holy Sacrifice of the Mass. He was thinking of the Levites, but the Levites purified, and a sacrifice offered in the name of Yahweh, known as such by all peoples. These considerations fully justify the Christian tradition which saw in this passage a premonition of the great change effected in worship by Christianity, and yet without the prophet departing from his own perspective." *Notes sur les prophéties messianiques des derniers prophètes,* Revue Biblique, 1906, p. 54.

The text of Malachi was already considered as a prophecy of the Eucharistic sacrifice in the *Didache,* chap. 14, then by St. Justin in his *Dialogue With Trypho,* chap. 41, 1–3. See above, p. 62.

*b) Participation in the Offering of the Mass through the Faith and
Charity of the Church Interceding for the Just and Sinners:
The Efficacy Is Said to Be "Ex Opere Operantis Ecclesiae"*

1. The first participation, namely through faith and charity, happens
according to *the depth of faith and charity* of not only those who immediately
offer it, but still more *of the entire Church*. This is in fact the charity of the
whole Church Militant, who through the Mass enters into the sacrifice of
the Cross in order to offer it, at each moment of time, for the salvation of
the world of which she is a contemporary. And the beneficence of this
offering being proportionate to the intensity and fervor of the faith and
love of those who—priests and faithful—offer with Christ, in Christ, and
through Christ, one would say that it is efficacious by reason of the
Church's devotion, *ex opere operantis Ecclesiae*.

2. It is efficacious in this manner, not only for those who, being in the
state of grace offer it for an explicit or implicit intention, but also for the
sinners throughout the entire world, whose conversion it implores.
"Insofar as it is a sacrifice," says St. Thomas, "the Eucharist has its effect
not only for those who offer it, but also for those for whom it is offered;
in these latter, what is required beforehand in them is not a spiritual life
in act but in potency only. Therefore, if they are found disposed, they
obtain grace by virtue of the true sacrifice from which every grace flows
to us; and consequently, it destroys mortal sin in them, not as a proximate
cause, but insofar as it impetrates the grace of contrition for them. When,
therefore, continues St. Thomas, it is said that it is offered only for
Christ's members, this means that it is offered for them that they might
become members of Christ."[14]

We must unwaveringly prefer this personal position of the
Sentences to the anonymous view recorded in the *Summa*, where it is
stated that we do not pray in the canon of the Mass for those who are
outside the Church.[15] We know the prayer for offering the chalice: "We
offer Thee, Lord, the chalice of salvation and beseech Thy clemency, that
it may ascend before Thy divine Majesty as a sweet fragrance, *for our
salvation, and for that of the whole world*." Now this supplication underlies
the canon before the latter is said; and it announces the very *consecration*

14   St. Thomas, *IV Sent.*, dist. 12, qu. 2, a. 2, quaest. 2, ad 4.
15   This opinion is reproduced by St. Thomas, *Summa Theologiae* III, qu. 79, a. 7,
     ad 2, where he cites a text of St. Augustine: "Who would offer the Body of
     Christ for anyone other than those who are members of Christ?"
         The text is exact but the sense goes beyond the mere words. Vincent Victor
     dared to promise to infants who die without Baptism "not only paradise, but
     even the Kingdom of God" because of the frequent oblations and sacrifices
     which will be constantly offered by the holy priests." To Victor St. Augustine
     responds: "Who would offer the Body of Christ for anyone other than those
     who are members of Christ?" *De anima et ejus origine*, I, chap. 9, n. 10.

of the chalice, and the Blood poured out "for you and for the many unto the remission of sins, *pro vobis et pro multis in remissionem peccatorum.*"[16]

3. What St. Thomas says of the effects of the Eucharist as a sacrifice joins and clarifies the text of the Council of Trent, which teaches "that this sacrifice is truly propitiatory, and that, by it, if we approach with a sincere heart and firm faith, with fear and reverence, contrite and penitent, we obtain mercy and find grace in seasonable aid (Heb. 4:16). For, appeased by this offering, the Lord, granting grace and the gift of penitence, remits even enormous crimes and sins, *crimina et peccata etiam ingentia dimittit.*"[17]

c) This Participation Varies but Is Infallible

The efficacy of the offering at Mass of the same sacrifice of the Cross by the charity of the Church varies; but it is infallible *ex opere operantis Ecclesiae.*

1. It *varies*, since at each moment of time it is proportionate to the intensity of this charity. It rises when there is in the Church more hope, more coredemptive suffering, more souls in the transforming union by whom the entire Church merits (in the strict sense of that term) the name "the Bride of Christ." It never has been so high as in the days of the new-born Church, when the Blessed Virgin assisted at the Mass of the Apostles, lifting up their offering by the force of her desire. And it ought to be said that it is there, on one hand, that one must look for the cause of the extraordinary diffusion of the first evangelical preaching.

2. It is, however, *infallible*. The Church Militant is not without sinners, but she is without sin. The Church is "without stain or wrinkle, or any such thing, but holy and immaculate" (Eph. 5:27). Never will she lack love. Never will she cease to be the Bride, in the strong sense of that term. Never will the gates of hell prevail against her. Consequently, never, at any point in time, will the valid offering of any Mass fall into nothingness, even one celebrated by the most miserable of priests and before the most ignorant laity who are totally closed off to things spiritual. It will always be mended, vivified in its roots by the great collective love of the Church. "Love," writes Tauler, "draws all to itself: every good work, every life, all suffering. It takes into its cup all that there is of good in the world, whether done by good or evil men. In fact, if your charity is greater than the charity of him who does some good, that good will belong more to you than to him who does it . . . . The measure of overflowing hearts is

---

This text, which concerns infants who die without Baptism, would not be able to be legitimately expanded to sinners. For the latter, insofar as death has not yet occurred, are members of Christ, at least in potency, as St. Thomas himself explains, St. Thomas, *Summa Theologiae* III, qu. 8, a. 3; such that one can and ought to pray and supplicate for them.

16 See above, p. 128.
17 Session XXII, chap. 2; Denz. 940.

poured out onto all the Church .... They allow nothing to be lost, whether it be of the smallest or greatest good—neither the smallest prayer nor the least pious thought or act of faith. They relate all to God with a lively love and offer all to the Heavenly Father."[18]

d) The Mass Is a Pure Offering and Without Stain Insofar as It Is Offered by the Pure Church

From this point of view we can respond with the words of the Council of Trent,[19] where, citing the prophecy of Malachi, it shows in the Mass "a pure offering, which can be stained by neither the unworthiness nor the malice of those who offer it."[20] And here we give these words a new, more mysterious, wider and more profound sense.

e) Participation at the Offering of the Mass through Sacramental Communion; Considered with Respect to Those Who Communicate, the Efficacy Is Said To Be "Ex Opere Operato"

Our entrance into the offering of Christ on the Cross can, moreover, be made through sacramental Communion.

Its measure, then, is not only that of our faith and love. The sacraments of the New Law, in effect, bring us grace: 1) certainly *depending* on our dispositions; 2) not according to that measure only, but *over and above* these dispositions; 3) and nevertheless *in proportion* to them, such that he who approaches with two or three receives four or six.

---

18 *Sermons de Tauler,* édit. Vie Spirituelle (Paris, 1930), II, pp. 189 and 193. Cited above, p. 104.

19 See above, p. 121.

20 It is justice to stigmatize the lack of awareness of those who celebrate or assist at Mass without love; but on the condition that we recall that every Mass is first of all offered by the Church, who is never without love.

   In *Missarum sollemnia* . . . , III, pp. 147–148, J.-A. Jungmann writes: "The sacrifice of the New Alliance . . . only becomes a truly pleasing homage to God if, among those who accomplish it, a minimum gift of their interior life really animates the exterior presentation. In this sense it is very appropriate that the strong words of the prophets, by which God rejects all of the people's external spiritless sacrifices, be applied even to the sacrifice of the New Alliance, when the latter is presented by unworthy priestly hands. It can happen that this most holy sacrifice finds itself more or less reduced to a reiteration, *hic et nunc,* of the sacrifice already offered by Christ—a reiteration deprived of its true sense in the order of salvation, if, contrary to its very raison d'être, it no longer translates a state of the Christian sacrificial soul, is no longer rooted in human soil, but isolated and suspended in a void." The author whom we cite felt, however, the need to add in a footnote the following: "This extreme case is, nevertheless, not entirely realized by the sole fact of an unworthy celebrant, provided that at least one of those assisting participate in the sacrifice with a fitting spirit. Furthermore, behind each Mass the universal Church is always present in some manner."

This is what is meant when—thinking here not of the minister who confers but rather the subjects who receive—it is said that the sacraments of the New Law act *ex opere operato* in order to communicate grace.[21]

5. The Efficacy of the Mass with Respect to Sanctity: 2) Descending Mediation

Christ's Passion is not only the meritorious and satisfactory cause of our salvation in the line of ascending mediation. It is also the efficient cause of our salvation in the line of descending mediation. These are the two distinct but inseparable aspects of one and the same mediation, the interdependent effects of which are mutually named and linked.

Christ, heard on the Cross, obtains from that moment on the fullness of inexhaustible grace, which is in Him and is poured out upon future generations as they come into existence; this is signified by the blood and water which flowed from His opened heart.

There again Christ's Passion, which the Mass renders present to us, acts in the manner of a universal sufficient, superabundant cause of salvation, the power of which needs to be communicated to us by faith and the sacraments.

At Mass we stand before the Source of all descending graces, like the Blessed Virgin and St. John at the foot of the bloody Cross.

The *efficient power* of the Mass is infinite. The *application* which happens by the Church is *infallible*: the now glorious Christ, coming to His Church with His Cross, will never find the Church insensible to His benefices. This application, however, varies and is *finite*. It is proportionate to the faith and love of the Church at each moment of time, and to the fervor with which she approaches sacramental Communion.

6. The Terminology of Cajetan: The Effect of the Mass Is Infinite with Respect to Sufficiency "Ex Opere Operato"; It Is Finite with Respect to the Application "Ex Opere Operantis"

In the work *De Missae celebratione*[22] Cajetan, faithful to St. Thomas, strongly affirms in a beautiful text that the power of the Mass is *infinite*, but that we never take hold of it except in a *finite* manner.

1. "Considered absolutely," he says, "the sacrifice of the Mass is the very immolation of Jesus Christ, the thing offered being Jesus Christ. It follows that the impetratory, meritorious and satisfactory power of this sacrifice is infinite. The *effect of the sacrifice of the Mass is infinite*, as is that

---

21 The sacraments of the New Law act *ex opere operato*, for they have their power from Christ, Who gives grace to the subject disposed to receive it. They confer grace beyond the personal disposition, but conformable and in proportion to it, although not without it, *ultra propriam dispositionem, conformiter tamen et proportionaliter ad illam, sed non sine illa."* John of St. Thomas, III, qu. 62; disp. 24, no. 29, édit. Vivès, IX, p. 152.

22 Rome, December 1, 1510. Qu. 2.

of the Passion. God loves the Mass more than He hates all the sins of the world. However, just as the effect of the Passion is infinite—in the sense that it *suffices* to redeem all men, not in the sense that it *in fact* redeems all men, *infinitas secundum sufficientiam et non secundum efficaciam*; again, just as the effect of the Passion acts in the manner of a universal Cause (that is indeterminate, and not in the manner of a cause determined to a particular individual, *secundum naturam causae universalis, indeterminatae scilicet, et non determinatae ad hunc aut illum*), so the sacrifice of the Mass is, by its very nature, of an infinite sufficiency and an indeterminate efficacy, *infinitae sufficientiae et indeterminatae efficaciae . . . .* It follows that the sacrifice of the Mass considered in itself, *ex solo opere operato*, does not have a particular effect with regard to any man whatsoever. It is pleasing to God, it renders thanks to Him, it is a memorial, etc."

2. "If, however, one considers the sacrifice of the Mass insofar as it is *applied* to this or that person, *its effect is finite.*" It is measured by our devotion. The Church draws from the infinite power of the Mass only according to the necessarily finite intensity of her desire. Through her love she touches the redemptive sacrifice present at Mass, and in proportion to this love she brings about a flowing forth of light, which inundates her and is poured out upon the entire world. St. John Vianney once said: "When our Lord is on the altar during Holy Mass, as soon as we pray to Him for sinners, He hurls down toward them rays of light in order to reveal their miseries and convert them."[23] This application, however, remains finite. The Church enters into the mystery of the Mass as into the sun, which overshadows her on all sides.[24]

7. Application and Fruits of the Mass

At each Mass *Christ in glory comes to us in order to touch us by means of His Cross* and in order to actualize for us His redemptive Passion: the universal, superabundant, and infinite cause of the world's salvation.

At each Mass *the Church enters into the drama of the redemptive Passion* in proportion to her faith and love. This is the first application, the direct

23 Francis Trochu, *Le curé d'Ars* (Lyon: Vitte, 1927), p. 619.
24 This teaching is accepted in substance by numerous theologians. Other theologians, nevertheless, think that the power of the sacrifice of the Mass is limited in itself and that this limitation is due to a restrictive decree of Christ. First of all, however, it will always remain rather difficult to prove the existence of such a decree. And one must especially not forget that, if the Mass is above all not a simple sacrifice of the Church but rather the very continuation, across time, of the redemptive sacrifice, it must act then as that sacrifice, in a manner of an absolutely universal cause. The devotion with which one participates in the offering of the Mass, with which also one communicates at Mass, would alone determine the measure (always finite), according to which this universal cause will be effectively applied.

participation of the sacrifice of the Cross procured by the Mass. This application, this participation, is immense but finite. It happens infallibly.

At each Mass the Church, united by her faith and love to the Passion of Christ, *begs for the world's salvation*. What she thus obtains by her supplication, what she draws in from Christ's Passion and which redounds upon men, is a second application, an indirect participation of the sacrifice of the Mass. This one is also finite, and is what theologians call the fruits of the Mass.

The question, "What are the fruits of the Mass?" is related to the question, "For whom is the Mass offered?"

8. What Are the Fruits of the Mass? Or, for Whom Is the Mass Offered?

a) The Mass Can Be Applied on Three Levels

By entering through the Mass into the sacrifice of the Cross, the Church, at each moment in time, can offer this sacrifice with Christ, in Christ and through Christ, while begging principally for the redemption of the world contemporary to it. From this perspective the Church will be heard, as we said, in proportion to the intensity of her desire; but she is allowed to distinguish her intentions.

The intention *of the Church Militant herself*, who prays at each Mass for all the faithful, both living and deceased, and for the salvation of the whole world, is the effect which theologians call the *general* fruit of the Mass. The intention *of the priest insofar as he is a minister of the Church* is the *special* fruit of the Mass (mentioned in the condemnation of errors of the Council of Pistoia). Finally, the *personal* intention, whether that of the priest or of the faithful, is the *particular* fruit of the Mass.

b) The Offering of the Church for One Universal Intention

1. The *Church herself*, first of all, draws in from the infinite treasure of each Mass all that the intensity of her love of the Bridegroom permits her to seize, in order that it might be poured out upon the world. She takes care that every Mass will be celebrated expressly and above all for the faithful both here below and in purgatory,[25] and for the salvation of the whole world. This is the *general fruit* of the Mass.

2. The prayers at Mass clearly manifest the universality of the co-redemptive intentions of the Church.

In offering the bread which he foresees will be changed by transubstantiation, the priest says: "Receive, Holy Father, Eternal and Omnipotent God, this spotless host, which I, Thy unworthy servant, present to Thee, my

---

25 The Council of Trent teaches that, according to apostolic tradition, the Mass "is offered not only for the sins, sufferings (expiatory), satisfactions and other goods of the *living* faithful, but also for *those who died* in Christ without having been fully purified." Session XXII, chap. 2, and canon 3. Denz. 940 and 950.

living and true God, for my innumerable sins, offences and negligences, and for all here present; as for all faithful Christians, both living and dead, *sed et pro omnibus fidelibus Christianis vivis atque defunctis*: that it may avail both me and them for salvation unto life everlasting."

In offering the chalice her intention expands to the ends of the earth: "We offer Thee, Lord, the chalice of salvation and beseech Thy clemency, that it may ascend before Thy divine Majesty as a sweet savor, for our salvation, and for that of the whole world, *pro nostra et totius mundi salute*."

And if Christ truly died for all men, how—regarding the words of the consecration of the chalice, "the Blood of the New and eternal Covenant, poured out *for you* and *for the multitude* unto the remission of sins,"—how can one keep from thinking that the words *for you* must designate those who have received the Gospel, and the words *for the multitude* all those who still do not know it?[26] The offering of the Mass goes beyond the frontiers of worlds: "When the priest celebrates, he honors God, gives joy to the angels, builds up the Church, aids the living, procures eternal rest for the deceased."[27]

3. According to the Council of Trent, even "the Masses where only the priest communicates sacramentally ought to be regarded as communitarian (*communes*), because the people communicate spiritually, and because the Masses are celebrated by the priest insofar as he is the public minister of the Church, not only for himself but for all the faithful who belong to the Body of Christ."[28] We add that this membership might already be in act or might still be in potency.

4. The application of the Mass is measured first of all by the fervor of those who, through Christ, with Christ and in Christ, pray for the salvation of the world. It is further conditioned, however, to a certain degree by the disposition of those very ones for whom we pray: by their present dispositions if they are living; by their previous devotion if they are dead.[29] "Be mindful, O Lord, of Thy servants and handmaidens . . . hose faith and devotion are known unto Thee."

c) The Offering of the Priest, Insofar as He Is the Minister of the Church, for a Special Intention

Independently of this general offering of the Mass for the whole world, which the Church makes in her own name as Bride of Christ, *the priest himself*, considered not as a simple individual moved only by his personal devotion, nor as the immediate minister of Christ as at the moment when he pronounces the transubstantiating words of consecration, but *insofar as*

26   See above, p. 123.
27   Thomas a Kempis, *Imitation of Christ*, IV, chap. 5.
28   Session XXII, chap. 6; Denz. 944.
29   "Defunctis, secundum praecedentem eorum devotionem . . . ," writes Cajetan, *De Missae celebratione*.

he is the immediate minister of the Church,[30] mandated by the hierarchical powers in order to confect the liturgy foreseen by them—as such the priest can freely offer the Mass for the good of those for whom he asks or for whom a stipend is given.

That which the Church has drawn in through the intensity of her love from the infinite depths of the Mass, she can attribute to the priest, insofar as he is her minister, leaving him the liberty of applying it for the ends of sanctification according to his intention. This intention constitutes the *special fruit* of the Mass; for it is especially taken up as the Church's responsibility.

It must be unwaveringly maintained (with Pope Pius VI in his condemnation of the Council of Pistoia) that such an offering, when it does not encounter any obstacle, procures for those for whom it is made a special application—a finite application of the infinite power of the Mass.[31]

According to the intention proposed by the priest, this finite application can be made either totally for one person or divided among several.

d) The Offering of Each Priest or of the Faithful for One Particular Intention

1. Finally, the *personal devotion* of the priest and of the faithful—whether they offer or contribute in some aspect to the offering of the Mass, whether they unite themselves by faith or by sacramental Communion—constitutes the third manner of participating in the infinite power of the Mass. These effects, which are drawn in and which constitute the *particular fruits* of the Mass, will also be distributed according to the proposed intentions.

2. Thus, each Mass is offered first of all by the Church, who, according to the intensity of her devotion, prays in general for the whole world; then, by the priest insofar as he is the minister of the Church and to whose responsibility the Church has left the special intention; finally, by the individual persons of the priest and faithful, whose intentions will be

---

30 See above, pp. 98 and 105.

31 Pope Pius VI's Bull *Auctorem fidei*, 28 August 1794, condemns as erroneous the thirtieth proposition of the Council of Pistoia, according to which, "the offering or *special application* of the sacrifice made by the priest at Mass brings no more to those for whom it is intended than for others"; and according to which, "no *special fruit* would come from this special application, made with the approbation or order of the Church, to certain persons or communities." Denz., 1530.

The Bull is referred to at the Council of Trent, session XXIII, *De reformatione*, chap. 1, which begins by recalling that "a divine precept orders all who have the care of souls to know their own flock and *to offer the sacrifice for them*, etc."

It is in conformity with this ordinance of the Council of Trent that the Code of Canon Law prescribes to pastors "to apply the Mass on all Sundays and obligatory Feast Days for the people who have been confided to their care," can. 339, § 1.

particular. This is the case each time the Blood of the Cross showers down upon the world.

9. A Text from the *Provinciales* on the Difference between the Mass and the Cross

1. The Mass is the Church's participation in and presence at the very immolation of the Cross by means of the unbloody sacrifice.

The bloody sacrifice of the Cross is of *infinite* power and is offered for all men.

The entrance of the Church into this sacrifice, her participation in and presence at this sacrifice (in other words, the application to her of this sacrifice) is *finite*. On one hand it is finite intensively; it corresponds to the devotion of the Church at a given moment. On the other hand it is finite extensively; it engages the Church at a given moment. And that is why this participation, this presence of the Church at the sacrifice of the Cross, this entrance of the Church into the sacrifice of the Cross must be reiterated unceasingly.

We insist, however, that the Church enters each time into the sacrifice of the Cross *in praying especially for the whole world contemporary with her*. The opinion which states that she prays only for those who are in communion with her must be dismissed. It is founded upon an unjustified extension of a text of St. Augustine.

2. Therefore, although the doctrine of Port-Royal on the Real Presence and transubstantiation stated in the *Sixteenth Provincial* is precise, we do not agree with the following:

> "And although this sacrifice is a commemoration of that of the Cross, there is however this difference: that the sacrifice of the Mass is offered only for the Church and the faithful who are in her communion, while that of the Cross was offered for the whole world, as stated in Scripture."[32]

The true difference between the Mass and the Cross is that the Mass is a finite participation at the infinite Cross—a finite presence of the whole Church and through her of the whole world contemporary with her. Masses multiply not the Cross, but the finite participation in the one and infinite Cross.

10. Mass in Honor of the Saints

1. Mass is not offered *for* the saints in heaven; for they are in a state of beatitude. The saints are those who offer with us for our good.[33] Mass is celebrated, however, *in their honor*, "in order to honor their memory," says

---

32 This proposition is taken by Pascal from *La théologie familière* of Saint-Cyran, *Cf. L'œuvre de Pascal*, édit. de la Pléiade (Paris, 1936), p. 624.
33 See above, p. 111.

Bossuet, "and to thank God for the glory which He has given them. For, why is it that Jesus Christ is offered, if not that He might merit glory for us? What then can we offer to God in thanksgiving for the saints, if not the same Victim through Whom they have been sanctified?"[34] The Council of Trent states: "Although the Church has the custom of celebrating at times Masses in honor and in memory of the saints, she teaches that the sacrifice is offered not to them but to God alone Who has crowned them."[35]

2. It is through Christ, with Christ and in Christ that thanksgiving is rendered to God for the saints. They are the docile members of Christ, putting up no defense against Him, those who have never said "no" to Him even in the very depths of their unconscious.

Christ's Passion is, in fact, the principle of all sanctity of every martyr: "*In this precious death of Thy just, O Lord,*" declares the Church, "*we offer that sacrifice from which martyrdom receives its every principle.*"[36] The voluntary death of Christians resembles the death of Christ; their martyrdom resembles His sacrifice; what happens to the members resembles what happened to the Head. The early French painted the beheading of St. Denis at the foot of Christ on the Cross. The spirit of Christ is poured out upon the martyrs. St. Stephen did not seek to imitate the last words of Christ; but the love which descended to him from Christ made him discover within himself two of these words. They were the words of pardon.

To offer Mass in honor of the saints is, again, to offer Mass in order to ask to love them more truly, more tenderly; to love more truly and more tenderly the Christ to Whom they have been configured (Rom 8:29), and with Whom they have been crucified (Gal 2:20), and the God of love Who showers down on them a ray of His purity.

11. Mass Stipends

Stipends serve as a witness of the interior gift of the faithful, a sign of their desire to divest themselves of something in order to participate more directly in the Savior's sacrifice of the Cross.

Will one try to rise up with the evil reformers of the Council of Pistoia against the usage of these Mass stipends or fees?[37] But it is in resting on the highest authorities that the Church believes herself to be able to approve a usage permitting "those who give spiritual goods to receive temporal ones."[38] For example, our Lord sent His disciples on their mission without allowing them to take anything along, "for the worker is worth his wages" (Mt 10:10), and St. Paul reminded the Corinthians of the right

---

34 *Explication de quelques difficulés* . . . , chap. 11.

35 Session XXII, chap. 3; Denz. 941.

36 Secret from Thursday of the Third Week of Lent, Stational Church of Cosmas and Damian.

37 Cf. the Bull *Auctorem fidei* of Pope Pius VI, no. 54; Denz. 1554.

38 Pius VI, Bull *Auctorem fidei*, no. 54; Denz. 1554.

of the apostles: "If we have sown for you spiritual goods, is it too much if we reap from you carnal goods?" (1 Cor 9:11 and 13–14). If, as the Church wills, her ministers are truly the laborers of the Gospel, if they live by the altar just enough to be crucified on the altar each day with Christ, then there will be no scandal except for the Pharisees.

12. Abuses

1. If the Mass, which is a perpetuation of the sacrifice of the Cross, calls for a minister and the participation of the faithful, is it surprising that their thoughtlessness, their negligence, even their sacrilege can appear?

The disorders began early on, during the time of St. Paul; and the conclusion which he drew from this was simply that this mystery ought not to be abolished: "Let each one," he said, "prove himself before he eats of this bread and drinks of this cup; for whoever eats and drinks without discerning the Body of the Lord, eats and drinks unto his own condemnation" (1 Cor 11:28–29).

2. The Mass must be celebrated by the priest and assisted by the faithful *worthily*. That is not to say that a mystery so sublime is ever celebrated or assisted by priests and people who are *worthy*. Indeed, how could we even think of such a thing? Before Communion, each of these, both the priest and the faithful, experience the irresistible need to confess their unworthiness: "Let not the partaking of Thy Body, O Lord Jesus Christ, which I, though *unworthy*, presume to receive, turn to my judgment and condemnation . . . " Only the saints could approach it without trembling; and they more than anyone feel themselves overwhelmed by the sight of such love. Others would appear with their ignorance, their distractions, their narrow-mindedness, their coldness. "They come down from Calvary and speak of frivolous things . . . " Ought this divine institution, then, be suppressed on account of these miseries?

Was this the very reason why Luther had to overturn the Mass? No. From the very beginning he had attacked the Mass in its essence, and for more hidden reasons whispered to him by the fallen angels.

CHAPTER 7

Transubstantiation

We shall recall briefly the discourse on the Bread of Life, where the Eucharistic mystery is promised, then the account of its institution, followed by the doctrine of transubstantiation and the Real Presence.

1. The Promise of the Eucharist

a) The Account of St. John Is Centered on the Future Institution at the Last Supper

St. John did not record the direct account of the institution of the Eucharist, which was already found in St. Paul and the Synoptics. The sixth chapter of his Gospel, however, with its discourse on the Bread of Life, has for its primary end the proclamation of the precise moment where Jesus, having then really entered into the bloody sacrifice of His Passion, would render that sacrifice sacramentally present under the appearances of bread and wine, in order that His faithful might be able to participate in it through consumption, as the Jews united themselves through consumption to the sacrifices which they offered to God. The discourse on the Bread of Life becomes fully intelligible to us only when read in the retrospective clarity of the Last Supper account; and it reaches its summit with verses 51–58, where the bloody sacrifice is predicted (Jn 6:51: "The bread which I shall give is My Flesh for the life of the world") as well as the manner in which one ought to participate in it (Jn 6:53: "Unless you eat the Flesh of the Son of Man and drink His Blood you will not have life in you"). This remained mysterious for those who heard Him in the synagogue at Capharnaum. It was not able to be for them but a warning, a first knock at the door of their heart. What was lacking to them, like Abraham before them, was the receiving without reserve of divine revelation in the night of faith, however incomprehensible it appeared to them: "Lord, to whom shall we go? You have the words of everlasting life." (6:68).

b) The Miracles of the "Passover of the Bread of Life" Proclaim the Miracle of the Last Passover

The Evangelist notes that "the Jewish feast of Passover was near" (Jn 6:4), and Jesus, having taken the bread, "gave thanks" (Jn 6:11), before multiplying it. He compels us to compare this "Passover of the

Bread of Life"[1] with the supreme Passover, where Jesus, having taken the bread and "given thanks" *in view of a more hidden miracle*, would give it to His disciples "saying, 'This is My Body given up for you'" (Lk 22:19).

"Jesus said to Phillip: 'Where will we buy bread for these to eat?' He said this to test him, for He Himself knew what He would do" (Jn 6:5–6). It seems that Jesus, fearing that the miracle would escape them, wished to draw the disciples' attention to the necessity of an intervention from the Divine Omnipotence.

The second miracle of Jesus, which took place while they were at sea, equally demonstrated that He possessed omnipotence and that one needs to abandon himself to Christ as one does to God.

The miracles of the Passover of the Bread of Life proclaim from afar the miracle of the last Passover, a bit like the miracle of John the Baptist's conception proclaims in St. Luke the miracle of the conception of Jesus.

c) The Bread of Life Is the God of Love Who Becomes Incarnate, Sacrifices Himself and Invites Us to Participate in His Sacrifice by Faith and Consumption

Jesus, having multiplied the bread, took the occasion to raise the minds of those around Him from the bread given for the life of the body to the bread given for the life of the soul, just as He had led the Samaritan woman a short time before from the desire for water which quenches thirst to that which satisfies the desires of the soul.

The bread from heaven, without which the soul would grow faint and not be able to live—neither now nor in the future—is God, the God Who "is Love" (1 Jn 4:8). We must take possession of Him; we must nourish ourselves on Him by faith and love. This is the first stage.

We must attach ourselves so firmly to Christ that we would even want to acquiesce to all the follies which His love moves Him to undertake in order to save the world.

The first "folly" is the mystery of the Incarnation: "By this hath the charity of God appeared toward us, because God hath sent His only begotten Son into the world, that we may live by Him" (1 Jn 4:9). With Jesus the bread from heaven appeared on the earth: "'Amen, amen I say to you; Moses gave you not bread from heaven, but My Father giveth you the true bread from heaven. For the bread of God is that which cometh down from heaven, and giveth life to the world.' They said therefore unto him: 'Lord, give us always this bread.' And Jesus said to them: 'I am the bread of life; he that cometh to Me shall not hunger, and he that believeth in Me shall never thirst. But I said unto you, that you also have seen Me, and you believeth not. Your fathers did eat manna in the desert, and are dead. This is the bread which cometh down from heaven; that if any man eat of it,

---

1   D. Mollat, S.J., *Évangile de saint Jean*, p. 96.

he may not die. I am the living bread, which came down from heaven. If any man eat of this bread, he shall live for ever'" (Jn 6: 32–36; 49–51). To come to Him, to believe in Him is to eat and to appropriate oneself to the bread of life and to hunger or thirst no longer. This is the second stage.

The second folly of divine love is the mystery of His sacrificial death on the Cross: "In this is charity: not as though we had loved God, but because He hath first loved us, and sent His Son to be a propitiation for our sins" (1 Jn 4:10). "This is He that came by water and blood, Jesus Christ. Not by water only, but by water and blood" (1 Jn 5:6). And here is the same affirmation in the discourse on the bread of life: "I am the living bread which came down from heaven. If any man eat of this bread, he shall live forever; and the bread that I give is My Flesh, for the life of the world" (Jn 6:51–52). We must follow Him even to that point, appropriating ourselves to Love crucified, eating Him, nourishing ourselves with Him through faith and love. But He will offer Himself in sacrifice as a propitiation for our sins. And as one united himself to the ancient sacrifices, *not only through faith and love, but also by identifying oneself with the victim through consumption, in order to become one with it*,[2] so Christ, entering into His redemptive Passion (we see this in the account of the Last Supper), wished to make Himself sacramentally present under the appearances of bread and wine, *in order that we might unite ourselves to Him not only through faith and love, but also through this mysterious consumption*, where each person receives more than, and yet proportionate to, what he himself brings. This is the third stage.[3]

Whence the solemn moments of the discourse on the bread of life, which immediately follow the proclamation of the redemptive sacrifice: "Amen, amen I say unto you: Unless you eat the Flesh of the Son of man and drink His Blood you shall not have life in you.

"He that eateth My Flesh and drinketh My Blood, hath everlasting life; and I will raise him up in the last day.

"For My Flesh is meat indeed and My Blood is drink indeed.

"He that eateth My Flesh and drinketh My Blood abideth in me and I in him.

"As the living Father hath sent Me, and I live by the Father; so he that eateth Me, the same also shall live by Me.

"This is the bread that came down from heaven. Not as your fathers did eat manna and are dead. He that eateth this bread shall live forever.

"These things He said, teaching in the synagogue, in Capharnaum" (Jn 6:53–59).

2   Cf. 1 Cor 10:16–22.
3   "If the eating and drinking in St. John is the eating and drinking of the institution of the Eucharist, then in St. John eating and drinking is through the mouth, since in the visible institution it is of that manner." Bossuet, *Méditations sur l'Évangile*, La Cène, I, 33.

d) Jesus Moves His Disciples Toward a Revelation, the Explanation of Which Would Have Been Premature at That Time

These words, which are illuminated in the perspective of the institution at the Last Supper, remained impenetrable to those who had heard them for the first time. They proclaim a mystery, which would undoubtedly be explained at a later time (that of Jesus' hour and the meaning of His redemptive sacrifice), *which the disciples were not yet ready to bear, but for which Christ already needed to prepare them,* and which they had then been asked to receive implicitly in the darkness of faith on the sole authority of Jesus.

Some murmured: "This saying is hard, and who can hear it?" (Jn 6:60). Others hesitated. Jesus Himself tried to persuade them. They were scandalized when He said that He "came down from heaven" (Jn 6:41). How they wanted to trust in Him! At the Ascension, when they saw Him "ascending up where He was before" (Jn 6:62), they understood that He is the bread from heaven.

They needed to go beyond the appearances, where flesh halted, and enter by faith into the depths of a life where the Spirit of God alone was able to lead our spirit: "It is the spirit that quickeneth; the flesh profiteth nothing. The words that I have spoken to you are spirit and life" (Jn 6:64).[4]

"After this many of His disciples went back and walked no more with Him. Then Jesus said to the twelve, 'Will you also go away?' And Simon Peter answered Him, 'Lord, to whom shall we go? Thou hast the words of eternal life. And we have believed and have known that Thou art the Christ, the Son of God'" (Jn 6:66–69).

e) "The Flesh Profiteth Nothing . . ."

1. The carnal sense, which is distinguished from the spirit of faith, cannot grasp the mystery; it profits nothing; hence the direct signification of Jesus' words. This is developed by St. John Chrysostom: *"The flesh profits nothing.* Did He say this about His own flesh? Please God no! Rather, of those who understand His words carnally. And what does it mean to understand carnally? It is to see nothing but the immediate and to think nothing beyond: this is carnal. Now it is not what one sees which one should judge. What is necessary is to contemplate all mysteries with the inner eye: this is spiritual. If he who does not eat the Flesh of Jesus and does not drink His Blood does not have life in him, how could it be true

---

4   "He asks them to come to Him for the sense of the words, which are spirit, that is, they surpass human understanding; and they are, nevertheless, life, a spiritual thing which is necessarily mysterious." M. J. Lagrange, O.P., *L'Évangile de Jésus-Christ* (Paris, 1928), p. 223.

"Man left to his own strength alone is unable to penetrate the mystery of the heavenly bread (cf. Jn 3:6). Only the Spirit, Who is God (Jn 4:24), can by speaking to man, introduce the sense of spiritual realities." D. Mollat, S.J., *Évangile de saint Jean*, p. 104.

that this Flesh, without which no one has life, profits nothing? You see then that, *The flesh profits nothing* signifies not the Flesh of Jesus, but their carnal manner of listening."[5]

2. The commentaries of St. Cyril of Alexandria and St. Augustine on this passage are more theological than exegetical. They both lead into the mystery of the Incarnation. Hear the following words of St. Cyril: "You are not wrong to deny to the flesh the power of giving life. Taken alone, in fact, it cannot bring life. . . . If, however, you scrutinize the mystery of the Incarnation and that of Him Who dwells in this flesh, you will admit, under pain of offending the divine Spirit, that it is able to give life; although, taken alone, the flesh profits absolutely nothing. . . . Your thoughts which I perceive are foolish. You imagine that, according to me, the body derived from the earth is by its nature life-giving. The flesh is, by its nature, incapable of vivifying; but let no one believe that in Christ it is found alone and isolated. It is in fact joined to the Word, Who, by His nature, is Life."[6]

Twelve years before, the commentary of St. Augustine developed the same thought in the West: "The *flesh profits nothing*, if it is alone. Let the spirit be joined to it, as charity is joined to knowledge, and it profits very much. For if the flesh profited nothing, the Word would not become Flesh in order to dwell among us. If Christ aided man much by becoming incarnate, how could the flesh profit nothing? The Spirit labored for our salvation through the flesh. The flesh was the vase. Consider what it contained, not what it was. . . . *It is the Spirit that gives life, the flesh profits nothing*—but the Flesh which I give to be eaten is not the flesh as they understood it."[7]

3. "The flesh profits nothing . . . " One of the most memorable misinterpretations in the history of exegesis will undoubtedly always be the grasping of these words (which are found in the Gospel of the Word Who became Flesh in order to *come* among us) in such a way that it ends up denying the entire sense given to that very Flesh of Christ, which *remains* among us in the Eucharist.

2. The Institution of the Eucharist

The institution of the Eucharist, to which St. John refers, is recorded in the three Synoptics and St. Paul.

a) The Gospel Texts

The hour of Jesus has come, that of the last Passover: "And He said to them, 'I have greatly desired to eat this Pasch with you before I suffer. For I say to you, that from this time I will not eat it, till it be fulfilled in the

5   *In Joannem*, VI, 63; Sermon 47; PG LIX, 265.
6   *In Joannis Evang.*, VI, 64; PG LXXIII, 601 and 604.
7   *In Joannis Evang.*, VI, 64; tract 27, no. 5.

kingdom of God.' And having taken the chalice, He gave thanks and said, 'Take and divide it among you. For I say to you, that I will not drink of the fruit of the vine, till the kingdom of God come'" (Lk 22:14–18).

Then the decisive moment: "And taking the bread, He gave thanks, and broke and gave to them saying, *'This is My Body, which is given for you. Do this for a commemoration of Me.'* In like manner the chalice also, after He had supped, saying, *'This is the chalice, the New Testament in My Blood, which shall be shed for you'"* (Lk 22:19–20).

St. Mark uses for the blessing of the cup a more direct manner: "And whilst they were eating, Jesus took bread; and blessing, broke and gave them, and said, *'Take ye. This is My Body.'* And having taken the chalice, giving thanks, He gave it to them. And they all drank of it. And He said to them: *'This is My Blood of the New Testament, which shall be shed for many.* Amen I say to you, that I will drink no more of the fruit of the vine, until that day when I shall drink it new in the kingdom of God'" (Mk 14:22–25).

Likewise St. Matthew: "And whilst they were at supper, Jesus took bread and blessed and broke, and gave it to His disciples, and said, *'Take ye and eat. This is My Body.'* And taking the chalice, He gave thanks, and gave to them, saying, *'Drink ye all of this. For this is My Blood of the New Testament, which shall be shed for many unto remission of sins.* And I say to you, I will not drink from henceforth of this fruit of the vine, until that day when I shall drink it with you new in the kingdom of My Father'" (Mt 26:26–29).

b) The Text of St. Paul

St. Paul's account is as follows: "For I have received of the Lord that which also I delivered unto you, that the Lord Jesus, the same night in which He was betrayed, took bread, and giving thanks, broke, and said, *'Take ye and eat. This is My Body, which shall be delivered for you. Do this for the commemoration of Me.'* In like manner also the chalice, after He had supped, saying, *'This chalice is the New Testament in My Blood. Do this, as often as you shall drink, for the commemoration of Me.'* For as often as you shall eat this bread, and drink the chalice, you shall show the death of the Lord, until He come. Therefore whosoever shall eat this bread or drink the chalice of the Lord unworthily shall be guilty of the Body and Blood of the Lord. But let a man prove himself, and so let him eat of that bread and drink of the chalice. For he that eateth and drinketh unworthily, eateth and drinketh judgment to himself, not discerning the Body of the Lord" (1 Cor 11:23–29).

c) Texts from the Liturgical Tradition

"The heart of the Eucharistic action and, through it, of the entire Mass, found in all the liturgies, is the account of the institution which contains the words of consecration. What strikes us most of all here is that the texts of the account never reproduce purely and simply one of the texts from Scripture; and this trait is of a particular clearness in the most ancient texts, which have been transmitted down to us and have been restored thanks to comparative studies. These texts go back to a tradition prior to Scripture. We touch upon here a consequence of the fact that the Eucharist was celebrated long before Paul and the Evangelists had picked up the pen. . . . We clearly have in such texts vestiges of the liturgical life of the first generation."[8]

The same fact helps explain the variations that we are able to find in the scriptural accounts of the institution. They must come from different liturgical practices where these texts had been used. In Luke and Paul the words over the bread and wine are separated by a meal. In Matthew and Mark they are joined—no doubt by the practice of the liturgical milieu.[9]

One can note also that the fundamental liturgical fact will be the point of departure of an evolution which orients itself in three directions: 1) either it will tend to render more perfectly symmetrical the two sides concerning the bread and wine respectively; 2) or it will strive to join the more possible scriptural texts; 3) or it will introduce some clarifications, both concrete—" . . . He took the bread in His sacred and venerable hands, and looking up to heaven, etc.," and theological[10]—The Blood of the New and eternal Covenant, the Mystery of Faith" (Roman Liturgy); "The night when He was delivered, or rather when He delivered Himself up" (Liturgy of St. John Chrysostom); "The night when He delivered Himself up for the life of the world" (Liturgy of St. Basil).[11]

3. The Prophesying of the Church

The Church adds nothing to these words. She accepts them in their fullness. The Christ Who speaks to her from without is the same Christ Who, living in her, moves her to desire and, in a certain sense, foretell His revelations.

If it is true that God so loved the world that He gave the corporal presence of His only Son, then the Church believes that she could love Him enough (if that is not something impossible in itself) in order for Him to leave her that corporal presence of that same only Son.

And if God had need of Christ's corporal presence (at that time subject to suffering) in order to gather men together around His redemptive sacrifice, which was still to be accomplished, the Church believes that (if it is not something impossible in itself) Christ's corporal presence—now glorious as it is—will be no less necessary and no less efficacious for gathering men together around His redemptive sacrifice,

8 J.-A. Jungmann, *Missarum Sollemnia* . . . , t. III, p. 111.
9 *Ibid.*, t. I, pp. 30–32.
10 *Ibid.*, t. III, pp. 11–114.
11 S. Salaville, A. A., *Liturgies orientales, La Messe* (Paris: Bloud et Gay, 1942), 4. II, pp. 18 and 22.

which is now accomplished. Such will it be until He comes again for the second Parousia.

But since Christ, on the day of His Ascension, left us in order to enter into heaven, where He is under His proper and natural appearances, it is clear that He cannot possibly be corporally present to us here below except in a mysterious manner, under appearances which are borrowed and foreign to His own.

The Church, rather than not conceiving these things—things which are foolishness in the eyes of man—foretells them in an obscure manner. When, however, she suddenly opens the Bible to the place where it states that, "Jesus, before the festival day of the Pasch, knowing that His hour was come, that He should pass out of this world to the Father; having loved His own who were in the world, He loved them unto the end" (Jn 13:1), and that, "the Lord Jesus, the same night in which He was betrayed, took bread, and giving thanks, broke and said, 'Take ye and eat. This is My Body, which shall be delivered for you. This do for the commemoration of me'" (1 Cor 11:23–24)—when the Church reads these words, how can she not feel her heart break? How can she not be heard to say quietly, "That is what I had thought; and yet it is more than what I had thought!"

The miracle of the continuation of Christ's corporal presence among us is what our religion calls the Word made Flesh.

4. From Christ's Real or Corporal Presence to Transubstantiation

a) The Knowledge of the Apostles Is More Perfect Than the Initial Knowledge of the Church

When one speaks of the development of dogma, one must distinguish between the revealed deposit in the thought of the Apostles and in that of the early Church.

The Apostles knew the mystery of Christ in an exceptional manner, in the incommunicable prophetic light of revelation (*apocalypsis*). It is in this light that they formed and read the statements transmitted to the faithful of their time. They had penetrated into the entire treasury. They were able to explain, formulate and express on demand that which had been shut up, unformulated and unexpressed.

Such was not the case for the early Church. She received from the Apostles the integral deposit of the Gospel through transmission—oral and written (*paradosis*). However, she did not inherit from the Apostles the infused prophetic light of revelation with which God had endowed them. The apostolic statements are as principles for the Church. They offer an explicit, determined and clear understanding; but whatever be the intensity of her adhesion to these statements, she is incapable of discerning in them all that they still contain implicitly, unformulated and unexpressed. Before her intelligence and faith the hidden riches of these statements become explicit only progressively, and not immediately (as they were for the Apostles). Many historical happenings and much time are needed in order for their virtual elements to be developed. Progress is made not by new *revelations*, but by new *explanations* of the evangelical revelation—a revelation given entirely at once by Christ to the Apostles. We speak not of the progress of "revelation," but of the progress of "dogma." For the directing of this progress the Magisterium, infallibly assisted by the Holy Spirit, suffices.[12]

b) The Initial Motherly Intuition of the Church, from Which All the Eucharistic Dogmas Begin

Those revealed statements, which came forth from the mouth or pen of the Apostles and which are the point of departure for dogmatic development, were, as such, understood by the early Church.

In the case of the Eucharist there is an initial glance from the Church's intelligence and faith which, falling upon the apostolic revelation of the Last Supper, its prophetic proclamation, the account of its institution and the precept of Communion, immediately encounters a truth so profound that it includes in advance (no doubt in an obscure, pre-conceptual and enveloped state) all of this mystery which will be made manifest conceptually throughout time. It in turn excludes in advance all misunderstanding or mutilation which will appear throughout time.

How do we describe this fundamental data, this "mother truth"? We say that it is the immediate, irrepressible certitude of a corporal presence of Christ, Who wills to be among us until the day of the Parousia—now hidden under the appearances of bread and wine in order that we might communicate in His bloody sacrifice of the Cross, as did His disciples at the Last Supper.

c) How This Dogma Develops

The Church keeps in her heart this "mother truth," living and unaltered. With the passing of time questions are posed and her teachers offer their responses. While remaining faithful to her interior certitude, the Church listens to them, sometimes granting her approval, other times discarding them. Finally, a doctrine on the Eucharist is made explicit.

It can happen that in the midst of this consideration a statement appears to the Magisterium to be so necessarily needed by the initial revelation that the latter would collapse if the former were denied. It would then be evident that the initial data truly and really pre-contained this statement, and that this statement can be considered as revealed.

In declaring a teaching as revealed the Church can add, in all truth, that she has always held and believed it; she had always believed, of

---

12 Cf. Our *Esquisse du développement du dogma marial* (Paris: Alsatia, 1954), pp. 40–42.

course, not in an explicit, conceptual and formulated manner, but in a manner implicit, pre-conceptual and pre-formulated. The given teaching had not been introduced from without; it was simply recognized that it had, in fact, always been really and truly included in the initial revelation—somewhat in the manner that the properties of a circle or a triangle are really and truly included in the definition of the circle or triangle before we actually recognize them.

d) In What Sense Has This Dogma Always Been Believed?

The Council of Trent would intend "to apply to the subject of the venerable and divine Sacrament of the Eucharist *the doctrine which the Catholic Church*—she being instructed by Jesus Christ our Lord Himself, and by His Apostles, and taught by the Holy Spirit Who informs her of all truth throughout the ages—*has always held and will keep until the end of time.*"[13]

The same Council would teach that "the Church of God has always believed, *semper haec fides in Ecclesia Dei fuit*, that immediately after the consecration the true Body of our Lord and His true Blood exist under the species of bread and wine, conjointly with His soul and divinity"; it clarifies also that the Body is present under the species of bread and the Blood under the species of wine directly in virtue of the words of consecration; and that the soul is present there in virtue of its natural connection and concomitance with the Body; and that the divinity is present in virtue of the hypostatic union.[14] It is clear that the Church has "always believed" these precise explanations implicitly and not explicitly.

The Council would present the doctrine of transubstantiation as "a constant conviction in the Church, *persuasum semper in Ecclesia Dei fuit*,"[15] although it needed ages in order to explain, conceptualize and formulize it.

The Council's intention was, by these texts, to assert in the course of time the inherent identity of the Church's Eucharistic faith. This faith certainly became more explicit with the passing of years, but in the same line and by a homogenous progress, conforming to the wish of St. Vincent Lérins' first *Commonitorium*,[16] which the [First] Vatican Council would make its own: "That the wisdom, knowledge and understanding of each and every one, from the individual to the entire Church, in every age, increase and progress greatly and intensely; but that they increase exclusively according to their genus, that is to say within the dogma itself, within the same sense, within the same thought, *in eodem scilicet dogmate, eodem sensu, eademque sententia.*"

13   Session XIII, 11 October 1551, prologue, Denz. 873.
14   *Ibid.*, chap. 3, Denz. 876.
15   *Ibid.*, chap. 4; Denz. 877.
16   Chap. 23.

5. The First Five Centuries of the Church

It is in the course of homogenous doctrinal development that the Church, progressively discerning what the words, "This is My Body, This is My Blood" required (words repeated at every consecration)—it is in the course of this development that the Church would proclaim that these words presuppose, under pain of losing their revealed sense, the conversion of bread and wine into the Body and Blood, and that it passes from the expressly revealed notion of a real or corporal presence of Christ to the implicitly and mediately revealed notion of transubstantiation.

The stages of this development can be followed during the first five centuries of the Church, for example, in Pierre Batiffol's book,[17] which presents and carefully analyzes Eucharistic citations by putting them in their proper context. One easily sees here the necessity which obliges the Church to deepen always the notion of the conversion of bread and wine into Christ's Body and Blood, in order to preserve the truth about the Real Presence.

a) Ignatius of Antioch, Justin, Irenaeus, Gregory of Nyssa

St. Ignatius of Antioch († c. 110) denounces to the citizens of Smyrna those who have gone astray, the Docetists, who "abstain from the Eucharist and prayer because they do not hold that the *Eucharist is the Flesh of our Lord Jesus Christ, the Flesh which suffered for our sins, the Flesh which the Father in His goodness has resurrected*. They, then, who speak against the gift of God (the Incarnation) die in their contentiousness. It would be better for them to have love, so as to share in the resurrection."[18]

The Real Presence, and at the same time the power of the words of consecration, are affirmed with force by St. Justin († c. 155): "This element is called by us the Eucharist. . . . We do not hold these things as common bread and drink. Incarnate by the Word of God, Jesus Christ our Savior took on flesh and blood for our salvation; *indeed, blessed by the prayer of His word, the food* by which our flesh and blood is nourished in view of a transformation, *is the Flesh and Blood of this same incarnate Jesus*, according to the teaching which we received. For the Apostles, in their recollections which are called the Gospels, teach us what had been thus prescribed for them: Jesus, having taken bread, gave thanks saying, *Do this in memory of Me, this is my Body*. And likewise having taken the cup, He gave thanks saying, *This is My Blood*."[19]

---

17 *L'Eucharistie, La présence réelle et la transubstantiation*, edition 5 refondue et corrigé, (Paris: Gabalda, 1913).
18 St. Ignatius of Antioch, *Epistle to the Smyrnians*, chap. 7, no. 1.
19 St. Justin Martyr, *First Apology*, chap. 66, nos. 1 to 3.
      Having analyzed the texts on the Eucharist before 150 A.D., Batiffol formulates ten conclusions, the last of which are: "8) . . . Although the word 'sacrifice'

The doctrine of St. Irenaeus († c. 200) is equal to that of St. Justin. The bread and wine, he says, "receiving the word of God, become (γίνεται, *fiunt*) the Eucharist, that is the Body and Blood of Christ."[20] We have here, notes Battifol,[21] "a formula of the presence, and at the same time a formula of the conversion."

In his *Catechetical Discourse* (c. 383), St. Gregory of Nyssa asks—and this in fact is the real problem—how the Body of Christ, while remaining one, can give the fullness of life to those who possess faith, shared by all without being divided. Thinking about the transformation of the bread he concludes: "We now then have reason to believe that the bread, sanctified by the word of God, is transformed, μεταποιεῖσθαι, *transformari*, into the Body of God the Word."[22] This is exactly correct. And yet this notion of transformation should be clarified more. Is Gregory already proclaiming the Catholic doctrine of "transubstantiation"? No. He ventures off on a wrong path. He is thinking of a "substantial transformation" of bread into the Body of Christ, as if the bread, at the moment of consecration, were assimilated by Christ.

b) Ambrose

The texts of St. Ambrose on the truth of the Real Presence and the prerequisite necessity of the conversion of the bread and wine are well known.

1. We read in his *De sacramentis* (recently restored)[23] the following: "You say perhaps, 'This is not ordinary! Before the sacramental words this bread is bread; and as soon as the consecration takes place the bread

---

is not pronounced, the idea of sacrifice takes precedence over that of covenant; for the wine is not used for aspersion, as it would seem normal if the blood is the blood of a covenant; but the wine is drunk. 'Drink,' and they all drank of it. And again, the bread is broken in order to be eaten; for in a sacrifice the victim, after having been offered to God, is food for the faithful who participate in the sacrifice; 9) The Eucharist, insofar as it is a supernatural gift, is, under the species of bread and wine, the Body of the crucified Christ, His Blood poured out on the Cross for us. The effect of the Eucharist in us is a communion with this Body and Blood. It is a principle of supernatural life; it is a pledge of immortality; 10) Finally, the Eucharist is a symbol of the union of the faithful. This symbolism was brought to light by St. Paul, by the *Didache*, by St. Ignatius. This symbolism, however, is accessory and a background, so to speak, especially if we consider that the Eucharist is not properly a meal but an image of a meal, and that this meal is not that of the 'brothers' of a same Church, but the *meal of the Lord.*" *Op. cit.*, pp. 160–161. This is an occasion to underline: a) that Christ wishes more than the Church that she gather around Him; b) that the union of communion in Christ surpasses all communitarian unions.

20 *Contra haereses*, V, chap. 2; PG VII, 1127; cf. 1125.
21 *Op. cit.*, p. 181.
22 *Catechetical Discourse*, chap. 37; PG XLV, 96. The text of Méridier, followed by Battiffol, *op. cit.*, pp. 401–402, is better than that of Migne.
23 Dom Bernard Botte, O.S.B., *Ambroise de Milan, De sacraments, Des mystères*, "Sources chrétiennes " See my response sent yesterday from the other chapters where this is cited: it is a collection. (Paris, 1949), *Introduction*.

becomes, *fit*, Christ's flesh. Prove it then. How is this bread able to be the Body of Christ? By what words does the consecration happen, and from whom are these words?' From the Lord Jesus. In fact, all that is said before is from the priest. Praises are offered to God; prayers are said for the people, for kings, for all others. As soon as the Blessed Sacrament is to be confected, *ut conficiatur*, the priest no longer uses his own words but the words of Christ. It is, therefore, the word of Christ which confects this sacrament. 'Which word of Christ?' Ah! That by which all things happen. . . . If, then, there is in the word of the Lord Jesus so great a force that that which was not begins to be, how more efficacious is it in making things which exist change into other things, *et in aliud commutentur*. . . . I tell you that, before the consecration it was not the Body of Christ; but after the consecration it is henceforth the Body of Christ. . . . You know then that, from bread is made the Body of Christ; and that the wine is poured with water into the chalice, but that it becomes Blood through the consecration of the heavenly word. But you say perhaps, 'I do not see the appearance, *speciem*, of blood!' There is there the symbol, *similitudinem*. Just as you take hold of the symbol of death, so you drink the symbol of blood, in order that no one who drinks would be moved by the blood which flows, *nullus horror cruoris*, and nevertheless the price of redemption is carried out. Know then that what you receive is the Body of Christ.[24]

2. The passages from *De mysteriis* are similar. Ambrose cites the miracles of Moses and Elijah, adding: "If the blessing of a man had a great enough power to change the nature, *ut naturam converteret*, what do we say of the divine consecration, where the very words of our Lord and Savior act? For this sacrament which we receive is produced by the word of Christ. If the word of Elijah had such power that it brought down fire from heaven, would not Christ's word have the power to change the nature of elements, *ut species mutet elementorum?* . . . Is not Christ's word, which is able to bring forth from nothing that which did not exist, is it not able to change, *mutare*, the things that are into that which they are not? It is no less difficult to give to things their first natures than to change natures, *mutare naturas*. . . . The Virgin gave birth outside the order of nature; and that which we bring forth, *conficimus*, is the Body born from the Virgin. Why search here in the Body of Christ for the order of nature. It is the true Flesh of Christ, which had been crucified, which had been buried; this then is truly the sacrament of His Flesh. The Lord Jesus proclaims it: *This is My Body!* Before the blessing by the heavenly words, another nature, *species*, is designated; after the consecration it is the Body which is signified. He said Himself that it is His Blood. Before the consecration it is called otherwise; after the consecration it is called Blood. And you say: *Amen*, that is, *It is true!* What the mouth pronounces the inner

24   St. Ambrose, *De sacramentis*, chap. 4, nos. 13 to 20.

spirit confesses; what the word expresses our hearts know."[25] There is that which one sees and that which one believes. That which one believes "is not what the nature forms, but what the blessing has consecrated; and the power of the blessing is greater than that of the nature, since the blessing changes the nature itself."[26] That which one believes is the Body of Christ. And this Body born of the Virgin, crucified and buried, St. Ambrose calls a spiritual body, because it does not fall under the senses, because it is food for the soul, because it is the Body of a God: "It is not a corporal food but spiritual. The Apostle also (1 Cor 10:3) said this regarding its type: 'Your fathers ate a spiritual food, they drank a spiritual drink.' For the Body of God is a spiritual body. The Body of Christ is the Body of the divine Spirit, for Christ is the Spirit."[27]

Thus, according to St. Ambrose, it is impossible to believe the evangelical revelation of the Real Presence without believing the miraculous conversion of bread and wine into the Body and Blood of Christ. These two notions are so directly united that to reject one is to reject the other. Whoever denies the Real Presence denies the conversion; whoever denies the conversion denies the Real Presence. What can we say but, if the first (Real Presence) is explicitly revealed in the Gospel, the second (the miraculous conversion) is found there also revealed, implicitly, but really and truly.

c) The Thought of St. Augustine

No sacramental heresy moved St. Augustine to treat the Eucharist directly. He speaks of it only incidentally.

1. St. Augustine believed in the Real Presence as much as his teacher Ambrose with whom he associated.[28] The bread which the baptized see on the altar, "once sanctified by the word of God, is the Body of Christ. The chalice, or better, that which the chalice contains, is the Blood of Christ."[29] There is no doubt regarding the truth of the corporal presence. Christ "took the flesh of Mary. It is in the flesh that He walked among us. It is the same Flesh which He gave to us to eat for our salvation; and no one eats it if he does not adore it beforehand."[30] An impossible thing for any man, "Christ bears Himself in His own hands, and speaking of His own Body declares: This is My Body."[31] The consecration of the bread

25   St. Ambrose, *De mysteriis*, chap. 9, nos. 52 and 54.
26   *Ibid.*, no. 50.
27   *Ibid.*, no. 58.
28   In this question of the Eucharist, however, St. Augustine seems closer to Cyprian and Tertullian than to Ambrose, whose *De sacramentis and De mysteriis* Augustine did not know. Cf. Batiffol, *L'Eucharistie . . .* , p. 453.
29   St. Augustine *Sermo CCXXVII.*
30   St. Augustine *Enarr. in Psalm. XCVIII*, no. 9.
31   St. Augustine *Enarr. in Psalm. XXXIII*, sermon I, no. 10. Not that there were two *bodies*, but two *presences* of His Body: one which has weight, the other which does not.

requires a miracle: man can prepare only bread and wine, but "in order for it to be sanctified in view of so great a mystery, the Spirit of God must work invisibly."[32] Those who worthily receive the Body and Blood poured out for the remission of sins become themselves the (Mystical) Body of Christ;[33] and one must be a part of this (Mystical) Body in order to understand the (Eucharistic) Body of Christ.[34] The Body of Christ is not given to us to be eaten in a carnal manner, like the flesh we see at the market,[35] but in a spiritual manner. What nourishes us is not what we see, but what we believe.[36] Baptized infants receive it.[37] Sinners, unworthy as they are, eat the Flesh and drink the Blood.[38]

2. At the same time, since the sign bears the name of what is signified, Augustine could write that the bread and the wine, by reason of their likeness to the Body and Blood, can be called the Body and Blood of Christ.[39] Thus the Eucharist is at the same time reality and figure.

The dynamism of the Augustinian thought passes without transition from the sign to the signified and from the cause to the effect: from the bread to the Eucharistic Body and from the Eucharistic Body to the Mystical Body. We will fall into serious errors if we forget this.

One initial error is that which Pascal pointed out. The argument states that the sacrament is a *figure* of Christ, and from there denies that it is the *presence* of Christ. "There is, then, a great number of truths, regarding both faith and morals, which seem repugnant, and which subsist completely in an admirable order. . . . The source of all heresies is the exclusion of some of these truths; and the source of all objections which would make us heretics is the ignorance of one of our truths. And ordinarily it happens that, in not being able to conceive the relation between the two opposed truths, and believing that confessing in one of them includes the exclusion of the other, they cling to one and exclude the other and think that we do the opposite. Hence the exclusion is the cause of their heresy; and their ignorance that we hold the other is the cause of their objections . . . The second example regards the subject of the Blessed Sacrament: We believe that the substance of the bread is changed, transubstantiated, into that of the Body of our Lord Jesus Christ and is really present. This is the first of the truths. The other is that this Sacrament is also a figure of [Christ's] Cross and glory, and a commemoration of both. The Catholic Faith understands both these truths which seem opposed. The heresy today, not grasping that

32 St. Augustine *De Trinitate*, III, chap. 4, no. 10.
33 St. Augustine *Sermo CCXXVII*.
34 St. Augustine *Sermo CCLXXII; In Joan., tract XXVI*, no. 13.
35 St. Augustine *In Joan., tract. XXVII*, no. 5.
36 St. Augustine *Sermo CXII*, chap. 5, no. 5.
37 St. Augustine *Sermo CLXXIV*, chap. 6, no. 7.
38 St. Augustine *Sermo LXXI*, chap. 11, no. 17.
39 St. Augustine *Epist., XCVIII*, no. 9.

this Sacrament contains at the same time both the presence of Jesus Christ and His figure, believes that one cannot admit one of these truths without excluding the other. They cling to this point alone: that this Sacrament is figurative—in this they are not heretics. They think that we exclude this truth; and that is why they offer so many objections regarding the passages of the Fathers who say as much. Finally, they deny the presence— and in this they are heretics."[40] Apropos of Zwingli, whom he does not name, Cajetan wrote that, "he boasts of the sign in order to deny that Christ's Flesh is contained in this sacrament. As if there were not present both, the sign and the signified . . . ; he uses one partial truth in order to exclude another, *ex veritate non integra, excludit aliam veritatem.*"[41]

A second error was pointed out by de Lubac. This argument states that the sacrament contains the *Mystical and ecclesial* Body of Christ, and from there denies that it contains His *real and sacramental* Body. The ecclesial Body, however, is precisely the effect of the sacramental Body. In St. Augustine the affirmation of the existence of the effect is, if not the only, at least the better proof of the existence of the cause. "Eucharistic realism, ecclesial realism: these two realisms stand one upon the other. Each is the pledge of the other. The ecclesial realism assures the Eucharistic realism, and this latter in turn confirms the former. . . . For Augustine the Eucharist is much more than a symbol, since in all truth it is that sacrament *quo in hoc tempore consociatur Ecclesia;*[42] and this is due to the fact that the water and wine of the sacrifice, as the water and blood which flowed from the Cross, are themselves the sacraments *quibus aedificatur Ecclesia.*[43] One cannot emphasize too much this line of reciprocal causality and guarantee between the two mysteries of the Church and the Eucharist, not only for the understanding of the dogma itself but also for that of the Christian past."[44] It is necessary to understand how and why the expression *corpus mysticum*, which very early on meant the real and sacramental Body of Christ, ended up signifying its effect, namely the ecclesial Body.[45] More precisely, it serves as a key to numerous passages of Augustine, for example to "his teaching on the Communion of the unworthy. These come forward and receive the sacrament. And what does the Lord do? *Non admittit ad corpus suum.*[46] Which ought to be

---

40 Pascal, *Pensées*, edit. Brunsvicg, no. 862. We made corrections according to the text of Zacharie Tourneur, no. 420.

41 Cajetan, *De erroribus contingentibus in Eucharistiae sacramento*, chap. 5.

42 "By which the Church is gathered together here below," St. Augustine, *Contra Faustum*, XII, chap. 20.

43 "By which the Church is built up," St. Augustine *De civitate Dei*, XXII, chap. 17.

44 Henri De Lubac, S.J., *Corpus mysticum, L'Eucharistie et l'Église au moyen âge*, (Paris, Aubier, 1944) pp. 288–290.

45 *Ibid.*, p. 294.

46 St. Augustine *Enarr, in Psalm.* LXVIII, *Sermo* 2, no. 6.

translated: *He does not incorporate them into His Body.* This is the usual perspective of St. Augustine, who always sees the ecclesial Body in the prolongation of the Eucharist."[47] The misinterpretation, which arose from some of these texts, is cleared up.

d) Cyril of Alexandria

In the East, St. Cyril, commenting on Matt. 26:27, wrote: "The Lord says, 'This is My Body,' and 'This is My Blood,' in order that you do not imagine that that which appears is a figure, τύπον, but that you understand well that, by the ineffable power of the omnipotent God, the offerings are truly changed, μεταποιεῖσθαι, *transformari*, into the Body and Blood of Christ; and we, participating in this, receive Christ's vivifying and sanctifying power."[48]

If the Body and Blood of Christ *vivify*, they are the Body and Blood of the *Word*.

Nestorius divides Christ; and as he asked whether Mary gave birth to flesh or to divinity, so he asks also whether we eat in the Eucharist Flesh or divinity. Why, he continues, did Jesus say, "This is My Body," and not, "This is My divinity broken for you"? Nestorius is easily recognizable as one who always and everywhere wishes to divide the hypostatic union.

Cyril's response is that we receive in the Eucharist not the simple flesh of a man, which could not be life-giving, but the *very Flesh—truly vivifying—of the Word.* The reality of the Eucharistic Body, says Batiffol, "is not the matter of discussion between Nestorius and Cyril, between Antiochians and Alexandrians, but only the divine power of this Body; in other words, the union of the divinity and the flesh."[49]

This recalling of a few testimonies which span from the earliest days until the Council of Ephesus is not meant to exhaust the Fathers' treasury regarding the Eucharist, but only to point out a first stage, where the Church everywhere realizes that the truth of her faith in the *Real Presence* implies a *miraculous conversion* of the bread and wine.

6. From the Patristic Period to the Lateran Council

a) The Work of Theologians and the Role of the Magisterium

When the Church recognized the fact that the Real Presence—which she always believed explicitly and conceptually—has as a necessary prerequisite, under pain of collapsing, a miraculous conversion of the bread and wine (and without any example), at that point she was able to define that this conversion, which she calls transubstantiation, was really pre-contained

---

47 De Lubac, *op. cit.*, p. 296.
48 St. Cyril of Alexandria, *Comm. in Mat., XXVI*, 27; PG LXXII, 452.
49 Batiffol, *L'Eucharistie . . .*, pp. 472–476.

in the primitive evangelical revelation; and she was then able to declare, in all truth, that she has always believed it implicitly and pre-conceptually.[50]

Eight centuries more would be needed after the patristic period in order for this recognition to result in the definition of transubstantiation—in 1215 at the Fourth Lateran Council.

During all this time the central and unfathomable mystery of the Real Presence—which was always believed in—would raise pressing questions, questions which in turn would bring forth responses. A huge task of doctrinal elaboration would follow. What the teachers and theologians bring forth will no doubt always be listened to, but the results of their own theological work will never be decisive.

The one power capable of judging in these matters—the power to discard the erroneous and to sanction what is authentic—is the magisterial power assisted by the Holy Spirit. It is the Magisterium, which, having examined and weighed all, will pronounce the solemn definition.

b) Three Principal Points with Which the Theological Elaboration Was Concerned

The preoccupations of these centuries of theological elaboration can be confined to three principal points:[51]

---

50 If one were to begin with the presupposition that *the Real Presence is metaphysically possible without transubstantiation*, and that consequently the notion of transubstantiation is not necessarily and *really included* in that of the Real Presence, but rather that it is *juxtaposed* to it, one would, we think, be led to an impasse. In order to remain Catholic one would have to maintain that transubstantiation needed from the beginning to be revealed explicitly and that it is "explicitly in every ecclesiastical tradition going back to Jesus and the Last Supper." Hence, 1) this view seems to us unsupportable from the point of view of the historian. In addition, 2) the theological presupposition which it requires, namely that the Real Presence is metaphysically possible without transubstantiation, is directly contrary to the teaching of St. Thomas, *Summa Theologiae* III, qu. 75, a. 2: "Et ideo relinquitur quod non possit aliter corpus Christi incipere esse de novo in hoc sacramento nisi per conversionem substantiae panis in ipsum" (see also a. 3). For these two reasons, one historical, the other theological, we cannot adopt the position of the "Roman theologian" referred to by Batiffol, *L'Eucharistie* . . . , pp. 500–508. The compromise, around which Batiffol rallied, seems to us unacceptable. He grants that the notion of transubstantiation is *explicit* from the beginning, but only in a *confused* state. To our eyes this seems to say that it is at the same time and under the same aspect explicit and implicit, conceptual and non-conceptual. We add that at the publication of P. Marin-Sola's book *L'évolution homogène du dogme catholique*, in 1924, Batiffol would express to the work's author the gratitude of the historians, "who during these past twenty years have had so much difficulty in verifying the formal implicitness of one or another dogma."

51 See the entry "Eucharistie" in the *Dictionnaire de Théologie Catholique*: F. Vernet, "Eucharistie du IX à la fin du XI siècle; J. De Ghellinck, *Eucharistie au XII siècle en Occident.*

1) One must clarify in the Eucharist that which is to be *believed* by faith and that which is *seen* by the sense. That which is *believed by faith* is the Body born of the Virgin Mary. If it is found, however, in a manner which is not evident to the sense, one would say that it is present in its proper substance, but not according to its proper mode. That which is *seen by the sense* is the appearance of bread, which signifies the Body, and the appearance of wine, which signifies the Blood. These are called the form or figure, natural qualities, accidental qualities, properties, and especially species or accidents, indeed accidents without their subject.[52] It was not in order to create a philosophical work and out of concern for agreement, but rather in order to safeguard the data of revelation and by proceeding in the light of faith that theologians would say that that which is believed is the *substance* of the Body of Christ and that which is seen is the *species* of bread. Finally, some distinctions would be made: that which is seen is the species of bread, that which is believed is the Eucharistic Body of Christ; the result of this is the Mystical or ecclesial Body.[53] In other words, that which is only the *sign* (the species), that which is the *reality and the sign* (the Eucharistic Body), and that which is only the *reality* (the Mystical Body).

2) We ought to clarify *the notion of change or conversion* of the bread and wine into the Body and Blood of Christ. We are not dealing with a simply superficial or accidental transformation. This much is evident; nor that type of substantial transformation as when the bread is assimilated by a living being (it is this type of change, one will recall, of which Gregory of Nyssa thought); nor a miraculous substantial transformation, as happened at Cana, where the wine did not preexist before the water, but drew its substance from it. It is necessary to arrive at something more secret, at a conversion which, with the species or accidents of the bread and wine remaining unchanged, brings about the passing from the substance of the bread to the substance of the Body of Christ, and which would come to be called transubstantiation ever since the first half of the 12th century.[54] Only then will be preserved the truth of the words of Jesus, Who taking the bread said, "This is My Body." Here again the process of clarification happens first from on high and in the light of evangelical faith with the only concern being the respecting of the transcendence; it does not begin, on the contrary, from below and for the purpose of reducing it to philosophy.

52   *Loc. cit.*, col. 1268.
53   Pope Innocent III underlines three aspects of the sacrament: "the visible form, the truth of the Body and the spiritual power. The *form* is the bread and wine; the *truth* is the Flesh and Blood; the *power* is the unity and charity. The first is the sacrament and not the reality; the second is the sacrament and the reality; the third is the reality and not the sacrament." *Epist.*, November 29, 1220, Denz. 415.
54   *Dictionnaire de Théologie Catholique, Loc. cit.*, col. 1289.

3) However, in lieu of speaking of such a mysterious change of bread and wine into the Body and Blood of Christ, would it not be simpler to suppose instead that the entire change happens on the side of Christ? We would then say that the bread and wine remain unchanged, but that the Body and Blood of Christ now descend from heaven into them. Berengarius, in the 11th century, was condemned for excluding the Real Presence. His disciples received it, but they were thinking of what would be called *impanation*, an *invination*. Is this explanation easier? In reality, it is disastrous.[55] It destroys the truth of Christ's words. He said, "*This* is My Body." He did not say, "*In this* is My Body, *In this* is My Blood." It also proposes for our adoration not *one* sole subsisting thing, but *two*: the bread and the Body of Christ. Finally, it renders the Real Presence contradictory, impossible, absurd. To seek a change in Christ and not in the bread is to replace the purely substantial sacramental presence with a local presence; it is to give to Christ as many bodies as there are places where He becomes present, and even contracts each of these human bodies to the dimensions of a small host.[56] Every attempt to maintain the Real Presence without transubstantiation is already doomed to failure.[57] In saying, on the contrary, that the *substance* of the bread changes into the *substance* of Christ's Body, which preexists and

---

55 This explanation of the real presence, which would later be taken up again by the Lutherans and Anglicans (Pusey, Gore, etc.) claims an association with a passage from St. Irenaeus, *Adversus haereses*, IV, chap. 18, no. 5: "The bread which is [produced] from the earth receives the invocation of God, and from then on is no longer ordinary bread, but the Eucharist composed of two things, one earthly the other heavenly." One of these two things would be bread, the other the Body of Christ. This is the Eucharistic theory of the two natures, of *diphysism*, or *consubstantiation*. This interpretation of Irenaeus, however, does not correspond to the text. He is combating here a Marcionite error, according to which there is no resurrection of bodies. If there is no resurrection of bodies, then one abstains from the Eucharist; for the Eucharist prepares our bodies for the resurrection: "When our bodies," continues Irenaeus, "receive the Eucharist, they are no longer corruptible; they have the hope of the resurrection." The reason is that the Eucharist does not contain dead flesh, but the living Flesh of the Lord. Here then are the two natures, one earthly, the other heavenly, Flesh and Divinity. Cf. Batiffol, *L'Eucharistie . . .* , pp. 173–179.

56 Cf. St. Thomas, *Summa Theologiae* III, qu. 75, a. 2.

57 Proposition 29 of the Synod of Pistoia, which wanted to *restrict the preaching of the Eucharist to two points* [1st Christ, after the consecration, is truly, really, and substantially under the species; 2nd, the entire substance of the bread and wine ceases, and only the species remain] *without mentioning transubstantiation*, was declared "pernicious" by the fact that it dismissed (by looking at them as purely scholastic) "both an *article* touching the faith and an *expression* consecrated by the Church in order to assure the profession against heresies." Pius VI, Bull *Auctorem fidei*, 28 August 1794; Denz. 1529.

remains unchanged now in heaven under its proper appearances—in saying this, one affirms a presence directly and purely *substantial* under the appearances of bread, and not a *local* presence. Each part of the appearances brings to us the substance of Christ's Body, and not some corresponding part of His Body. It is clear that to divide the appearances is not to divide the Body of Christ, but to multiply its presences. At the moment when Jesus said for the first time, "This is My Body," there were two substantial presences of His one preexisting unchanged Body: the first natural, durable, under its proper appearances, and therefore local; the other derived, sacramental, temporary, under borrowed appearances, and therefore not local—let us say by mode of pure substance.

7. Transubstantiation Defined by the Council of the Lateran and by the Council of Trent

1. It was in 1215, at the Fourth Lateran Council, that the word "transubstantiate," used for three-fourths of a century, appeared for the first time in a solemn profession of faith: "The universal Church of the faithful is one, outside of which no one is saved; and in which the very same One Who is the Priest is also the sacrifice, Jesus Christ, *Whose Body and Blood are truly contained in the sacrament of the altar under the species of bread and wine: the bread having been transubstantiated into the Body, the wine into the Blood by the divine power*; in order that, by consuming the mystery of unity, we may have a share in Him, since He has had a share in us."[58]

2. On October 11, 1551, when the Council of Trent defined transubstantiation again, it took care, as we have seen, to declare that that has always been the sentiment of the Church; and the reason it gave is that the Real Presence has always been believed. Does believing (explicitly) in the Real Presence already imply (implicit) belief in transubstantiation? Yes, if one holds with the Council that the Real Presence is realized only by transubstantiation. Here is the text of the fourth chapter, session XIII: "*And because Christ our Redeemer said that that which He offered under the species of bread was truly His Body; for this reason it has always been held in the Church*, and the holy Council declares it once again that, by the consecration of the bread and wine is produced *a conversion of the entire substance of the bread into the substance of His Blood*. This conversion has rightly and truly been called by the Holy Catholic Church *transubstantiation*."[59] The second canon explains that it is a conversion absolutely without example, that the substance of the bread and that of the wine do not remain, that only the species of the bread and wine remain: "If anyone says that, in the most Holy Sacrament of the Eucharist, *there remains the substance of the bread and wine* with the Body and Blood of our Lord Jesus

---

58 Caput *Firmiter;* Denz. 428.
59 Denz. 877.

Christ, and denies *this marvelous and unique conversion* of the entire substance of bread into the Body, and the entire substance of wine into Blood, *not allowing anything to subsist but the species of bread and wine*, a conversion which the Catholic Church calls by the most appropriate name 'transubstantiation', let him be anathema."[60]

8. The Technical Formulation of the Dogma

a) The Dogma of Transubstantiation, Like the Christological and Trinitarian Dogmas, Produces from the Faith a Technical Formulation without, However, Enslaving It to Any One System

We see here how the Church's Magisterium proceeds. It does not seek to give precedence to any one system of philosophy, but, on the contrary, to block the road to each enterprise of rationalization, so subtle as it might be. It seeks also to maintain with all its integrity, with all its profundity, let us say with all its scandal, the unimaginable sense of these simple evangelical words, "Take, this is My Body."

Concerned with dissipating deviations and storming them in their strongholds, the Church's Magisterium does not hesitate to produce from true belief a technical formulation,[61] alone capable of excluding ambiguity. It continues to act spontaneously, as did the Fathers of the first centuries who, in order to preserve the transcendence of the revealed deposit against the attempts of rationalization and syncretism, and in order to define the

---

60 Denz. 884.
61 It would take six provincial councils held under four different popes, between 1050 and 1079, in order to put an end to the equivocations of Berengarius. See the note in Denz. 355. It is true that the first profession of faith proposed lacked precision, which stipulated that the Body of Christ "is truly touched and broken by the hands of the priests and ground by the teeth of the faithful." St. Thomas, *Summa Theologiae* III, qu. 77, a. 7, ad 3, will later add that "that which is broken and ground is the sacramental species, under which is truly the Body of Christ." In the *Lauda Sion we sing: He who takes It does not split It, nor break or divide It; whole and entire It is received. Each one takes It, thousands take It; the same for each. It is taken but not consumed.* Cajetan, *De erroribus contingentibus in Eucharistiae sacramento* (1525), chap. 3, notes that the sense of the condemnation was simply that "the Flesh of Christ is eaten not only in sign, but in the sacrament of the Eucharist which contains it." And Bossuet, *Histoire des variations*, XV, no. 130, writes: "There was no one who did not understand that the Body and Blood of Jesus Christ was broken in the Eucharist in the same sense that one says that one is torn, or one becomes wet, when it is actually the clothes which he wears"; and he cites Berengarius' adversary, Guitmund d'Aversa (c. 1075), saying, "that the Body of Jesus Christ was totally in the entire sacrament, and totally in each particle; everywhere the same Jesus Christ, inviolable and indivisible, Who communicated Himself without dividing Himself, as the word to a hearer, and as our soul to all our members."

great Trinitarian and Christological dogmas, needed to clarify in a technical manner the notions of paternity and filiation, of generation and procession, of subsistent relation and consubstantiality, of person and nature. They made use of conceptual elaborations, which they found fitting for their explanations, critiquing these concepts beforehand in the light of faith and separating them from all that does not immediately apply to their project. They would mold them as needed for the service of the Faith. These concepts manifested the Faith; they in no way enslaved it.[62]

b) The Reality Which It Defines Is Known Both on the Level of the Spontaneous Knowledge of the Believer and on the Level of the Elaborated Knowledge of the Theologian

The dogmas of which we speak, among which must be placed transubstantiation, while remaining identical in their essential signification, in their universal value of truth, can be understood at two levels of our intellectual knowledge: the level of spontaneous knowledge and common sense; and the level of analyzed and elaborated knowledge.[63]

At these two moments there is the same reality which is grasped, the same unfathomable revelation to which the spirit of the believer adheres, according to the measure of the intensity of his own faith. At the first moment my knowledge, partly implicit, circumscribes more largely the zone of mystery. I must respond instinctively to any questions which it might raise. At the second moment my knowledge, explicit, circumscribes strictly the zone of mystery, and allows me to respond conceptually to the questions raised.

It is true, then, that the dogma begins by being expressed in formulas from the common sense. The dogma uses the signification which

---

62 St. Thomas, *Summa Theologiae* says of sacred doctrine, "that it receives its principles immediately from God through revelation, and that, by this fact, it does not depend on other sciences as an inferior depends on a superior; but that it uses them as inferiors and helpers. . . . Certainly not in order to fill in a lacking or insufficiency which it carries with it; but in view of the weakness of our intelligence, which is led more easily into the domain of things which surpass our natural reason by way of those things known to reason." St. Thomas, *Summa Theologiae I*, qu. 1, a. 5, ad 2. If the revelation is divine, and divinely assisted, its entrance into different cultural milieus will no doubt provoke different problems, but without affecting the quality of the responses given.

63 Cf. Ambroise Gardeil, *Le donné révélé et la théologie* (Paris: Gabalda, 1910), p. 110. It is by building on this distinction—fundamental, in his opinion—between the natural intelligence with its own native power and the intelligence perfected by the intellectual virtues, namely by those acquired qualities or energies which are special to the genius, artist, philosopher, etc., that Jacques Maritain propagates today the idea of a "liberal education for all." See his work *Sur quelques aspects typiques de l'éducation chrétienne*, in *Nova et Vetera*, 1956, no. 1, pp. 1–24.

these formulas immediately carry. It suffices, therefore, to enlighten the knowledge of the faithful and to open for them the great doors of love. It is not true, however, to say that it cannot reach a greater precision. To the extent that error refines dogma, dogma pursues error into its den. It is then formulated in an elaborated and technical language, but without ceasing to remain within the confines of the spontaneous intelligence and accessible to it to a certain degree. There is no esotericism in Christianity.

c) No Dogmatic Slavery to a Culture

Nevertheless, as we have said, dogmatic definitions do not enslave the dogma to a system even when formulated in a scientific language. They can borrow notions such as nature, relation, substance and person from metaphysical systems, but they do this by disregarding the context to which they belong, by critiquing them according to the proper exigencies of the faith, by taking them up into a light superior to that of all philosophies. "Far from being enslaved to these concepts, revelation makes use of them; it *utilizes* them as in all orders the superior *utilizes* the inferior, in the philosophical sense of the word, that is in the sense of ordering toward an end. Before making using of these concepts and terms, Christ, through the Church, judged and approved them in a completely divine light, which is not measured by time but by eternity."[64]

9. The Technical Notion of Transubstantiation Can Be Rendered Accessible to the Common Sense to a Certain Degree

We shall try to show precisely by which way the dogmatic notion of transubstantiation—which no doubt represents an elaborated and technical notion—can nevertheless be rendered accessible to the common sense of the faithful.

a) Matter for the Philosopher and for the Physicist

One must first of all discard as an illusion the thought that the theories of contemporary physics have been able to reduce to nothingness the philosophical notion of matter and remove all weight from the pre-philosophic and pre-scientific notion which the common sense possesses.

"The expression, structure and constitution of matter does not have the same signification for the philosopher and the physicist. For the philosopher this expression is related to the structure or constitution of matter as *substantial being*; for the physicist it is related to the structure or constitution of matter as *phenomena*, or insofar as a coherent representation of it can be elaborated by our process of observation and measure.

---

64   R. Garrigou-Lagrange, *Le sens commun, la philosophie de l'être et les formules dogmatiques* (Paris: Beauchesne, 1909), partie I, chap. 3; edit. 1922, Nouvelle Librairie Nationale, partie 3, chap. 3, p. 358.

"Both concepts of the constitution of matter are valid, but not on the same level or plane. It is clear that we must not try to fuse one with the other or find in one the principles or foundations of the other.

"When the physicist speaks of matter (or mass) and energy and declares that matter can be transformed into energy and vice versa, he is in no way thinking of what the philosopher calls the substance of material things—this substance, considered in itself (abstracted from its accidents) is purely intelligible and cannot be known by sense or any means of observation and measurement. The matter and energy of the physicist are physico-mathematical entities elaborated by the mind in view of expressing the reality; this corresponds symbolically to that which the philosopher calls the *proper accidents* or the structural properties of the material substance (quantity and quality). What we can say, then, *from the philosopher's point of view or from ontological knowledge* is, that the material substance considered in one or the other of the elements of the periodic table (which is revealed to us in a mere symbolic manner, under the aspect of the atom of the physicist) possesses in virtue of its proper accidents or structural properties a certain *organization in space* (which is revealed to us in a symbolic manner under the characteristics of the system of electrons, protons, neutrons, etc. of the physicist) and a *specific activity* which derives from its very essence (and which is revealed to us in a symbolic manner as 'energy' invested in the system in question). Then, when it is a case of atomic transmutations, the change which is produced in the system of electrons—for example, the loss of an electron due to some atomic bombardment—will be regarded by the philosopher as a *symbolic image* (in the field of physico-mathematical entities) of what constitutes ontologically the ultimate disposition of the matter, which determines the substantial change the instant that the previous substance is 'corrupted' and the new substance is 'generated.'"[65]

We see clearly now where the difference lies between the philosophic and scientific notions of matter.

b) *Substance and Substantial Transformations*

Whether we are intellectuals and philosophers or not, there exists in each one of us a notion of material being which will accompany us throughout our life. It is the fruit of an initial glance of our intelligence, which discovers in sense data the surrounding universe. It constitutes for the intellectual and the philosopher a pre-scientific, pre-philosophic data, both of whom will always be obliged to presuppose but also to critique and analyze, each according to the light and order of his proper research; for, this

---

65 Jacques Maritain, *La philosophie et l'unité des sciences, in Quatre essais sur l'esprit dans sa condition charnelle,* nouvelle edition revue et augmentée (Paris: Alsatia, 1956), pp. 253–254; cf. also p. 217.

notion of material being blocks, with an extremely rich but completely indifferent intellectual view, a whole host of imprecisions, superficial inferences and hasty conclusions. One can discern in this initial data a sort of rudimentary metaphysic of "common sense," and at the same time all the prejudices and utilitarian carvings of the "vulgar sense." It is an ore in the unpolished state.

By this first glance we come soon enough to distinguish in the universe different essences (inanimate matter, plants, animals, men). We distinguish furthermore (this is the point which interests us here) in the visible universe, on one hand types of bonds, centers of condensation, nuclei of permanence; and on the other hand manners of superficial and changing beings. The experience which we have of the continuity of our own self and the changeability of our states is particularly enlightening here. But it is only when philosophy will have born these facts of common sense to its proper terrain, critiquing and analyzing them in the light of being, and showing that it is impossible to think of a movement without something mobile, a modification without something modified, an action without an agent, and that the division of material being is made into being capable of existing *in itself* and being which is capable only of existing *in another* (in short, between what is called *substance* and *accident*)—only then will philosophy be rendered intelligible and impose itself as necessary. We see that this distinction, while surpassing in precision the common sense, will not be completely inaccessible to it. A more meticulous analysis will allow one on one hand to circumscribe clearly the substance and distinguish it from an aggregate (a cup of water represents not one alone but millions of substances); and on the other hand one is allowed to recognize in that which is called bread and wine not aggregates of uniform substances, but mixtures of diverse substances.

It is the same for the notions of *accidental change* and *substantial change*. A piece of wax changes shape, a rod of iron is stretched or cooled: these are accidental changes or transformations. A sheep eats grass and what was grass becomes the sheep; something of the grass passed into the sheep, but precisely by ceasing to be grass. The change, the transformation, is here more profound; it bears upon the essence of the being. One essential part subsists;[66] another essential part—that which differentiates the herb—gives way to that essential part which differentiates the sheep. We say that the essential or substantial form of the grass gave way to the

---

66 To this essential non-differentiating element is given, in a very technical sense, the name prime matter (*hyle*). It is common to all material substances, and not revealed by chemical analysis, but one that is purely philosophical and intellectual. The essential specifying element is called form (*morphe*); hence the name *hylomorphism*. On the use of scientific facts by the natural philosopher in the establishment of hylomorphism, see: *La philosophie et l'unité des sciences*, in *Quatre essais* . . . , J. Maritain, op. cit., pp. 245 and following

essential or substantial form of the sheep. This is a transformation which is not accidental, but essential or substantial. This notion of substantial transformation, while surpassing in precision the view of the common sense, is not, nevertheless, totally inaccessible to it.

At Cana, when the water changed into wine, it was from the water itself (it was not from nothing) that the different substances which constitute wine were suddenly and miraculously made. There is, therefore, a substantial transformation of a *miraculous character*. This notion of a miraculous substantial transformation is itself accessible, in a way, to the common sense.

c) Transubstantiation

We come now to the mystery of transubstantiation. The second canon of session XIII of the Council of Trent states: "If anyone says that, in the most Holy Sacrament of the Eucharist, there remains the substance of the bread and wine with the Body and Blood of our Lord Jesus Christ, and denies this marvelous and unique conversion of the entire substance of bread into the Body, and the entire substance of wine into Blood, not allowing to subsist only the species of bread and wine, a conversion which the Catholic Church calls by the most appropriate name 'transubstantiation', let him be anathema."[67] Something is going to change and give way, namely the entire substance of bread and wine; and something is going to remain, namely the species of bread and wine.

a) If Christ ate bread and wine, there would be on one hand an increase and change in Him. On the other hand, with regard to the bread and wine, they would not disappear totally. Something of them would pass into Christ, and something would disappear. The substantial form of the bread and wine would give way to the substantial form animating Christ's Body and Blood. There would be then, as is the case with all nutrition, a substantial transformation. Here however we are dealing with something totally different.

For, on the one hand, neither at Cana nor now in heaven does Christ eat transubstantiated bread and wine. He preexists transubstantiation and is unchanged by it. The entire change of the bread and wine will take place by Him without affecting Him in any way. It is a little like when, at the moment of creation, all change—however so extraordinarily real—happens to the world and by God, not to God and by the world. At the moment of the Incarnation, all change happens to Christ's humanity by the Word, not to the Word by Christ's humanity. At the moment of our justification, all change happens to us by the Holy Spirit, not to the Holy Spirit by us.

---

67   Denz. 884. That which everyone calls the substance of bread and the substance of wine presents itself to the analysis of the philosopher of nature as a determined mixture of diverse substances, as we have noted above.

On the other hand, regarding the bread and the wine, it is their entire substance which is changed here. At the beginning they are bread and wine; at the completion there is *nothing* of the substance of the bread and wine and their composing essential parts (form and matter). It is changed *completely* by the Body and Blood of Christ, Who preexists and does not undergo any change. It is impossible, therefore, to confuse the natural mystery of *substantial transformation*, which happens in nutrition, with the supernatural mystery of *transubstantiation*, which is absolutely unique. It is clear that at least this difference is perceptible, in a way, to the common sense.

b) The entire *substance* of bread changes. It disappears certainly not into nothing, but into the Body of Christ (*desinit in corpus Christi*), Who preexists and remains unchanged. Nevertheless, something of the bread remains, namely the *species*, which the Council of Trent expressly distinguishes from the substance. It is easy to know what the Council of Trent calls the *species* of bread. It is what the Council of Constance, in its condemnation of Wycliffe, called the *accidents* of the bread.[68] The synonymous use of the two terms is traditional. We said that the distinction between the substance and accidents was not intelligible to the common sense. The accidents of the bread are all of its exterior and empirically observable manifestations, all its properties, mass, quantity, quality. The substance of bread being totally changed and converted, disappearing into the substance of the Savior's Body, has left the accidents without a subject of inherence which they had, and the most fundamental of which is expanse. The divine power, which sustains the accidents both by and in the substance, will henceforth sustain them immediately. This is a direct corollary of transubstantiation; it is required in order for the words of the Savior to be true: "This is My Body." The accidents of the bread, however, scooped out of their substance, acquire from this fact a relation of capacity to that in which their substance was changed, converted, disappeared; that is to say to the preexisting and unchanged Body of Christ. There is not only a relation *of sign to the thing signified*, which can be established between the bread and Christ's Body without transubstantiation; there is furthermore a relation *of containing to contained*,[69] which can happen only by transubstantiation.

---

68 See the first two propositions of Wycliffe, condemned in the eighteenth session of the Council of Constance, May 4, 1415, as contrary to Catholic doctrine. "The material substance of bread and the material substance of wine remain in the sacrament of the altar." "In this same sacrament, the *accidents* of the bread do not subsist without the subject." Denz. 581 and 582.

69 The dimensions of bread acquire a "relation of capacity," *habitudo continendi*, with respect to Christ. L. Billot, S. J., *De Ecclesiae sacramentis* (Rome: 1915), p. 426. "The conversion provokes a *real* relation between the species of bread and wine and the Body of Christ, and a relation *of reason* between the Body of Christ and the species of bread." R. Garrigou-Lagrange. O.P., *de Eucharistia* (Turin: 1943), p. 108. Cf. St. Thomas, *IV Sent.*, dist. 11, qu. 1, a. 3, quaest. 1, ad 3.

10. The Sacramental Presence, Or by Mode of Substance

a) It Follows Upon Transubstantiation

What is meant here by "relation of capacity"?

It is certainly not a question of local capacity, where each part of the containing species corresponds to a part of the thing contained, namely the Body of Christ. For, 1) How would the dimensions of a small host be commensurable with those of Christ's body? and, 2) Christ, whether in the Cenacle or in heaven, having not changed locally, cannot be locally under the species.

It is a question, then, of a capacity of a totally different order. According to this capacity, Christ, once in the Cenacle and now in heaven, becomes present where He was not, without changing locally, without losing His proper quantity, and yet not by means or mediation of this quantity, but by a pure change of the substance of bread into the substance of His Body. Such is the new presence, not local but sacramental, not by way of quantity and according to quality, but by way of substance and according to substance. There is one sole presence strictly but rigorously required, if one is to believe in the words once pronounced by Christ Himself in the Cenacle and now by His priests: "This is My Body." Christ, whether in the Cenacle or now in heaven, is present in Himself, according to nature, by mode of quantity. And He is present a second time under the sacramental species, according to transubstantiation, by mode of substance. There is no other case of such a corporal but non-local presence. For when we seek how one being, without changing himself, can become present where he was not, the examples which come to mind do not concern any corporal beings, but rather God, Who becomes present in the world through creation, in Christ by the Incarnation, and in the sinner by sanctification.

b) There Is a "Presence in Place," but This Is Totally Different from a "Local Presence"

The sacramentarians of Zwingli and Calvin, adversaries of belief in the Real Presence, feigned to combat simultaneously both Lutherans and Catholics, attributing to both the erroneous thesis of a local presence of Christ in the Eucharist. In the Eucharist Catholics adore Christ Himself. The glorious Christ is present under the accidents and dimensions of the host without any change taking place in Himself,[70] but only on account of a

---

70 It is this which explains that the same Christ, without bi-location or multi-location, can really be present in several places, and that several hosts or fragments of hosts are not several Christs (something absurd), but rather several presences of the one and only Christ. A reality x cannot really become present to a reality A except by a change that is real. This change, however, can be a modification of either x and A, or simply of x which enters into a

change of the substance of bread into the substance of His preexisting Body. The whole reason, therefore, for the Real Presence is transubstantiation. We must add also that, if Christ is present *under the dimensions of the host*, it is assuredly not this *local* presence that we know and according to which each part of a body is co-extensive with each part of the place it occupies. Besides, it would be contradictory for the Body of Christ to be co-extensive with the place a small host occupies. What we know is a *non-local* presence, *by way of substance, of which we have no examples, but the impossibility of which no mind can demonstrate*. That is, the Body of Christ, which is in heaven by a local presence, each of its parts being co-extensive with a part of its proper place, which He Himself created—this Body acquires a new, profoundly mysterious presence in another place. (This is the mystery of the Real Presence.). For the changing of the substance of bread into the preexisting Body of Christ gives to the accidents and dimensions of the host the privilege of containing, yet without inhering in it, the substance of the Body of Christ, and by this all that goes with it. Thus therefore, *that which* Catholics adore in the Eucharist, the *reality* to which belongs their faith and love, *is Christ alone. There is for them no more bread* in the consecrated host; and the accidents and dimensions of the bread remain only in order to circumscribe the mysterious presence of Christ.

c) The Notion of Presence Is Analogical or Proportional

1. The notion of presence, of contact, is an analogical or proportional notion. It signifies in the proper sense presences, contacts essentially different but proportionately similar.

   God is present to the world. In the *natural order* He is present to all things by His *knowledge*, penetrating into their very depths; by His *power*, His *strength*, giving them all that there is of their being; by His *essence*, sustaining them immediately and constantly in their existence. These three divine presences are essentially different and proportionately similar. The presence of knowledge is in the line of intelligence what the presence of power is in the line of acting, and what the presence of essence is in the line of being. In the *supernatural order* God is present, more mysteriously and intimately still, by His *indwelling* in the souls of the just. And finally, He is present in the loftiest manner conceivable by His *Incarnation* in

---

relation with *A*, which remains unchanged. Thus, therefore, in creation God became really present to the world because *the world* began to depend on Him. At the moment of the Incarnation, the Word was made Flesh because a *human nature* began to subsist in Him. In the Eucharist, the Body of Christ is really present not by a displacement of it, but by *the changing of transubstantiated bread*, the accidents of which begin to contain His Body. All of these examples of real relations are similar by only *one* of their terms. But here they are no more than comparisons. The multiplication of mirrors multiplies the presence of the original figure. The multiplication of hearers multiplies the presence of the one word.

Christ, the human nature of Whom is united personally to the Word. These two new presences are analogical and proportionate not only to the three aforementioned presences, but to each other.

An *angel*, a pure spirit, is not in itself in a place, but it can be active there (operative or virtual contact); and then its presence is limited to the point of its power's application. Between the presence of God's infinite power and the angel's finite power there is a relation of analogy, of proportion.

A *body* is present in a place in a totally different manner than an angel, namely, by way of place or dimension—each part being co-extensive with the surface of the surrounding body (quantitative contact). To speak of the presence of an angel or the presence of a body in a place is neither a univocal nor absolutely equivocal manner of speaking; it is a manner that is analogical and proportional, and nevertheless proper and true.[71]

Even the notion of presence of a *body in a place* can be analogical, proportional. This is where evangelical revelation intervenes.

2. The Eucharistic presence is, in fact, a presence of Christ's Body *in* a place, but not *by way* of place or dimension. It is a real and true corporal presence, but of a new character. Before the consecration the substance of bread, which sustains the species or appearances of the bread, is found in the place by reason of its dimensions, directly, *by way of place or dimension*.[72] After the consecration the substance of *the Body of Christ*, along with the

---

71 "There are different possible manners of finding oneself in a place; consequently, the notion of presence is not univocal. Let us suppose that a man is possessed by a demon. In this portion of space which this human body covers are present the following: the body itself, the soul which informs the body, the evil angel which possesses it, and finally God Who sustains the existence of the body . . . However, it is not by a simple play on words that we employ the term *presence* when speaking about the body, the soul, the angel and God. It is easy, nevertheless, to find a proportionately common element among them: the *relation* of contact with a place." M. T. –L. Penido, *Le role de l'analogie en théologie dogmatique* (Paris: Vrin, 1931), p. 442.

72 These are the words of St. Thomas. It is true that he had just said a few lines above that even before the consecration "the substance of bread was under its own dimensions, not by way of place, but by way of substance," *Summa Theologiae* III, qu. 76, a. 5. His thought is, that the substance *as such*, transcending quantity, a) can by a miracle be separated from quantity; b) that it happens that even corporeal substances—we must add, at least some of them—can manifest a sort of independence with relation to quantity, and remain for instance whole and entire under a variable quantity, "as human nature is wholly in a man, whatever be his dimensions," *Summa Theologiae* III, qu. 76, a. 1, ad 3. To say that a corporeal substance is found under its own proper dimensions "by way of substance" signifies therefore, that it *can* be found wholly under variable dimensions. But this is true only with restrictions, relatively, coming fully from the presence of Christ's Body through a relation with the borrowed dimensions of bread. The Body of Christ, which is a corporeal substance, is wholly under each portion of species of bread, as the

Word Who is united to it personally, is contained under the species or appearances of bread *in an essentially different manner*. Now it no longer sustains these appearances and thus enters into *direct* contact with the place; but rather, it assumes the veil of these borrowed appearances in order to enter thus into *indirect* contact with the place—now no longer *by manner of place*, of dimension, of co-extension of each of the parts of its proper expanse with the corresponding part of the surrounding body, but in a more secret manner, the entire undivided Body of Christ (and consequently Christ Himself, the Word made Flesh) being present under each divided piece of species or appearances, and each divided piece of species or appearances containing the entire undivided Body of Christ. This is what is called the corporeal presence in a place, not by way of place, but *by way of substance*.[73] Between these two corporeal presences there is an analogy, a proportion: just as before the consecration the bread is in the place by manner of dimension and by means of its proper dimensions, so proportionately after the consecration the Body of Christ, without having undergone any change in itself, is in the place by manner of substance and by means of the borrowed and assumed dimensions of bread.[74]

3. "This is My Body . . . This is My Blood . . ." *This is the evangelical revelation itself*, rigorously and strictly understood, *which requires that we confess*, under the appearances of bread and wine, *the presence of Christ's Body and Blood by way of substance*.

According to the very words of consecration, the *bread* is really changed into the Body of Christ: here is faith. But the *accidents*, the *dimensions* of the bread remain: here is evidence.

---

human soul, which is a spiritual substance, is found wholly in each part of the human body. Cf. St. Thomas, *Summa Theologiae* I, qu. 8, a. 2, ad 3.

Morever, it cannot be said that the substance of water, for example, is indifferent to quantity, that a drop of water is no less than a cup of water. We know today that there are, in both cases, millions of molecules of water, each of which has absolutely the same unchanging quantitative exigencies.

73   The dimensions of bread being subjected in the substance of bread, "the *bread* is found in the place *locally*, being in contact with the place by means of its proper dimensions. But the *substance of Christ's Body* enters into contact with this same place by means of borrowed dimensions; and, for the proper dimensions of Christ's Body, by an inverse relation, they enter into contact with this place by means of the substance, which is incompatible with the notion of a body present *locally* in a place." St. Thomas, *Summa Theologiae* III, qu. 76, a. 5.

74   "The substance of bread enters into contact with the place, on account of the dimensions which are proper to it, which not only contain it but are subjected in it and extend it in space; whereas the substance of Christ's Body is present there by means of dimensions which are foreign to it and do not directly affect it. Bread and Body have contact with the same place, and nevertheless one is found locally and the other not locally: a similarity within a dissimilarity. Here is the analogy." M. T.-L. Penido, *op. cit.*, p. 445.

The words of consecration do not say, then, that the dimensions of the bread are changed into the *dimensions* of Christ's Body. They say rigorously and strictly that a substance is changed into a *substance*. And therefore, in virtue of the evangelical words of consecration, one must hold that it is primarily, directly and immediately the *substance* of Christ's Body which is under the sacramental sign. The Body of Christ is in the sacrament by way of *substance*.[75]

4. The natural dimensions of Christ's Body are present in the sacrament, but they are there by way of substance.

Transubstantiation, as we have said so many times, is something unique. It is a change, a conversion of only the bread. It is the bread which is *changed* into the Body of Christ, which preexists and remains *unchanged*. The Body of Christ is therefore not separated from its proper dimensions by transubstantiation. They are no longer modified or altered. They extend the Body of Christ in space in heaven, but they do not extend it in space here below. They are really found with Him under the sacrament, not, as we have just seen, directly in virtue of the words of consecration, but indirectly by concomitance. That is to say, these dimensions of Christ's Body are not able to enter into contact with the place where the sacrament is primarily, directly, immediately and according to their proper mode and the mode which they have in heaven; but only secondarily, indirectly, mediately and according to the mode which is proper to the substance. They must, under this precise relation, fully bend to the exigencies of the presence by way of substance; such that they will be, like the substance, contained completely as under each piece of the species which is divided. St. Thomas proposes an image here: the sight of a rose reminds one of perfume. It is therefore the same perfume which exists directly for the sense of smell according to its proper mode, as that which exists indirectly for the sight according to another mode. Thus the dimensions of the Body of Christ enter into contact with the place of the sacrament, not according to their direct and proper mode, but according to an indirect and totally different mode.[76] It is a contradiction to hold that *the same Body of Christ*, which exists in heaven *with* its dimensions, exists here below *without* its dimensions, or with other dimensions other than its own, for example dimensions adjusted to those of the small host; it is a contradiction to hold that Christ is simultaneously *endowed* and *deprived* of His own proper dimensions. It is no contradiction, but rather a mystery, to hold that the Body of Christ exists, both here below and in heaven, *with its proper dimensions*, which *in heaven* enter into direct contact with the place according to their proper mode, and which *here below* enter into only indirect contact with our place according the mode of the substance, being deprived of direct contact with our place. In reality, *to be*

75 St. Thomas, *Summa Theologiae* III, qu. 76, a. 1, ad 3; and a. 4.
76 St. Thomas, *Summa Theologiae* III, qu. 76, a. 4, and ad 1.

extended or not, to have one's proper dimensions or not, *intrinsically* affects the corporeal substance. The simultaneous co-possibility of yes and no is contradictory. But *to enter into contact with the place* affects one only *extrinsically:*[77] it is not contradictory for some thing, endowed with its own proper dimensions, to have simultaneously different contacts with different places.

It is not contradictory, as we have just seen, for one and the same body, like the Body of Christ,[78] to be present in virtue of transubstantiation in two places with its own proper dimensions: in the first place locally, and in the second place not locally and by way of substance.

It would be contradictory, however, and metaphysically impossible for the same body to be present in two places locally. In fact, *"the same body"* signifies no-division; *"in two places locally"* signifies division.[79]

d) It Is Defined by the Council of Trent

Here is how the Council of Trent speaks of the two presences of Christ: one natural and by way of quantity, the other sacramental and by way of substance. "The holy Council teaches and confesses openly and irrevocably, that in the august Sacrament of the Eucharist, after the consecration of the bread and wine, our Lord Jesus Christ, true God and true man, is truly, really and substantially contained under the species of these sensible realities. For it is not repugnant for our Savior Himself to sit always at the right hand of the Father in the heavens[80] *according to His natural manner of existing*, and nevertheless, be present to us in numerous places *sacramentally, by His substance*, according to a manner of existing which, although we hardly can express it in words, is able to be conceived of by the mind in the light of faith as something possible for God, and which we must firmly believe."[81] And the corresponding canon states: "If anyone denies that in the sacrament of the Most Holy Eucharist are truly, really and substantially

---

77 Cf. St. Thomas, *Summa Theologiae* III, qu. 76, a. 5, ad 3.

78 In itself and absolutely speaking, transubstantiation could have for its point of departure another substance other than bread, and for its term another substance other than Christ's Body. St. Thomas, *IV Sent.*, dist. 10, qu. 1, a. 1, ad 8.

79 St. Thomas, *IV Sent.*, dist. 44, qu. 2, a. 2, quest. 3, ad 4.
   It would not be contradictory for *two bodies to be in one and the same place* through the effect of divine omnipotence: one locally with its proper dimensions, and the other not locally and miraculously deprived of its own dimensions. It is such a miracle, says St. Thomas, supposed by the dogma of Mary's virginal conception and the entering of Christ through the closed doors of the Cenacle. Jn XX, 19. Cf *IV Sent.*, dist. 44, qu. 2, a. 2, quest. 3, and ad 4; III, qu. 54, a. 1, ad 1.; *Evang.In Joan.*, XX, 19.

80 On this image *of the right hand of the Father*, which contains a most precise reality, namely the glorification of the Messiah outside of our historic era, trials and sufferings, see Ps. CX (CIX), 1, Mk. 12:36, 16:19; Mat. 20:23; Act. 7:55; Rom. 8:34; Eph. 1:20; Heb. 1:3 and 13, etc.

81 Council of Trent, session XIII, chap. 1, *On the Real Presence of Our Savior Jesus Christ In the Most Holy Sacrament of the Eucharist*, Denz. 874.

contained the Body and Blood, soul and divinity of our Lord Jesus Christ, and consequently the entire Christ; and if he holds that they are there only in sign or figure, or by their power, let him be anathema."[82]

11. The Consequences of the Sacramental Presence or by Mode of Substance

a) The Body of Christ Is Not Multiplied

The Catholic teaching on the Eucharist is nothing but a strict and rigorous development of the word of the Savior, but understood in all its profundity: "And having taken the bread and given thanks, He broke the bread and gave it to them saying, '*This is My Body*, given for you; do this in memory of Me'" (Lk 22:19). *This*, that is to say the thing, the existing substance, which before the act was bread, is now, after the action, a *Body*, the *Body of Christ*. What one sees, the appearances, are always those of bread. What one believes, the existing substance, is that of Christ's Body. Christ in the Cenacle does not change, neither do the accidents of bread. The conversion is a unique type, a conversion of the substance of bread to that of the Body of Christ. It does not result in two bodies of Christ, but two presences of the one Body of Christ: the one unchanged, original, under its natural appearances; the other new, dependent, under sacramental appearances. Thus now, when priests dispersed over five continents pronounce the words of consecration over the bread, they do not multiply the Body of Christ, but rather the sacramental presences of Christ's Body.

b) It Is Not Divided

In the Cenacle, when Christ breaks the consecrated bread in order to give it to His disciples, what He divides are the sensible appearances, which are the sign, the sacrament of His Body (*signum, sacramentum*); He does not divide the substance present under these appearances, the reality (*res*). And what are multiplied are the real presences of that one reality, of that unique substance. Thus it still is today:

> Fracto demum sacramento,
> Ne vacilles, sed memento,
> Tantum esse sub fragmento,
> Quantum toto tegitur.
>
> Nulla rei fit scissura:
> Signi tantum fit fractura:
> Qua nec status, nec statura
> Signati minuitur.[83]

---

82 Canon 1, Denz. 883.

83 S. Thomas, *Lauda Sion*. ["Though the Sacrament has just been broken, fear not, but remember: there is as much contained in one fragment as in the whole. No rending of the reality but only of the sign takes place; neither the state nor the stature of what is signified is lessened."]

c) It Ceases to Be Present the Moment the Species Are Altered

When the species of bread and wine are altered under the influence of physical or chemical agents, the sacramental presence immediately ceases; and as Christ came without suffering any change, so He departs without any change. It is under the species of bread and wine, not under those of any another body, that Christ gave Himself at the Last Supper; and it is to these same species alone that He attaches His sacramental presence.[84]

d) Under the Species Christ Is as He Is in Himself

The consecrated species have a relation of capacity in regard to Christ as He is in Himself: in the Cenacle, in regard to the mortal Christ; now, in regard to the glorious Christ. The sacramental presence reflects as in a mirror the natural presence. If Christ is mortal or glorious naturally, He is necessarily the same sacramentally.

e) The Presence in Virtue of the Words and the Presence of Concomitance

The same Jesus Who said to the daughter of Jairus, "Little girl, I say to you, arise" (Mk 5:41), to Lazarus, "Come out" (Jn 11:43), to the sinful woman, "All your sins are forgiven" (Lk 7:48), and Whose words confect what they signify, is He Who, having taken the bread, said, "This is My Body," and taking the cup, "This is My Blood." *In virtue of these words* His Body is immediately present under the species of bread and His Blood under the species of wine. However, the Body and Blood of Christ now no longer being separated, His Blood is mediately joined to His Body *by concomitance* under the species of bread, and His Body mediately joined to His Blood under the species of wine. Such that whoever receives the Body necessarily receives the Blood, and whoever receives the Blood necessarily receives the Body. And to receive the Body and Blood of Christ is to receive them with the soul which vivifies Him and with the divine Person in Whom His human nature subsists.

Listen to the teaching of the Council of Trent: "The Apostles, having not yet received the Eucharist from the hand of the Lord, already believed nevertheless that His Body was present to them. And there has always been in the Church of God this faith that, immediately after the consecration, the true Body of our Lord and His true Blood exist under the species of bread and wine, together with His soul and divinity. But it is in virtue of the words, *vi verborum*, that the Body is under the species of bread and the Blood under the species of wine. Whereas, if the Body is under the species of wine and the Blood under the species of bread, and the soul equally under both species, it is in virtue of this natural connection, this

---

84 Are the extravagant imaginations of certain medievals, born from the neglect of this simple consideration, even worth the effort to refute?

concomitance, *vi concomitantiae*, by which the parts of Christ the Lord, now risen from the dead never to die again (Rom 6:9), are united among themselves. With respect to the divinity, it is by reason of this wonderful *hypostatic union* with the body and soul that it is present. It is true, therefore, that each of the two species contain as much as the two together. It is Christ in His totality and integrity Who exists both under the species of bread and each of its parts and under the species of wine and its parts."[85] And the corresponding canon states: "If anyone denies that, in the venerable sacrament of the Eucharist the entire Christ is contained under each species, and when they are divided under each part of each species, let him be anathema."[86]

12. The Revealed Foundation of This Entire Doctrine

Such are the rigorous consequences of the doctrine of the substantial presence. To deny this doctrine of the substantial presence, one would have to deny also the truth of one of the following three propositions: 1) This is My Body; 2) This is no longer bread; 3) The visible appearances of the bread do not change. The first of these three is immediately revealed. The second is revealed in the first; for if the bread remains, the proposition, *This* is My Body, will be false, and the true proposition would be, *Here* is My Body. The third is immediately obvious.

13. Protestantism, Which Broke with Transubstantiation, Separates the Subject from the Real Presence

Protestantism abruptly broke with transubstantiation. What would happen then to the doctrine of the Real Presence? Two opposed camps were established: one of Luther, and the other of those whom Luther would call the "sacramentarians," to which Zwingli belonged. Calvin would try to unite the two without being able to separate himself from the latter.

So as not to lose ourselves in a world of equivocations, let us distinguish right from the beginning three types of presences: 1st, *presence of sign* alone—Jesus is present by a "sign" in the immolation of the Pascal lamb (Jn 19:36); 2nd, *presence of power* or *presence of efficiency* alone—Jesus is present by "power" in the house of the centurion into which He did not enter (Lk 7:2–10); 3rd, *substantial presence*—Jesus is present "substantially" in the house of Simon the Pharisee, where the sinful woman threw herself at His feet (Lk 7:36–50).

Zwingli and Calvin[87] hold only that the first two presences in the Eucharist; yet they do not hesitate to call them the substantial presence,

---

85 Session XIII, chap. 3; Denz. 876.
86 Canon 3; Denz. 885.
87 It is the presence of power more than the presence of sign which Calvinism seems to profess today: "The texts, Synoptic, Johannine and Pauline, conceive the whole presence of Christ in the sacrament with the most serious realism.

throwing everything into confusion. Luther confessed the substantial presence as we do; but as soon as he tries to justify it, it disappears into his doctrine of the ubiquity of Christ's Body.

a) Luther

Luther was struck by the clarity of the Gospel words, "This is My Body." He believed unwaveringly that the Body of Christ was really and substantially present in the Eucharist. But he rejected just as firmly the Catholic understanding of transubstantiation. For Luther, the bread is not converted; it remains unchanged. It is, therefore, the Body of Christ which changes. It comes locally to the bread and unites itself with the bread. There are two substances in the Eucharist: the bread and the Body of Christ. This is the thesis of Eucharistic diphysism, consubstantiation, or impanation. It was a return to a position rejected in the Middle Ages as erroneous. He first had to bend the text of the Gospel, "This is My Body," to mean "This is some bread where My Body is." Then was reborn the henceforth insoluble problem: Is the Body of Christ, Who is in heaven at the right hand of the Father, able to be in time on the earth and in different places and enclosed in a little host? Here is the famous response of Luther: "After the Resurrection the glorified Body of Christ participates in the mode of existence of God Himself. He is therefore present everywhere. He is in the air which we breathe, in the bread which we eat. He is not, however, bound to these things. Such that we do not eat the Body of Christ when we eat bread, even though He is found there by His infinity and His omnipotence. In the Eucharist, on the contrary, the Body and Blood of Christ are bound to the bread and wine in virtue of the divine Word Who established the sacrament. Such that those who consume the bread and wine, really eat and drink the Body and Blood of Christ, and regardless of the

---

The words by which our Lord defined the sacrament, the repetition of the word *is* present in the text of the institution (Mt 26:26–29), clearly underlines this realism: This *is* My Body, This *is* My Blood. However, one ought not give to this *is* the sense of identity . . . But neither must this *is* be taken in the sense of *signifying* what some have at times tried to substitute in order to preserve the spiritual character of the holy meal. One would weaken too much the intimate line, which Christ willed to mark between Himself and the material elements which represent Him. If it is not necessary to confound in one identity the Body and bread, the Blood and wine, neither is it necessary to disassociate them; for Christ is not only represented to us in the Eucharist, He is also present to us. He is not only recalled to us, He is also communicated to us. And His presence is only of the spiritual order, since it is delivered over to the material elements of bread and wine." J.-PH. Ramseyer, article *Eucharistie*, in *Vocabulaire biblique* (Neuchâtel-Paris: Delachaux et Niestlé, 1954), p. 97. In order to deny the substantial presence, those texts are cited where Jesus says that He is the door, the way, the vine (Jn 10:7; 14:6; 15:1; and Jn 6:63: "The flesh is of no avail."). On this last text see above, pp. 136.

dispositions of those who communicate."[88] Either Luther expands to infinity the human nature of Christ, or he ends up contenting himself, as did his adversaries, with only a presence of power.

b) Zwingli

From the beginning Zwingli leaned toward a purely symbolic notion of the Eucharist. He thought that he could begin with St. John (namely with the words "The flesh is of no avail") in order to overturn the realism of the

88 This summary is by Maurice Goguel, *Luther* (Paris: La Renaissance du Livre), s. d., p. 25—And, here are some lines (less injurious) from that same work, from the section, *Que ces paroles: "Ceci est mon corps" restent inébranlables contre les fanatiques*, 1527, where Luther responds to the Zwinglians, who deny both the real presence and the ubiquity, and who cite Scriptural passages where Christ is at the right hand of God, not everywhere: "Even if Christ, at the moment of the Last Supper, had not said and formulated, 'This is My Body,' the affirmation, 'Christ is at the right hand of God,' would oblige one to admit that His Body and His Blood are there (in Communion) as well as in every place. There is no need, as it is, for the transubstantiation or for the transformation of the bread into His Body; nor is it necessary that the right hand of God be transformed into all things in order to be present in them . . . If the Body of Christ is everywhere, you certainly will not eat it . . . I said above that the hand of God is everywhere, and that nevertheless it is not a part of anything, it is incomprehensible and beyond every creature . . . The rays of the sun are so near you . . . You can halt them, keep them from penetrating the window, but cannot stretch out your hand and seize them. It is the same with Christ. He is everywhere, but He does not allow Himself to be taken or seized. He can break free; you hold the casing but the core escapes. Why? Because, that God is there and that He is there for you are two different things. He is there for you when He puts forth His Words and binds Himself saying, 'Here you will find Me.' When you have this Word, you can with certitude grasp and possess Him and say, 'Here I possess you.' Because Christ is at the right hand of God He is also, in the manner of God's right hand, in all things and beyond all things . . . You will not seize Him, though He is in your bread—at least He does not bind Himself to you—and though by His Word He invites you to a particular feast, and means by His Word the bread which you must eat, that which is in Communion . . . Here there is certitude: 'This is My Body; When you eat, it is My Body which you eat and nothing more. Why? Because I wish to bind Myself here by My Word, in order that you might not be obliged to search for Me everywhere I am. You would be too small for such a task; you could not seize Me without My Word.'" *Op. cit.*, pp. 144–146.

Thus the Zwinglians argue against Luther, that since Christ is *at the right hand of God*, as Scripture attests, His Body cannot be in the Eucharist. And Luther responds that, *the right hand of God*, the hand of God, the divine omnipotence, is everywhere, and therefore the Body of Christ is everywhere. It is true that it is unknowable, but it is *everywhere as unknowable*; He can *be made knowable in the Eucharist*. The exegetical equivocation of Luther on the "right hand of God" is pitiable. And what ought we to say of the metaphysical perspective of the immensity of Christ's real Body to which such exegesis leads?

words of the Last Supper. According to Zwingli these are to be understood
as a trope. The sacramentarians are in agreement on that point. Their
question is where to search for this trope. For Carlstadt, it is in the word
This, by which Christ designates Himself. For Oecolampadius, *My Body*
means *the symbol of My Body*. For Zwingli, *is* means *signifies*. Christ is contained under the bread only if He is sought there by faith. To believe that
His Body and His Blood have been given for us is to eat His Flesh and
drink His Blood in spirit. Whoever believes has Christ's Body and Blood
present to himself; for, faith in Christ Jesus is not understood without
including His Body and Blood. At the Last Supper the Body of Christ was
substantially present in the hearts of the believers, *substantiell gegenwärtig
im Herzen*. We see here which Lutheran formulas of compromise the
Zwinglians singled out without adopting their thought. For Zwingli there
is no other alternative: either the eating of raw flesh, or spiritual consumption by faith. He never was able to understand that the Body and
Blood of Christ could be truly received under a spiritual mode in a spirit
of faith and love.[89]

89   On the Eucharistic doctrine of Zwingli and its evolution, see J.-V.-M. Pollet,
     O.P., *Dictionnaire de Théologie Catholique*, article "Zwinglianisme," col. 3800
     and 3825Ð3842. The same author writes (col. 3841): "From the Catholic position,
     one could not cite a more peremptory refutation of the Zwinglian teaching than
     that presented by Cajetan in his *De erroribus contingentibus in Eucharistiae
     sacramento* (1525). It treats, beyond the positions of Zwingli on the subject of
     the Eucharistic, his notion of faith, which is a key point in the system; and by
     that, it has the value of a general critique. Cajetan formulates twelve theses
     extracted from the *Commentaire*."
         The work of Cajetan, *De erroribus . . .* was meant to instruct the nuncio on the
     errors of Zwingli's pamphlet *De coena Domini*, though the title was never
     mentioned. Here is an abridgment of the first four of Cajetan's twelve theses:
     1) *The Lord, in John 6, speaks not only of the loving faith which it is necessary to have
     in Him, but also of the spiritual eating of Him in the sacrament of the Eucharist*. We
     distinguish in the Eucharist three aspects: the sacrament which we adore; the
     sacramental eating alone, common to both the good and the bad, of which St.
     Paul speaks in 1 Cor 11:27; the spiritual eating proper to the good. It is true
     that John does not speak of the second aspect, but he does speak of the other
     two, the spiritual eating (6:56) and the sacrament which Jesus would later
     institute. For he strongly distinguishes the obligation to eat the Flesh and
     drink the Blood (6:53). It is false, then, to say that the spiritual eating of the
     sacrament is excluded by St. John.—2) *The words "the flesh is of no avail" (Jn 6:63)
     exclude neither the corporeal presence of Christ in the Eucharist nor the true spiritual
     eating of His Body*. The Zwinglian interpretation, a thousand times repeated, is
     directly contrary to the context (6:54). It is the flesh carnally eaten which is
     excluded; but the true Flesh of Christ eaten spiritually gives eternal life.—3)
     *It is false to say that Catholic theologians teach that in the sacrament of the Eucharist
     the Body of Christ is received under a corporeal and perceptible mode*. The Body of
     Christ is believed by faith; the species are perceived by the sense. The first
     confession of faith proposed to Berengarius signifies simply that the Body

c) Calvin

Calvin, who rose up with equal vehemence against both the Catholic doctrine of transubstantiation and the Lutheran doctrine of consubstantiation,[90] did not depart from Zwinglianism: "If we direct our glance and thought toward heaven *and ourselves, transported there in order to search for Christ in the glory of His kingdom,* as the signs guide us to come totally to Him: *in this way we will be distinctly filled by His Flesh under the sign of bread, nourished by His Blood under the sign of wine,* in order that our joy in Him might be full. For although He has carried away His flesh from us and risen in body to heaven, nevertheless He is seated at the right hand of the Father, that is, He reigns in the power, majesty and glory of the Father. This reign is in no way limited to any one place, and it is in no way so determined that Jesus Christ does not *show forth His power* everywhere He pleases in heaven and on earth, that He does not declare Himself *present by power and strength,* that He does not always *assist* His own, breathing His life into them, *sustaining* them, *strengthening* them, granting them *vigor* and *protecting* them no less than when He was corporeally present—*in short, that He does not nourish them with His own Body, the participation of which He grants to them by the power of His Spirit.*"[91] If the ancients spoke of a conversion, "it was not in order to signify that the bread and wine disappear, but that they must be thought of as other than common provisions, which are only for feeding the stomach."[92]

---

of Christ is eaten not only in sign but in the sacrament of the Eucharist which contains it.—4) *Theologians do not err in saying of faith, that it comes from man's judgment and choice; and that it extends even to sensible things.* Certainly faith comes from God as a gift, Eph 2:8 (efficient and formal cause), but it is given to him who receives it, not to him who refuses it (dispositive and material cause). Faith is of things invisible, Heb 11:1, but it descends even to things visible. In the mystery of the Incarnation the eyes see only the Body of Christ, while faith alone believes the union of the Word with that sensible Flesh. In the mystery of the Eucharist the eyes see only the species, while faith alone believes in the inexpressible union of these species with the Body of Christ. *The major sophism of Zwingli is his denying that faith descends to the sensible.* For him Christ is the object of faith only according to His divinity. In the name of *sola fides,* which he used against Luther, he refuses to believe in the corporeal presence of the Eucharist . . . When Cajetan, a little further on, in 7), encounters the Zwinglian proposition that *nothing bodily falls under faith,* he marvels at an equal aberration, so contrary to the Creed: We believe that Christ was born, crucified, died, buried and rose from the dead; we believe in the resurrection of the body and all these corporeal things.

90 He reproaches Lutherans and Catholics for detracting from Jesus' heavenly glory by "dragging Him down to us" and by "binding Him to earthly creatures;" and he reproaches Lutherans for granting Christ an infinite body. *Institution chrétienne* (Genève: 1888), livre IV, chap. 17, no. 20.

91 *Ibid.,* no. 19.

92 *Ibid.,* no. 14.

Such is the thought of Calvin.[93] With respect to his language, he has no difficulty in admitting that, for the Body and Blood, "it is in no way by imagination or thought that we receive them, *but the substance is truly given us.*"[94] He adds a little later: "I agree with the promise of Jesus Christ. He states that *His Flesh is food for the soul and His Blood drink.* I offer Him, therefore, my soul, that it may be filled with such food. He commands me at His holy supper, *to take, eat and drink His Body and His Blood under the signs of bread and wine.* I doubt neither that He gives me what He promises nor that I receive it."[95]

93 Listen how Pascal summarizes it in his *Seizième Provinciale*: "Everyone knows that the heresy of Geneva consists essentially in believing that Jesus Christ is in no way contained in this sacrament; that it is impossible that He be in several places; that He is only truly in heaven and that it is only there where He ought to be adored, and not on the altar; that the substance of bread remains; that the Body of Jesus Christ in no way enters into the mouth or the bosom; that He is eaten only through faith, and thus the evil in no way eat Him; and that the Mass is certainly not a sacrifice, but rather an abomination." Édit. Pléiade, p. 622.

94 *Inst. chrét., loc. cit.,* no. 20.

95 *Ibid.,* no. 32.

In his *Petit traité de la sainte Cène,* 1540, Calvin, who was thirty years old at the time, sets out to teach the heads of both parties of the Reform, and to proclaim finally the true doctrine of the Last Supper. Both sides have failed. Luther, because "dealing with the corporeal presence of Christ, he seems to admit that Christ leaves it such that the world can then comprehend it. For in condemning transubstantiation, Luther said that the bread was the Body of Christ insofar as it was united to it." Zwingli and Oecolampadius, "for, although they did not deny the truth, however, they did not teach so clearly what they thought. I believe that, in placing too much weight on maintaining that the bread and wine are called the Body and Blood of Christ because they signify them, they neglected to add that they are such signs that the truth is joined to them; thus, they protest that they in no way obscure the true Communion which the Lord gave to us in His Body and Blood through this sacrament." *Recueil des opuscules c'est-à-dire des traits de M. Jean Calvin* (Genève: 1566), pp. 193–194.

His *Catéchisme,* 1542–1545, has the following: "*The Minister*: 'Do we have at the Last Supper simply the testimony of the things said above?' *Child*: 'Insofar as Jesus Christ is the truth we ought not doubt that the promises which He made at the Last Supper would be accomplished, and that that which is there signified is true. Thus, according to what He promises and represents, I do not doubt that He makes us participants in His own substance in order to unite us with Himself in one life.' *Minister*: 'But how can this happen, seeing that the Body of Jesus Christ is in heaven and that we are on this earthly pilgrimage?' *Child*: 'It is by the incomprehensible power of His Spirit, Which joins things separated by distance of place.' *Minister*: 'You do not mean, then, that the Body is enclosed in the bread and the Blood in the chalice, do you?' *Child*: 'No, rather that in order to have the truth of the sacrament, it raises our hearts to heaven on high, where Jesus Christ is in the glory of His Father, and Whom we await in our redemption; and we do not seek for Him in these corruptible elements.'" *Op. cit.,* p. 235.

d) Calvin Fails to Reconcile Lutherans and Zwinglians

Calvin, who had tried to reconcile Lutherans and Zwinglians, ended up colliding violently with the first (we are reminded here of his disputes with Westphal and Heshusius)[96] and found himself once again among the second, with whom he never really differed except in appearance. For Calvin as for Zwingli, when Jesus instituted the Last Supper He spoke symbolically, He used metonymy, He called the bread His Body and the wine His Blood, the sign taking the name of the thing signified because it granted the thing signified, the substance of the signified. And how did it grant it? Essentially there was for Calvin only one possible way, which presented itself under three different modalities. The substance of Christ is given to us, on one hand, in the administration of the two sacraments, Baptism and the Last Supper, and, on the other hand, in the preaching of

---

In the *Accord* passed in 1549 and 1554 between ministers of the Church of Zurich and master Jean Calvin, the minister of the Church of Geneva, proposition 22 states the following: "*We reject, then, as evil expositors those who insist rigorously on the literal sense of those words, 'This is My Body, This is My Blood.'* For we hold as well-known that *these words must be interpreted soundly and with discretion: namely, that the names of that which the bread and wine signify are attributed to them.* And this ought not to be found as something new or strange, that *by a figure which we call metonymy* the sign borrows the name of the truth it represents, seeing that such ways of speaking are more than frequent in Scripture; and we in speaking thus posit nothing which the best and most approved teachers of the ancient Church have already said before us." The twenty-fifth proposition explains that, since the Body of Christ "is contained in heaven as in the space of a place, it is necessary that there also be a long distance between Him and us, as heaven is far from the earth"; and proposition twenty-six says that "if it is not licit to attach by our false imaginings Jesus Christ to bread and wine, it is even worse to adore Him as being present there." *Recueil des opuscules . . .* , pp. 1142 and 1478.

96 The conflict was fatal. Calvin made use of the expressions "corporeal presence," *substantial presence*, the common usage of which had always signified what the Eucharistic presence alone possessed, in order to designate a presence of a completely different nature, one which has always been called the *presence of power*. How could the Lutherans not accuse him of equivocation after such ill treatment? Listen to his response to Heshusius: "That schoolboy of Iena reproaches me for using subtleties, sophisms and even enchantments, as if there were some shades or variations to my words or some obscurity in my manner of speaking. When I say that the Flesh and Blood of Christ are offered to us *substantially* at the Last Supper, I speak with regard to the manner in which Christ's Flesh is living: namely, insofar as Christ, by the incomprehensible *power* of His Spirit, transmits to us the life of His own substance, in order that He might live in us and that His life in us might be shared with Him. By this, Heshusius believes that there is some insinuation in this language, when I speak plainly and satisfy the intended hearers." *Op. cit.*, p. 1702.

the Word. In these three cases, the sign of the sacraments and the sign of the Word elevate our spirits and our faith to Christ in heaven, Who transmits to us the life and power of His own substance.[97]

e) The Equivocation: The Presence of the Sign Given as a Real Presence

The equivocation causes no trouble for the sacramentarians. We know that Zwingli said that, at the Last Supper, "the Body of Christ is substantially present in the heart of the believer," and that Calvin said that "the substance is truly given to us." Others baptized the "Real Presence" as the presence of the thing signified in the sign—the presence of a far away friend in his image or in the object which reminds us of him: *without seeing that the presence of the thing signified in the sign is a presence "in alio" but not immediate, intentional but not physical, one of reference but not contact, of knowability but not reality.*[98] And why stop with so beautiful a slope and

---

97　"But just as God established all fullness of life in Jesus in order to communicate it to us by His means, so He ordered the *Word* as an instrument through which Jesus Christ with all His graces would be dispensed to us ... Jesus Christ is the sole food on which our souls are nourished. But because it is given to us through the Word of the Lord, which He willed to be used as an instrument, it is also called bread and wine. Yet that which is said of the Word belongs also to the sacrament of the *Last Supper*, by means of which the Lord brings us to the communication of Jesus Christ." *Petit traitf de la sainté Cène, Op. cit.*, pp. 176–177. The sixth and seventh articles of the *Accord* with the ministers of Zurich speak of "the spiritual communication which we have with the Son of God, when dwelling in us by His Spirit He makes us participants in all the goods residing in Himself, for which we have been ordered to testify, *regarding both the preaching of the Gospel and the use of the sacraments*, namely *Baptism* and the holy *Supper* ... The foundation of their office is that, through them, God bears witness to His grace, representing and confirming them before us. For *although they do not signify anything to us except what has been proclaimed to us by the Word*, nevertheless, it is a great and singular good which God places before our eyes, as the living images which touch our sense better, as if we were brought to the thing itself." *Op. cit.*, pp. 1139 and 1475.

98　Far from us is the thought of diminishing the *mystery of the sign*: "There is a certain presence—the presence of knowability—of the thing signified in the sign. It is there in another being, *in alio esse*. Here is a point of doctrine of capital importance on which depend many truths and which must be noted as absolutely characteristic of the passage. Thus there is a charge of signification with which statues of the gods overflow. The god did not exist; but all the cosmic and psychic forces, the attractions and passions which assume a symbol in him, and the idea which the artists and the contemporaries make of him, all this was *present* in the statue, not by a physical mode, but *in alio esse*, and according to the presence of knowability. For it was made precisely in order to make him known, in order to communicate him. In our museums this pagan charge is sleeping; it is always there. An accident happens, the meeting of a soul sensitized by some unconscious charge: the contact will be sent,

not speak of "transubstantiation" of bread when, at the Protestant Last Supper, without changing *nature*, it is diverted from its profane *usage* in order to signify and therefore, shall we say, grant the Body of Christ, the substance of Christ's Body?[99]

When so much is conceded to Catholics, it is surely not aimed at misusing their vocabulary. It is rather, thought Bossuet, that in these areas the error tries to mimic the truth: "The Arians and Socinians say as we do that Jesus Christ is God, but improperly and by representation, because He acts in God's name and by His authority. The Nestorians say that the Son of God and the Son of Mary are the same person; but as an ambassador is one with the prince whom he represents. Could it be said that they have

---

it will be able to awake and strike this soul in an unforgettable manner." Jacques Maritain, "Signe et Symbole," in *Quatre essais sur l'esprit dans sa condition charnelle*, nouvelle edition (Paris: 1956), p. 68.

The mystery of the Eucharistic presence, however, is incomparably more than that. "In his work on the Creed, F. Th. Vischer looked to it for an eminent example of one of the poles which his theory attributed to the creed. In reality, nevertheless, there is by no means an example of identity between the sign and the signified which we find there. The sacred words, 'This is My Body,' do not state an identity, they work (as an instrumental cause) a change (transubstantiation). Far from resting on an identity between the sign and the signified, the sacrament of the Eucharist adds to the relation between the sign and the signified that of a cause and effect, and supposes the intervention of the First Cause producing the most radical change conceivable, a change which touches being insofar as it is being." *Ibid.*, p. 80. On the opposition between sacramental sign and magical sign, see *ibid.*, p. 106.

99 F.-J. Leenhardt, in *Ceci est mon corps*, no. 37 of *Cahiers théologiques*, (Neuchâtel: 1955), tries today to acclimate into Protestantism the word *transubstantiation* in order to signify that Christ, at the Last Supper, simply conferred a new sense on the bread: "When therefore Jesus said, '*This is My Body*,' He did not intend to speak of the crude thing considered in a Greek and profane manner. He speaks of the thing which is perceived and grasped in its profundity by faith. He speaks thus because he refers to an end which transcends the thing. It is no doubt only bread; but this common thing, which is a piece of bread, Jesus Christ makes an instrument of His presence for those who are able to go beyond the simple sensible reality." But "it remains understood, that on the level of its material composition, this thing always remains identical with itself. The bread remains bread" (p. 30). The bread remains bread, but its *substance* is said to be changed by the fact that the word of Christ gives it a new *destination*, a new *finality*, other than that of bread, and which is to perpetuate its corporeal presence among men. "In order to know the substance of the reality it is necessary to have a deep knowledge of it, going beyond the 'what' of things to the 'why' of things. The substance of the reality is in the divine intention, which is realized in it. Faith alone knows this dimension of things, their invisible and eschatological reality. Faith alone is suitable to learn what things are in the will of God, which is their destination, their raison d'être and what is essential to their being, their final substance" (p. 31).

the same foundation as the Catholic Church and that they differed only in their manner of expression? On the contrary, we would say that they are the same in their manner of speaking but not in their manner of thinking. ... Thus it is in the discourse of Calvin and the Calvinists regarding *proper substance* and other similar expressions."[100]

f) Christ Would Have Spoken Using Images

Christ, therefore, spoke with the use of images when He said, "This is My Body given for you," and "This is My Blood, the Blood of the Covenant poured out for the multitude unto the remission of sins." St. Paul spoke

---

We present two remarks: 1) Opposed here is that which a thing is by its *being* and that which it is by its *destination*. The destination is legitimate; but at the same time, one destroys everything in calling a substance not that which a thing is by its being but what it is by its destination. Elijah, says James, "was a man like us"; before God and before men he was by his being, by his nature, by his substance, not an angel but a man. By his vocation, by his destination, Elijah was a prophet. "The Word was made Flesh." He took on our being, our human nature, our human substance. He carried it away into the heavens, transfigured, but not transubstantiated. This is the "thingism" of the evangelical message. There is no distinction between Greek and Hebraic thought which holds up. We must choose to be or not to be a Christian. 2) Another element of confusion must be dissolved. It is exactly true to say that the Body of Christ is the organ, the instrument of His presence; but *directly*. In virtue of the hypostatic union the Body of Christ is an instrument conjoined to the person of Christ (as my hand is an instrument *conjoined* to my person); it is an integral part of Christ's person, the *organ,* in the proper sense, of Christ's person. Jesus was thus present with Simon the Pharisee, or Martha and Mary. If it is said with M. Leenhardt, that the bread, remaining bread, is the organ, the instrument of Christ's presence, it is not directly but *indirectly*. The bread cannot be but an instrument *separated* from the person of Christ (a stick is an instrument *separated* from my person). It cannot be an integral part of Christ's person; the word *organ* is used here *improperly*. In the first case, "This is My Body" means, "This is no longer bread, it is My Body in the proper sense." Here we have the immediate presence, the real presence, the substantial presence, and here we have transubstantiation. In the second case, "This is My Body" means, "This is bread which mediates My Body, which is presented as being My Body. This is bread in the proper sense. It is My Body only in an improper sense, by figure of speech, which gives the same name to the instrument and the agent, to the transmitter and to the cause, to the sign and the thing signified." Here we have the mediate presence, the presence *in alio*, or the presence of the sign, the presence of another substance by interposition. *And there is, then, no trace of transubstantiation*. Calvin, in rejecting transubstantiation, was right with respect to M. Leenhardt.

A mother who contemplates a photo of her child—this is a presence of sign. A mother who embraces her child in her arms—this is a real presence, a substantial presence.

100 *Histoire des variations . . .* , IX, no. 72.

with the use of images when he said, "Whoever eats or drinks the cup of the Lord unworthily eats and drinks judgment to himself, not discerning the Body of the Lord." What, then, would words be without images?

14. Can One Reject Transubstantiation and Still Preserve the Real Presence?

1. The refusal of the Catholic doctrine of transubstantiation by Protestantism has introduced a division even within its own bosom. On one hand, Lutheranism strives to maintain the Gospel revelation of the Real Presence, despite the difficulties of granting to this presence an explanation which does not throw the mind into the impossible and contradictions. On the other hand, the sects and reformed branch, obeying an interior logic of the movement of dissidence, repudiate along with the dogma of transubstantiation the Gospel revelation of the Real Presence; and they think, whatever be their manner of expressing it, that Jesus spoke in images at the Last Supper.

Does the Gospel revelation of the Real Presence really and necessarily contain the Catholic dogma of transubstantiation? We know the Catholic Church's response to this question, a question which directly confronts the attitude of Lutheranism.

2. There are other problems in need of clarification. Is it possible, in regards to the Lutheran, to propose an explanation of the Real Presence which would be less unacceptable than the fictional ubiquity of Christ's Body? Is it possible, in regards to the Catholic, while accepting the Tridentine formulation of the Eucharistic doctrine, to propose an explanation not thought of by its authors? These are secondary questions.[101]

---

101 Leibniz tried to respond to the first question; and Descartes to the second.

Descartes, *Méditations, Quatrièmes réponses*, responds without appearing to know about an error of Wycliffe, which was condemned at the Council of Constance—he does not accept that the accidents of bread can be separated from their substance. That which one sees in the Eucharist, the species, the surface, is a network of tiny bodies having figure and movement, under which is found the bread which will replace the Body of Christ: "There is nothing incomprehensible or difficult in the fact that God, the Creator of all things, can change one substance into another, and that this latter substance remains precisely under the same surface under which the former was contained." Édit. Pléiade, p. 359. A great difficulty remains. If, as Descartes desires, the essence of bodies consists in extension, the Body of Christ cannot be in the Eucharist, where we see the extension of bread. In a confidential letter written much later, to a Pére Mesland, Descartes abandoned this first position in order to maintain that the bread remains after the consecration (another error of Wycliffe condemned at the Council of Constance); but the soul of Christ, more than His own Body, annexes itself to this bread as a Body which can be called His own. Thus two bodies would be given to Jesus' soul, counters Bossuet, and that which we receive in the Eucharist *would not be the*

15. "God So Loved the World That He Gave His Only Son"

a) In Image or in Truth?

What exactly is this great secular dispute about? It is about that very same thing which has been disputed since the birth of Christianity—a dispute which will last as long as Christianity. It is always the scandal of a God Who so loved the world that He gave His only Son in a gift so incredible, so complete, so irrepressible that it can be explained by nothing except that kind of folly which is inspired by the passion of love.

But is God, Who is infinite, able to fall in love with a finite and even sinful creature? Is it even conceivable that God could have a Son? Is the Word, Who was in God from the beginning, able to be God and distinct from God? Can God be born of a woman and remain among men? Can He deliver us from evil by allowing Himself to be nailed to a Cross?

These facts, which are so contrary to likelihood, so scandalous to reason: are they nothing more than foolish constructs (no doubt touching) of the eternal dream of suffering humanity? It is true that they are written in the Gospel. But how exactly are they to be received? Is it not clear that they are speaking in a figurative manner and ought to be received as such, and that to want to take them word for word is to commit oneself to absurdities, which God, Who is the Author of reason, cannot ask reason to receive?

---

one born of the Virgin, but of the bread to which His soul is annexed. Cf. *Dict. Théol. Cath.*, "Eucharistiques (Accidents)," col. 1424 and following. The two explanations of Descartes lack, if not the word, then at least the reality of transubstantiation, understood according to the sense of the Council; and by this fact they render the real presence impossible. The second seems to meet up with the explanation given in 1305 by Jean de Paris, *Dict. Th. Cath.*, art. "Eucharistie," col. 1309. See also the explanation of transubstantiation condemned by the Holy Office, July 7, 1875, Denz. 1843–1846.

More interesting are the views of Leibniz, in his *Système théologique*, chap. 14. He admits a real distinction between the essence and the dimensions, the qualities, the mass: the essence, the substance of a body, is deprived by a miracle of its dimensions, qualities, accidents. He concludes (and this is where, in our view, he introduces impossibilities), that the Body of Christ, present in heaven with its accidents, can at the same time transport itself without its accidents into other places. According to St. Thomas, *two bodies*, the one with its accidents the other without its accidents, can by a miracle coexist in *the same place* (Christ entering the Cenacle through closed doors); but it is a contradiction to say that the *same body* can by displacement exist simultaneously *with its accidents and without its accidents*. Even an angel, which is not circumscribed by a place but becomes present to it by the application of its power, can be present in only one place at one time. Cf. Saint Thomas, *Summa Theologiae* I, qu. 52, a. 2; and *Summa Theologiae* II, qu. 76, a. 5, ad 1, where he shows that *the Eucharistic presence is not the same as that of the angel in a place*. Leibniz's explanation, which also is replete of the true notion of transubstantiation, renders, by this fact, the real presence impossible.

b) The Scandal of Christian Preaching

And nevertheless, always, in every place and at every time, ever since the disputes on the consubtantiality and nevertheless real distinction between the Father and the Word, on the personal unity in the Christ of two natures, human and divine, on the truth of the mystery of a God Who died on the Cross—ever since then, Christianity has refused to reduce to mere figures the solemn attestations of Scripture. Each time Christianity rejected as a betrayal the explanation by figure, by trope, which let fall between the cracks the very divine substance of the Gospel message. Christianity is sustained in time just as it entered: by preaching a folly of God which is holier than all human wisdom. And furthermore, in absolutely refusing to tone down the scandal of the divine revelations, in not permitting one to be able to interpret them within the "limits" of some type of "reason," Christianity affirmed moreover (and here is the significance of theology), that if these revelations remain impenetrable to reason, they are nevertheless not absurd, that they are able to be beyond reason without being contrary to it, that it is not for the mystery to be dissolved into reason but for reason finally to adore the mystery. "The last journey of reason is to recognize that there is an infinity of things which surpass it; it is but a weakling if it fails to learn this. If there are natural things which surpass reason, what could be said of the supernatural?"[102]

c) The Revelation of the Eucharist Is but a Moment of the Christian Mystery

Again, if God so loved the world that He gave it the corporeal presence of His only Son, would He not love it so much that He would leave His Son in it? Would He take Him away at the Ascension? When He receives His Son back into the heavens in order to seat Him at His right hand, would He not (without taking anything away from His glory) find some marvelous means of secretly bringing Him to us in the midst of this exile, on this bloodstained planet, where His Kingdom and that of the prince of darkness confront each other?

In fact, we know that, "on the night He was betrayed, the Lord Jesus took the bread, and giving thanks, broke it saying, 'This is My Body, which shall be delivered for you.' Do this in memory of Me. . . . ' Whoever eats the bread and drinks the chalice of the Lord unworthily, shall be guilty of the Body and Blood of the Lord" (1 Cor 11:24–27). What Jesus Himself did at first, He continues to do through His disciples until He comes again. His Body is given for us, His Blood poured out for us; they are present as food and drink; in such a way, in the Israel according to the flesh, one ate the victim in order to become one offering with it (1 Cor 11:18). He is now glorious, but He comes with His Cross, that is, under the

102 Pascal, *Pensées*, edit. Br., no. 267.

sign of His supreme love. We might fear that His glory will judge us without saving us; it is necessary that He touch us through the veil of His
sorrows, through that Blood which alone can wash away sins, through an
agony so desolate that it allows the most guilty among us to dare to
approach Him in order to be consoled.

The real Incarnation, the real redemption, the participation in the
redemptive sacrifice through the real eating of the Victim in faith of
love: these are the successive moments of a unique and unheard of
mystery of divine love. "God," writes St. Paul, "Who is rich in mercy,
for the sake of His love by which He loved us, while we were dead
because of our sins, brought us to life through Christ" (Eph 2:5). And
the Savior said all in these words: "God so loved the world that He
gave His only Son, that all who believe in Him might not perish but
have eternal life" (Jn 3:16).

16. Two Testimonies

a) Anne de Gonzague de Clèves

At the end of his funeral oration for Anne de Gonzague de Clèves,
Bossuet cites these words of that same Princess of Palatine: "It is believ-
able that a God Who loves infinitely gives proofs proportionate to the
infinity of His love and power, and that what belongs to the omnipotence
of God far surpasses the capacity of our feeble reason. This is what I say
to myself when demons try to surprise my faith; and since it has pleased
God to teach my heart that His love is the cause of all that we believe, this
response persuades me more than any book." Bossuet adds to this: "Do
not ask who has united in Jesus Christ heaven and earth and the Cross
with all its greatness: God so loved the world! Is it unbelievable that God
loves and that His goodness is communicated? What would courageous
souls not do for the love of glory? What would worldly souls not do for
the love of riches? What would anyone who is moved by love not do? No
cost is too great: neither danger, nor labor, nor pain. Just consider the
marvels of which man is capable. If man, who is but a weakling, attempts
the impossible, would not God, in order to satisfy His love, do something
extraordinary? With good reason, then, we say in all mysteries, 'God so
loved the world . . . *Et nos credidimus charitati quam habet Deus in nobis*'
(1 Jn 4:16). There is the complete faith of Christians, there the cause and
summary of the entire Creed. It is there that the Princess of Palatine
found the resolution of her old doubts. God loved—it is to say all."
Bossuet cites again these words: "If God, she said, did such great things
in order to declare His love in the Incarnation, what would He not do in
order to consummate that love in the Eucharist, in order to give Himself
now not in a general way to human nature, but to each member of the
faithful in particular?"

b) The Mass Here Below

In his work *Consécration de La Messe là-bas*, Paul Claudel thinks of those who, with Rimbaud, having expected from a poetic mind a power, secrets, an absolute which it is not made to give, have ended up by making that same poetic mind impossible and, what is worse, have led their own soul astray. And from then on they must aim toward a more august mystery:[103]

> "Rimbaud, why are you leaving and why are you once again in these pictures,
> The child who leaves home towards the row of pine trees and towards the storm?

> What you were seeking so far away, the Eternity of this accessible life all makes sense,
> Raise your eyes and fix them in front of you, it is there, and look at the Azyme in the monstrance.

> A furious spirit against the cage, full of cries and blasphemies,
> It is by another path that we will direct our feet toward Jerusalem.

> You did not deceive yourself when you were thus devouring things, poet without the power of the priest,
> This is, here is one of those things immediately capable of serving as a veil for the Being.

> This object between the paper's dried flowers, it is that which is the Supreme Beauty,
> These words so used that they are no longer heard, it is in them that there was truth.

> What will raise the dead, the word, but is it then something which wears out or dies?
> May the priest proclaim it, this bread is enough for it to remain.

> The word which is the whole Man, this man which is God at the same time,
> We have but to open our lips to receive Him in our mouth.

---

103 Journet criticizes here the abuse of poetic inspiration, that is when poets try to substitute it for religion, thinking it can comprehend all things. The only words which can do such a thing are not those of the poet, but of the priest, namely the words of consecration: Hic est . . . etc. In this poem Paul Claudel criticizes the poet Rimbaud for attempting such a thing. In a conference given to religious sisters (1974) Journet relates that Rimbaud died after having received the sacraments of the Church. [Translator's note]

The one who from our flesh made Himself flesh, the Cause
accessible to me in one body,
I finally see, with my own eyes, that the supreme possession is
possible!

Possible not only for our soul, but for our body!
Possible for the whole man from this life one, who knows that he
is more powerful than death!

The veil of things on this point has just become transparent for me,
I embrace the Substance at last by means of the Accident!

I now understand the failure of this thing so often attempted,
The combination of our soul with things created!"

CHAPTER 8

Communion

1. Communion with Christ Creates Communion Among His Members

a) The Text of the Apostle, "One Bread, One Body"

"The cup of benediction which we bless, is it not communion with the Blood of Christ? The bread which we break, is it not communion with the Body of Christ? Since there is but one bread, we are, though many, but one body, for we all partake of the one bread" (1 Cor 10:16–17)

The cup of benediction which we bless. It is twice blessed: it results from a benediction, that same one which Christ pronounced at the Last Supper. This is why it contains Christ's Blood. It is also a cause of benediction. For how does it not bless the Christ Who allows us to receive it? *Is it not communion with the Blood of Christ?* The Blood of Christ is a unifier. It grants us, who enter into communion with Him, to enter in communion with each other as well.

The bread which we break, is it not communion with the Body of Christ? Since there is but one bread, we are, though many, but one body, for we all partake of the one bread. The Body of Christ is called bread because of the appearances which cover it; more profoundly, because it gives life to the world (Jn 6:33). It is one bread, a unifier capable of uniting all to Him, beginning with those who receive it. The sacramental Body of Christ is the cause of unity of Christ's Mystical Body.

According to the Apostle, it is through the Body and Blood that we have communion—that is to say, it is through Christ in the act of His bloody sacrifice, just as at the Last Supper. It is there, in fact, that the supreme and permanent source of the Church Militant's unity resides.

b) To Communicate Is to Be Associated in the Transubstantiating Movement Which Goes from the Bread and Wine to Christ

We said that transubstantiation multiplies the presences of Christ, not Christ Himself. It is a change which goes from the bread and wine to Christ, Who preexists and remains unchanged.

To communicate by the bread and wine, which has changed into Christ, is not to multiply Christ with the contact of our multiplicity, but to unify our multiplicity with the contact of His unity. It is not to draw to oneself a particular Christ, but rather to be thrown together with the one Christ.

Along with the image of the movement of transubstantiation, which in the ontological order goes from the bread and wine to Christ, there is communion, a movement in the moral order, which has for its purpose the leading forth from the multiplicity of presences of Christ to the one Christ by means of the one Cross.

It is impossible to communicate with Christ in such a way without forming His Mystical Body and Kingdom.

2. The Sacramental Sign and the Signified

a) The Species Are Pure Sign; Christ Is the Reality and the Sign; The Mystical Body Is the Pure Reality

We recall here that theology distinguishes three aspects of the Eucharist.

1. There is *that which we see*, that is the species of bread and wine. Insofar as their signification remains determined by the words of consecration, they designate both the Body of Christ given for us as well as the Blood of Christ poured out for us. This is *pure sign, pure symbol, pure sacrament*.

2. There is *that which we believe*, that is the Body signified by the species of bread and the Blood signified by the species of wine. As the sacramental presence refers entirely and constantly to the natural presence, Christ is found under the species of bread and wine such as He is at the moment of transubstantiation. He was able to suffer at the Last Supper; He is now glorious in heaven. It is by means of His Cross, however, that He wills to come to us and draw us to Himself. Christ sacramentalized, that is the glorious Christ with His Body given for us and His Blood poured out for us: this is the supreme *reality* signified and contained by the sacramental species.

3. This is the supreme reality, not the ultimate reality. The Body and Blood are united to those who participate in them, and in addition they unite together the participants themselves with each other. Thus the sacramental Body of Christ creates around Him the Mystical Body or ecclesial Body of Christ. And if the cause is a natural sign of its effect, the sacramental Body, which is the reality, the supreme reality, will also at the same time be a sign—a reality *and a sign*. The Mystical or ecclesial Body will be pure effect, the *pure and ultimate reality*.

The Mystical or ecclesial Body is, therefore, *contained in the Eucharist as the signified in the sign and the effect in the cause*. The sacraments of the New Law really contain the grace they signify.[1] Nevertheless, unlike the true and sacramental Body of Christ, the Mystical or ecclesial Body *is not contained substantially in the Eucharist*. It is precisely under this association and vis-à-vis the sacramental Body that we say that it is the "reality not contained."

---

1   St. Albert the Great says of Christ sacramentalized, that He "signifies, causes and *contains* the grace of our incorporation, which is what is ultimate in the sacrament according to the Catholic Faith." *De Eucharistia*, dist. 6, treatise 3, chap. 1, no. 2; edit. Borgnet, XXXVIII, p. 413.

b) Christ Sacramentalized Is the Common Good of the Entire Church

Christ is in the sacrament in order to create and reassemble around Himself His Mystical or ecclesial Body.

However, it is more precious to Him alone than to the whole ecclesial Body. Apropos of St. Paul's text: "God did not spare His own Son, but handed Him over for us" (Rom 8:32), St. Thomas maintains that "God loves Christ not only more than the whole human race, but also more than the entire universality of creatures," since He "gave to Him the name above every other name" (Phil 2:9). St. Thomas also says that, if He nevertheless delivered Him up to death for the salvation of the human race, it was ultimately in order to make for Him a crown of all those Whom He will have loved and saved.[2] There is not more sanctity in Christ and His Mystical Body than in Christ alone. There are new partakers in this sanctity of which Christ is the source.

Christ is in the sacrament as the greatest good of the Church: "The common spiritual good of the entire Church is contained substantially in the very sacrament of the Eucharist."[3]

c) He Is the Cause of the Church's Unity

The entire Church is gathered around the sacramentalized Christ as her center.

It is the corporeal presence of Christ which raised up the Church in Palestine; it is the same corporeal presence which sustains her in the world.

Humanity, sinful as it is, has the need to approach Jesus in order to feel itself forgiven (Lk 7:36–50), like the woman with the flow of blood who touched Him in order to be cured: "And Jesus said, 'Who touched Me?' And all denying it, Peter and those with Him said, 'Master, the multitudes crowd and press upon You, and do You ask, Who touched me?' But Jesus responded, 'Somebody touched Me; for I know that power is gone out from Me'" (Lk 8:44:46).

d) The Sacramental Realism Is Guarantee of the Ecclesial Realism, and Vice Versa. The Protestant Counter-proof

1. It has been said that, in this association of the sacramental Body with the ecclesial Body, of the cause with the effect, sometimes one of the terms is emphasized, at other times the other of the terms: "Today, more than anything else, it is our faith in the *Real Presence*—clarified, thanks to centuries of controversy and analyses—which leads us to faith in the

---

2   St. Thomas, *Summa Theologiae* I, qu. 20, a. 4, ad 1.
3   "Bonum commune spirituale totius Ecclesiae continetur *substantialiter* in ipso Eucharistiae sacramento." St. Thomas, *Summa Theologiae* III, qu. 65, a. 3, ad 1. Christ is in the other sacraments by virtue of the *instrumental power* which He communicates to them; He is in the Eucharist *substantially*.

ecclesial Body: efficaciously signified by the mystery of the altar, the mystery of the Church must have the same nature and depth. Among the ancients the perspective was often the opposite. The emphasis was habitually put on the effect rather than the cause. But the ecclesial realism, for which they everywhere offer us the most explicit witness, guarantees us at the same time—when there is a need—their Eucharistic realism. For the cause must be adequate to its effect . . .

2. "In virtue of the same internal logic—and this counterproof has its price—those who, in modern times, exhaust the traditional idea of the Church as the Body of Christ, find themselves exhausting as well the reality of the Eucharistic presence. It is in such a way that Calvin endeavored to establish the same idea of the *virtual presence* of Christ in His sacrament and in His faithful. His reason is the same in both cases: *for He is in heaven and we are here on earth.* And the pastor Claude, while wishing to exclude the testimony which the apologists draw from the Fathers in favor of the Catholic doctrine of the Eucharist, finds himself compelled to contest the significance of their texts concerning the Church. How, in fact, will the Church be truly built up, how will all her members be gathered into an organism which is truly one by means of a sacrament which contains only in symbol Him Whose Body she must become and Who alone can bring about her unity? . . . A *Real* Presence, because *realizing.*"[4]

3. The Three Ways of Communicating

a) Spiritual and Sacramental Communion

The Corinthians asked St. Paul about food consecrated to idols. Can it be eaten? The Apostle's response is twofold: it is forbidden to take part in a banquet of sacrifice—that would be idolatry (1 Cor 10:14:22); in private meals, however, these foods may be eaten, provided it does not cause scandal (1 Cor 10:23; 11:1).

It is in explaining the first point that St. Paul reveals to us the sense of the Eucharistic Communion. He distinguishes the worship of Christians from that of the Jews and Gentiles. In both there is a sacrifice and a communion with the sacrifice through the eating of the victim.

The Jews offered victims to the true God, the Gentiles to idols. The idols are nothing in themselves; at most they are substitutes for the demons. To eat the victim offered to idols, to become one with it through consumption in order to offer oneself with it is to perform an act of idolatry. Hence the first words of the Apostle: "My beloved, flee idolatry" (1 Cor 10:14). Like the Jews and the Gentiles, the Christians have a sacrifice to which they are to unite themselves through the eating of the Victim. Hence the words cited above: "The cup of benediction

---

4   Henri de Lubac, *Corpus mysticum, L'Eucharistie et l'Église au moyen âge* (Paris: 1944), pp. 289–290.

which we bless, is it not communion with the Blood of Christ? The bread which we break, is it not communion with the Body of Christ?" (1 Cor 10:16). Are Christians going to desert the cup of the Lord for that of demons, the table of the Lord for that of demons?

Here is the text of the Apostle: "Consider Israel according to the flesh. Are not they that eat of the sacrifices partakers of the altar? What then? Do I say that what is offered in sacrifice to idols is anything? Or, that the idol is anything? But the things which the heathens sacrifice they sacrifice to devils, and not to God. And I would not that you should be made partakers with devils. You cannot drink the chalice of the Lord and the chalice of devils. You cannot be partakers of the table of the Lord and of the table of devils. Do we provoke the Lord to jealousy? Are we stronger than He?" (1 Cor 10:18–22).

The thought is clear. There is a sacrifice to which Christians are to unite themselves not only by faith and love, but also by the eating of the Victim, an act which faith and love move them to perform: communicating with the Body and Blood of Christ, drinking of the Lord's cup and partaking of His table. This is the Communion in the one sacrifice of Christ, which is at once spiritual and sacramental.

b) The Communion of Sinners Which Is Sacramental Only

St. Paul distinguishes from the spiritual and sacramental Communion that which is "sacramental only"[5]—the Communion of the sinner, who in receiving the Body and Blood of Christ, eats and drinks to his own condemnation: "For as often as you shall eat this bread and drink this chalice, you shall show the death of the Lord until He comes again. Therefore, whoever shall eat this bread and drink the chalice of the Lord unworthily, shall be guilty of the Body and Blood of the Lord. But let a man prove himself, and so let him eat of that bread and drink of the chalice. For he that eats and drinks unworthily, eats and drinks judgment to himself, not discerning the Body of the Lord" (1 Cor 11:26–29).

To these unworthy Communions the Apostle relates the sicknesses and even the corporal deaths which occurred among the Corinthians, considering them as salutary warnings of the Lord, Who chastises bodies in order to save souls: "Therefore, there are many infirm and weak among you and many sleep. But if we are judged, we are chastised by the Lord, that we be not condemned with this world" (1 Cor 11:30–32).

c) The Communion by Desire Which Is Spiritual Only

Theologians call the desire to be united to Christ's Passion by means of the Eucharistic mystery perpetuated among us a communion which is "spiritual only." St. Francis said to his friars: "When you pray, say, 'Our Father' and,

---

5   This is the name given it by theologians. Cf. St. Thomas, *Summa Theologiae* III, qu. 80, a. 1, 3, 4.

'We adore Thee, O Christ, here and in all the churches in all the world, and we bless Thee because by Thy holy Cross Thou hast redeemed the world.'"[6]

d) These Three Ways of Communicating Are Distinguished by the Council of Trent

The Council of Trent would henceforth be able to distinguish three ways of communicating: the first, sacramental only, which is sacrilege; the second, spiritual only, which is very holy, but inchoate, skeletal; the third, spiritual and sacramental, which is full, perfect: "Our predecessors distinguished wisely and exactly three manners of receiving this holy sacrament. The first, they teach, receive it only *sacramentally*, such as sinners; the second, only *spiritually*, those who, under the impulse of a faith living and acting through charity (Gal 5:6), form in themselves the desire to receive this heavenly bread and experience in themselves the fruits and benefits; finally the third, *sacramentally and spiritually*, those who test and prepare themselves to approach this divine table, vested in the wedding garment" (Mt 22:11 and ff.).[7]

We read further on: "The holy Council desires that at each Mass the faithful present communicate not only *spiritually*, by interior desire, but also *sacramentally*, by receiving the Eucharist, which brings to them more abundantly the fruits of this sacrifice."[8]

e) St. Francis of Assisi and the Eucharist

Spiritual Communion leads by its very nature to sacramental Communion, where it finds its completion.

St. Francis of Assisi implores the leaders of the people "to receive with love the most holy Body and Blood of our Lord Jesus Christ in His holy memory."[9]

Regarding St. Francis, Thomas of Celano says that "he burned with love, even down to the very marrow of his bones, for the sacrament of the Lord's Body; and he remained struck with wonder before this mercy full of charity, and especially before this charity so merciful. Not to attend at least one Mass every day, provided he was not hindered, was for him a grave fault. He communicated often and so piously that his piety was communicated to others. He brought to this most holy act all his meditation; he made to God the sacrifice of all his body, and in receiving the

---

6   Thomas of Celano, *Vita prima*, chap. 17. "When the Friars passed before a church or saw one from afar, they turned toward it and prostrated themselves in body and soul saying, 'We adore Thee, O Christ . . . '" *Ibid.*, St. Francis relates, at the beginning of his *Testament*, how he was inspired to write this prayer, *Les Opuscules*, trad. Ubald d'Alençon (Paris: Poussielgue, 1905), p. 94.

7   Session XIII, chap. 8; Denz. 881; see also canon 8, Denz. 890.

8   Session XXII, chap. 6; Denz. 944; see also canon 8, Denz. 955.

9   St. Francis of Assisi, *Lettre IV, Aux chefs des peoples*, dans *Les Opuscules*, p. 151.

immolated Lamb he immolated his own spirit in the fire which always burned on the altar of his heart."[10]

He begs his friars "to manifest every manner of respect and honor to the most holy Body and Blood of our Lord Jesus Christ, through Whom all in heaven and on earth are pacified and reconciled with the Omnipotent Father."[11] He stipulates that "in every place that our Lord Jesus Christ is intentionally left behind or abandoned we will lift Him up and put Him in a precious place."[12] Celano writes: "Because Francis loved the Body of Christ, he cherished that country and desired to die there on account of the respect it had for holy things."[13]

He demands of those friars who are priests, that they celebrate "with a holy and pure intention, and not for an earthly motive . . . and that their entire intention, insofar as the grace of the Almighty permits, be centered on the Sovereign Lord alone, and seek only to please Him. . . . If anyone acts otherwise, he becomes another traitor, another Judas; he is responsible for the Body and Blood of the Lord."[14] His devotion for the Eucharist moved him to render to priests honors overwhelmingly great: "He often said, 'If I should happen to meet at the same time a saint descended from heaven and a poor old priest, I would first render my homage to the priest, and I would bow and kiss his hands. I would say, Wait St. Lawrence, for these hands touch the Word of Life and possess a superhuman power.'"[15]

4. Sensible Contact with the Species and Spiritual Contact with Christ

a) The Fleeting Union Through Consumption Is the Symbol and Cause "Ex Opere Operato" of The Lasting Union of Charity

Consumption, where food becomes the proper substance of the living being—in other words union by assimilation—is the most direct and most intimate union which can be found in the order of bodies.

Now this natural union by way of assimilation is, in the Eucharistic Communion, only the sacrament, that is the sign and means of a most lofty and supernatural union. *The sensible contact of the Christian with the visible sacramental species, which he consumes* and where Jesus is invisibly but really, not locally but substantially, present—this sensible contact *is the symbol* (no doubt expressive but quite imperfect) *and the means, the instrument of an invisible, spiritual contact.* Here the fervent soul—such as

10 Celano, *Vita secunda*, chap. 152.
11 St. Francis of Assisi, *Lettre II envoyée à la fin de sa vie au chapitre general et à tous les Frères, Opuscules*, p. 137.
12 St. Francis of Assisi, *Lettre V aux clercs sur le respect du corps du Seigneur et sur la propreté de l'autel, Opuscules*, p. 153.
13 Celano, *Vita secunda*, chap. 152.
14 St. Francis of Assisi, *Lettre II, Opuscules*, p. 138.
15 Celano, *Vita secunda*, chap. 152.

the sinful woman in the house of the Pharisee (Lk 7) or Mary of Bethany (Mk 14; Jn 12)—encounters Christ by faith and love. Christ in turn, in order to draw the soul further into His own redemptive Passion, pours down the most intimate, the most Christ-conforming of His graces, where the soul is perfected and consummates its spiritual life here below.

The encounter with the Savior is fleeting, momentary; for His corporeal presence in us lasts only as long as the sacramental species remain unaltered. This, however, is enough for the Christian soul "ex opere operato;" that is, certainly not independent of his own dispositions, and yet beyond and proportionate to them. Such that those who approach with two receive four, and those who approach with three receive six—the same sort of lasting participation in Christ's charity, the same sort of entry into the mystery of His Cross which He wanted to communicate to His disciples on the evening of the Last Supper.

b) To Encounter Jesus Is to Encounter the Trinity

All the significance of the sacramental encounter with Jesus is contained in St. John: "Unless you eat the Flesh of the Son of Man and drink His Blood you shall not have life in you. Whoever eats My Flesh and drinks My Blood has eternal life, and I will raise him up on the last day. For My Flesh is food indeed and My Blood drink indeed. Whoever eats My Flesh and drinks My Blood remains in Me and I in him . . ." (Jn 6:53).

And to encounter Jesus is to be thrown immediately by Him, as He said, into the very heart of the Trinity: "If anyone loves Me he will keep My word, and My Father will love him and We will come to him and take up Our abode in him" (Jn 14:23).

5. Incorporation into Christ by Baptism and the Eucharist

a) Incorporation Begins at Baptism

1. "Those He foreknew He also predestined to be made conformable to the image of His Son, that He might be the firstborn of many brothers" (Rom 8:29). Conformity to Christ in glory presupposes conformity to Christ in grace. This conformity is normally given by Baptism and the Eucharist; and it is into Christ's Passion that these two major sacraments endeavor to incorporate us—the first in an initial manner, the second in a consummate manner.

2. Baptism is the sacrament which initiates us into the depths of the mystery of Christ. The grace which it communicates is a participation in that grace which, in order to redeem and save the world, moved Jesus in His Passion, Death and Resurrection. It strives, therefore, to produce in us analogous effects, to move us in Jesus' Passion, Death and Resurrection, in order to redeem the world along with Him. The entire journey, which demands from us the death of the old man and the birth of a new man, a true member of Christ—this entire journey, the exigencies of which can at times

be terrible (think of the sufferings of the martyrs or the mystics' dark night of the sense and soul), is inscribed as it were and pre-contained in the grace of Baptism, as a flower is contained in a seed and seeks to blossom.

3. This is the teaching of the Apostle: "Do you not know that we all, who are baptized in Christ Jesus, are baptized into His death? For we are buried together with Him by Baptism into death; that as Christ is risen from the dead by the glory of the Father, so we also may walk in the newness of life. For if we have been sowed in the likeness of His death, we shall be also in the likeness of His resurrection. Knowing this, that our old self is crucified with Him, that the body of sin may be destroyed, that we might serve sin no longer. For he that is dead is justified from sin. Now if we have died with Christ, we believe that we also shall live with Him . . ." (Rom 6:3–8).

b) The Full Incorporation of the Eucharist

What Baptism begins, the Eucharist seeks to consummate; what has been planted tends of itself toward full blossom. The Eucharist is a new moment destined to make one enter more into the Savior's Passion, to incorporate one more intimately into His redemptive sacrifice. Did not the Passion begin when Jesus instituted the Eucharist and gave it to His disciples? "The Lord Jesus, the same night He was betrayed, took bread, and giving thanks, broke it saying, 'This is My Body, which shall be delivered for you; do this for the commemoration of Me.' In like manner also the chalice, after He had supped, saying, 'This chalice is the New Testament in My Blood; do this, as often as you shall drink it, for the commemoration of Me.' For as often as you shall eat this bread and drink the chalice, you shall proclaim the death of the Lord, until He comes again" (1 Cor 11:23–26). To proclaim the death and resurrection of the Lord is to agree to enter alive into the wake of His Death and Resurrection.

c) The Eschatological Character of the Eucharist

As Israel on its journey toward the Promised Land was sustained by the water from the rock and the manna, so the Church on its way toward the Fatherland of the final ends is mysteriously strengthened by Baptism and the Eucharist (1 Cor 10:1–5). The eschatological character of our sacraments culminates in the Eucharist. It contains the Body of the Resurrected One, Who promised to raise us up on the last day (Jn 6:39–40, 54). The first Christians spontaneously saw in the Eucharistic presence of the glorious Christ an anticipation of His appearance at the end of time.

d) The Desire of Co-redemption in Marie of the Incarnation and St. Catherine of Siena

To eat this bread and drink the cup is to eat and drink, along with the Body and Blood of the Savior, His great desire to save the world: "I have greatly desired to eat this Pasch with you before I suffer" (Lk 22:15).

One can guess that it is in the great souls opened to the things of heaven where nothing, consciously or unconsciously, creates an obstacle to the divine influx—that in these souls are found the full effects of the sacraments; that in them will be manifested the nature of the sacramental, Christ-conforming graces poured out on the world in order to build up the Mystical Body of Christ. And this will happen more in the Eucharistic Communion than in any other sacramental encounter, if it is true that it is the sacrament par excellence of the spiritual life's consummation, the sacrament of the unity and gathering of the Church around the redemptive sacrifice.

In speaking of the trials which accompany her love, Marie of the Incarnation declares that the greatest relief which her soul can find is in daily Communion, where it is assured that it possesses the life of Jesus: "Not only does faith live what He says, but it makes one experience what He is, by a bond and union of love, which He allows it to enjoy in an indescribable manner. When everyone around Him would have said that what is in the Host is not the most adorable Word Incarnate, she would die in order to assure them that it is Him."[16] It is, without a doubt, those contacts which inspired her to urge God to hear the redemptive supplication of Christ: "O Father, why do You delay? It was so long ago that my Beloved poured out His Blood! I ask in the interests of my Bride. Keep Your word, O Father, for You promised Him all the nations."[17]

Two and a half centuries later, after a night of vigil, St. Catherine of Siena, having been enlightened about the loss of souls and the tribulation of the Church, and yet confident that God knows how to provide in times of such evil, ardently awaited the hour of Mass: " . . . because in Communion the soul most sweetly tightens the bonds between it and God and knows its truth better. It is in God and God is in it, as a fish in the sea and the sea in the fish." She then addressed to the Eternal Father her huge requests for the reform of the Church and the salvation of the whole world.[18]

e) St. John of the Cross and St. Benedict Joseph Labre

1. Christians who approach the Eucharist know that it is an inexpressible mystery, that the image which they form of it from their Communions is, even in the best cases, poor compared to what remains unexpressed. They know that they must remind themselves that here below we know divine things only by seeing at the same time that there is always more to be discovered and that we must unceasingly try to go further. "Try to content yourself not with what you know of God," said

16   Marie of the Incarnation *Écrits spirituals* (Paris: Desclée De Brouwer, 1930), t. II, p. 222.
17   *Ibid.*, p. 311.
18   St. Catherine of Siena, *Libro della divina dottrina*, chaps. 1 and 2.

St. John of the Cross, "but with what you do not know of Him. Do not dwell on putting your love and your delights in that which you know or experience of Him; put them rather in that which you are unable to understand or experience of Him. This is what is called searching for God in faith."[19] Well-known is his poem on the hidden Source, which he composed in his prison cell in Toledo:

> That eternal source is well-hidden
> In living bread in order to give us life
> But it is night
>
> It is there crying out to every creature
> Which drinks from this water but not in light
> For it is night
>
> This living source to which my desire carries me
> I see it in this bread of life
> But it is night[20]

He is fascinated by the mystery of the Real Presence. "At night," records Alphonse of the Mother of God, "the saint had the custom of going down in his cape before the Most Blessed Sacrament. After remaining a long time in prayer on his knees on the steps of the altar, he placed his head on his folded cape to rest a little while. Then he returned to his prayer."[21] Martin de Saint-Joseph relates: "One day, around the year 1580, the holy Father said the Mass at the convent of Baeza. After having communicated, he remained completely absorbed with chalice in hand. He was so outside of himself that he did not even succeed in finishing the Mass, and left the altar." Then a woman from the congregation cried out, "Call the angels, that they might come and finish this Mass!"[22]

2. And what saint's life was more intensely animated, more silently stunned by the Eucharistic mystery than that of St. Benedict Joseph Labre, who went in search of the Real Presence in all the churches of Rome as soon as they opened for Benediction or exposition of the

---

19 St. John of the Cross, *Cantique spirituel, second texte*, Silverio, t. III, p. 202.

20 Silverio, t. IV, p. 324. French translation by Lucien Marie de Saint-Joseph, p. 1238.

21 Bruno de Jésus-Maria, *L'Espagne mystique*, Paris, 1946, Arts et métiers graphiques, p. 157.

22 *Ibid.*, p. 192. Regarding those who seek sensible experiences from Communion, he said: "If they do not receive some sensible taste or sentiment, they think they've done nothing, judging very basely of God. They do not understand that the least of the benefits of this Most Blessed Sacrament is that which touches the sense, and that *the invisible gift of grace which It gives is the greatest*; and this is in order that we look with the eyes of faith, which God often deprives of taste and other sensible savors." *La nuit obscure*, I, chap. 6. Silverio, t. II, p. 382. French translation by Lucien Marie de Saint-Joseph (Paris: 1949), p. 504.

Blessed Sacrament, and who came to be known as *the poor man of Forty Hours?*

One century later, Charles de Foucauld would raise up for us from the Sahara the secret of that "poor man's" love, by making it echo once again: "How I love Rome! It is in that city where there are the most tabernacles, where Jesus is corporally present the most. One of my dreams would be to reestablish worship in the little *Quo vadis* chapel on the Appian Way."[23]

6. The Threefold Symbolism of the Eucharist Reveals Its Effects to Us

a) The Bread and Wine Indicate the Body and Blood of Christ

1. The effects of the Eucharistic Communion are multiple: They have the liberty and unpredictability of an entry of God into the soul. They can by turns console and distress the soul, illuminate and submerge it by eddies coming from the night of our Savior's agony. They can confound it by the sight of its own weakness and needs. They can reveal to it the passion of the Church, crucified on five continents and in humanity's distresses. Nevertheless, all multiplicity of its effects tends toward one end: the consummation of the spiritual life.

Eucharistic Communion gives life: "Unless you eat the Flesh of the Son of Man and drink His Blood, *you shall not have life in you*" (Jn 6:53); but it gives it in a different way than Baptism, with new modalities which are proper to it. What are they? The direct way to take by surprise the secret of sacramental graces is to become attentive to the symbolism of each sacrament. Let us allow ourselves, then, to be instructed by the symbolism of the Eucharist.[24]

2. The bread and wine, over which are pronounced the words of consecration and the appearances of which subsist, signify primarily the Body and Blood of Christ—Christ born of the Virgin is present in this sacrament. We know, then, that what visibly happened in the world with the Incarnation happens in an invisible manner in each of the faithful with Holy Communion. He desires to give Himself to each one, you and me, after having been given to all.

Christ now glorious, however, continues to be signified under the appearances which are separated from the bread and wine, as at the Last Supper when His Body was given for us and His Blood poured out for us. Therefore, it is by means of the act of His bloody sacrifice that He continues to come to us. And by asking us to eat His Body and drink His Blood He invites us, in our turn, to enter mysteriously into the drama of His Passion and into the work of redeeming the world.

---

23 René Bazin, *Charles de Foucauld* (Paris: Plon, 1921), p. 224.
24 This is what St. Thomas did, *Summa Theologiae* III, qu. 79, a. 1.

b) The Bread and Wine Indicate Nourishment and Comfort

More than the material repast which preceded it, what St. Paul calls "the meal of the Lord" (1 Cor 11:20) is obviously the "participation in the one bread" (1 Cor 10:17).

In the ancient sacrifices the eating of the victim was both a nourishment and a comfort. Here the sacramental species signify that what eating and drinking are for the biological life, Eucharistic Communion is for the spiritual life. It comforts, vivifies, raises up, inebriates:

> Dedit fragilibus
> Corporis ferculum
> Dedit et tristibus
> Sanguinis poculum
> Dicens, "Accipe
> Quod trado vasculum
> Omnes ex eo bibite"[25]

Elsewhere St. Thomas writes: "This sacrament confers grace with the virtue of charity. St. John Damascene therefore compares it to the burning coal which Isaiah saw (Is 6:6). The coal is not simply wood, but wood and fire. Thus the bread of Communion is not simply bread, but united to the Godhead.

"St. Gregory the Great says that the love of God is not idle, that wherever it goes it works great things. Yet, if we consider the particular power of this sacrament, grace and the virtue of charity, it is not only conferred with respect to its habit (*habitus*), it is, an addition, moved to act, in the sense of St. Paul's words (2 Cor 5:14): '*The love of Christ compels us.*'

"This is the reason why the soul is spiritually comforted by the power of this sacrament; for it is spiritually delighted and inebriated by the sweetness of divine goodness, according to the words of the *Canticle of Canticles* (5:1): *Eat, O friends, and drink, and be inebriated, my dearly beloved.*"[26]

c) The Bread and Wine Indicate a Union of Many

Sacramental Communion, explains St. Thomas, nourishes us spiritually, uniting us to Christ and to His members, as food is united to him who consumes it.[27] To become one with Christ is, to the same degree, to

---

25 St. Thomas, Hymn *Sacris solemniis*: "*For their fragility—a repast of His Body— For their sadness— He gave a cup of His Blood—Saying, "Take—the cup I give you—Drink of it."*

26 St. Thomas, *Summa Theologiae*, III, qu. 79, a. 1, ad 2.

27 St. Thomas, *Summa Theologiae* III, qu. 79, a. 5. It is Christ Who is the stronger and Who changes us into Him, not conversely.

build His Church. The union of charity, which assimilates the faithful to Christ and unites them to each other, as participating in the one Bread (1 Cor 10:17), the very union of the Mystical Body, is also symbolized by the sacramental species. It has long been a consideration of ours. The grains of wheat and the grapes, united by baking and fermentation to make one sole bread and one sole wine, become from then on indiscernible and inseparable. Thus it is with Christians united by charity.

The prayer of the *Didache* is well-known: "Regarding the Eucharist, we render thanks in this way. First for the chalice: 'We give Thee thanks, O Father, for the holy Vine of Thy Servant David, that Thou hast made known to us through Jesus Thy Servant; glory to Thee forever!'

"Then for the breaking of the bread: 'We give Thee thanks, O Father, for the life and knowledge Thou hast made known to us through Jesus Thy Servant; glory to Thee forever!'

"*As this bread, once scattered among the hillside, has been received in order to become one whole, thus may Thy Church be gathered from the ends of the earth into Thy Kingdom; for Thine is the glory and the power through Jesus Christ forever . . .*

"Come Lord, to deliver Thy Church from every evil and to perfect her in Thy love. Gather together from the four winds this sanctified Church into Thy Kingdom Thou hast prepared for her; for Thine is the power and the glory forever! May grace come and may this world pass away!"[28]

Considering the ecclesial Body, St. Augustine would later write: "The Lord Jesus signified His Body and Blood by elements which unify a multitude in them: one made from innumerable grains, the other from innumerable grapes."[29] And it was the ecclesial Body (no doubt an effect of the sacramental Body) that he was speaking about when that same doctor said: "O sacrament of piety, O sign of unity, O bond of charity."[30]

d) The Eucharist Gives Eternal Life and Erases Sin

1. The Savior explains that the life given through Eucharistic Communion is eternal life. It begins here below in grace, blossoms into glory, and will have the power to transfigure bodies: "Whoever eats My Flesh and drinks My Blood will have eternal life, and I will raise him up on the last day" (Jn 6:54). Communion prepares the eschatological Kingdom.

2. It is furthermore clear that, by enkindling charity in the soul, sacramental Communion also destroys at the same time venial faults,

28 *Didache*, chap. 9, nos. 1–4, chap. 10, nos. 5 and 6.
29 St. Augustine, *In Joan. Evangel.*, XXVI, no. 17.
30 *Ibid.*, no. 13.

and even mortal faults, if the latter are found in one who is not conscious of them.[31]

e) The Reasons for the Institution of the Eucharist According to the Council of Trent

We saw under what three general titles St. Thomas, in his *Summa*, draws up the principal scriptural and patristic data concerning the effects of sacramental Communion.

The Council of Trent touched on the same points when it stated the reasons for the institution of this sacrament: "At the moment when He was to leave this world to go to the Father, the Savior instituted this sacrament, a memorial of His wonders, where He poured out all the riches of His love for men. He gave us the precept of receiving it, in order to honor His memory and to announce His death, until He comes again to judge the world.

"He willed that we receive this sacrament as *spiritual food*, which supports and fortifies our souls, making them live with the very life of Him Who said, 'Whoever eats Me will live by Me,'[32] and as *the antidote* which delivers us from our daily faults and preserves us from mortal sins.

"He willed furthermore that it be for us *a pledge of future glory* and eternal happiness; and *the symbol of that one Body* of which He is Himself the Head, and to which He desires that we be joined as members by the most intimate bonds of faith, hope and charity, in order that we might all have the same sentiment and that there might be no division among us."[33]

f) The Missal's Three Prayers Before Holy Communion

The effects of Eucharistic Communion can be read in the very beautiful prayers, the hymns of St. Thomas like the *Adoro Te, Anima Christi,* etc., composed throughout the ages by Christian piety in order to aid one in preparing for Communion and giving thanks afterwards. We translate here only the three prayers from the Missal which precede the priest's Communion:

"Lord Jesus Christ, Who said to Thine Apostles, *I leave you peace, My peace I give you*, look not upon my sins but upon the faith of Thy Church; and deign to grant her that peace and unity which is in accord with Thy will.

---

31   St. Thomas, *Summa Theologiae* III, qu. 79, a. 3, and 4.—We ought constantly to thwart Lutheran equivocations. To approach Communion *with the confidence of not communicating unworthily* if one has confessed, has been prepared by prayers, exempt from being conscious of any mortal sin ... may be understood in two different ways: *This confidence keeps us from a sacrilegious Communion*—this way is *Catholic. This confidence*, and not the sacraments, *is itself justifying*; and this way is *Lutheran*, but contrary to the Apostle, 1 Cor 4:4: "My conscience reproaches me of nothing, but I am not justified by that." Cajetan, *Responsio super quinque Martini Lutheri articulos*, article 3, Rome, June 6, 1521.

32   John 6:57.

33   Session XIII, chap. 2; Denz. 875.

"Lord Jesus Christ, Son of the living God, Who, according to the will of Thy Father, with the cooperation of the Holy Spirit, hast by Thy death given life to the world; deliver me by this Thy most sacred Body and Blood from all my iniquities and from all evils; and make me always cleave to Thy commandments, and never allow me to be separated from Thee.

"Let not the partaking of Thy Body, O Lord Jesus Christ, which I, though unworthy, presume to receive, turn to my judgment and condemnation; but let it, through Thy mercy, become a safeguard and remedy, both for soul and body."

g) "Post-Communion"

But who could speak of the infinite tenderness of this dialogue between the soul and its God? There is a world of silence of which only the poet can speak.

> "One experiences himself as the tiny thing that he is
> That he knows himself to be
> Now he knows it in the spirit
> And in the soul and in the body
> He sees this emptiness with a simply joy
> In this emptiness there is a light
> It comes from somewhere else
> It signifies nothing but this emptiness
> And this other place
> One is defenseless but also fearless
> It is the repose of him who is without defense
> And who wishes no longer to defend himself
> Not even his own life perhaps
> The entire treasury of past sufferings
> Always present
> Rest in peace and raise a song of help
> To mercy
>
> My misery is with me as a thing
> The weight of which it would take a miracle to remove."[34]

7. Communion Under One or Two Species

a) Communion Under One Species Alone Is Justifiable Only in the Light of the Real Presence

1. We recall the words of the proclamation of the Eucharist: *"Whoever eats My Flesh and drinks My Blood* has eternal life and I will raise him up on the last day"* (Jn 6:54).

And the words of institution: "And while they were eating, Jesus, having taken the bread and said a blessing, broke it and giving it to the disciples, said, *'Take. Eat.* This is My Body.' And having taken the chalice

---

34   Raïssa Maritain, *Portes de l'Horizon*, in *Aux creux du rocher* (Paris: Alsatia, s. d.). See also Verlain, *Mon Dieu m'a dit . . .* ; Claudel, *Communion* in *La Messe là-bas*.

and given thanks, He gave it to them saying, '*Drink ye*, for this is My Blood, the Blood of the Covenant . . . '" (Mt 26:26–28).

We must eat the Flesh and drink the Blood. It is the formal precept of Christ.

2. Is it possible to justify from this the use of Communion under only one species in the Latin Rite?

We offer a brief response.

No, if one denies the Real Presence. For to eat the bread and drink the wine, then, would not be to eat the Body and drink the Blood of Christ in order to be united in the consumption to the same immolated Victim; it would be, rather, to perform a simply figurative rite, which, split in two, would lose all significance.

Yes, if one believes in the Real Presence. For, to eat the bread and drink the cup would be to eat the Body and drink the Blood of Christ. He is now glorious. We know "that Christ once risen from the dead dies no more, that death no longer has power over Him" (Rom 6:9), that His Body and His Blood are no longer separated, that where His Body is there also is His Blood, *and that henceforth in receiving Him under one species alone, bread or wine, one receives Him entire*, as He is now in glory. We eat His Flesh and drink His Blood.

The abandonment of Communion under both species would begin in the twelfth century in the West. The factor which contributed most decisively to the propagation of the new usage was "the explanation of the dogma, clearly showing Christ totally present under each species *by concomitance*."[35]

b) The Sacramental Symbolism Is Safeguarded in Communion Under Only One Species

The glorious Christ wills to come to us only by means of the act of His sacrifice. This is why the species of bread and wine, separated on the altar, recall for us His Body given for us and His Blood poured out for us, respectively. We receive Him whole and entire under each of the species, which are disjoined, in order to symbolize His bloody death. The essential symbolism of the sacrament, revealing its spiritual effects, is also (and this is the second point) a comfort, a refreshment, a communication of life. This symbolism is protected under the one species of bread: "This is *the bread* come down from heaven; not as your fathers ate the manna, and are dead. Whoever eats *this bread* will live forever" (Jn 6:58).[36]

---

35   J. –A. Jungmann, *Missarum sollemnia* . . . , t. III, p. 318.

36   St. Thomas would say that the nourishment and drink being ordered to one refreshment, the sacrament of the Eucharist is *materially many* (bread and wine), but *formally and finally one* (spiritual refreshment), *Summa Theologiae* III, qu. 73, a. 2.

The third symbolism, that of the multiplicity of the faithful gathered into the Church's unity, is manifested by both the bread uniting in cooking the multitude of grains of wheat, and by the wine uniting in its fermentation the multitude of grapes.

c) Therefore, the Question Belongs Not to Divine Law But to Ecclesiastical Law

Therefore, Communion under one or two species is not a question of divine law, of validity or invalidity, but a question of ecclesiastical law, of licit or illicit. There are three possibilities according to divine law. The Church, for grave reasons, prefers one among the others.

d) The Diverse Disciplines of the Church

What course has it taken throughout the centuries?[37]

1. From apostolic times until the twelfth century Communion under *two species* prevailed almost universally in the East and the West.

Parallel to this custom we find the practice of Communion under only one species, especially outside of churches. Communion under the *species of bread* was authorized quite frequently in private homes during the first centuries. It was the Eucharistic bread which was carried to the absent, which the anchorites kept, which was given to the sick. It was distributed even in the churches, as texts from the East and the West testify. It is only the species of bread which was received at the Masses of the Pre-sanctified, celebrated during Lent on all days of fasting.

During the same period Communion was given to infants under the *species of wine*, the only one possible for them.[38]

2. It was in the thirteenth century that the practice of Communion under one species alone prevailed in the West, both for the laity and for the priests who did not celebrate the Mass.

---

37 On this point, cf. E. Dublanchy, *Dictionnaire de Théologie Catholique*, article "Communion (sous deux espèces)," col. 554–566.

38 *What ought to be said regarding the necessity of Eucharistic Communion for the salvation of infants?* That which is said about the necessity of receiving Baptism in *fact* and by *desire* is valid here, according to the data of theology of the Eucharist. Hence the words of the Savior: "Amen, amen I say to you, if you do not eat the Flesh of the Son of Man or drink His Blood, *you will not have life in you*" (Jn 6:53). However, also according to theology, while the desire for Baptism is impossible for infants, *the desire* for the Eucharist is pre-contained and prescribed in the baptismal grace which they receive, as the bud is pre-contained in the seed, and the grace of consummation in the grace of inchoation. Cf. St. Thomas, *Summa Theologiae* III, qu. 73, a. 3; qu. 79, a. 1, ad [insert number?]. The Council of Trent would be able to declare that it is not necessary to give Communion to infants *in fact*. Session XXI, chap. 4 and canon 4. Denz. 933 and 937.

St. Thomas notes that, having considered the increasing number of the faithful in certain regions and the number of elderly and infants among them, it was decided that Holy Communion no longer be given under the species of wine for fear of spilling the Precious Blood.[39]

e) The Decisions of the Council of Constance and the Council of Trent

On July 15, 1415, the Council of Constance (session XIII) defended the legitimacy of this practice against a reaction raised by advocates of the chalice, called "calixtins."[40]

On July 16, 1562, the Council of Trent (session XXI) defined the following: 1) No obligation of divine law exists for the laity and priests who do not celebrate the Mass to communicate under both species; 2) The Church has the power, provided the substance of the sacraments is preserved, to determine at each epoch the best manner of dispensing the sacraments; 3) Communion under one species alone gives us the whole Christ and the true sacrament.[41]

f) A Text of L. Duchesne

In his response to the *Encyclical of Patriarch Anthime* of September 29, 1895, L. Duchesne wrote the following: "The latest liturgical grievance concerns the *use of the chalice*. It is certain that, in suppressing Communion under the species of wine, or rather in reserving it more or less to only priests, the Roman Church broke with a previous practice. She did not do this without regret or opposition; but she felt the need to disregard it for grave reasons, which I will not try to explain here.

"The encyclical of the patriarch reproaches the Church for having violated a divine precept formally proclaimed in the Gospel. This is quite extraordinary; for the Roman Church recognizes that she has no more right than the Greek Church to tamper with things of divine law.

"Let us consider this a bit more. The Gospel text invoked by His Beatitude is taken from the passage of the Last Supper in St. Matthew. The Savior, presenting the chalice to *His Apostles*, says to them, 'Drink ye all.' By this invitation addressed to all the *guests* of the Last Supper the

---

39 St. Thomas, *Summa Theologiae* III, qu. 80, a. 12.—This new practice [i.e. Communion under one species] is most certainly more favorable for frequent Communion.

40 Denz. 626—"Communion from the chalice was more or less forgotten when movements of opposition attempted to revive the practice and make of it the symbol of their demands. Initially refused, it was granted in 1433 for Bohemia, and in 1564, after the Council of Trent, for the Germans under certain determined conditions; but, as a consequence of bad experiences the concession was revoked for Bavaria in 1571, for Austria in 1584, and for Bohemia and universally in 1621." J.-A. Jungmann, *Missarum sollemnia . . .* , t. III, p. 319.

41 Session XXI, chap. 1, 2, 3, canon. 1, 2, 3; Denz. 930–932, 934–936.

Patriarch makes a precept inculcated to all *Christians* of every age. This is an exaggerated exegesis. It is refuted not only by the text at hand, but also by the parallel passage found in St. Mark: 'He took the chalice, gave thanks and gave it to *them*; they *all* drank of it.' Who are they? Clearly the Apostles.

"There is here no precept from the Lord. Moreover, do we not know that the practice of Communion under only the one species of bread goes back, albeit as an exception, to the earliest times? The Eucharist which the Christians kept in their homes during times of persecution, that which was ordinarily given to the sick, even that which served for private Communions outside of the church was the Eucharist under the species of bread and that alone. The Liturgy of the Pre-sanctified, common to the Latin and Greek rites, but more frequently to the latter, excludes the consecration of the wine. Here, as in Baptism,[42] the Latin Church, inspired by circumstances, allowed the exceptional form to pass to the state of ordinary form. She did not exceed her right here."[43]

8. Holy Reserve

The consecrated Hosts which had not been distributed to those who assisted at Mass were kept in churches as a "holy reserve."[44]

These could be brought to the sick and the weak, as well as the dying, as Holy Viaticum, at every hour of the night or day, in order to comfort them in their passage to eternity.[45]

The faithful would come to visit this mysterious Real Presence, which transforms our churches and without which life would seem no longer bearable.

The Eucharist would be carried in procession in regions of faith, as a memory of the times when our Savior, in His pilgrim state, walked the streets of Palestine and was asked to bless the crowds.

To those who wonder what exposition or benediction of the Blessed Sacrament can add to its hidden Real Presence in the tabernacle, we respond that these solemnities and ceremonies are two sacramentals by which the Church the Bridegroom, enveloping in her prayer the prayer of her children, hopes to open their hearts to more devotion and fervor.

42   Once given by immersion, then by pouring.
43   *Églises séparées* (Paris: Fontemoing, 1896), pp. 102–103.
44   The Council of Trent dismissed the error which claimed that the real presence lasted only as long as the time of Communion and that wishing to preserve the Eucharist would therefore be in vain. Session XIII, 11 October 1551, chap. 6 and canon 7; Denz. 879 and 889. The real presence lasts as long as the species of bread and wine are not altered.
45   The custom of bringing Communion as Viaticum is solemnly attested already by the thirteenth canon of the First Council of Nicea, in 325. Cf. Denz. 57.

In the course of time, notes the Encyclical *Mediator Dei*, there appeared new manifestations of the Eucharistic cultus, "as for example daily visits of devotion to the Blessed Sacrament, benediction of the Blessed Sacrament, solemn processions in towns and villages, Eucharistic congresses, public adoration of the Blessed Sacrament, sometimes brief other times lasting forty hours, or even continued throughout the entire year in different churches, each taking a turn."[46]

9. "Veils Which Cover God"

In his fortieth letter to M. de Roannez,[47] at the end of October, 1656,[48] Pascal wrote: "If God continually revealed Himself to men, there would be no merit in believing; and if He never revealed Himself, there would be little faith. . . . This strange secret into which God withdraws, impenetrable to the sight of men, is a great lesson to bring us to the solitude far from that same sight of men.

"He remained hidden under the veil of the nature which hides Him from us until the Incarnation; and when He had to appear, He was hidden even more by cloaking Himself with humanity. He was more recognizable when He was invisible than when He became visible. And finally, when He willed to fulfill the promise He had made to His Apostles to remain with men until His final coming, He chose to remain in the strangest and most obscure secret of all, which is the species of the Eucharist. It is this sacrament which St. John calls in the Apocalypse (2:17), *a hidden manna*; and I believe that Isaiah saw Him in this state when he said in the spirit of prophecy (Is. 45:15), *Truly Thou art a hidden God*. There is there the last secret where He can be . . ."

Certain people "seeing natural effects, attribute them to nature without thinking that there is an Author of nature." Others, "seeing a perfect man in Jesus Christ, have not thought to seek there another nature: *We did not think it was Him*, says Isaiah (63:3)." And finally, others, "seeing the perfect appearances of bread in the Eucharist . . . do not think to seek another substance."

"All things cover some mystery; all things are as veils which cover God. Christians must recognize Him in everything."

After three hundred years Pascal was echoing one of the verses of the *Adoro Te*:

> In cruce latebat
> Sola Deitas
> At hic latet simul
> Et humanitas
> Ambo tamen credens

46   AAS 1947, 569.
47   Édit., Br., p. 214.
48   Translator's Note: In Journet's original French version the date given here is 1956, which is an obvious misprint.

Atque confitens
Peto quod petivit
Latro poenitens[49]

10. The Church Instinctively Closes Around the Real Presence

It is certain that the Church, to the extent that she goes forth in time, feels the need to gather more and more around the Eucharistic Presence. She senses also around herself the increasing powers of the Antichrist; but at the same time, the charity which lives in her allows her to discover evermore clearly the secret dispensation of Christ Who, having founded her by His corporal presence, wills to accompany her with that same corporal presence throughout her earthly pilgrimage. It is easy to multiply the signs of this initial knowledge of the Church and of her progression in time. We have already given many in this chapter, and here are a few more.

a) Two Inscriptions from the Second Century

1. Ever since her beginning the Church has known in a profound and mysterious manner that the center of her unity resides in the sacrament where Christ, now glorious, draws her unto Himself by the mystery of His redemptive Cross.

Recall the teaching of St. Paul: "The cup of blessing which we bless, is it not communion with the Blood of Christ? The bread which we break, is it not communion with the Body of Christ? Since there is only one bread, we are all one body, for we all participate in the one bread" (1 Cor 10:16–17).

2. The inscription of Abercius, discovered in 1883 in Hieropolis and dated from the end of the second century, shows the Church united by the seal of Baptism and the banquet of the Eucharist. Abercius, the seventy-two year old Bishop of Hieropolis in Phrygia, had the idea of writing his epitaph under the veil of symbolism, the key for which has been given to us by Christian archaeology. He traveled to Rome and to the Euphrates. Everywhere he was received by the brethren; the Faith gave him to eat, along with bread and a delicious wine, a Fish caught by a pure Virgin (Mary? The Church? Both?):

"My name is Aberkios. I am a disciple of a pure Pastor, Who feeds his flock of sheep on the mountains and plains. He has two very great eyes which see everything. It is He Who teaches me the faithful Scriptures. He sends me to Rome to contemplate a Kingdom and see a

---

49 *Hidden on the Cross—Deity alone—Here hidden also—His humanity—But believing in both—And confessing—I seek what he sought—The penitent thief. On the literary and textual tradition in the Adoro Te, see Dom. A. Wilmart, Auteurs spirituals et texts dévots du moyen âge latin* (Paris: Bloud et Gay, 1932), pp. 361–414. Another prayer from the same period is the *Anima Christi, Ibid.*, p. 367, note 6.

Queen in vestments and shoes of gold. I see there a People who bear a shining Seal. I also saw the plain of Syria, and all the towns, and Nisibe beyond the Euphrates. Everywhere I found brothers. I have Paul for (a companion?) . . . . And the Faith guided me everywhere. *Everywhere it nourished me with a Fish of a very great source, pure, caught by a holy Virgin. It allowed me to eat it unceasingly with my friends. It has a delicious wine which it gave along with bread.* I, Aberkios, have sought to write these things at the age of exactly seventy-two years. May every friend who reads this pray for Aberkios." The text is related by Pierre Batiffol.[50]

3. The same author compares the first inscription with a funeral inscription of Pectorius, discovered in 1839 in Autun and dating from the same period. The first six verses of the work form an acrostic on the word *Ichtus* (=fish, the symbol for Christ):

"O divine race of the heavenly Fish, receive with a respectful heart the immortal life among mortals in the divine waters. Beloved, refresh your soul with the eternal streams of the Wisdom which grants riches. Receive the sweet nourishment as the honey of the Savior of the saints. Satiate your hunger; you hold the Fish in your hands."[51]

b) Two Medieval Saints: Thomas Aquinas and Nicholas of Flue

1. We have two of St. Thomas' encounters with the Eucharist: one marks the end of his writings, the other the end of his life.

"One day while celebrating Mass in the chapel of St. Nicholas in Naples, Friar Thomas was overwhelmed with an extraordinary emotion. After Mass he no longer wished to write or dictate anything. He stopped his work with the beginning of his tract on Penance, in the third part of his *Summa*. And when Br. Reginald learned of it, he asked, 'Father, why are you abandoning so great a work, undertaken for the praise of God and the enlightenment of the world?' Br. Thomas responded, *'I am no longer able.'* Br. Reginald, fearing therefore that Thomas had become over-whelmed with the mental stress involved in such a work, encouraged him. But Friar Thomas responded, *'Reginald, I am no longer able, for all that I have written appears to me as straw.'* And having repeated these words, added, *'. . . at the price of that which has been shown and revealed to me.'*"[52]

Having left Naples in order to attend the Council of Lyon, he was overtaken by a sickness and understood that his hour had come. He was taken to the Cistercian monastery of Fossa Nova. After some days, "he wished to receive the Body of our Savior. And when It had been brought to him, he genuflected and adored the Host with words of bountiful and admirable adoration, and rendered thanks. Before receiving the Body he

50 Dict. Théol. Cath., article *Abercius*, col. 57.
51 *L'Eucharistie* . . . , p. 183. At that time the consecrated bread was placed in the right hand of the communicant, with the left hand underneath.
52 Deposition of Bartholomeus of Capua.

said, '*I receive Thee, price of my soul's redemption. I receive Thee, Viaticum of my journey, for the love of Whom I have studied, kept vigil, labored, preached and taught. I have never said anything against Thee; or if I have, I am unaware of it. And I have not been obstinate in my thought; but if I have said anything incorrect, I leave all to the correction of the Roman Church.*'"[53]

2. Two centuries later, when St. Nicholas of Flue, who could not read, made use of the humble image of a wheel to explain to a pilgrim, who had come from Nuremberg to visit him in the solitude of Ranft, the mystery of the Trinity and the universe, he summarized in just three marvels the entire activity of God from without—every divine work: the marvel of the shortness of life, which was very bitter for Jesus, however, when Judas betrayed Him with a kiss; the marvel of the small Infant and the Virgin; the marvel of the small Host which the priest elevates above the altar.

St. Nicholas lodged under a wooden shed joined to the chapel. The upper cell, where he always stayed, had a low ceiling. Two small windows opened to the landscape: one toward the road, the other toward the river. A third small window looked toward the altar of the chapel, where his friend, the pastor of Kerns, sometimes came to say Mass, and where he was able to contemplate the small Host which explains the entire reason for the world's creation.[54]

At the time of St. Nicholas of Flue there lived in a monastery of Flanders another contemplative, Thomas à Kempis (1399–1471), the author of *De imitatione Christi*, the fourth book of which is a dialogue of love with Christ in the Blessed Sacrament.

c) Modern Times: Teresa of Avila and Charles De Foucauld

1. It is very moving to consider the manner in which St. Teresa covered Spain with her foundations. She first needed (it goes without saying) to obtain Episcopal authorization. That, however, was just the beginning. Innumerable and apparently insurmountable difficulties would arise on all sides as soon as it was learned that a new convent was trying to be established in one of those cities, where the means of living were already limited. She had to make use of the element of surprise. The saint would arrive without anyone awaiting her, accompanied by some nuns and a priest, most often her faithful Julien of Avila. Throughout the entire night they would hastily work with some drapery to prepare something which resembled a chapel—often in the most miserable of places. The first thing in the morning they would open the door, ring a bell, celebrate Holy Mass, receive Holy Communion and install the Blessed Sacrament. After this the convent would be founded; for it was the accepted custom that

53   *Ibid.*
54   Cf. our *Saint Nicolas de Flue*, Neuchâtel, La Baconnière (Paris: Seuil, 1947, second edition), pp. 40 and 64.

one could not expel a community once a Mass had been said and the Blessed Sacrament was permanently installed. In such a way small Carmels of the Reform were established everywhere by the saint—Toledo, Salamanca, Albe de Tormez, Segovia, Burgos—in order to revive the spiritual flame, which always burns secretly in the heart of the Church. Each of these "enclosed gardens" of the great Church transports, by repetition of the unbloody rite of the Last Supper, the rays of the bloody Cross to the heart of a world in distress.

2. In his makeshift hut in Nazareth, Charles de Foucauld dreamed of buying the Mount of the Beatitudes in order to "keep at the summit a tabernacle where the Most Blessed Sacrament would be perpetually exposed," and, having become a priest, "he would himself be the poor chaplain of this poor sanctuary." Faith in the Word of God and His Church, he continues, "are practiced equally everywhere, but there in the Mount of the Beatitudes, in the nakedness and isolation. . . . I will be able to do infinitely more for my neighbor through one single offering of the Holy Sacrifice . . . by the setting up of a tabernacle which, through the presence of the Blessed Sacrament alone, would invisibly sanctify the surroundings, as our Lord sanctified the house of John the Baptist while still in the womb of His Mother . . ."[55]

Much later, while alone in Hoggar, when he did not dare celebrate Mass if he lacked a server, he wrote: "I am happy, happy to be at the feet of the Blessed Sacrament every hour, happy with the great solitude of this place, happy to be and to do—except for my sins and shortcomings— what Jesus wills; happy, above all, with the infinite pleasure of God . . . Prayer and penance! The longer I go, the more I see there the principal means of action on these poor souls. What am I doing in their midst? The great good which I do is that my presence procures that of the Blessed Sacrament. . . . Yes, there is at least one soul, between Tombouctou and El Goléa which adores and prays to Jesus . . ."[56]

"The journey to Hoggar will be an extreme sweetness thanks to the solitude, especially now that I have some books—and I do not lack the Mass. I always have the Blessed Sacrament of course. I renew the holy species when a Christian comes by and I can say Mass. I never believe in the right to communicate myself outside of Mass. If I am mistaken in this, hasten to write me; it would change my situation infinitely, for it is here a question of the Infinite."[57]

The marshal Lyautey had assisted at a Mass of the Father at Ben-Abbès: "His chapel, a poor passage with columns, covered with reeds. For an altar, a plank. For decoration, a panel of cotton with an image of Christ,

55 René Bazin, *Charles de Foucauld*, pp. 174–175.
56 *Ibid.*, p. 350.
57 *Ibid.*, p. 352.

and some candles of tinplate. We stood in the sand. Well, I have never seen Mass said as it was said by the Father of Foucauld! I thought I was in the Thebaid. It is one of the greatest memories of my life."[58]

d) Conclusion: The Cross and the Glory

We said that the Church, while going forth in time, learns always more and more explicitly about, and marvels all the more at the mysterious dispensation, according to which He Who founded her by His corporeal presence wills to accompany her all along her earthly pilgrimage by that same corporeal presence. He is now glorious, but hidden and accessible only under the signs of His Passion.

"It seems to me that Jesus Christ allowed only His wounds to be touched after the Resurrection: *Noli me tangere*." Pascal goes on: "It is necessary for us only to unite ourselves to His sufferings."[59] Yes, but insofar as they open up to the immediate splendor of His Resurrection. "I wish to know nothing among you but Jesus Christ, and Him Crucified" (1 Cor 2:2), said the Apostle. And it is thus possible for us to unite ourselves to His sufferings and Resurrection only by beginning to unite ourselves to his joys: "Behold, I announce to you a great joy which will be for all men: Today, in the City of David a Savior is born to us, Who is Christ the Lord" (Lk 2:10–11). The sacramentalized Christ unceasingly unites Himself to His Church by every path of His life, begun with the Annunciation, immolated on the Cross, risen for always—by His joys, sufferings and His glory.

The best way for the Church to know so intensely that the mystery of the bloody Cross exists in order to open up to the mystery of glory is by contemplating the glorious Christ under the symbol of His Passion, as He dwells in our tabernacles. Sometimes even the Cross can seem to disappear momentarily before the glory and be absorbed into it. Then the Church, like St. Catherine of Siena before the crucifix at Pisa, believes she can see the streams of Blood coming from Christ's wounds, changing into rays of glory the moment she touches them.

This is the mystery which she tries to sing of in the Liturgy of Easter, of the Ascension, of All Saints—the holy nostalgia of heaven, the first fruits of which she communicates to her poorest children.

---

58 *Ibid.*, p. 305. A doctor friend, returning from the opening of the hospital of San Giovanni Rotondo, said, "After one Mass of Padre Pio one can no longer assist at Mass as before."

59 *Pensées*, Edit. Br., no. 554.

CHAPTER 9

The Settings of the Mass

1. The Names of the Mass

a) The First Names: Breaking of the Bread, Eucharist, Sacrifice

1. "Having taken the bread and given thanks, *He broke it* and gave it to His disciples saying, 'This is My Body given for you. Do this in memory of Me'" (Lk 22:19). The *breaking of the bread* is the first term which serves to designate the rite which the disciples would reproduce.

The Acts of the Apostles describes for us that the converts of Pentecost were "assiduous in the teaching of the Apostles and fraternal communion, in the *breaking of the bread* and the prayers" (Acts 2:42). "Each day, in one heart, they frequented the Temple and *broke the bread* in their homes, taking their nourishment with joy and simplicity of heart" (2:46). Further on we are shown that the Christians reunited the first day of the week for the "breaking of the bread" with Paul (20:7, 11).[1]

The breaking of the bread, by which the president of the assembly opened the ceremony, announced much less the meal preceding the celebration of the mystery than the participation in the sacramental bread of which St. Paul speaks: "The bread which we break, is it not communion with the Body of Christ" (1 Cor 10:16).[2] It designates "the Lord's Supper" (1 Cor 11:20).

2. "And having taken the bread and *given thanks* . . . " (Lk 22:19). The term *Eucharist* appears, apropos of the liturgy of the Last Supper, since the end of the first century. It has, in St. Justin's writings, two uses.

Jesus, about to redeem the world, took bread and gave thanks. Thus do Christians. The mystery which they celebrate is a *thanksgiving* of the redeemed. The preface of the Mass will be the invitation to thanksgiving.

---

1 According to Joseph-André Jungmann, "the most recent research has established decisively that these three passages deal with the Eucharist." *Missarum sollemnia* . . . , t. I, p. 33, note 16.
   It is a different case in Acts 27:35 and Luke 24:30. According to Pascal: "He is given to be communicated: as mortal at the Last Supper, *as resurrected to His disciples at Emmaus,* as ascended into heaven to the whole Church." *Pensées,* edit. Br., no. 554. We must, therefore, ignore the italicized proposition.

2 Jungmann, *op. cit.,* t. I, p. 213.

But in the midst of this mystery the bread and wine are changed; hence, the Eucharist designates in addition, in St. Justin, *the prayer by which the bread and wine are consecrated*, and finally *the bread and wine consecrated*.[3]

3. The celebration of the Last Supper is circumscribed in its most profound mystery by the term *sacrifice*, which is found in St. Ignatius of Antioch, and which seems to have been common in Africa at the time of Saints Cyprian and Augustine; or equivalent words like *offering* or *oblation*, which prevailed elsewhere.[4]

b) Secondary Names: The Lord's, Liturgy, Synaxis, Mass

"In addition to those terms which go to the very heart of the matter, we ought not be surprised if we meet others which, according to the law of religious language, express the sacred action only with a certain reserve, as though from a distance."[5]

The rite of the Last Supper, being something sacred, was called *Sacrum*, or "the Lord's," *Dominicum*.

From the point of view of the celebrant's role, the name *service*[6] was used, a *liturgy*, a *service*, an *action*.

From the faithful's point of view two names would arise. First, the name *synaxis*, signifying the *gathering* of Christian people centered on the mystery of the Eucharist. Then, the name which would replace all others, Mass, *missa*, *missio*, *dimissio*, originally signifying the *dismissal* given at the end of a gathering. It appeared with this meaning toward the end of the fourth century.[7] But the dismissal did not take place without a blessing. In the fifth century the word *missa* came to designate the blessing which the Mass brought, and the word took on its current meaning.

c) The Sense of the Word "Mass"

The Church, in fact, would not be the Church if, having borrowed from the current language the word *missa* in order to grant a solemn dismissal to the catechumens after the sermon and to the faithful after Communion, she did not also fill them with a blessing and hence a mission.

"Whether it is a question of the Mass itself or of some other ceremony, the conclusion normally included an ecclesial and religious act, a dismissal in which the Church, before having sent here children on their way, drew them back to her once again as a mother in order to bless them. Such was the case in the first years of Christianity. According to the *Apostolic Constitution* of Hippolytus, the catechumens are always sent away with an imposition of the hands; and this practice remained in use for centuries,

---

3   *Ibid.*, pp. 47 and 214; and Batiffol, L'*Eucharistie* . . . , pp. 13–15.
4   Jungmann, *op. cit.*, t. I, pp. 50–51, 214–215.
5   Jungmann, *op. cit.*, t. I, p. 215.
6   In *German text Amt. Ibid.*, p. 217.
7   *Ibid.*, p. 218. Cf. Dom B. Botte, *L'ordinaire de la Messe*, pp. 146–149.

both in the Mass and outside. It exists in another form until our present day. This comes as no surprise, for it is founded on the very nature of the Church who, by reason of her holiness, is a treasury of graces and blessings for her members. As the word *missa*, when found at first to be the conclusion of a divine service, often included a blessing, so the same word would designate the final blessing, and then the blessing in general."[8]

By extension the name *missa* is used for the entire divine service, which closes with a blessing. The celebration of the Eucharist becomes a *missa* par excellence. It is clearly attested in the most widely separated parts of the Latin area (Italy, France, Africa) that, from the middle of the fifth century, the word *missa* is used univocally for the Mass. The word, in the official language of the Church, is employed normally without an adjective: *fit missa, celebratur missa*. "It preserves so much internal splendor that it has no need for decoration. At the time of its formation its sense must have been close to the Greco-Coptic γιασμός, a sanctifying action; for it is the celebration in which the world is sanctified."[9]

2. The Settings of the Mass in the First Centuries

a) The Initial Supper and the Setting of the Jewish Passover

At the solemn Passover of the Jews, which celebrated the flight from slavery in Egypt to the freedom of the Promised Land, and which essentially comprised the blessing of the unleavened bread, the eating of the lamb, the blessing of the third and final cup; at this Passover Jesus, on the evening of Holy Thursday, superimposed a new and perfect Passover, where He Himself, entering into His Passion, Death and Resurrection, inaugurated the definitive flight which would redeem humanity from the servitude of sin and transfer it into the freedom of the Kingdom of God. He blessed the bread and wine, but in so doing He transubstantiated them. The immolated Lamb signifies Christ Himself, the "Lamb of God," whose bloody sacrifice is already begun, and Who, as such, makes Himself present sacramentally under the consecrated species of bread and wine in order that He may be eaten.

The setting of the initial Supper is that of the Jewish Passover. St. Paul teaches that the bread was given first, then the meal, then the cup (1 Cor 11:25). But the proclaiming Passover would fade away before the splendor of the definitive Passover, the figure would disappear before the reality, the promise before the fulfillment:

> In hac mensa novi Regis
> novum Pascha novae Legis
> Phase vetus terminat.

8 Jungmann, *op. cit.,* t. I, p. 219. Our *Ite missa est* is replaced during Advent, Lent and Passiontide by the formula *Benedicamus Domino.*

9 *Ibid.,* p. 220.

Vetustatem novitas
umbram fugat veritas
noctem lux eliminat.[10]

This setting of the Jewish Passover, so strongly immersed in the temporal, is no longer of use from that moment on, except for the celebration of that first Christian Passover. And as the Christian Passover borrows the Old in order to insert into it the purely spiritual and universal splendor of its message, it cannot help at the same time but to burst it open.

b) The First Eucharistic Gatherings: The New Testament, the Didache, St. Ignatius of Antioch, St. Justin

1. The converts of Pentecost continued to frequent the Temple, and it is in their *individual houses* that they celebrated the breaking of the bread (Acts 2:46). On one Sunday evening at Troas a long sermon of St. Paul preceded the breaking of the bread (Acts 20:7 and 11).

The rite of the breaking of the bread seems, in memory of the Last Supper, to have been preceded by a common meal. Thus at least it was at Corinth at the time of St. Paul (1 Cor 11:18–22).

2. The *Didache* (first century Syria) recalls the Lord's precept and connects the sacrifice of the Christians with the pure offering prophesied by Malachi. In chapter fourteen we read the central testimony on the Eucharist: "Gathered together on the day of the Lord, break bread and give thanks, after having first confessed your sins in order that your sacrifice may be pure. He who has a difference with his neighbor must not be joined to you before being reconciled so as not to profane your sacrifice. For of this the Lord spoke, Malachi 1:11 and 14: *'Offer to Me in every place and time a pure sacrifice; for I am a great King, says the Lord, and My Name is revered among the nations.'*"

It is believed that the text in chapters nine and ten speaks of the agape, which undoubtedly at times followed the Eucharist:

Listen to the hymn from chapter nine: "Regarding the Eucharist, we render thanks in this way. First for the chalice: 'We give Thee thanks, Our Father, for the Holy Vine of David Thy servant, which Thou hast made known to us through Jesus, Thy Servant. To Thee be the glory for evermore!' Then for the breaking of the bread: 'We give Thee thanks, Our Father, for the life and knowledge which Thou hast made known to us through Jesus, Thy Servant. To Thee be the glory for evermore. As this broken bread was scattered over the hills and then, when gathered became one mass, so may Thy Church be gathered from the ends of the earth into Thy Kingdom; for Thine is the glory and the power through Jesus Christ forever!'

---

10 *In this meal of the New King—The New Passover of the New Law—The Old is finished—-Newness banishes the Old—Truth flees the shadow—Brightness disperses the night.* St. Thomas, *Lauda Sion.*

"May no one eat or drink of your Eucharist unless he be baptized in the name of the Lord; for it is to such that the Lord said, *'Do not give what is holy to the dogs.'"*

In the tenth chapter we read: "After you have taken your fill of food, give thanks as follows: 'We give Thee thanks, O Holy Father, for Thy holy Name which Thou hast enshrined in our hearts, and for the knowledge and faith and immortality which Thou hast made known to us through Jesus, Thy Servant. To Thee be glory for evermore.

"'Thou, Lord Almighty, hast created all things for the sake of Thy Name and hast given food and drink for men to enjoy, that they may give thanks to Thee; but to us Thou hast vouchsafed spiritual food and drink and eternal life through Thy Servant. Above all, we give Thee thanks because Thou art mighty. To Thee be the glory for evermore.

"'Remember, O Lord, Thy Church: deliver her from all evil, perfect her in Thy love, and from the four winds assemble her, the sanctified, in Thy kingdom which Thou hast prepared for her. For Thine is the power and the glory for evermore. *May Grace come, and this world pass away!* Hosanna to the God of David! If anyone is holy, let him advance; if anyone is not, let him be converted. Marana tha! Amen.' But permit the prophets to give thanks as much as they desire."[11]

Here, as at Corinth, a common meal, an agape came to precede the Eucharistic Communion.[12]

The testimony of the *Didache* seems, with its personal tone, to have been written outside of the common Eucharistic liturgy, like the one found in St. Ignatius and St. Justin.

3. It is the unity of the Church, gathered together in each city around one single Eucharistic celebration, presided over by the bishop surrounded by his clergy, which St. Ignatius of Antioch (c. 110) never ceases to advise to his correspondents: "May the Lord reveal to me that you—the entire community of you—are in the habit, through grace derived from the

11 *Ancient Christian Writers—The Works of the Fathers in Translation.* Vol 6. James A. Kleist, S.J., Ph. D.; New York: Newman Press, 1948). Edited by Johannes Quasten, S. T. D. and Joseph C. Plumpe, Ph. D.

12 "Since the beginning without exception, as we see in the First Epistle to the Corinthians, the Eucharistic supper had been preceded by an ordinary meal taken in common. This was called the *agape.* This practice, however, contained too many inconveniences to last. The *liturgical agape* disappeared, or very nearly, less than one hundred years after the first preaching of the Gospel. With respect to the *agape of charity*, it continued , above all at funerals, until the fifteenth century at least." L. Duchesne, *Origines du culte Chrétien* (Paris: De Boccard, 1920), p. 50.

When the evening meal was suppressed, the celebration of the Mass was moved to the first hours of the morning, when Christ rose from the dead, in order to signify that the mystery of Redemption opens up to that of the Resurrection.

Name, of meeting in common, animated by one faith and in union with Jesus Christ—Who in the flesh was of the line of David, the Son of Man and the Son of God—of meeting, I say, to show obedience with undivided mind to the bishop and the presbytery, and to break the same Bread, which is the medicine of immortality, the antidote against death, and everlasting life in Jesus Christ."[13]

"Take care, then, to partake of one Eucharist; for, one is the Flesh of Our Lord Jesus Christ, and one the cup to unite us with His Blood, and one altar, just as there is one bishop assisted by the presbytery and the deacons, my fellow servants."[14]

4. In his first *Apology* St. Justin wrote, in Rome around the year 155, the following description of the Christian assemblies, which meet on Sunday: "And on the day called Sunday, all who live in the cities or in the country gather together to one place, and the memoirs of the apostles or the writings of the prophets are read, as long as time permits; then, when the reader has ceased, the president verbally instructs, and exhorts to the imitation of these good things. Then we all rise together and pray, and as we before said, when our prayer is ended, bread and wine and water are brought, and the president in like manner offers prayers and thanksgivings, according to his ability, and the people respond, saying *Amen*; and there is a distribution of each, and a participation of that over which thanks have been given, and to those who are absent a portion is sent by the deacons. And they who are well to do, and willing, give what each thinks fit; and what is collected is deposited with the president, who succours the orphans and widows, and those who, through sickness or any other cause, are in want, and those who are in bonds, and the strangers sojourning among us, and in a word takes care of all who are in need."[15]

c) The Anaphora of Hippolytus

The Eucharistic liturgy in the beginning was not fixed in every detail. According to St. Justin, he who presided was able to improvise. The author of the *Didache* indicates the same. In around 215, Hippolytus, it is true, wrote an anaphora[16] which was very successful in the East, but he foresaw that its words would be able to vary.

The structure of the Eucharistic liturgy was, nevertheless, fixed from the very beginning. Four principal moments can be discerned: the *act of*

---

13 "Letter to the Ephesians." *Ancient Christian Writers—The Works of the Fathers in Translation.* Vol 1.
14 "Letter to the Philadelphians." *Ancient Christian Writers* . . . etc. Vol 1.
15 "First Apology," LXVII. *The Ante-Nicene Fathers.* Editors Rev. Alexander Roberts, D.D. and James Donaldson, LL. D., Vol. 1
16 *The anaphora*, that is the *offering*, in reality corresponds to our *Roman Canon.*

thanksgiving, the *institution account*, the *anamnesis*, or the memory of the Savior's Death and Resurrection (an expectation of the Parousia), and finally the *epiklesis*, or the invocation of the Holy Spirit over the community. "Such are the elements of the schema which we find in all the ancient liturgies."[17] They are easily recognizable in the anaphora of Hippolytus:

"The deacons present to the bishop the offering and, he, placing his hands on it, says this *thanksgiving*: 'The Lord be with you!' And all respond: 'And with your spirit!' 'Lift up your hearts!' 'We turn them up toward the Lord!' 'Give thanks to the Lord!' 'It is right and just!' And he continues thus: 'We give Thee thanks, O God, through Thy Beloved Son Jesus Christ, for having sent Him in these final days as Savior, Redeemer and Messenger of Thy will. He is Thy Word, inseparable from Thee, through Whom Thou hast created, and in Whom Thou hast been pleased. Thou hast sent Him from heaven into the womb of a Virgin, and, conceived in her, He has become incarnate, and manifested as Thy Son by His birth of the Holy Spirit and the Virgin. It is in order to fulfill Thy will and win for Thee a holy people that He extended His hands, during the days of His Passion, in order to deliver from suffering those who believe in Thee.

"'It is at the moment that He voluntarily delivered Himself to the Passion in order to destroy death, break the chains of the devil, tread hell under His feet, establish a testament and manifest His Resurrection, that taking bread and giving Thee thanks, He said, *Take, eat, this is My Body broken for you*. In the same way the cup saying, *This is My Blood poured out for you. When you do this, do this in memory of Me.*

"'*We commemorate therefore His Death and Resurrection*, we offer Thee bread and wine, and give Thee thanks that Thou hast judged us worthy to stand before Thee and serve Thee.

"'And we beseech Thee *to send Thy Holy Spirit* upon the offering of the Holy Church. Grant to all the assembled saints who receive it to be filled with the Holy Spirit. May their faith be strengthened in the truth. And may we praise and glorify Thee through Thy Son Jesus Christ, through Whom be glory and honor to Thee, Father, united to the Son and Holy Spirit, in the Holy Church, now and for evermore. Amen.'"[18]

Although with these great lines it reproduced the Roman tradition, the anaphora of Hippolytus is a personal composition, which would take up its position in the liturgy only by passing through Egypt.

What exactly was the text of the primitive Mass in Rome? We do not know. Equally ignorant are we of the date when the Eucharistic

17   Dom Bernard Botte, *L'ordinaire de la Messe* . . . , pp. 15–16.
18   Dom. B. Botte, *Hippolyte de Rome, La Tradition apostolique*, text and French translation (Paris: 1946), pp. 30–33. The Greek text of the *Apostolic Tradition* is lost; the Latin translation which we have is fragmentary.

liturgy ceased to be in Greek. We can write, as did St. Ambrose at the end of the fourth century, that the Roman Canon "arose out of the darkness of prehistory."[19]

3. Liturgical Rites and Languages[20]

a) The Origin of Liturgical Rites

The two principal liturgical centers are Rome and Antioch. The Egyptian rite of Alexandria seems to be connected to the Roman rite by way of the anaphora of Hippolytus. To the Syrian rite of Antioch is related the Gallican rite, introduced in the fourth century in the West, whose center of development seems to have been Milan. Therefore, there were four principal types of liturgies in the fourth century: the Syrian and Alexandrian in the East, and the Roman and Gallican in the West.[21]

In the West the Roman rite prevailed, with variations in practice among the ancient monastic orders. The Galllican rite, after having made some contributions to the Roman rite, ended up being almost entirely eliminated.[22] It survived, nevertheless, in the Ambrosian (Milan)[23] and Mozarabic (Toledo) rites.

In the East the Byzantine rite prevailed; it is thus named because it received its definitive form in Byzantium. It could be called Syro-Byzantine from its Syrian origins. It is certain "that the formulations of the two so-called Byzantine Masses, of St. Basil and St. John Chrysostom, are the result of a slow historical labor accomplished on the liturgies coming from Syria."[24] It is also called the Greco-Slavonic rite. This Byzantine rite,

---

19   Dom B. Botte, *L'ordinaire de la Messe . . .* , pp. 16–17.

     Regarding Gregorian Chant, "it seems rather easy to confirm that the majority of the chants currently in use for the Mass already existed by the fourth century, whether in Rome itself or in the great Churches in union with Rome." Dom Germain Morin, *Les véritables origines du chant grégorien* (Abbaye de Maredsous: 1912), p. 55. The origins of Roman chant are Syro-hellenistic (Antioch) and Jewish (services of the synagogues). *Ibid.*, p. 51.

     On the pilgrimages to the East and their influence in art, see Émile Male, *La fin du paganisme en Gaul et les plus anciennes basiliques chrétiennes* (Paris: 1950), chap. 3.

20   "I will take the liberty of recalling the rules, often forgotten or poorly understood, of the French practice, according to which the term *rite* is used to designate both the liturgical families (the Roman *rite*, the Oriental *rite*), as well as the ceremonies themselves (the *rites* of the Churches, the *rites* of Baptism, the *rite* of the blessing of bells)." Dom A. Wilmart, O.S.B., Annotations on *Le génie du rit romain*, of E. Bishop (Paris: Art catholique, 1920), p. 70.

21   L. Duchesne, *Origines du culte Chrétien*, pp. 56 and 96.

22   *Ibid.*, p. 101.

23   *Ibid.*, p. 92.

24   Severien Salaville, des Augustins de l'Assomption, *Liturgies orientales, La Messe*, t. I, p. 12.

however, contains numerous deviations from ancient rites. The primitive *Alexandrian* type would give birth to: *a)* the Coptic rite; and *b)* the Ethiopian rite. The *Antiochian* or Syrian type would engender: *a)* the Western Syrian rite, which survives under two forms, the pure Syrian (practiced by the Monophysite Jacobites and by Catholics) and the Maronite (practiced by Monothelites and by Catholics); *b)* the Eastern Syrian rite, followed by the Nestorians and Chaldean Catholics; and *c)* the Armenian rite, in use among the Monophysite Armenians and the Catholic Armenians.[25]

b) The Plurality of Rites in the Unity of the Church

Just before the proclamation of the encyclical *Mediator Dei* (November 20, 1947) Pope Pius XII wrote: "In this Encyclical we are concerned primarily with the Latin liturgy. It is not that we have less respect for the venerable liturgies of the Eastern Church, whose rites have been handed down by ancient and glorious texts; they are equally dear to us, *pari ratione carissimi.*"[26]

The concern to keep vigilant watch over the ancient rites has in fact always appeared to the sovereign pontiffs as a mark of the Church's catholicity, capable of welcoming into her unity every form of legitimate worship. Pope Benedict XIV's encyclical on the Oriental rites (26 July 1755), where he recalls the innumerable witnesses of previous popes, was written "in order to manifest to all the benevolence with which the Apostolic See regards Oriental Catholics. In fact: 1) it prescribes that those of their rites which offend neither the Catholic religion or decorum be conserved at all cost; 2) it does not require dissidents returning to the unity of the Church to abandon their rites, but only to refuse and renounce their errors;[27] 3) it ardently hopes that their different nations will be prosperous and not destroyed; and, to sum up much in a few words, that all become Catholics, but not that all become Latins, *omnesque (ut multa paucis complectamur) catholici sint, non ut omnes latini fiant.*"

c) The Latin Rite and the Byzantine Rite

1. The boundaries of the rites are not those of the Church. The Latin rite is housed completely within the Church. The Byzantine rite is associated both with the Catholic Church and to an even greater extent with dissident christendoms.

And the boundaries of the rites are not those of the languages.

25 On the probable development of the Eucharistic celebration in the first century, its progress from Justin to Hippolytus, and the differences of the liturgies in the Eastern world in the fourth century, etc., see also *La structure de la Messe au cours des siècles*, in the work of J.-A. Jungmann, *Missarum sollemnia . . .* , t. I, pp. 29 and ff.

26 AAS 1947, p. 524.

27 We believe we are rendering faithfully the thought and intention of Benedict XIV by translating *schismatici* by "dissidents" and *haereses* by "errors."

2. Latin is the liturgical language for three rites: the Roman rite throughout the whole world, the Ambrosian rite in Milan, the Mozarabic rite in Toledo.

Nevertheless, the Roman rite itself is not tied to Latin. It can use other languages.[28] It was translated into Paleoslavonic for the Churches of Croatia and Dalmatia. In 1615 Pope Pius V, upon the request of St. Bellarmine, authorized a Chinese version of the Roman rite.[29] It is clear that different versions could be made in both ancient and modern languages.

The language which even in the West served for the spread of Christianity was Greek. The Roman Church spoke and prayed in Greek even until the middle of the third century. Only Africa and Spain have always spoken and prayed in Latin. The prestige of Imperial Rome, imposed on the barbarians, brought about the triumph of the use of Latin in the West. Greek, on the other hand, reigned as master in the East after Justinian.[30]

3. The Byzantine rite, like the Roman, preserves a character of universality. Its original language is Greek; but it has been translated into Old Slavonic, Georgian, Arabic, Romanian, and even into Japanese, Korean, Chinese, Hungarian, English, French . . .

Other Oriental rites, on the contrary, eventually coincided so directly with ethnic and linguistic formations that they have practically become nationalized: such as the Armenian, Coptic, Ethiopian and Syrian rites.

4. The Byzantine and Latin rites are different expressions of one single faith. The Byzantine rite is more demonstrative, more emphatic, and is more fitting to the peoples of the East; it will be able to play an important role when the hour of Asia's conversion finally comes.[31] The Latin rite is more restrained, condensed, and adapted to the ethnic and historical

---

28 We now know that the first Mass translated into Slavonic by Cyril and Methodius was the Roman Mass. Cf. J.-A. Jungmann, *Missarum sollemnia* . . . , t. I, p. 114.

29 This concession did not reach those who begged for it. It was asked for again in 1631, under Urban VIII, but was not granted. Cf. Jungmann, *op. cit.*, t. I, p. 211. Later, a Chinese missal, translated by P. Buglio, was printed in Peking in 1670 and put into use. In 1680, however, because of quarrels over the question of Chinese rites, the Congregation of Rites refused to approve it. See Cyrille Korolevskij, *Liturgie en langue vivante, Orient et Occident*, (Paris: Édit. du Cerf, 1955), pp. 150–152.

30 C. Korolevskij, *op. cit.*, pp. 15–17.

31 "To sum up my thought (and I am not the only one with such an idea), I would say that it is certain that the Oriental rite, more full of pomp, more cohesive, is better than the Roman rite for the peoples of Asia. The Roman rite can be more practical, but colder and too much adapted to the Western mentality. A Russia relieved of bolshevism, of caesaropapism, of Byzantine formalism, united to Rome and having rediscovered in this union the vitality which was lacking to the ancient Church of the Tsars (a Church enslaved to

conditions of the West; it seems that it has already resolved the problem of the insertion of the mystery of the Mass into strongly technical civilizations by combining dignity with sobriety.[32]

We are not opposing here one rite against the other. We regard the Byzantine and Latin rites as two versions (among possible others) of an ineffable mystery, which goes beyond them. Both are capable of introducing faithful and loving souls into the depths of this mystery. The rites are not made for the purpose of being contemplated and compared as works of art; they are as so many doors which must be passed through in order to enter into the Holy of Holies.

d) The Use of Sacred Languages in the Liturgy

1. The distinction between sacred and modern languages exists even in the East, where spoken Greek and Slavonic do not perfectly coincide with liturgical Greek and Slavonic. In the West, however, the use of Latin as the principal liturgical language gives it a special importance.

It is evident that the liturgical languages have primarily been the common languages. They became sacred only with time, especially due to a version of Scripture which was approved originally by the Church and then passed into current usage.

2. The sacred languages bring with them the witness of the Church's constancy in time and her unity in space.

Moreover, there is no doubt that a sacred language can allow revealed doctrine to be expressed in a more certain, more pure and more stable manner than modern languages, whose sense can be imperceptibly modified. The fixity of sacred languages is a factor of orthodoxy.

We can add here as well a consideration of the linguistic order. One distinguishes in a language its social and banal role as a means of communication, and then its artistic and mysterious role as a means of expression, as well as its power of evocation. Hence, "in all religious and sacred languages the communication is held in check—in a more or less

---

civil power and often a political instrument) would be able to convert all of Asia." Cyrille Korolevskij, *op. cit.*, p. 228. See the moving *Méditations sur la divine liturgie* of Nicolas Gogol, present by Pierre Pascal (Paris: Desclée De Brouwer, 1952).

32 "There is nothing which consoles me, which pierces my heart, impassions and overwhelms me as the Mass which is celebrated among us. I could assist forever at Mass without ever leaving . . . It is the greatest act on earth . . . Words impatiently hasten to fulfill their mission. They pass rapidly; for they are parts of an integral action. Rapidly, because they are the formidable words of the sacrifice: the work is just too great to be delayed . . . Rapidly, because the Lord Jesus passes with them, as He passed along the lake, calling now this one, now that one . . . " John Henry Cardinal Newman, *Loss and Gain*, chap. 20.

complete manner—to the profit of expression."[33] With the Latinization of the Eucharistic liturgy in Rome the Church found the just mean between two extremes. She was attentive first of all to the establishment of the social element of communication, but at the same time concerned (according to the wish of St. Hilary) with differentiating the liturgical language from the current language in order to raise man out of the mundane and evoke the presence of the mystery.[34] It follows that "there will always exist a certain tension between the essential tasks of the liturgical language: the task of communication and that of religious expression."[35]

3. If one wishes not to run into disorder and anarchy, these questions of tension must be resolved by the supreme canonical authority; and it is clear that its decisions can vary according to differences of time and place. The father of a family, says St. Thomas, is not fickle in asking his children to wear warm clothes in winter and light clothes in summer.[36]

e) Latin and Modern Languages

1. "Although the Mass contains great instruction for the people, it nevertheless has not seemed *expedient* to the Fathers that it be celebrated everywhere in the vernacular language," said the Council of Trent. And the corresponding canon states: "If anyone says . . . that the Mass must be celebrated *only* in the vernacular . . . let him be anathema."[37] The Council did not find it expedient that the Mass be celebrated in the vernacular. Furthermore, it intended to condemn the error that states that the validity of the Mass depends upon the faithful's understanding of the liturgical prayers.

Regarding the role of Latin in the Roman rite, the Encyclical *Mediator Dei* says the following: "The use of the Latin language in a large part of the Church is a sign of the manifest and brilliant unity, and an efficacious protection against every corruption of original doctrine.

"Nevertheless, in several of the rites (ceremonies) the use of modern languages can be very profitable for the people.

"It belongs, however, to the Apostolic See alone to grant such use. Without its counsel and approbation it is forbidden to do anything in this regard, for the organization of the sacred liturgy depends entirely on the Apostolic See's judgment and decision."[38]

33 Christine Mohrmann, *Le latin liturgique, in L'ordinaire de la Messe* . . . , by B. Botte and Chr. Mohrmann, p. 33.
34 *Ibid.*, pp. 35 and 36.
35 *Ibid.*, 36 and 48.
36 III, qu. 61, a. 4, ad 3.
37 Session XXII, chap. 8 and canon 9; Denz. 946 and 956. On the circumstances of this decree, see C. Korolevskij, *op. cit.*, pp. 142–145.
38 AAS 1947, p. 545.

2. This text of the Encyclical underlines, first of all, the advantage of a liturgy in Latin: it is a sign of unity;[39] it is a producer of orthodoxy; and we can add that it is a bearer of beauty.[40]

The misfortune is that the Latin language has ceased to be understood by the people.[41] This can certainly be remedied to some degree. The Council of Trent ordered pastors of souls to explain often (either by themselves or through others) to the faithful, within the Mass,[42] what is being read, and especially to emphasize the mystery of the sacrifice, in order that the children may not beg for bread without anyone there to break it for them.[43] Today, in regions where everyone knows how to read, a hand missal with a translation of the text can be given to the faithful.[44] Need we go further? Some seem to think so: "The necessity of rendering the liturgy more accessible to the people (if one wishes to keep in the practice of their religion the many who are distancing themselves more and more) brings about attempts which are not always pleasant and which only incite more the desire for a reform. The Holy See has taken this into account and has made some concessions for certain parts of the Ritual, especially

---

39 It is a privilege of the Byzantine-Slavonic rite to make use of sacred languages still easily understood by the people. The effort, however, required by the Latin liturgy to elevate us out of our national languages is, in a sense, salutary. It constantly recalls the supra-national catholicity of the Church in a world which sees the rise and fall of the basis of nationalities.

40 What would become of the *Exultet or the Lauda Sion* if they were translated and sung in German or French? We understand why Pius X (and after him Pius XII) recalled "the law according to which the words of the liturgy must not be chanted in the vernacular." AAS 1955, p. 17. See also below, p. 245.

41 Even in Italy. The first of the "five wounds" of the Church which were denounced by A. Rosmini in his work dedicated to the Catholic clergy, (A work entitled *Delle cinque piaghe della santa Chiesa*, which appeared in Lugano in 1848, and was immediately placed on the Index)—the first of these "five wounds" was the incomprehension of the liturgy by the faithful; and the only remedy which he sees to this evil is the suppression of Latin. The other four wounds were: 2) ignorance among the priests, 3) lack of unity among bishops, 4) the nomination of bishops, 5) the distribution of ecclesiastical goods. Rosmini wrote at a time when translating the Missal was not permitted.

42 Especially during the sermon, clarified by Pius XII. AAS 1955, p. 17.

43 Session XXII, chap. 8, Denz. 946.

44 The Church has set Latin aside for herself while Protestantism has adopted the vernacular languages. The translation itself of liturgical prayers into these languages ends up becoming suspect. Perhaps that is the reason why, along with a too severe interpretation of the Council of Trent, that the translation of the Missal into French was condemned successively by the Faculty of Theology of Paris in 1655, by the Assembly of the French Clergy in 1660, then by Alexander VII on January 12, 1661. In 1857, Pius IX renewed the prohibition, but with the accompanying sanctions. It was in 1897, under Leo XIII, that it was definitively abandoned. See C. Korolevskij, *op. cit.*, p. 157;

in mission countries. That is where we are at the present moment. This is a beginning, but one which is open to developments."[45]

4. The Current Roman Setting of the Mystery of the Mass

The celebration of the sacrifice of the Mass is accomplished at the moment of *consecration*. It is preceded by the *offertory* and followed by the *Communion*. Here we have the three integral parts of the liturgy of the Mass. A sort of portico, the *fore-Mass*, of a catechetical nature, gives access to this sacrificial liturgy. The distinction between the fore-Mass and the Mass corresponds, at least to a certain extent,[46] to that which took place in the earliest days between the Mass of the Catechumens and the Mass of the Faithful.

a) The Catechetical Liturgy of the Fore-Mass[47]

The catechetical liturgy prepares us for the sacrifice, where the mystery of faith is accomplished: primarily at the first stage by prayer, then at the second stage by readings from Sacred Scripture, which are intended to instruct and nourish the faith.

1. *The first stage: prayer*. The liturgy begins at the foot of the altar and continues to the altar.

a) Two ancient rites contain in seminal form the prayers which the priest says *at the foot of the altar*—when he advanced up to the altar, he prostrated before it.[48] The altar was the "table of the Lord." When it was made of stone, it seemed more the image of Christ, the "cornerstone" and "spiritual rock." Finally, there was added to it the relics of the martyrs, imitators of Christ.[49]

The entrance to the altar is accompanied, since about the year 1000, by the recitation of Psalm XLII (XLIII) *Judica me* ("Judge me, O God"), the central verse of which sings of the eternal youth which God grants to souls who seek Him: "I will go up to the altar of God, the Giver of triumphant

---

J.-A. Jungmann, *Missarum sollemnia* . . . , t. I, pp. 185 and 206. Pius XII gave his signature of approval to translations of the liturgy into the vernacular; see his encyclical *Musicae sacrae disciplina*, December 25, 1955. AAS 1956, p. 17. It would be necessary, then, to have in each language a single translation of the Bible approved for liturgical usage.

45   C. Korolevskij, *op. cit.*, p. 221. The author, a priest of the Byzantine Rite, is a Consultor of the Sacred Congregation for the Oriental Churches, the Oriental Liturgical Commission, and the Commission for the Oriental Canonical Codification.

46   J.-A. Jungmann, *Missarum sollemnia* . . . , t. II, p. 6.

47   All the historic and liturgical information which we present here is borrowed, except where otherwise indicated, from the monumental work of Joseph Andre Jungmann.

48   *Op. cit.*, t. II, p. 39.

49   *Ibid.*, p. 66.

happiness." God alone, by dividing us from ourselves, can destroy in us the iniquity which ravages us.

In order to accentuate the confession of this unworthiness there is joined a little later a *Confiteor* with its reply; this is followed by the prayer *Aufer a nobis*, which the priest says while going up to the altar: "Take away from us our iniquities, we beseech Thee, O Lord, that we may be worthy to enter with pure minds into the Holy of Holies." Kissing the altar the priest prays: "We beseech Thee, O Lord, by the merits of Thy Saints, whose relics are here, and of all the Saints, that Thou wouldst vouchsafe to forgive me (us) all my (our) sins."[50]

b) At the altar begins a prayer more ancient than the previous, a preparation for the reading of Holy Scripture. It envelops with one movement the *Introit*, part of a psalm initially chanted during the solemn entrance of the clergy; the litany of the *Kyrie*, in which the people participate; sometimes the *Gloria in excelsis*, an ancient canticle of the early Church; and it finishes and culminates in the *Prayer* called the *Collect*, because the priest sums up in it the prayer of the people. The rite of entry reaches its completion with the *Collect*, as the presentation of the offerings will be completed by the *secret*, and the Communion by the *Postcommunion*.[51]

The priest then calls to the people (*Dominus vobiscum*) who gather around him (*Et cum spiritu tuo*), and invites them to unite themselves to the prayer or collect (*Oremus*).[52] The Roman prayers, sober and measured, are Catholic, responding at one and the same time to the greatest needs of the world and the most intimate needs of our hearts. The characteristics are as follows: 1) they are pronounced by the priest, but not in his own name, rather in the name of the whole Church; 2) they are addressed to God considered in the ineffable simplicity of His mystery, *Deus, Domine, Omnipotens Deus, Omnipotens sempiterne Deus*, not to one of the Divine Persons in particular; 3) they have the same movement: invocation, recalling of the mystery of the day, a supplication connected to this mystery; 4) they appeal each time, according to the Gospel precept, to the mediation of Christ, and continually put before our eyes the design of the world's redemption.[53] Listen to the collect from Christmas: "O God, Who hast made this most holy night shine forth with the splendor of the true Light. Grant, we beseech Thee, that we, who have known the Mysteries of His light on earth, may enjoy His happiness in heaven. Who with Thee, God the Father, lives and reigns in the unity of the Holy Spirit,[54] forever and ever. Amen." And from Easter: "O God, Who, on this

50   *Ibid.*, pp. 10–12; 14.
51   *Ibid.*, p. 119.
52   *Ibid.*, pp. 121–123.
53   Batiffol, *Leçons sur la Messe*, pp. 123–124.
54   On the true Trinitarian character of the conclusion of prayers, see B. Botte, *L'ordinaire de le Messe* . . . , pp. 133–139.

day, through Thine only-begotten Son, hast conquered death, and thrown open to us the gate of everlasting life, give effect by Thine aid to our desires, which Thou dost anticipate and inspire. Through the same Jesus Christ, our Lord, Who lives with Thee, God . . ." And the collect of the Fourth Sunday after Easter: "O God, Who makest the faithful to be of one mind and will. Grant to Thy people to love what Thou dost command and to desire what Thou dost promise, that, amid the changes of the world, our hearts may there be fixed where true joys are to be found. Through Our Lord Jesus Christ . . ." And finally, the collect from the Fifth Sunday after Pentecost: "O God, Who hast prepared for them that love Thee such good things as pass understanding. Pour into our heart such love toward Thee, that we, loving Thee in all things, and above all things, may obtain Thy promises, which exceed all that we can desire. Through Our Lord Jesus Christ . . ."

2. *The second stage: the readings.* Formerly and up until the time of St. Augustine, the fore-Mass began immediately after the readings. They are still as important as ever. The catechesis, which they constitute, is the object of the fore-Mass, as the sacrifice, which they prepare one for, is the proper object of the Mass. The readings transmit the message of faith before the mystery of faith is accomplished. Thus the Scriptures, the Word of Christ, proclaim the Eucharist, the presence of Christ. These are the two treasures of the Church.[55] Readings had been used in the synagogue, where they formed the main part of the Sabbath. In the Christian Divine Office the reading of the Old Testament prepares that of the New.[56] Our Masses of Lent draw up striking relations between the Old and New Testaments. As in the Jewish liturgy,[57] since the time of the first Christians the readings have been explained to the people by a homily.

The *Creed*, preceded by the sending away of the catechumens, was inserted into the solemn Mass in the East at the beginning of the 8th century, and into the Roman liturgy in the 9th century. Being a solemn profession of faith made by the faithful, it was meant more to open the imminent sacrificial action than to close the liturgy of the fore-Mass.[58]

---

55   Cf. Jungmann, *op. cit.*, t. II, pp. 7 and 153.—"Without these two things I would not be able to live; for the Word of God is the light of my soul, and His Sacrament the bread of life. They can also be called two tables placed side by side in the treasury of Holy Church . . . " *De imitatione Christi*, IV, 11.

56   Around the 12th century the Epistle side was distinguished from the side of the Gospel. Supposing that a church faced east, the bishop, seated at the base of the apse, had on his right, that is to the north, the deacon who turned toward the people to read the Gospel. Whence the practice of reading the Gospel into the north. JUNGMANN, *op. cit.*, t. II, pp. 178–183.

57   Jesus entered the synagogue in Nazareth on the Sabbath, read and commented on a text of Isaiah (Lk 4:16–21). See also the discourse of St. Paul at Antioch (Acts 13:14).

58   Jungmann, *op. cit.*, t. II, pp. 240–241.

b) The Sacrificial Liturgy of the Mass

The catechetical liturgy of the fore-Mass prepares the sacrificial liturgy of the Mass.

The sacrificial offering is accomplished at the moment of the *consecration*, when Christ now glorious appears under the separated appearances of bread and wine in order to draw us into the drama of His bloody Passion, as He did the disciples at the Last Supper. This sacrificial offering is situated at the heart of an ensemble of prayers called the "canon" in the West and "anaphora" in the East. The canon constitutes the immediate Eucharistic action in the liturgy. It is followed by the *Communion* prayers and preceded by those of the *offertory*.

The offertory and the prayers of the offering can be related principally to the Father, the sacrificial drama to the Son, and the effusion of graces at Communion to the Holy Spirit.[59]

1. *The Offertory.* The offertory acts as an initial anticipation, or rather as a prelude to the canon.[60] It consists essentially in the

59 See the study done by Sévérien Salaville, on the "Épiclèse eucharistique," in the *Dict. De Théol. Catholique*: "A work common to the Three Persons, transubstantiation is not attributed especially to the Holy Spirit except in virtue of an appropriation explained by the Fathers, and in particular by the formula of St. Gregory of Nyssa touching the divine action in general." But why in the Eastern liturgy does the invocation of the Holy Spirit come after the consecration? Would it not be logical for it to precede the consecration? "At first glance, yes. And yet there is, against this *a priori*, the universal fact of the epiklesis at the place which we stated. This universal fact and this unchanging place must have their reason for existence. One must look for this reason, we believe, in another fact, a liturgical fact and one of profound theological inspiration: it is the existence in the canon of the Mass of the very distinct triple euchology (prayer): the euchology of the Father, the euchology of the Son, the euchology of the Holy Spirit. The *preface* is the act of thanksgiving (εὐχαριστία) to God the Father, the gratitude for His work of creation and conservation. The part which extends from the *Sanctus* to the epiklesis is that of the Son accomplishing the work of redemption. The *epiklesis* marks the sanctifying action of the Holy Spirit, but above all the special operation which was just accomplished by the word of the Son in the elements, as happened formerly in the womb of the Virgin by the word of the Angel and of Mary." Liturgists, in fact, distinguish an *epiklesis* of the *consecration* and an *epiklesis of Communion*. It is the place of the first which causes difficulty. Why does it come after the words of the Last Supper? "The epiklesis cannot be related only to the moral sanctification of the faith and to the *Communion*; it must be attached to the very act of the *consecration*. It must be understood as an invocation of the Holy Spirit . . . Who with the Father and the Son works the transubstantiation at the moment when the priest pronounces the Gospel words. It is placed after these words, 1) in order not to interrupt the exact reproduction of the Savior's Last Supper" and to give "an explanation of the act already accomplished;" 2) in order to ask that the sacrifice be profitable to the Mystical Body. Col. 293–297, 278.

60 Jungmann, *op. cit.*, t. II, pp. 379–380.

presentation to God of bread and wine mixed with a little water, which will be transubstantiated.

The texts of the offertory, which express humility, repentance, invocation and supplication, have come together over time.

This whole rite of offering is finally recapitulated in the prayer called the *secret*, as the rite of entrance is summed up in the collect, and the rite of Communion in the post-communion.[61]

The secret, no doubt, owes its name to the simple fact that it is said in silence. Formerly it was, like the canon, said out loud. Toward the end of the 8th century, under the influence of the Franks, the silence seemed to be a more holy preparation for approaching God.[62]

Let's listen to the secret for the Feast of Epiphany: "Look graciously, we beseech Thee, O Lord, upon the offerings of Thy Church, in which are no longer offered gold, frankincense, and myrrh: but He, Who by these same gifts was signified, is sacrificed and received, Jesus Christ, Thy Son, Our Lord, Who lives and reigns . . ." That of the Saturday before the Fourth Sunday of Lent: "Be appeased, we beseech Thee, O Lord, to accept our offerings; and in Thy goodness move our rebellious wills to turn toward Thee. Through Jesus Christ, Our Lord, Who lives and reigns . . ." That of the Mass of St. Gregory the Great: "Grant, we beseech Thee Lord, that through the intercession of Blessed Gregory, this offering might be profitable for us, for it is when it is offered that Thou deignest to pardon the sins of the whole world."[63]

2. *The Canon or the Great Prayer.* The canon consists of two distinct movements. One, which forms the setting of the canon, is that of an upward motion of *thanksgiving* or eucharist, leading from the words of *consecration* to their completion in the *anamnesis* and praise. The other is the sentiment of a silent descent of the sacred and ineffable mystery of the Last Supper into our midst. These two movements seem to have inverse exigencies: the first invites us to a public and open participation; the second seems to call for a participation of silence and adoration—hence the more recent practice of pronouncing the canon in a low voice.[64]

a) *The Thanksgiving* or *Eucharist* begins with the solemn dialogue which opens the preface. It is followed by a profound adoration expressed by the *Sanctus*. At the end of the 4th century, Rome, following the example of the East, placed between the *Sanctus* and the consecration the intercessory prayers: *Te igitur, Memento, Communicantes, Hanc igitur.* Here we pray for the Holy Catholic Church, in order that she might be preserved from without and unified from within.[65] We mention by

61   *Ibid.*, pp. 369, 371, 381.
62   *Op. cit.*, t. III, pp. 8, 48.
63   See other Secrets above, pp. 52, 115, 131.
64   Jungmann, *op. cit.*, t. III, p. 6.
65   *Ibid.*, p. 65.

name her servants, that is, those who are her heads: the pope and bishops. We commemorate the faithful, not only those present but those everywhere who unite themselves in spirit to the central offering of the Mass. The needs of the dead are remembered as well.[66] Those in the Church here below, who "render praise to the eternal God, living and true," form a communion of intention with the Blessed Virgin Mary, Mother of Our Lord Jesus Christ, with the apostles, martyrs and all the saints of the heavenly Church.[67] Finally, just before the culminating point of the sacred action, the *Hanc igitur* of St. Gregory the Great sums up again the supreme prayer of the clergy (the servants—*servitutis nostrae*) and the entire people (the family—*cunctae familiae tuae*) and the permanent need of Christendom, namely divine peace here below, perseverance at the moment of death and the final salvation of all men: "Dispose our days in Thy peace, preserve us from eternal damnation, and rank us among the number of Thine Elect."[68]

b) *The Consecration.* The consecration is introduced by the *Quam oblationem*, where we beseech God to change the bread and wine into the Body and Blood of His Beloved Son:[69] "Which oblation do Thou, O God, vouchsafe in all respects to bless, approve, ratify, make perfect and acceptable; that it may become for us the Body and Blood of Thy most beloved Son Jesus Christ Our Lord."[70]

The miracle of transubstantiation is due to the divine omnipotence, an omnipotence ordinarily attributed to the Father but common to the Three Divine Persons. This omnipotence, nevertheless, acts through the humanity of Christ. It enters immediately on the scene with the narration of the institution: "Who, the day before He suffered, took bread into His sacred and venerable hands . . ."

We are now truly at the heart of the Mass. But up until this narration one must make allowance for that which is the sacred liturgy of the Church and that which is the divine liturgy of Christ. Recall the words of St. Ambrose: "All the rest which had been said before was said by the priest: he offered praises to God, he prayed for the people, for kings, for all. When he is about to confect, *ut conficiatur*, the venerable sacrament,

---

66 *Ibid.*, p. 75.
67 *Ibid.*, p. 382. We must add the end of the *Memento* to the beginning of the *Communicantes* and read, according to Jungmann: *Tibi reddunt vota sua, aeterno Deo vivo et vero, communicantes et memoriam venerantes* . . . The word *communicantes*, placed in the canon as a testimony, clearly recalls the great text of 1 Peter 4:13: *Communicantes Christi passionibus, gaudete* . . .
68 *Ibid.*, pp. 99–101.
69 Jungmann considers this prayer as the consecrating epiklesis of the Roman Mass. *Ibid.*, p. 106.
70 *Ibid.*, p. 106. On the sense of the word *rationabilem* translated here by the word "perfect," see B. Botte, *L'ordinaire de la Messe* . . . , pp. 79 and 122.

the priest no longer uses his own words but the words of Christ. It is the word of Christ, then, which confects this sacrament."[71]

This liturgy of the Church is the context in which are inserted the very words of Christ. They alone are efficacious with regards to transubstantiation and the perpetuation of the redemptive sacrifice.[72] It can be rather striking that these liturgical narrations of the institution, and especially the more ancient, never purely and simply reproduce one of the narrations from Scripture. The reason for this is, as has been said, that they precede the redaction of Scripture. The Eucharist was celebrated before St. Paul and the Evangelists had picked up the pen.[73]

The liturgy of Christ consists in the efficacious words of transubstantiation. With each renewal of the unbloody rite of the Last Supper the now-glorious Christ comes silently to touch us by means of His Cross. The word "liturgy" takes on a different meaning, we believe, when it passes from the level of the canonical cultic dispositions of the Churches to the level of the bloody sacrifice celebrated one time in order to save the world, and applied, rendered present, to each succeeding generation. Christ's sacrifice transcends all liturgical settings of the East and West. It is at the same time and eminently, infinite adoration and infinite thanksgiving, infinite offering and infinite supplication, infinite praise and infinite propitiation, an act of infinite worship and an act of infinite love. All the prayers of invocation, of offering, of thanksgiving, which the liturgies distinguish and multiply before and after the very sacrifice of Christ, will never be but feeble reflections of the theandric Liturgy of the Savior in the broken mirrors of our hearts.

c) *The Anamnesis or Commemoration.* What just took place? The first concern of the Church, who once again returns to the path of the Great Prayer, is to define that path.[74] We just *commemorated* what Christ did at the Last Supper, consecrating bread and wine according to His command: "Do this in memory of Me." And if He then changed the bread and wine into His Body and Blood, it was in order to permit His disciples to *participate in His bloody sacrifice*, to enter with Him into the offering of His bloody sacrifice. Whence the two elements of the *Unde et memores*. First the *commemoration*: "Wherefore, O Lord . . . calling to mind the blessed Passion of the same Christ, Thy Son, Our Lord, and also His Resurrection from the Dead and His glorious Ascension into heaven . . ." Then the *supplication*, not that the redemptive sacrifice be acceptable in itself, but that it be acceptable insofar as it is presented by us today. We beseech the Divine Goodness to accept it without separating us from it, to deign to incorporate

---

71   *De sacramentis*, chap. 4, 14.
72   See above, p. 113.
73   Jungmann, *op. cit.*, t. III, p. 111. See above, p. 138.
74   *Ibid.*, p. 136.

us into it. This supplication is continued in the *Supra quae*, which recalls that the sacrifices of Abel, Abraham and Melchizedek were already accepted. In the *Supplices* we ask that the gift, which we desire to make of ourselves by uniting ourselves to Christ, be fully acceptable, that is, according to an image borrowed from the Apocalypse (8:3–5), transferred by the angels to the throne of God. But it is here, in its second half, that the *Supplices* takes a new turn, and expresses the desire that the carrying of our sacrifice to the altar of heaven have the effect of a bountiful communion.[75] The anaphora is completed and Communion is sought. The *Nobis quoque* will act as a continuation of the *Supplices*, from which it seems to have been separated by a later insertion of the *Memento* of the dead. Finally, a prayer of praise to God, Who by His created word sanctifies, vivifies and blesses, is completed in the trinitarian doxology: "Through Him, with Him, in Him, in the unity of the Holy Spirit, all honor and glory be Thine, God all-powerful Father, for ever and ever. Amen."

3. *Communion*. The *Pater*, which by its solemnity seems to respond to the preface and to continue the canon, in reality inaugurates the liturgical cycle of Communion. From earliest times it has served to prepare the neophytes for their first Communion. It is the Lord's Prayer which one recites with trembling in order to implore pardon for one's sins before receiving the consecrated bread, the Lord's Body. The need for pardon is made felt up until the *Libera nos* which follows.[76]

The *fractio* of the host marks off the priest's share, then the part belonging to the people, which serves also as a holy reserve, and finally, the part which is kept in order to be dropped into the chalice, which signifies the unity of the Church—a unity in time, by joining the Mass of yesterday with that of today, and a unity in space, by joining the Mass of the bishop to that of his priests.[77] The breaking of the host was later related to the Death of Christ, and its mingling in the chalice to His Resurrection.[78]

At Rome, during the first thousand years, the prayer of the priest, as we noted, was addressed to God, Who was adored in the mystery of His unity. The invoking of Christ in the *Kyrie* was reserved for the congregation. Similarly, the *Agnus Dei*, an invoking of the immolated Christ, was, ever

---

75 *Ibid.*, p. 155. It is truly an epiklesis, an invocation to the Divine Omnipotence, but this time an *epiklesis of Communion*, not an *epiklesis of consecration*. However, in a wider sense one can give the name epiklesis to all the prayers which follow the anamnesis. See above, p. 293. The signs of the cross over the Eucharistic bread and wine seem to have had primarily an indicative sense. They seem today to signify the desire to bless by means of Christ's sacrifice those who present the sacrifice. *Ibid.*, pp. 157–158. Let us say that, made over Christ, the blessings come down from Him to us. See above, p. 114.

76 Jungmann, *op. cit.*, pp. 202 and following.

77 *Ibid.*, p. 235.

78 *Ibid.*, p. 245.

since its beginning in 8th century, a hymn chanted by the people during the breaking of the bread.[79]

The three prayers to Christ in preparation for the priest's Communion are not of Roman origin. They began to appear in the 9th century.[80]

The Communion of the priest is followed by that of the faithful. Up until the 4th century the faithful communicated at every Mass; and even more often than that, since the Mass was limited to Sunday, and the consecrated bread was preserved in order to be communicated each day.[81] Later, Communion became rarer, especially (a strange thing!) in the countries where the war against Arianism obliged one to insist on the reverence due to the transcendence and divinity of Christ. The end of the Middle Ages and the Council of Trent once again favored frequent Communion. Thus, for two thousand years we see alternately prevailing two opposing views: while faith brought the baptized to regard the bread from heaven as his daily bread, reverence made him afraid to approach the holy mysteries rashly.[82] Due reverence, however, ought not to engender estrangement.

Toward the 13th century there was spread out before the communicants who knelt before the altar a cloth held by two acolytes. The altar, which is first of all the place of the sacrifice, is also the table of the Lord.[83] In the 17th century our table of Communion would replace the ancient rood screens. It is "the noble task of the builder of churches to know how to suggest by the disposition and style that an intimate relation unites this table of Communion to the true holy table, and that by kneeling at the one we ascend to the other."[84]

As we mentioned before, there is a parallelism between the entrance procession which concludes with the *collect*, the offertory procession which concludes with the *secret*, and the Communion procession which concludes with the *postcommunion*. These three prayers are conceived

79   *Ibid.*, p. 263.
80   *Ibid.*, p. 274.
81   *Ibid.*, p. 291.
82   *Ibid.*, pp. 294–297.
83   From the theological point of view, *the notion of sacrifice takes precedence over that of a meal*. The whole notion of meal is based on one's participation in the immolation of the victim. To those who tend to subordinate the sacrifice to the Communion of the faithful, the Encyclical *Mediator Dei* responds that, "the Eucharistic sacrifice consists by its very nature in the *unbloody immolation* of the Divine Victim, an immolation which is mysteriously indicated by the separation of the sacred species and by their oblation made to the eternal Father. *Holy Communion* assures its integrity, and its goal is to allow one to participate sacramentally. Nevertheless, though it is absolutely necessary from the part of the minister who offers the sacrifice, it is only strongly recommended to the faithful." AAS 1974, 563.
84   *Ibid.*, p. 308.

according to the same style.[85] Listen to the postcommunion for the Friday after Ash Wednesday: "Protect, Lord, Thy people, and in Thy clemency purify us from all sins; for no adversity will harm us, if no iniquity rules us. Through Jesus Christ . . ." And that of Easter: "Pour forth upon us, O Lord, the spirit of Thy love, that those whose hunger Thou hast satisfied with the Sacraments of Easter may in Thy kindness be one in heart. Through Jesus Christ . . ." And finally that of Pentecost: "May the infusion of the Holy Spirit, O Lord, cleanse our hearts, and render them fruitful by the inward sprinkling of His dew. Through Our Lord Jesus Christ, Who lives and reigns with Thee in the unity of the Holy Spirit . . ." The entire doctrine of the Church regarding the effects of Communion could be found in an analysis of the postcommunion prayers. We beg Christ to come to accomplish His redemptive work in those who receive Him; to aid them in the order of means and in the order of ends, in things temporal and spiritual, for the present and the future, in body and in soul. We pray that He might make us increase in charity, that He might allow us to serve Him, to remain faithful to Him, never to be separated from Him. We pray that, after having been given to us under sacramental signs, He might reveal Himself to us in our heavenly homeland with faces unveiled.[86]

The conclusion of the Mass is a final benediction. It was expressed in the early days by the "Prayer Over the People," which today terminates our Masses of Lent. This final benediction gives signification to the Roman rite's *Ite missa est* and the *Go in peace* of the Eastern rites. The Prologue of St. John was considered a text especially rich in benediction.[87] Let us say that it quickly tears away the veil which hides the Fatherland from us, and that it unfurls above our heads the immensity of the creative and redemptive plan of the God of love.

5. The Transcendence of the Mystery and Liturgical Tensions

a) Liturgical Dilemmas

1. The mystery of the Mass is beyond its own liturgical expressions. Legitimate and necessary as they are, they still remain by their very nature inadequate to the task. They represent but partial truths; and a tension is created among them.

---

85 *Ibid.*, p. 358.

86 Cf. *Ibid.*, pp. 360–361.

87 When Jacques Cartier landed in Canada, the Indians brought to him the blind, the lame and the paralytics. Then, "seeing the faith of that people, he read the Gospel of John, namely the *In principio*, making the Sign of the Cross over the sick, praying to God that He would grant them a knowledge of our holy Faith and our Savior's Passion, and the grace to receive Christianity and Baptism." Cited by Etienne Gilson in his Discourse at his reception into the Académie Française, *Doc. Cath.* (1947), col. 867.

Ought we to insist, first of all, on the primordial, enveloping and supremely efficacious role of Christ's sacrifice in the liturgy? Or ought we, on the contrary, to accent the secondary role of the sacrifice of the Church and the participation of the faithful?

Ought we to underline that which separates the priest from the faithful, namely the divine and inalienable privilege of the power of Orders? Or ought we rather to note the grace of union with Christ, and in addition, the grace of communion among all the faithful, both priests and laity—the more divine and final end of the power of Orders?

Ought we to fix our attention on the stability, solemnity and poetry of the liturgical language, or rather to throw ourselves into profane languages?

Ought we to adore in silence the ineffable mystery of the world's redemption made present in our midst, or rather to have it proclaimed to the people?

Ought we to preach the unimaginable sanctity of sacramental Communion and the preparation required if one does not wish to eat and drink to one's own condemnation, or rather to insist on the misery of a people who must beg for sacramental Communion, even with regards to preparation and the very desire for this Communion?

> I engrave the degrees of Thy mercies—from fall to fall
> I learn to recognize Thy humble heart in my own faults
>
> And Thy unbearable sweetness—Lamb of God
> Which melts that which it touches or destroys it like fire . . . [88]

Ought we to exalt and lose ourselves in the spirit of the crowd through the chant and unceasing rotation of collective exercises, or rather to close the door and enter into our interior and question ourselves regarding the truth of our faith, hope and charity?[89]

Ought we to accept the chant and music as means to open the soul to prayer and things divine, as St. Thomas did,[90] or rather to point out the dangers of dissipation which they can bring, as St. Augustine did—but only

---

88 Raïssa Maritain, *La vie donnée* (Paris, s. d., Desclée de Brouwer).

89 The purpose of the ceremonies of the Mass is, according to the Council of Trent, "to elevate the souls of the faithful to the contemplation of the mysteries hidden in this sacrifice." Session XXII, chap. 5; Denz. 943.

90 "Salubriter fuit institutum ut in divinas laudes cantus assumerentur, *ut animi infirmorum* magis provocarentur ad devotionem." ["The use of music in the divine praises is a salutary institution, that the souls of the faint-hearted may be the more incited to devotion."] St. Thomas, *Summa Theologiae* II-II, qu. 91, a. 2. Notice the words we placed in italics. [Translator's note: The original French edition incorrectly cited this quote as coming from the Prima Secundae.]

after having explained to us how he himself wept in Milan upon hearing the sweet melodies of the Church?[91]

2. We see the tensions which have given birth to diverse rites reappearing within the same rite. Looked at with the eyes of faith and contemplation, the mystery of redemption continued in each Mass is one, perfect, unchangeable, infinitely simple, embracing in its horizon the universality of time and space, absolutely transcendent with respect to its liturgical forms, which have but a secondary value. But the good order and life of the ecclesial community needs precisely these liturgical forms. They make up the object of pastoral power, which must be concerned with the changing needs of the faithful, and the law of which is to go forth in time and space according to the way one travels, emphasizing at each turn one or another aspect of the mystery. Each of these partial and temporary liturgical forms will have faithfully served when it will help introduce a faithful soul into the universe of God, Who exceeds it.

b) Liturgy and Dogma

Since the liturgical expressions are surpassed by the fullness of the mystery, then it is not the liturgy as such which will be the supreme authority when it is time to define the essence of the sacrifice of the Mass.

In a more general order, the axiom affirming that prayer rules belief is true only in a subordinate manner. It is rather that faith, and with it hope and love, rules prayer.

Having cited the axiom, *Legem credendi lex statuat supplicandi*, that the rule of prayer is the rule of believing, Pius XII explains its meaning: "The sacred liturgy, consequently, does not decide or determine independently and of itself what is of the Catholic Faith. More properly, since the liturgy is also a profession of eternal truths, and subject as such to the supreme teaching authority of the Church, it can supply proofs and testimony, quite clearly, of no little value, toward the determination of a particular point of Christian doctrine. But if one desires to differentiate and describe the relationship between faith and the sacred liturgy in absolute and general terms, it is perfectly correct to say, *Lex credendi legem statuat supplicandi*—let the rule of belief determine the rule of prayer."[92]

---

91 "Quantum flevi in hymnis et canticis tuis, suave sonantis Ecclesiae tuae vocibus, commotus acriter." ["How I wept uncontrollably, moved as I was by Thy hymns and canticles, the sweet sounds of Thy Church."] *Confessions*, IX, chap. 7, no. 14. On this text was written for us the following: "The liberating action of the music suddenly delivers one from fear of effort and from distractions, from strange images, and from the distance between time and eternity. The burning love transports the soul and enlightens the faith. The conquered heart brings us the sweetness of tears."

92 Encyclical *Mediator Dei*, AAS 1947, 541.

c) The Gentleness of the Unbloody Sacrifice

1. One could love a grand Mass chanted outside in plain-chant by some unknown people; or a Mass of Easter or of Pentecost in a Benedictine abbey, when the contained yet contagious nobility of the liturgical chant wins the hearts of the faithful, who fill the nave. Or one could also love a Cistercian Mass in the melancholy peacefulness of dawn, with the austere, sorrowful, heart-rending supplication of the *Kyrie*, the prostrations which throw a man to the ground as the only reminder of the Incarnation, or the repetition of the *Agnus Dei*, the sound of the bells which announce to the world beyond the cloister the moment of consecration, the sanctuary lamp which flickers because someone has received some of its light, as Christ's heart must flutter when a soul seeks love from it—the whole drama of the bloody Cross and the world's redemption is transported in the ineffable silence, the gentleness, the peace of the unbloody sacrifice.

It is this mystery of the presence of the bloody sacrifice under the veil of the unbloody sacrifice which Grunewald's reredos at Colmar evokes, when he places the chalice of the Mass and the brilliant whiteness of the immaculate Lamb close to the swollen and bleeding feet of the immense Crucified Christ.

> On the altar are accomplished Thy Mysteries
> Lord of the ordered rites
> Lord of Scriptures, Lord of sacred chants . . .
>
> Thou Who turns not the poor away,
> Thou comest to us in Thy sweetness
> In Thy love, in Thy power—move away a bit Lord
>
> Move away a bit if Thou wilt that I live
> Am I the flaming bush, which burns without being consumed?
> I am a heart adrift . . .[93]

2. It happens that the circumstances of time and place allow the Mass suddenly to reveal the unimaginable depths of its mystery to those who assist with an extraordinary intensity. Think, if you will, of that Mass at dawn in Graham Greene's novel, *The Power and the Glory*, feverishly improvised in the heart of the Mexican forest, when the police begin to surround the village; or at that solemn celebration of the Church's last Pentecost with which Msgr. Benson ends his novel, *Lord of the World*. Or, leaving the world of fiction behind, think of those Masses said at night on the cots of prisons—a little bread and wine miraculously concealed by some priests, surrounded by a few of the faithful eager to communicate sacramentally one last time before they die.

93   Raïssa Maritain, *La vie donnée*.

6. The Churches

a) The Church, the House of the Christian People

1. One of the more revolutionary traits of Christianity is the fact that it has freed cultures from their necessary bonds to determined places, holy mountains or sacred woods, or even their ties with the Temple in Jerusalem. The faithful people are themselves the Temple of God (2 Cor 6:16; 1 Cor 3:16). Wherever it is has spread, from the rising of the sun to its setting, a new sacrifice is offered (Mal 1:11). The true sanctuary is no longer on Mount Garazim or in Jerusalem, but wherever true adorers adore in spirit and in truth (Jn 4:21).[94]

2. Men need houses; Christ needed an upper room. The living temple of the faithful will build, according to its proper structure, the houses it will need. The word which signifies the Christian assembly, *ecclesia*, would come to signify the house, *church*, where that assembly would come together and commemorate the redemptive Death of Christ and be filled with His Spirit. As the hymn from the *Didache* states, the church of stone will be the image of the living Church. It will contain, therefore, the people and the clergy, a *nave* and a *choir*. When all turn to pray toward the place where Christ has risen, it will be a "nave" sailing toward the east.[95]

The *altar*, which replaces the table where the offerings are laid, is between the nave and the choir, and is primarily the place of the celebration of the sacrifice, the center toward which all else converges. It is, in a secondary manner, the table where one communicates in the sacrifice. Even in the round churches the altar is placed in the east, not the center. The Middle Ages move the altar to the choir; and the east isolates it from the people by the iconostasis. In the churches of religious communities and canons, the choir is made larger and becomes a second church, where the divine office is recited: a rood screen separates it from the nave. The Baroque Period would replace the rood screen with the Communion table and reestablish the unity between the choir and the nave, but without changing the place of the altar.[96] Thus, the table where the offerings are placed is no more than a movable accessory. It would become less and less important. It was the altar, and then the Lord's table, which our present table of Communion recalls. Today, says Pius XII, "to wish to return the altar to its primitive form would be to veer from the right path."[97]

3. Summing up the evolution of what is called "the spatial exigencies of the Eucharistic celebration," J.-A. Jungmann writes: "The inner power

---

94   Cf. J.-A. Jungmann, *Missarum sollemnia . . .* , t. I, p. 307.

95   *Ibid.*, p. 308. The majority of the Roman basilicas face the west. "The orientation of the churches was first toward the east, then the west." *Ibid.* [Translator's note: There is here a play on the Latin word *navis*, which means ship.]

96   *Ibid.*, pp. 309–311. See above, p. 224.

97   Encyclical *Mediator Dei*, AAS 1947, 545.

and depth of the Christian Mass magnificently reveals itself in the fact that, spiritual to the point of not being fettered by necessity to a place, it has nevertheless found its expression in space, in masterpieces of architecture and sculpture throughout the world, more than any other idea of human history."[98] Every page of Emile Mâle's work illustrates this fact with knowledge and love.

b) The Church, Even More So the House of Christ

1. Still more than the house of the Christian people, the church is the house of Christ.[99] A mystery, a presence, fills even the poorest of the Catholic churches. The church is inhabited. It does not live primarily by the motion of the comings-and-goings, which the crowds bring to it. A church is, rather, the very source of life and purity for those who enter within its walls. It possesses a real presence, the corporal presence of Christ, where Love Supreme touched our human nature in order to contract an eternal wedding with it, the hearth of a radiance capable of illuminating the entire drama of time and human affairs.

Everyone can enter in and personally encounter the Jesus of the Gospel. Everyone, no matter how ignorant they might be, and even though the memory of whose faults and whose secret interior trials can be overwhelming—everyone can dare to approach, as did the sinful woman in the house of Simon the Pharisee. Everyone can cry out to him, as did the blind man from Jericho: "Lord, that I might see!"

When an honest man asks us what he must do to find the Truth, before being able to explain to him the Christian catechism and mysteries, before also throwing him into the crowd of believers, where he will feel strange and where the Church which he does not yet know might appear to him to be equal to all others—before all this, we can ask him to go and sit awhile each day in an empty church, just him and the Gospel. Later, when he understands that the Real Presence is the raison d'être of the Church's permanence in space and time until the end the world, then his eyes will open to the Catholicity of the mystery of the Church, and her most humble attempts to gather men around Christ will become clear to him.

---

98 J.-A. Jungmann, *op. cit.*, p. 307.

99 The first churches of Jerusalem recall the mysteries of Christ's life: the Holy Sepulcher, the Resurrection, the Ascension. All the churches of Rome, until the fifth century, were dedicated to Christ.

Pope Sixtus III (432–440) was the first to consecrate a basilica to the Virgin Mary, built on the Esquiline Hill. As the Blessed Virgin contained the beginnings of the mystery of the Incarnation, so the Notre-Dames of the world house its permanence in space and time.

When a church is dedicated to the Blessed Virgin or to the saints, it is always because of their close intimacy with the mystery of the redemptive Incarnation.

2. There are too many ugly churches in our day to speak unreservedly with the Psalmist of the beauty of the house of God. Beauty is ardently desired. It certainly does not fetter the power of prayer; but it's another thing when it concerns the meeting of a soul with Christ in the Sacrament. There can be a harsh attack, even savage at times—a ray from the bloody Cross which tears the soul in its very depths.

There is no church sadder than that church in London, in which the heroine of Graham Greene's *The End of an Affair* takes refuge one stormy night; and it is from the depths of that ugliness that she fails to see Jesus approaching—Jesus, Who was acquainted with indescribable agony, an agony given to Him in order that He might make His supreme and decisive act of love.

Each Mass is, by means of the Cross of Christ, a great blessing, a silent explosion of love, a grand descent of God into the world in order to prevent it from perishing and to prevent evil from completely prevailing over the good. And in return, each Mass provokes, in a hidden part of the world, a response of love, which, by means of the Cross of Christ, ascends back up to God.

St. Thomas remarks, concerning the mystery of the Incarnation[100] (yet the principle is valid in every circumstance), that, when it is a question of mutual relations between God and the world, it is important to consider first and foremost the downward movement of the divine plenitude toward man; and only afterwards that which is as a feeble echo, namely the upward movement by which men thus predisposed turn toward their God.

---

100 St Thomas, *Summa Theologiae* III, qu. 34, a. 1, ad. 1.

APPENDIX I

Two Papal Documents

A. The Teaching of the Encyclical "Mediator Dei" on the Nature and Offering of the Mass

The encyclical *Mediator Dei et hominum, On the Sacred Liturgy,* November 20, 1947,[1] contains four parts: *I. The Nature, Origin and Progress of the Liturgy; II. Eucharistic Worship; III. The Divine Office and the Liturgical Year; IV. Practical and Pastoral Directives.* The second part, reserved for the mystery of the Eucharist, is subdivided into four sections: *1. The Nature of the Eucharistic Sacrifice; 2. The Participation of the Faithful in the Offering of the Eucharistic Sacrifice; 3. Holy Communion; 4. Eucharistic Adoration.* There is a very brief schema of the first two sections, where the common teaching of the Church regarding the Eucharist is authoritatively proposed, which we believe would be useful to present here in order to show the doctrine's logical and organic order. It is a little more developed than the table of contents.[2]

1. Recall the doctrine of the Council of Trent, according to which Christ institutes the Eucharistic sacrifice in order that the bloody sacrifice, which must be accomplished on the Cross, be represented; that the commemoration of that bloody sacrifice be perpetuated until the end of time; that its power be applied to us.

2. This is no simple commemoration, but a true and real sacrificial act, where, by an unbloody immolation, the Sovereign Priest does that which He did on the Cross, offering up His very self.[3]

3. The Priest at the Mass is the same as on the Cross, but now He offers Himself through the hands of His ministers. The Priest is Christ. The ministers act in His name. Through the priestly consecration the ministers are assimilated to the Sovereign Priest. They possess the power to act in the name and power of Christ.

---

1   AAS 1947, 521–600.
2   It is found at the end of the encyclical, AAS, p. 598.
3   Further on the Encyclical responds to those who wish to see the culminating point of the Mass in the moment of Communion and the common meal: "the Eucharistic sacrifice consists, by its very nature, in the *unbloody immolation* of the Divine Victim—an immolation which is mystically indicated by the separation of the sacred species and their oblation to the Eternal Father. *Holy Communion* assures its integrity and has for its end sacramental participation . . ." AAS, p. 563.

4. The Victim is the same, but under a different presentation. On the Cross Christ offered Himself to God along with all of His sorrows; the immolation happens by His bloody death. On the altar the sacrificial action of the Redeemer is made manifest in an admirable manner through the exterior signs of death: the Body and Blood are really present through transubstantiation. Their separation is represented. Death really happens at Calvary; the commemorative manifestation of the death is reenacted on each altar, where Christ is represented in the state of a victim.

5. The ends of the sacrifice are the same on the Cross and at the Mass: the homage of praise and adoration of the Cross is continued in the Eucharistic sacrifice, to which is united the Church here below and the Church in heaven; the thanksgiving of Christ rendered to the Father, in recognition of the love by which He loved us, continues from the Cross to the Mass; the expiation, propitiation and reconciliation of Christ offered on the Cross for the sins of the whole world are continued at the Mass, where He offers Himself for our redemption; the impetration and supplication begun on the Cross continues on our altars.

6. The sacrifice of the Cross has fully redeemed the world and has prepared a pool, as it were, in which the whole human race can be purified. In order that men, each and every one of them, might be suited to this treasure, to enter into living contact with the Cross, to plunge into this pool, Christ arranged it that they should gain access to this by the sacraments, by the Eucharistic sacrifice, which is the supreme means whereby the merits of the Cross are distributed; for, men are in constant need of the Blood of redemption.

7. Only the priest can act in the name of Christ in order to carry out the unbloody immolation by which Christ is made present on the altar in the victim state. In other words, he is the only minister of Christ for the offering, which is accomplished by transubstantiation.

8. In a more limited sense we can call the offering the act by which the Divine Victim, already present on the altar, is offered to God the Father for the spiritual welfare of the entire Church. The faithful can participate in this second offering made by the priest in two ways: 1) They offer it first of all *through the hands* of the priest—the minister at the altar represents Christ, Who as Head offers the sacrifice in the name of all His members, in the name of His whole Church; 2) They offer it also *in union* with the priest—certainly not by consecrating with him, but in joining their acts of praise, supplication, expiation and thanksgiving to those of the minister and the High Priest.

9. The faithful must unite themselves not only to Christ the Priest but to Christ the Victim as well. The faith and devotion with which they participate at Mass will move them to become like unto Christ, Who offers Himself for the world. The Pontiff reminds new priests that they must be conscious of what they have become; they must imitate what they do; they must put to death in themselves their vices and concupiscences. It is

especially at Mass that the words of the Apostle are applied to the priest: "I am crucified with Christ; and I live, no not I, but Christ Who lives in me" (Gal 2:19–20).

B. An Allocution of Pope Pius XII to the Participants of the International Congress of Pastoral Liturgy

In the closing Allocution, given in French (September 22, 1956) to the participants of the *International Congress of Pastoral Liturgy*,[4] the Holy Father judged it "useful to mention some important points, which are currently being discussed in the liturgico-dogmatic field" and which he "holds dear to his heart." He groups them under two headings.

1. The Liturgy and the Church

The *liturgical activity*, in which the hierarchy and the faithful participate together, as rich and as vast as it is, does not cover all of the *cultic acts* of the Church, which include not only *liturgical* acts, but *private* acts of worship as well: "The liturgy, however, is not *the whole Church*. It does not exhaust the field of her activities. There is, in addition to public worship (that of the community), a place for private worship, which the individual renders to God in the secret depths of his heart or expresses by external acts, and which possesses as many variations as there are Christians, although it proceeds from the same faith and grace of Christ. Not only does the Church tolerate this form of worship, but she fully recognizes and recommends it, without ever taking anything away from the preeminence of the liturgical cult."

Acts of worship, on the other hand, represent but one part of the Church's *pastoral activities*. The pastoral functions of teaching and governing regulate the truth and order of worship. "They extend to the world beyond. In order to see this one has only to take a glance at canon law and what it states about the pope, the Roman Congregations, bishops, councils, the Magisterium and ecclesiastical discipline."

In conclusion, the Holy Father notes two types of excess: first, those who tend "to give religious and pastoral teaching an exclusively liturgical sense"; second, those who tend "to place on the liturgical movement limits which do not pertain to it."

2. The Liturgy and the Lord

The Holy Father touches on three principal points:

I. "ACTIO CHRISTI"—1. *The Mass is the sacrifice of Christ*. More than an act of the faithful the Mass is an act of Christ: "The objective of the liturgy of the Mass is to express in a sensible way the grandeur of the mystery which is accomplished therein; and current efforts are striving to permit the faithful to participate in a manner as actively and as intelligently as

4   AAS, 1956, 711 and following.

possible. Although this objective is justified, we risk bringing about a loss of respect, if we take the focus from the principal act and turn it to the splendor of other ceremonies."

The principal action is noted by the Council of Trent, session XXII, chap. 2. "In this divine sacrifice which is accomplished at Mass, that very same Christ is contained and immolated in an unbloody manner Who is offered once and for all on the altar of the Cross in a bloody manner. . . . It is really one and the same Host; it is the same Priest Who now offers through the ministry of the priests, Who offered Himself on the Cross, the only difference being the manner of offering."

2. *The priest insofar as he is the minister of Christ*—In his *Allocution* of November 2, 1954 (AAS 1954, 668–670), Pope Pius XII explains that the priest alone, who celebrates the Mass and possesses the role of Christ, sacrifices, and not the people or the clerics or even other priests who take an active part in the sacrifice. It would be an error, then, to think that one sole Mass, at which a hundred priests devoutly assist, could be equal to a hundred Masses. "It is a question of offering the Eucharistic sacrifice. There are as many acts of Christ the High Priest[5] as there are priests who celebrate, not priests who assist at the Mass."[6]

"After this," the *Allocution* continues, "the central element of the Eucharistic sacrifice is that where Christ intervenes by offering Himself, *seip-sum offerens*—to use the words of the Council of Trent. This takes place at the consecration, when, in the same act of transubstantiation worked by the Lord, the celebrating priest assumes the role of Christ, *est personam Christi gerens*. Even if the consecration is carried out with simplicity and without splendor, it remains the central point of the entire liturgy of the sacrifice, the central point of Christ's act, Whose role is assumed by the celebrating priest, or, in the case of a true concelebration, by the celebrating priests."

3. *The question of concelebration*—This moved the Pontiff to distinguish between two types of concelebrations: the first, *properly called*, which results in consecrating the bread and wine; the second, *improperly called*, which results in "offering the host placed on the altar," to use an expression from *Mediator Dei*.

"In the case of a concelebration *in the proper sense* of the word, Christ, instead of acting through one minister, acts through several. On the contrary, in a *purely ceremonial* concelebration, which a layman can do, there is not a simultaneous consecration."

---

5   There are as many transubstantiations worked by Christ as there are unbloody sacrifices, and, we should say, as many presences of the one bloody sacrifice.

6   [Translator's note: One cannot conclude from these words of Pius XII that a concelebrated Mass is more than one sacrifice, more than one act of Christ. Pius XII is making a distinction here between the priest who celebrates Mass and the priest who just assists. Journet's footnote makes this clear: "There are as many transubstantiations worked by Christ as there are unbloody sacrifices . . . etc."]

In order for there to be a concelebration in the proper sense, it is not enough—contrary to what "certain contemporary theologians" think—to have and to manifest the desire to make one's own the words and actions of the celebrant. The concelebrants must themselves say over the bread and wine: *This is My Body, This is My Blood*. If they do not, their concelebration is purely ceremonial."

"We repeat: the decisive question for concelebration, as for the Mass said by only one priest, is not what fruit the soul draws from it, but rather what is the nature of the act posed.[7] Does the priest, as a minister of Christ, perform the *act of Christ sacrificing and offering Himself* or not?"

II. "PRAESENTIA CHRISTI"—1. *The Holy Father dismisses an insufficient explanation of transubstantiation and the true presence.* "Certain theologians, while accepting the teaching of the Council of Trent on the true presence and transubstantiation, interpret the words of Christ and those of the Council in such a way that nothing of Christ's presence subsists but a sort of shell emptied of its natural content. In their opinion, the essential real content of the species of bread and wine is *the Lord in heaven*, with Whom the species have a so-called real and essential relation of capacity and of presence.[8]

"This speculative interpretation gives rise to serious objections when one presents it as fully sufficient; for, the Christian sense of the faithful, the constant catechetical teaching of the Church, the words of the Council, and above all the words of our Lord require that the Eucharist contain the Lord Himself. The sacramental species are not the Lord, even if they have a so-called essential relation of capacity and presence with the substance of Christ in heaven. The Lord said, *This is My Body, This is My Blood*. He did not say, *This is a sensible appearance which signifies the presence of My Body and My Blood*. Undoubtedly, it can happen that the sensible signs of a real relation of presence be the sensible and efficacious signs of sacramental grace; but it is a question here of the essential content of the *Eucharistic species*, not their sacramental efficacy. One cannot say, then, that the above-mentioned theory does complete justice to the words of Christ, that the presence of Christ in the Eucharist signifies nothing more, that it suffices in order to say in all truth regarding the Eucharist, *It is the Lord* (cf. Jn 21:7)."

7　Following the Fathers (St. Ambrose) and St. Thomas, we made a clear distinction between two essentially distinct actions of the celebrant: 1) the first, by which he acts insofar as he is the *minister of Christ*, in order to consecrate the bread and wine into Christ's Body and Blood; 2) the second, by which he acts insofar as he is the *minister of the Church*, in order to accomplish and direct the other liturgical functions. It is under the second title that he can dispose the special fruit of the Mass.

8　The consecrated species have a relation of capacity with the glorious Christ, *not insofar as He is in heaven by* His natural presence, but *insofar as He is here below* by His sacramental presence. See above, p. 161.

"The *Roman Catechism* . . . neither mentions nor proposes the theory summarized above; still less does it affirm that the theory exhausts the sense of Christ's words and fully explains them. One can continue to search for scientific explanations and interpretations, but they must not depart, so to speak, from the Christ of the Eucharist, nor leave in the tabernacle nothing but the Eucharistic species preserving a so-called real and essential relation with the true Lord, Who is in heaven. It is surprising . . . that, regarding this notion of a so-called scientific presence of Christ, one does not hesitate to declare: *This truth is not for the multitude.*"

2. *The relation between the altar and the tabernacle*—"The altar has prominence over the tabernacle because it is on the former that the Lord's sacrifice is offered. The tabernacle certainly possesses the *permanent sacrament*, but it is not a *permanent altar*; because the Lord offers Himself in sacrifice only on the altar during the celebration of Holy Mass, and not after or outside of the Mass. In the tabernacle, on the other hand, He is present as long as the consecrated species is preserved, without nevertheless offering Himself unceasingly. We have the complete right to distinguish between the offering of the sacrifice of the Mass and the cult of adoration, *cultus latreuticus*, rendered to the God-Man hidden in the Eucharist."

However, "it is one and the same Lord Who is immolated on the altar and honored in the tabernacle, and Who pours down His blessings from there." "He who adheres to the teaching of the Council of Trent" on the due worship of Christ in the Blessed Sacrament (Session XIII, canons 6 and 7), "does not attempt to formulate objections against the presence of the tabernacle on the altar. . . . To separate the tabernacle from the altar is to separate two things which must remain united by their origin and their nature. The manner in which one could place the tabernacle on the altar without preventing the celebration facing the people can receive different solutions, concerning which the specialists will give their opinion. . . . The most enthusiastic and convinced liturgist must be able to understand and appreciate what the Lord in the tabernacle represents for the pious faithful, be they simple or lettered folk."

III. "INFINITA ET DIVINA MAJESTAS CHRISTI"—1. *The liturgy and the Person of the Word.* "The mediation of the infinite, supreme and divine majesty of Christ can certainly contribute to the deepening of the liturgical sense."

2. *The liturgy and the past*—"With regard to the past, one must avoid two extreme positions: a blind attachment and a complete disregard. There are in the liturgy immutable elements, a sacred content which transcends time; but there are also transitory elements, capable of variation, at times even defective."

3. *The liturgy and the present*—"The liturgy bestows a characteristic imprint on the life of the Church and even on the daily religious attitude.

We notice especially the faithful's active and conscious participation in liturgical acts. On the part of the Church, the current liturgy bears a concern for progress, but also for preservation and defense. It looks back to the past without imitating it slavishly; and it is created anew in the very ceremonies themselves, in the popular chant and construction of churches. Nevertheless, it would be superfluous to recall once more that the Church has grave motives for maintaining firmly in the Latin rite the unconditional obligation for the priest celebrant to employ the Latin language; and also, that when Gregorian chant accompanies the Holy sacrifice, it be done in the language of the Church. . . . The current liturgy also concerns itself with numerous particular problems regarding the relations between the liturgy and the religious ideas of the present world, the contemporary culture, social questions and psychology."

APPENDIX 2

Theological Approaches to the Mystery

We would like to present in a very sober manner two epochs: that of the Medieval Period, which joins the Fathers to the Scholastics; and that of the post—tridentine theologians.

I. Medieval Period

1. From Paschasius Radbertus to Peter Lombard

We do not wish here to improve upon the patient and erudite work of M. Lepin,[1] but rather, by borrowing his translation, to present some texts of theologians from that first period (that is from the 9th century to the first half of the 12th).

St. Paschasius Radbertus, Abbot of Corbie, composed (in 831) and published (in 844) his important treatise, *De corpore et sanguine Domini.*[2] Here is an often-repeated passage from book 9: "*This oblation is taken up again each day, although Christ, after having suffered once on the Cross, has at the same time saved the world by this one unique Passion* and by raising it to life, no longer needs ever again to be subject to death. The wisdom of God has judged this necessary for several reasons. First of all, because we sin everyday—at the very least those sins without which human infirmity cannot live. For, if all sins have been pardoned at Baptism, the weakness of sin does not cease to subsist in the flesh. . . . *Thus, because we fall each day, each day Christ is mystically immolated for us*, and His Passion is presented to us in a mysterious way, in order that He Who conquered death by dying one time, might remit each day our recurring sins by these sacraments of His Body and His Blood."[3]

Étienne de Beaugé (†1136): "We fall everyday, but *we are raised up and restored by the immolation which is reiterated on the altar*. Not that Christ is killed again, *but His Passion is re-presented, He being present.*"[4]

Durandus of Trobarn (†1088): "It is correct to call that which represents the Passion of the only Son, carried out in the past, a similitude or figure.

---

1   M. Lepin, *L'idée du sacrifice de la Messe d'après les théologiens depuis l'origine jusqu'à nos jours*, Paris, Beauchesne, 1926. The first chapter is entitled *La première speculation théologique sur le sacrifice de la Messe* (From Paschasius Radbertus, 9th century, to Peter Lombard, 12th century).
2   St. Paschasius Radbertus, PL CXX, 1267–1350.
3   Cf. Lepin, *op. cit.*, p. 48.
4   *Ibid.*, p. 130.

However, it is a similitude or figure full of truth and grace, *plena admodum veritate et gratia. . . .* We proclaim each day the death of Christ, in order that by that death we might more easily obtain the propitiation of the Father. Thus the mystery of salvation, *at the same time that it signifies the death of the Lord, brings about human reconciliation, reconciliationis humanae effectivum.*"[5]

Alger of Liège (†1130). If we compare the Cross and the Mass, "there is no difference with respect to the Real Presence of Christ, but only with respect to His immolation. . . . Only His oblation on the Cross was real; that which takes place each day on the altar is figured. *Nevertheless, there is the same salutary grace from both.* Both are just as true, just as sufficient and always necessary, because in both there is the same true omnipotent Christ."[6]

2. Peter Lombard

Peter Lombard, Bishop of Paris (1164), speaks only in passing about the sacrificial character of the Eucharist:[7] "It was asked whether what the priest does is properly called a sacrifice or immolation, and whether Christ is immolated each day, or if He was immolated only once. To this we may briefly respond that what is offered and consecrated by the priest is called a sacrifice and immolation, because it is the memory and representation of the true sacrifice and holy immolation accomplished on the altar of the Cross. Christ died on the Cross and was immolated there one time only, but each day He is immolated in the sacrament, because in the sacrament there is a remembrance made of that which was accomplished one time . . .

"The Host capable of saving us was offered in Christ one time only. And we, then, do we not make an offering each day? Yes, we make an offering each day, but it is a memory of His death; and there is only one Host, not several. How one and not several? Because Christ was immolated only once. Now this sacrifice is the exemplar of ours: it is always the same Victim which is offered, and this is why it is the same sacrifice. Or would one say that, because it is offered in many places, there are therefore many Christs? No, but rather that there is but one Christ only, complete in both places; and just as there is everywhere offered only one Body, so there is only one sacrifice.[8] Christ offered one Host; we offer it now. However, that which we do is a memorial of His sacrifice. And it is not because it is insufficient that it is reiterated, for it perfects man's salvation; but rather, because we sin daily out of our weakness.[9]

5   *Ibid.,*p.130.
6   *Ibid.,*p. 130.
7   Peter Lombard, *IV Sent.,* dist. 12: *Whether the Eucharist is a sacrifice, and whether Christ is immolated each time?*
8   This passage, attributed by Peter Lombard to St. Ambrose, is actually reproduced by St. John Chrysostom. See above, p. 45.
9   This last thought goes back through Paschasius Radbertus to St. Ambrose. See above, p. 45.

"Whence we see that that which happens on the altar is a sacrifice and is called such. We see that Christ was offered only once and that He is offered everyday, but in one manner then and another manner today, *Christum semel oblatum et quotidie offerri, sed aliter tunc, aliter nunc*. We see that the power of this sacrament is the remission of venial sins and the perfection of virtue."[10]

3. Albert the Great

St. Albert the Great (†1280): "Christ is truly *immolated* each day when we offer this *sacrifice* to God the Father. It is the same act of offering which is signified by the word *immolation* and by the word *sacrifice*; but the first word brings to mind the reality offered, while the second word the effect produced. The same reality offered for us continues to exist. We therefore continue to *immolate* and to *sacrifice*," but without crucifying Christ.

"There is an immolation not only in figure but in truth, that is the offering of one immolated reality through the hands of the priests.... Properly speaking, the immolation is the offering of one reality sent to death in honor of God."

To the objection that this does injury to the Cross, which was offered for all sins always, Albert the Great responds that "it is the same reality which is always offered and in view of the same effect."[11]

Listen as well to these beautiful texts: "This sacrifice is offered *to* the Father; it is offered *by* the Son, our High Priest; *that which* is offered is Christ in His human nature with His Body and His Blood; it is offered *for* all men.

"The divine wisdom has united Him Who is offered and Him Who offers: They become one personal Being. Divine wisdom has united Him Who offers to Him to Whom the offering is made: the Father and the Son are one in Deity. Divine wisdom has united Him Who is offered to those for whom He is offered: Christ and men are of the same nature....

"He Who offers and He Who is offered cannot not be acceptable. The same goes for those for whom He offers, since they are of the same nature as Him and the Blood of Christ has purified them from every obstacle.... We have therefore no need of many offerings: that which was offered one time only sufficed for all men....

"The Son alone is the worthy Priest of such a sacrifice and of such an offering. We pontiffs and priests are but vicars of the Uncreated Word Who, whenever we repeat His words, accomplishes the offering.... Once purified, we simply are taken up in this same offering in order to be acceptable to the Father.... This sacrifice will always please Him; for, being absolutely perfect, no other can ever succeed it."[12]

10 In the French edition of this book Journet gives credit here to M. LEPIN for the use of his French translation.
11 St. Albert the Great, *IV Sent.*, dist. 13.
12 St. Albert the Great, *De Eucharistia*, dist. V, chap. 3: *De hujus sacrificii acceptabil-itate*, edit. Borgnet, t. XXXVIII, pp. 347–348.

4. Conclusion

These few texts, which are concerned with the precise nature of the Mass, suffice for our present purpose, though one can easily add to them. They bear witness to what we know to be the faith and constant certitude of the Church: 1) They maintain the double scriptural revelation concerning the absolute sufficiency of the sacrifice of the Cross and the necessity to reiterate the rite of the Last Supper each day; 2) They open up a way which allows one to reconcile these two revelations, by confessing the essential unity of the sacrifice of the Cross with the Mass; 3) They present the Eucharistic sacrifice as a means by which men, incorporated one by one into the sacrifice of the Cross, see the work of their redemption accomplished. Theological elaboration, lofty as it might be concerning the Real Presence and transubstantiation, is here still quite sober. It distinguishes between the bloody immolation and unbloody immolation, the latter made again and again through the ministry of the priests.

II. Post-Tridentine Theology: Principal Types of Solutions

Our intention here is not to look at all the opinions of every post-tridentine theologian concerning the Eucharistic sacrifice,[13] but rather, to examine as briefly as possible the principal types of solutions concerning the central point, namely that of the very essence of the sacrifice of the Mass.

Christ is Priest and Victim both at the Mass and on the Cross; but at Mass in order that He might offer Himself in an unbloody manner. This unbloody offering is a real and true sacrifice. Why? We respond: because it brings us, under the sacramental and unbloody species, Christ now glorious along with the redemptive sacrificial act of His bloody Cross. This is the way we have explained it. But here are some other responses.

1st Type: Theories Which Seek in the Mass a Sacrificial Destruction Distinct from That of the Cross: Bellarmine, Salamanticenses, De Lugo, Lessius

The first type of solution consists in seeking in the Eucharist an immolation, a destruction distinct from that of the Cross, which the glorious Christ would offer to the Father in order to commemorate the immolation of the Cross. This is the way followed by several of the great post-tridentine theologians. And here we can divide them into two groups.

1. Certain of these theologians think they find this destruction most of all in the *Communion of the priest*, which would belong, therefore, to the very essence of the sacrifice.

---

13   For this one can read the work of M. Lepin, *L'idée du sacrifice de la Messe...*, *Deuxième Partie, Du concile de Trent à nos jours*, pp. 335–720.

For St. Bellarmine (1542–1621), the consecration consists in three moments: 1) A created thing (bread) which becomes consecrated (the Body of Christ); 2) This consecrated thing is offered to God by being placed on the altar; 3) It is offered under the appearances of bread in order to be consumed, and it is here where the destruction, necessary to the nature of a sacrifice, intervenes.[14]

The Salmanticenses teach that if there is a sacrifice, there must be a destruction of it. They do not see it taking place in the consecration. It must, for them, be situated in the Communion of the priest, where Christ loses His sacramental existence.[15]

For Cardinal De Lugo (1583–1660), Christ is certainly not destroyed substantially in His corporal being by the consecration, but He is destroyed with respect to His human mode of existing. Christ, in fact, is in the sacrament under a humbled state, incapable of exercising His proper human acts, and capable of being taken as nourishment. This reduction, sufficient to constitute a true sacrifice, will be consumed at Communion.[16]

One can say in response to the above opinions, that transubstantiation is a change from the bread to Christ, not vice versa. Christ's presence is given to us under the sacramental species; it is taken away from us through the alteration of the sacramental species, without Christ Himself being affected in His being. It is Christ, now in His heavenly glory, Who begins or ceases to be sacramentally present to us. The traits of humility and weakness, under which He appears or disappears, affect not Christ, but the borrowed appearances which veil His glory.

2. Others think they find this destruction above all in the *consecration*, in which they enclose the entire essence of the Mass. For Lessius (1554–1623), Christ is mystically killed by the fact that, in virtue of the words of consecration, there is on the altar His Body and His Blood in two different parts. It is true that the Body and Blood are no longer really separated, and that the Blood is joined to the Body and Body to the Blood; but, says Lessius, it is by concomitance, that is to say accidentally.[17] St. Bellarmine, whose opinion we mentioned above, had flatly rejected this: if the killing is not real, the consecration is not a true sacrifice; if the killing is real, the consecration is a sacrilege.

The merit of these solutions of the first type is the fact that they preserved the true and proper sense of the notion of sacrifice in general[18]

---

14 St. Robert Bellarmine, *De Missa*, I, chap. 27.
15 Salmanticenses, *De Eucharistiae sacramento*, disp. 13, dub. 2, no. 30. The author of this part of the *Cursus theologicus* is the Carmelite John of the Annunciation (†1701).
16 Cardinal John De Lugo, *De Eucharistia*, disp. 19, sect. 5.
17 Leonard Lessius, S.J., *De perfectionibus divinis*, XII, chap. 13, no. 97.
18 There is a sacrifice only when the thing offered is altered. St. Thomas, Summa *Theologiae* II–II, qu. 85, a. 3, ad 3; qu. 86, a. 1.

and the notion of Christ's sacrifice in particular. The Cross is a true and proper sacrifice of Christ, Who gives His life. At the Last Supper, at the Mass, there is, under the sacramental appearances, the true and proper sacrifice of Christ. All of this is exactly right. But how is it explained? Is it that the one redemptive immolation is really and sacramentally present at the Mass? They do not think of this. They think rather of an immolation, a real destruction of Christ, equivalent to that of the Cross. If this were true, the sacrifice at the Last Supper and at the Mass would be compared to that of the Cross, certainly different numerically but the same at least in species. However-and here is the difficulty-there is no real destruction of the glorious Christ.[19]

2nd Type: The Mass Is a Sacrifice Numerically and Specifically Distinct from the Sacrifice of the Cross: Suarez

For Suarez (1548–1617), the sacrifice of the Mass consists in the consecration. The following elements belong to the essence of the Mass: 1) the double consecration of the bread and wine, which mystically signify the bloody separation of the Body and Blood on the Cross; 2) the destruction of the substances of the bread and wine, offered as the matter from which comes the sacrifice; 3) first and foremost the presence of Christ under the sacramental species, the end of the sacrifice. The Mass, therefore, is a very new sacrifice, since the priest, far from immolating the Victim, actually brings it into existence. It has for its end not a destruction, but rather a production (*effectio*) and a presentation (*praesentatio*). We see immediately that it is quite different from the Cross. According to Suarez,

---

19 Everyone today admits that the essence of the sacrifice of the Mass is situated in the moment of the consecration, and that the reason for Communion is to allow us to enter more deeply into the sacrificial drama.

We clarify here two casuistic points related to the consecration.

1) *Can one consecrate only one species?*—"Although the consecration of the bread does not depend on that of the wine," says St. Thomas, "the priest who does not have wine available must decide not to celebrate, and not transgress the custom of the Church by consecrating only bread. The consecration would be valid, nevertheless, if he were to consecrate only one species, *quamvis etiam si una tantum specie consecraret, consecratum esset.* However, he would sin gravely." *IV Sent.*, dist. 11, qu. 2, a. 1, quaest. 1, ad 4. The only thing to do in such cases would be to communicate spiritually, *IV Sent.*, dist. 8, qu. 2, a. 4, quaest. 3, ad 3. In the *Summa*, St. Thomas contents himself with saying: "In the case where either bread or wine is lacking, one must not consecrate one without the other; for the sacrifice will not be accomplished, *quia non esset perfectum sacrificium.*" III, qu. 74, a. 1, ad 2. (Further on he says that, without bread made of wheat the sacrament would not be accomplished, *perfectum. Ibid.*, a. 4) The sacrifice is accomplished only if the priest has the intention of doing that which Christ did. *But would there, then, be a valid consecration if the priest decided to consecrate only one species? We can doubt it.* "At the heart of our historical exposition," writes

there is an *essential* difference between the bloody sacrifice constituted by the Passion and real Death of Christ and the unbloody sacrifice constituted by the presence of Christ's Body under the sacramental species. He says that it is not enough that the sacrifice be the same, that the reality offered be the same; for the sacrifice consists not in the permanent reality, but in the action which one exercises over it. If these actions are completely different in nature, even if they are exercised over the same reality, the sacrifices will be essentially different. With respect to the effects of the Cross and the Mass, they differ here as well: the Cross works our redemption *quoad sufficientiam*; while the Mass applies to us the fruits of the Cross *quoad efficaciam*. Likewise, it is by way of application and efficiency that the Mass, essentially different from the Cross, is a propitiatory sacrifice.[20]

Without commenting here on the well-known words,[21] according to which Suarez "learned the whole School," we must recognize that his influence was great. Of the three moments, which, according to Bellarmine, constitute the essence of the Mass, Suarez retains the first two: the destruction of the bread and the position of Christ. He does not hold

---

A. Michel, "we have met some authors who hld for the reality of the sacrament even with the consecration of one species. The majority, however, claim that the consecration of two species is necessary for the existence of the sacrifice. Not that the consecration of only one species to the exclusion of the other would be necessarily ineffective—this question can also be asked—but because the consecration under two species appears to be required in order for the sacrifice of Jesus Christ, such as He instituted it, to be verified . . . And so the Church understands it, considering the double consecration as necessary for the sacrifice, and never allowing it to be dispensed with, however grave be the reasons one might propose in order to consecrate one species without the other. And the law of the Church on this point is so grave that Canon Law forbids *consecrating one matter without the other even in a case of extreme necessity*, can. 817." *Messe*, Dict. de Théol. Cath., col. 1260. Cf. from the same author *Les décrets du concile de Trente*, in *Histoire des Conciles*, Hefele—Leclercq, Paris, 1938, Letourney et Ané, t. X. p. 395: "The near unanimity of theologians recognizes that Communion under two species is a divine right for the celebrant."

2) *The validity of the consecration.*—Certain theologians say that the consecration, in order to be valid, must be for the quantity of bread and wine destined for the Communion of the faithful, and that it must be made in view of the end of sanctification. St. Thomas thinks, on the contrary, that it will be valid even when it is for a greater quantity, *but falling nevertheless under the actual perception of the minister*, and even when it is made for sacrilegious ends. *IV Sent.*, dist. 11, qu. 2, a. 1, quaest. 3, ad 1; *Summa Theologiae*, III, qu. 74, a. 2.

20　III, qu. 83, a. 1; disp. 75, sect. 1, no. 8–12; sect. 4, no. 2; sect. 5, nos. 6, 11; sect. 6, nos 7–15; disp. 76, sect. 1, nos. 4–6.

21　That is, the words of Bossuet regarding Suarez, namely that, according to him, all of Scholasticism is found in Suarez. [Translator's note]

onto the third, namely the necessity of destruction. Wherefore, the definition of sacrifice will be changed when one passes from the sacrifice of the Cross to the sacrifice of the Mass. At the Cross, the sacrifice is a destruction, a death; at the Mass, the sacrifice is a sanctification, a glorious sacramental presence. Suarez would declare quite clearly that the sacrifice is essentially different at the Cross and at the Mass. The same Christ is certainly Priest and Victim at both; but that does not suffice, for the sacrificial action is essentially different in each.

Theologians for the most part shy away from these conclusions of Suarez, however logical they might be. Despite everything else, a hidden instinct moves them to maintain the unity of the sacrifice on the Cross and at the Mass. Suarez's merit is in posing, or in posing anew, the question regarding the unity of the sacrificial act. He resolved it negatively. How can it be resolved positively? Here also Suarez would open a path. He showed that one could change the definition of the sacrificial act: he called a sacrificial act both that which resulted in the death of Christ on the Cross, and that which results in the Mass, in the sacramental presence of Christ. Why would he not seek—but this time in the heart of Christ—an act which would be common to both moments of the Cross and the Mass, for example the interior and enduring act of the offering, by which Christ offers Himself to His Father ever since the moment of the Incarnation? And why would Suarez not call sacrificial this enduring act of the offering— this act which is really distinct from the transitory act by which Christ, when His hour had come, offered His death once only and "gave His life in order to take it up again" (Jn 10:17)? All difficulties would have henceforth fallen away. At the Cross and at the Mass there would be the same Priest, the same Victim, the same sacrificial act. Yes, but the very notion of the sacrifice of Christ would be changed once again; and this not without difficulties.

Let us stop here for a moment to recall an important point.[22] We clearly distinguish that which is the sacrifice of Christ in the *proper* sense (the redemptive sacrifice) from that which is the sacrifice in the *improper or metaphorical* sense (acts of adoration, of praise, of thanksgiving, of offering, which filled the entire earthly life of Christ).

If the unbloody sacrifice contains sacramentally the reality of Christ and His bloody sacrifice, one must say by this same reason that it is a true and proper sacrifice: not another *sacrifice* than the one sacrifice, but another *presence* than this sacrifice. What is analogous is the notion of the *presence* of the one sacrifice: a presence which is natural on the Cross, and sacramental at Mass. The notion of *the sacrifice of Christ* is univocal. We say equally that each consecrated host is Christ because it contains Christ truly, really, substantially. It is, again, the notion of Christ's presence

22 See above, p. 49.

which is analogous: natural in heaven, and sacramental among us. It is not the notion of Christ which is analogous.

The general notion of *sacrifice*, taken in its true and proper sense, can certainly be analogous. There is nothing univocal here; there is only the relation of analogy when we speak of the poor sacrifices of the Old Testament and the theandric sacrifice of Christ on the Cross. But the *sacrifice of Christ*, His redemptive and propitiatory sacrifice for the sins of the whole world, is unique. If, therefore, we call the sacrifice of Christ those acts of His of adoration, praise, thanksgiving and offering, which took place before the redemptive sacrifice and which continue in heaven, then we would pass from the proper and true sense to the improper and metaphoric sense.

3rd Type: The Mass as the Sacrifice of the Church Appropriating Itself to Christ in Heaven: De la Taille, Lepin

For P. Maurice de la Taille, S.J., the heavenly Christ, by reason not of His wounds but of His previous immolation, His temporal act of offering, one which is valid for always and which does not need to be repeated, has passed to the state of victim on the eternal altar. He has passed to the state of victim on the eternal altar. He is in a perpetual state of immolation, consumed by divine glory. He is formally a perpetual host. He is "theothyte." At Mass this host becomes ours. The newness is completely on the side of the Church alone; by her act of offering she is appropriated to the Body of Christ which was once capable of suffering. There is not here the act of Christ. To say that Christ offers by us signifies that our power of offering comes from Christ as the principal Cause, and that our act of offering depends on the act formerly accomplished by Christ. Christ, being "theothyte," can be offered by us from that moment on. In this sense His offering incorporates our offering; it gives us the power to offer the Body and Blood as our own host.[23]

Thus, according to de la Taille, there is no sacrificial act of Christ at the Mass;[24] there is Christ in glory, improperly called a sacrifice. The only act

---

23 Maurice de la Taille, S.J., *Mysterium fidei* (Paris, Beauchesne, 1921), pp. 151, 173–180, 195, 200, 295–303.

 According to P. de la Taille, the Passion of Christ is a true sacrifice, possessing one invisible element (the offering of the human race to God) and two visible elements (1) the Victim, sanctified by the hypostatic union and sacrificed; 2) the immolation or passion, which leads to death). *Nevertheless, he lacks the third visible element necessary for the sacrifice*, namely the liturgical offering. But it is found at the Last Supper, such that *the Last Supper and the Cross constitute by their union one and the same sacrifice. Op. cit.*, p. 104. Almost no one follows P. de la Taille on this idea of the imperfection of the sacrifice of the Cross.

24 This position of de la Taille is rightly contested by R. Garrigou–LaGrange, *An Christus non solum virtualiter sed actualiter offerat missas quae quotidie celebrantur*, in *Angelicum*, 1942, pp. 105–118. See above, p. 243.

which is called sacrificial there is that of the Church. It consists in offering up Christ in glory, and not in immediately entering into participation in His redemptive sacrifice.

According to M. Lepin, who inspired the "French School," one distinguishes in the oblation itself the interior act, which is the gift of self to God, and the exterior act, which is a secondary rite of presenting a thing to God (simple oblation), or of giving a thing to God with or without immolation (bloody sacrifice or unbloody sacrifice). The sacrifice of Christ, then, includes a continuous interior oblation which is signified exteriorly: on the Cross, by the offering of His Passion; during His earlier life, by the offering of Himself independently of all suffering; in heaven, by the offering of His glorious Body which was already immolated at His Passion. The sacrifice of the Mass is defined as "the oblation which Christ made of Himself and which the Church makes of Christ under the signs representative of His past immolation." The Church, by her liturgical offering, makes present—in order to be incorporated into it from the consecration to Communion—the sacrifice of heaven, adapted to our earthly conditions, that is, under the figurative immolation which recalls the sacrifice of the Cross. The definitive moment of the sacrifice is the offering, which Christ makes of Himself at the moment of consecration; the figurative immolation is the condition of the present form of His sacrifice.[25]

Thus, one calls the sacrifice of Christ something other than what Scripture calls the sacrifice of Christ. The one act which redeems the world, which Jesus called His hour, is no longer the sacrifice of Christ. It is joined to a permanent sacrifice as a secondary rite, a passing accident. The logical order is saved, but the mystery of the Gospel is lost.

4th Type: The Invisible Offering of the Glorious Christ in the Sacrament, Joined to an Exterior Sign of Immolation, Is Sufficient to Constitute a Real and Proper Sacrifice: Billot, Garrigou-Lagrange

What is necessary, according to Cardinal Billot, for there to be a true and real sacrifice of Christ? His response is twofold. If Christ is offered under His natural appearances, the real immolation is required in order to signify His interior act of offering. But if Christ is offered under sacramental appearances, the mystical immolation, that is to say the double consecration, is sufficient to signify His interior act of offering, and hence to constitute with it a real and true sacrifice. We clarify, that the mystical immolation constitutes the sacrifice not simply insofar as it represents the offering of the Cross (the thesis of Vasquez), still less insofar as it kills Christ (thesis of Lessius), but insofar as it renders Christ present under an

---

25 M. Lepin, *L'idée du sacrifice de la Messe d'après les théologiens, depuis l'origine jusqu'à nos jours* (Paris, 1926), pp. 737–758.

external bearing of death and destruction. From this fact it is apt to signify outside of the invisible sacrifice, that is to say the interior offering, and to constitute with it a true sacrifice. This is not the redemptive sacrifice; it is another sacrifice of Christ, directly impetrative. And it is called propitiatory because it makes supplication that the merits and satisfactions of the Cross be applied.[26] The same teaching is taken up again by R. P. Garrigou-Lagrange, who sees in the permanent interior act of Christ's offering the soul of the sacrifice, whether on the Cross or at the Mass; such that the sacrifice of the Mass is not only similar to that of the Cross, as roses of this year resemble in species those of last year, but it is individually the same sacrifice, but in substance only.[27]

What ought one to think of these views? Of all the modern theologians Cardinal Billot is certainly the one who understood most profoundly the teaching of St. Thomas, according to whom transubstantiation happens from the bread to Christ, Who preexists and remains unchanged. If, therefore, Christ was in heaven in the act of offering a present sacrifice, true and proper, it is clear that transubstantiation would bring us this sacrifice. We would add that, in changing a little of the common interpretation and by recalling De Lugo, the double consecration would represent, then, not so much the past sacrifice of the Cross as this present sacrifice in heaven. The Mass would undoubtedly be a true and proper sacrifice. But is Christ in heaven in the act of offering a present true and proper sacrifice? Wherever Christ exists under His proper appearances—Billot admits this—His interior offering does not become sacrificial in the proper sense unless it is signified outwardly by a real immolation, a destruction. Is it possible to find in heaven a real immolation, a destruction of Christ? How then could transubstantiation bring us, under the appearances of bread and wine, a true and proper present sacrifice of the heavenly Christ? It is here, in our opinion, that the theory runs aground.

Perhaps there is another way. Let us consider Christ Himself with His perpetual interior act of offering as being substantially a true and proper sacrifice. The external signification by a real immolation of Christ living

---

26 Cardinal Louis Billot, *De Ecclesiae sacramentis* (Rome: Typog. Pont., 1915), t. I, pp. 588, 628, 634. The 1924 edition is more brief on these points. On the other hand it combats, without naming him, the thesis of de la Taille (1921), and affirms that the oblation of the Last Supper must be considered as *completely distinct from* the sacrifice of the Cross, and not an essential or integral *part of* it. The author declares a little later—as did Suarez—that, properly speaking and understanding by the term "sacrifice" the sacrificial action, the Mass and the Cross *"non possunt esse unum, nec numerice nec specifice"* (cannot be one, neither numerically or according to species), p. 604.

27 R. P. Garrigou—Lagrange, O.P., *L'amour de Dieu et la Croix de Jésus* (Paris: edit. du Cerf, 1929), t. II, p. 856; *De Eucharistia* (Turin: Berutti, 1943), p. 286.

in this world would therefore be accidental to this interior sacrifice, as would His mystical immolation while living in heaven. One could say, then, that the sacrifice of the Mass is the same individually as that of the Cross, but in substance only. Yes, one could say this. But at what price? The sacrificial act of Christ is placed primarily and substantially in His perpetual interior act of offering. The real and bloody immolation of the Cross, then, can no longer enter into the definition of Christ's sacrifice except accidentally.

The definition of the sacrifice as the exterior sign of an interior offering must be interpreted correctly. The offering and the sacrifice are ranked by St. Thomas[28] among the exterior acts of religion. An interior act of reverence or adoration results in a thing given; this is the exterior act of offering. An interior act of reverence or adoration results in a thing destroyed; this is the exterior act of sacrifice. The gift and the sacrifice, always presupposing the interior act of religion which inspires them, are exterior acts differing specifically. We ought not to confuse them with each other or with the interior act of religion which animates them. These are exterior acts, not interior, and they are specifically distinct from each other. These exterior acts translate and signify, each in their own way, an interior act of religion; but they are not merely signs. An interior act of religion joined to a pure sign would never make an exterior act of offering or sacrifice. Christ inters into the world with a heart full of interior acts of adoration. When He says, "Behold I come to do Your will, O God" (Heb 10:5–7), He signifies this interior act. He has not yet accomplished His sacrifice; He will accomplish it on the Cross. He will not take up a new sacrifice once in heaven. It seems that one forgets these distinctions when one thinks that the mystical immolation, considered a pure sign and united to Christ's interior offering, suffices to constitute a present sacrifice of the glorious Christ; or whenever one places the very substance of His sacrifice in the interior act of the glorious Christ.

5th Type: The Mass Is a Presence of the Sacrifice of the Cross by Way of Representation and Application: Vonier, Lépcier, E. Masure, G. Rohner

We can rank within our last group theologians who attribute to Christ no other sacrifice than the unique sacrifice of the Cross, and who confess that the Mass is one real and proper sacrifice because it transports to us the very reality of the bloody sacrifice under the unbloody appearances.

1. Dom Vonier, O.S.B., recalls that the Mass is not a natural sacrifice, but a sacramental one. It represents the natural sacrifice and, as sacramental signs in the new economy are efficacious, it renders that natural sacrifice present. The Eucharistic Body under the species of bread and the

28   Thomas Aquinas, *Summa Theologiae* II-II, qu. 85, a. 3, ad 3; qu. 86, a. 1.

Eucharistic Blood under the species of wine represent Christ's natural Body and Blood as they were on Calvary. Such, in the final analysis, is the true value of the sacramental representation. And such a representation suffices in itself to constitute the sacrifice, for it represents Christ in that period of His life when He was nothing other than a sacrifice, since His Blood was separated from His Body. Here we see already the singularity of Dom Vonier's teaching. He affirms—and he is correct—that the sacrifice of the Cross is present at Mass; but for him the sacrifice of the Cross is not the offering of Christ, but rather the dead Christ, not the sacrificial act, but rather its result. Christ, says Vonier, may be considered in three successive phases or states: 1) in His mortality, from His birth to His death on the Cross; 2) in His death, from Good Friday to Easter; 3) in His immortality, beginning with Easter. The Mass represents the second phase by the fact that it perpetually renders it present among us; the Mass does more than offer up the Body and Blood, it immolates the Christ of Calvary. It is the Christ of the second phase, absolutely the same, Who is found on the altar. We think neither of the mortal Christ nor of the immortal Christ when we speak of the immolated Christ. We think of the dead Christ. In virtue of the sacrament, the Eucharist contains neither the mortal Christ nor even the dying or glorious Christ. It contains Christ such as He was immediately after His death, although without the gaping wounds.[29] Today on the altar, in virtue of the sacrament, we possess Christ in the second phase of His personality, that of His death; but in virtue of concomitance, we possess also the entire third phase of His personality, that of His glory. However, when we speak of the sacrifice we consider only the second phase of Christ's personality.[30]

That there is in virtue of the words of transubstantiation only Christ's Body under the species of bread, and in virtue of concomitance His Blood and soul, and in virtue of the hypostatic union His divinity—this is the very teaching of the Council of Trent. The presence of concomitance and that of the hypostatic union will not contradict what the words of consecration affirm, but rather complete it. Where the Body is directly present, the Blood, soul and divinity can be indirectly present. There is no difficulty with this. But how can there not be a simple contradiction in saying that Christ is present in the sacrament at the same time under the phase of His death, or the real separation of His soul from His Body, and under the

29 Is this correct? Yes, if the words of consecration had been pronounced at the time of Christ's death (And why then exclude the "gaping wounds"?). But no, if they are pronounced at any other time. All the words say is, that the bread and wine are changed into the Body and Blood; they say nothing regarding the relationship of the Body and Blood to each other or to the soul. To make them speak thus is to fall into the thesis of Lessius.

30 Dom Vonier, O.S.B, *La clef de la doctrine eucharistique*, trad. Du R. P. Roguet, O.P. (Lyon, edit. de l'Abeille, 1942; Paris: edit. du Cerf, s.d.), chap. 13.

phase of His glory, or the indissoluble union of His soul and Body? The one Christ can simultaneously *be present twice*: in heaven where He is naturally, and here below where He is sacramentally. The notion of presence affects Him only extrinsically. The theologian can contemplate Him in His mortal phase or in His glorious phase; but does the theologian forget that Christ cannot be simultaneously *dead and living*, living in heaven but dead here below?

What we must say is, that the Mass brings us the substantial presence of the glorious Christ—the Christ Who comes to touch us by means of the unique redemptive act whereby He willed to draw us to Himself, to associate us with the path of His Life, Passion, Death and Resurrection. The sacramental appearances of His Body given for us, His Blood poured out for us, communicate that which they signify, namely the drama of the redemptive Passion—a drama forever in the past with respect to its sensible envelopment, but perpetually present by its spiritual contact and power. Dom Vonier rightly underlines the importance of the notion of *representation*. However, St. Thomas writes, it is the notion of application, the notion of participation in the fruits of the Passion which is principal and which explains that Christ is truly immolated at Mass. The notion of *application* is certainly indicated in the teaching of Dom Vonier, but it alone would have allowed him to teach without contradiction that the Mass can give us simultaneously Christ in glory and His sacrifice of the Cross.

2. We find a few similar ideas among Cardinal Alexis-Marie Lépicier, of the Order of the Servants of the Blessed Virgin Mary. The power and formal reason of the Eucharistic sacrifice is, he says, derived from the Passion and Death of Christ, not from the fact that they are simply represented (*in actu signato*), but from the fact that they are actualized, insofar as the glorious state of Christ permits it (*in acto exercito*). The formal reason of the sacrifice of the altar consists not in any immolation whatsoever, but in the same immolation accomplished on the Cross. The power of the immolation on the Cross goes forth into our sacrifice on the altar, as the power of a seed goes forth into the plant. The sacrifice of the Mass draws its formal reason from the immolation of the Cross. The plan of the Savior was that His death on the Cross should actually flow into each of the Eucharistic sacrifices which would be celebrated throughout time. In such a way the contact of the Cross comes to us, not without an intermediary (not without the mediation of helpers), but by the mediation of the unbloody rite (and by mediation of power). Hence the Cross and the Mass do not make two sacrifices, but only one. It is most certainly true to regard the Mass as the sacrifice and immolation of Calvary. One must assist at the sacrifice of the Mass as one would assist at the sacrifice of the Cross. The effect of the Passion and Death of Christ is therefore applied to us at Mass. The Eucharistic sacrifice is

neither a restoration nor a simple commemoration of the Cross, but rather a commemoration in act, an actual application, a continuation of the Cross.[31]

3. Although the presentation of Canon E. Masure[32] is associated more with *types 2, 3 and 4* listed above, nevertheless he strongly insists on the numerical unity of the sacrifice of the Cross, the Last Supper and the Mass.

The Eucharist is at the same time *mystery* and *sign*.[33]

The *mystery* is before the sign or sacrament.[34] The mystery is a reality of the divine invisible and supernatural world, namely the reality of our redemption and our religion. This mystery is incarnate, that is to say, rendered present and visible in a Victim.[35] The Victim is Christ Who, being offered and immolated, is eternally in this state of victim, oblation and immolation.[36] The historic immolation of Christ is henceforth eternal.[37] The sacrifice begun on Calvary is crowned in heaven, where it is never completed because it is consummated there.[38] On this point the teaching of Masure does not seem to differ essentially from that of de la Taille.

At a given moment, nevertheless, the question is posed of knowing whether the "historic death" of Christ is that which is rendered present to us at Mass. A positive response is not excluded. The author, however, who seeks for help here only from "modern philosophy," simply concludes that the preceding states survive in subsequent states.[39]

The role of the *sign* is to contain and communicate that which it symbolizes.[40] The Mass does not need to bring about the sacrifice of Calvary, since it already exists. The Mass recommences it insofar as it makes it ours, places it at our disposition, presents it to our adoration.[41]

It is in explaining the role of the sign that Masure "seeks a passage way" between Dom Casel and Dom Vonier.[42]

31 Cardinal Alexis-Marie Lépicier, *De sacrosancto sacrificio eucharistico* (Paris, Lethielleux, 1917), pp. 112–115.
32 Canon Eugène Masure, Director at the Grand Séminaire de Lille, *Le sacrifice du Corps mystique* (Paris: Desclée De Brouwer, 1950), 206 pages.
33 P. 21.
34 Pp. 17, 45.
35 We will see in the "mystery" *the Redeemer first and foremost*, more loved than all the redeemed and drawing them all in His wake; and *not first and foremost the mystery of our alliance*, "incarnated" and realized in a Victim.
36 P. 151.
37 Pp. 57, 71.
38 Pp. 83, 85.
39 Pp. 23–24, 37, 71.
40 Pp. 17, 23.
41 Pp. 28, 31, 38, 39, 57.
42 Pp. 37, 71.

From Dom Casel he retains that, in the mysterious pagan religions, the mystery is before the sign and rite, which communicates it to us.[43] But he excludes the idea that the rite of the Mass, by "performing" the mystery of Christ's Passion, would have to recommence it.[44]

From Dom Vonier he retains that the mystery is present on the altar under the species of a ritual immolation.[45] But he excludes the idea that the resemblance, the representation, can suffice to make real the sacrifice of Calvary. Following the author, the fact that, along with this resemblance, the Mass is the sacrifice of the Cross, there is a substitution, thanks to transubstantiation, of one victim (bread and wine) for another (Christ's Body and Blood), the conversion of one sacrifice (bread and wine) into another (Christ's Body and Blood).[46] He frequently insists on the idea (suarezian) of one sacrifice, one immolation, of bread and wine,[47] only to finish by saying that this immolation is only sacramental, not real, because the bread and wine are not the victim of the true sacrifice.[48]

The sacramental sign is not only a *rite*, which can be repeated indefinitely and efficaciously.[49] Dom Casel's position here must be completed by using that of de la Taille and by affirming that the sacramental sign is still a *gesture*, that is to say the visible expression of an interior movement, first of all of Christ at the Last Supper, then that of the Church at Mass.[50] "It is a gesture which makes up a part of the mystery of which it is a sign. It one time previously, at the Last Supper, launched and provoked the sacrifice of Calvary by making it inexorable. It will continue each morning on our altars, not only by representing, but by making this sacrifice, at the command of the same spiritual forces, divine and human, which it brings to the sacrifice, because it issues forth from Christ. In this sense we can and must say that the Mass recommences and renews the sacrifice of Calvary. Christ is the Head, the Church His Body. The action of the latter continues to be the very same action of the former."[51] Masure nevertheless seems to distance himself even from de la Taille when he considers as *minimizing* the "liturgist tendency, the French School," according to which the

43 Pp. 18, 37.
44 P. 71.
45 P. 37.
46 P. 72.
47 Pp. 38–39, 64, 72, 79–81, 89.
48 P. 91.
49 P. 21.
50 Pp. 22–25.
51 P. 25. It is said elsewhere that, "the Mass renews the sacrifice of Calvary. It does not exactly have to make it, since it already exists. But it recommences it insofar as it is ours . . ." p. 29. It is in the improper sense that one can speak of renewing and recommencing that which has been declared eternally present.

Mass "is rather *the sacrifice of the Church* uniting herself to Christ in order to offer herself (the drop of water in the chalice), in order to offer Christ or to permit Christ to offer Himself."[52]

The first effect of the sign was *the real presence of the sacrifice and of the Victim of the Cross*: "On one hand, the Mass must place the sacrifice of the Cross on our altar today, in and under a representing symbol, in order that this sacrifice might become ours and be present to us, in order that we might possess it as realized under our eyes and in our hands, in a manner both sensible and true: this is the *sacramentum-et-res*."[53] The second effect of the sign will be *the spiritual fruits of Christ's sacrifice*: "On the other hand, this celebration must obtain for our souls the communication of all the spiritual and invisible fruits of this same sacrifice: this is the second result, which we have the right to expect from the accomplishment of this liturgy, the *res-et-non-sacramentum*: this effect is always a bit uncertain, not on the side of God, but on the side of our dispositions, which can thwart it by placing obstacles in its path, and which always condition and limit it according to their own strength."[54]

4. The most attentive recent study of St. Thomas' thought on the nature of the sacrifice of the Mass is, according to our knowledge, that of Gebhard Rohner, which appeared in *Divus Thomas* (Fribourg, Switzerland).[55]

The author begins with the text of St. Thomas: "The sacrifice which is offered each day in the Church is not another one than that which Christ Himself offered, but its commemoration," Summa Theologiae, III, qu. 22, a. 2. It is not a question of a simple and bare representation: "The sacraments of the New Law contain and cause that which they signify," III, qu. 62, a. 1, ad 2. The separation of the Body and Blood is therefore not only signified, but contained and caused as well, in the sense that the sacrifice of the Cross is rendered present, but enveloped under the exterior appearances of bread and wine. "Christ was offered one time only *in Himself*, and nevertheless is offered each day for the people *in the sacrament*," III, qu. 83, a. 1, following St. Augustine. Thus the sacrifice of the Mass is the same sacrifice of the Cross. It is the blood sacrifice which is present under the sacramental envelopment. The thought of St. Thomas would become that of the Council of Trent, according to which, there is at the Mass and at the Cross one and the same *Victim*, one and the same *offering*. Rohner believes one can add also, one and the same oblation, one and the same *sacrificial act*. We agree with him, though we would not dare say that this is expressly formulated by the Council of Trent. Only the "mode of offering," the

52 P. 93.
53 P. 41.
54 *Ibid.*
55 Gebhard Rohner, *Die Messapplikation nach der Lehre des heiligen Thomas* (December 1924), pp. 385–410; (March 1925), pp. 64–91; *Messopfer-Kreuzesopfer* (March 1930), pp. 3–17; (June 1930), pp. 145–174.

Council adds, is different. This difference does not concern the sacrifice, but the mode in which it is offered. On the Cross it is offered *without* the sacramental envelopment; at the Mass, *under* this envelopment. It is always good to cite Cajetan here. It is not exact, then, to say that the bloody sacrifice is *renewed* in an unbloody manner. It is the exterior rite which is renewed: the sacrament, the consecration, the celebration of the sacrifice of the Cross. The sacrifice of the Cross is itself placed in the hands of the Church in order that she might offer it in Christ, with Christ, through Christ; in order that in the reconciliation with Christ we might ourselves be able to reconcile God with us and with the world. The sacrifice of the Cross acts in a manner of a universal cause of salvation, which must be applied to each generation by faith and the sacraments of faith.[56]

There are two concepts of presence in space and time: one is valid for God, the other for men. Just as many consecrated hosts make for us many presences of the one Christ in space and time, so many Masses make for us many presences of the one sacrifice in space and time. The "presentiality" with regard to God is not incompatible with the "passingness" of men. "When St. Thomas, with the Fathers and the Council of Trent, speaks of *the past Passion of Christ signified by this sacrament*, he expresses himself according to the human concepts of time and space. The suffering of Christ is in fact past; that which is present are the consecrated species and the power of the sacrament. When he says that *the true sacrifice of the Cross*, or *the Passion of Christ*, or *Christ Who suffered*, is contained in the sacrament not only in figure or sign but in truth and reality, this containing and this presence are understood according to the divine concept of containing and presence *in eternity*. One cannot conclude, then, from the expression *past Passion* that *Christ Who suffered* would be present to us only in sign. . . . In God's eyes all is present. Yet God says, 'That which *for you* is past, I will make it *present again for you* under the species of bread and wine, in virtue of My omnipotence, through transubstantiation . . .'As it is true that the visible species are in space and time, so it is true—and more so—that *Christ Who suffered* is found present *according to the mode of eternity*."[57]

Moreover, we are not going to believe that in the sacrament Christ is at the same time both living and dead: "*The blessed Passion of Christ, His Resurrection from Hell, His glorious Ascension into heaven*," recalled in the anamnesis of the Roman Canon, are contained in the sacrament not as juxtaposed (*nebeneinander*), but as successive (*nacheinander*). The Eucharist, according to St. Thomas, signifies the past sacrifice, the unity of the Church, the heavenly glory: *recolitur memoria Passionis ejus, mens impletur gratia, et futurae gloriae nobis pignus datur*, III, qu. 73, a. 4. "It causes, therefore, these three things in the order that they are signified. The *Passion* of

56   *Loc. cit.*, 1924, pp. 385–397.
57   *Loc. cit.*, 1930, pp. 152–153.

Christ is past. It remains as such according to our concept of presence in time and place; but it becomes present to us according to the divine concept, transcending time and space . . . *Grace* is signified and contained as present. . . . Heavenly *glory*, insofar as it is possessed, is future. This glory is also in the sacrament, signified and caused as to be acquired, if it is true that the same Passion of Christ, the cause of our glorification, is contained within: 'Whoever eats My Flesh and drinks My Blood *has* eternal life.'"[58]

Rohner believes that the teaching of St. Thomas on the physical causality of Christ's humanity and the sacraments can be the key to resolving the problem of the essence of the sacrifice of the Mass.[59] His doctrine of the numerical identity of the sacrifice of the Cross and the Mass being equal, as it is, to that of Dom Odon Casel, must have to face the same adversaries. This gives him the occasion not only to render homage to the great monk, Maria—Laach[60] (as if he needed it), but also, in the last pages, to rectify that which still remains a bit obscure in his views and those of his collaborators, touching notably on the relations between the Holy Spirit and Christ.

None of the theological opinions which we have summarized have been directly condemned by the Magisterium. It is clear, however, that whatever elements of truth they might contain, they all cannot be true at the same time, and that, as soon as the theological reflection centers on the ineffable mystery of the Mass, one must make a choice.

---

58 *Loc. cit.*, p. 166.
59 *Loc. cit.*, pp. 168 and 172.
60 It goes without saying that one can find the general ideas of Dom Casel debatable, not only on the evolution of culture, but also on the significance of the pagan mysteries. One might prudently consult on this latter point the book of E.-B. Allo, *L'Évangile en face du syncrétisme païen* (Paris, Bloud, 1910), and the works of Père LaGrange on *Les mystères d'Éleusis et le christianisme*, and *Attis et le christianisme*, in *Revue Biblique* (1919), pp. 157–217 and 419–480. The theory of Casel is explained and critiqued by Antonio Piolanti, *Il miserio eucaristico* (Florence: Libreria Editrice, 1955), pp. 354–364.

Index of Proper Names

About the Author

Charles Journet, the great Swiss theologian and cardinal of the Church, first wrote this work on the Mass over 40 years ago; yet his ever-ancient-ever-new insights into the sacrificial nature of the Mass are most needed today, when this aspect of the sacrament is so often misunderstood or neglected.

The Mass is the "unbloody presence of the one unique bloody sacrifice of the Cross". This is the fundamental principle upon which Journet develops his theology of the Mass. Guided by the teachings of the Fathers, St. Thomas Aquinas and the Magisterium of the Church, and supported by his own rich spiritual life, Journet plumbs the depths of this unfathomable Mystery and presents It to the reader with a clarity rarely equaled.

Journet also presents an historical survey of explanations of the Mass—both orthodox and heterodox; and against this backdrop he brings out in bold relief the identity of the sacrifice of Calvary with that of the altar. Such an identity, Journet notes, is perfectly expressed in the Church's own liturgical prayer: "As often as the memorial of this Victim is celebrated, the work of our redemption is wrought."

This classic in sacramental theology is now made available to English readers for the first time ever. Journet's original format—with its many subsections—has been retained for easy reading. Also included is a wealth of footnotes for the scholar. This English edition includes a Preface by Bishop Salvatore Cordileone, Auxiliary Bishop of San Diego, California.

The translator, Fr. Victor Szczurek, is a Norbertine priest from St. Michael's Abbey in Orange Country, California. He is presently on the faculty of St. Michael's Abbey Seminary and is the Headmaster of St. Michael's Preparatory School. He recently also published an English translation of Journet's *Theology of the Church*.